Eighteenth-Century British and American Rhetorics and Rhetoricians

CRITICAL STUDIES AND SOURCES

Edited by

Michael G. Moran

D0075314

GREENWOOD PRESS
WESTPORT, CONNECTICUT • LONDON

Library of Congress Cataloging-in-Publication Data

Eighteenth-century British and American rhetorics and rhetoricians:
    critical studies and sources / edited by Michael G. Moran.
        p.   cm.
    Includes bibliographical references and index.
    ISBN 0–313–27909–8 (alk. paper)
        1. English language—Rhetoric—Study and teaching—Great Britain—
    History—18th century.   2. English language—Rhetoric—Study and
    teaching—United States—History—18th century.   3. English
    language—Rhetoric—Textbooks—History—18th century.   4. Rhetoric—
    Great Britain—History—18th century.   5. Rhetoric—United States—
    History—18th century.   6. English language—18th century—
    Rhetoric.   7. Rhetoric—1500–1800.   I. Moran, Michael G.
    PE1405.G7E43   1994
    808'.0071'041—dc20   93–35838

British Library Cataloguing in Publication Data is available.

Library of Congress Catalog Card Number: 93–35838
ISBN: 0–313–27909–8

First published in 1994

Greenwood Press, 88 Post Road West, Westport, CT 06881
An imprint of Greenwood Publishing Group, Inc.

Printed in the United States of America

The paper used in this book complies with the
Permanent Paper Standard issued by the National
Information Standards Organization (Z39.48–1984).

10 9 8 7 6 5 4 3 2 1

To My Parents:
Jane and Tim Moran

EIGHTEENTH-CENTURY BRITISH AND AMERICAN RHETORICS AND RHETORICIANS

CONTENTS

PREFACE

I became interested in eighteenth-century rhetoric while a graduate student in English at the University of New Mexico during the 1970s. At the time, I wanted to write my dissertation on the application of the century's rhetorical theory to Edmund Burke's *Reflections on the Revolution in France*; however, nobody in the department felt qualified to direct a dissertation in rhetoric, and I turned to other topics. After finishing my Ph.D. in 1978, I took a postdoctoral fellowship in composition theory at the University of Kansas and spent the next ten years teaching composition and technical writing and researching issues related to writing and writing theory. I never lost interest in eighteenth-century rhetoric, though, and when I began teaching eighteenth-century British literature at the University of Georgia, I combined my interests in the century and rhetorical theory. The result is this book.

The period has not received the scholarly attention it deserves. In fact, many of the minor figures have received little scholarly attention to date (a situation that this book attempts to remedy). This fact is not surprising considering that literary scholars working in the eighteenth century have been historically more concerned with traditional literary genres than with the rhetorical theory developed by a small group of Scottish intellectuals and often forgotten English and American rhetoricians. The tendency to forget these theorists was complicated by the fact that many of them—Adam Smith is the striking example—were not creative writers but philosophers, social commentators, critics, and theologians. Therefore, much of the early and most important work done about these figures was carried out not in English but in speech departments, whose primary interest concerned the spoken word. Consequently, much available research approaches rhetoric from that important angle.

Now, however, a new group of scholars with parallel interests has begun to attend to eighteenth-century rhetorical theory. This group consists of composition scholars interested in rhetorics of the written word. These scholars have found in eighteenth-century rhetoric the beginnings of their own discipline, for these early rhetoricians, especially those in Scotland, caused three important shifts in American and English views of language. First, they emphasized issues of literary criticism, the study of what they called belle lettres; second, they expressed a direct interest in helping college students and others speak and write well; and, third, they sowed the seeds for the first modern English departments. Composition scholars, therefore, find the roots of their profession in the eighteenth century, and this interest promises to lead to more research into the century's contributions to writing theory and the establishment of a broad-based approach to English studies. It is my hope that this book will contribute to this movement.

There are many people who helped make this volume possible. I would like to give special thanks to Marilyn Brownstein, Greenwood's recently retired Acquisitions Editor, who encouraged the project from the outset. I would also like to thank Dr. George F. Butler, Acquisitions Editor, for his suggestions that have made the book better than it would have been. Thanks also go to Winifred Bryan Horner of Texas Christian University and Thomas P. Miller of the University of Arizona for their suggestions early in the proposal stage. I would like to thank my Research Assistant, Patricia L. Watson, for help checking references and proofing the manuscript. I especially thank the English Department at the University of Georgia for encouraging me to return to teaching eighteenth-century literature and to develop courses in the period's rhetorical theory.

As usual, special thanks go to my wife, Mary Hurley Moran, who has always encouraged my work, and my daughter, Alison Moran, who loves to write.

INTRODUCTION

The purpose of this reference volume is to provide introductory entries on all major and many minor eighteenth-century British and American rhetoricians. The book is intended to be used not only by the expert, but also by students entering the field and scholars in related fields who need an introduction to the rhetoric and rhetoricians of the period. Each entry offers a brief biography of the rhetorician followed by an analysis of the figure's rhetorical theory and an up-to-date bibliography of the primary and secondary works on the figure. Although the figures are arranged alphabetically for easy reference, users can also read the volume through from beginning to end to get a sense of the major statements in rhetoric of the period. While not every minor rhetorician appears in the volume, the editor has attempted to offer a broad survey of representative figures of the period. The editor has also attempted to include representative figures of all major schools of rhetorical theory from the century, including neoclassical, stylistic, elocutionary, belletristic, psychological-philosophical rhetorics, and women's rhetoric.[1] While these categories overlap and some theorists can fit into more than one, the categories do offer a useful overview of the directions rhetoric took during the century, and a few words about each will provide an intellectual context for the figures in the book.

NEOCLASSICAL RHETORICS

Although most of the rhetoricians of the century were familiar with classical rhetorical theory, many of them rejected, modified, or developed this theory. However, a few theorists, the neoclassicists, worked closely within the tradition. For the most part, these rhetorics either restated classical theory or used it as their organizing principle. These works tended, for instance, to address at least some of the five arts of Ciceronian rhetoric—invention, arrangement, style, memory, and delivery—although not all neoclassical rhetorics necessarily discussed all of them. The two rhetorics most completely in the classical tradition were John Ward's *A System of Oratory* (1759) and John Holmes's teaching text for grammar school students, *The Art of Rhetoric Made Easy* (1739) (Howell 696). By far, the most important of the two was Ward's book, which consists of the lectures that he delivered at Gresham College. Opened in 1597, Gresham taught what we would now call "nontraditional students"—older students who wanted to hear lectures on various subjects without being confined to rigid degree programs with examinations and such. It is interesting that Ward thought, as his lectures demonstrate, that these students would benefit most from a reinterpretation of Ciceronian rhetoric. His book emphasizes the topics of invention, the use of enthymemic and syllogistic reasoning, and the tropes and figures of rhetoric in its approach to style. While Ward's rhetoric is a detailed and elaborate restatement of classical theory for the adult, Holmes's book is a distillation of classical theory for the child. Like any distillation, Holmes left much out, and his approach was to make it possible for his young students to memorize the basic dictates of the classical tradition through question and answer formats and mnemonic devices. A third important neoclassical rhetoric is John Lawson's *Lectures Concerning Oratory*, published in 1758. Based on lectures given at Trinity College in Dublin, Lawson's book is a looser restatement of classical doctrine than Ward's. In fact, much of Lawson's work attempted to apply classical principles to eighteenth-century British culture, as when he modified classical doctrine to help his students become better writers and deliverers of sermons, a genre unknown to the ancients.

STYLISTIC RHETORICS

A second tendency in the century was stylistic rhetorics, best represented by such theorists as John Stirling, Thomas Gibbons, and Anthony Blackwall, all of whom discussed style by means of figures of speech. Since these writers worked within the classical tradition of instruction in style, they could be considered an offshoot of the neoclassical school. However, as the titles of two of the books suggest, Stirling's *A System of Rhetoric* (1733) and Gibbons's *Rhetoric; or, a View of Its Principal Tropes and Figures* (1767), these rhetoricians used the term "rhetoric" in a much narrower sense than Ward did. In fact, both books clearly continue the seventeenth-century tradition that reduced rhetoric largely to style, giving to logic the canons of invention and arrangement. Stirling wrote his book to help elementary students learn the figures of speech so that they could better read the Latin classics. The first half of the book consists of a discussion—in English rhymed couplets (to help students memorize the material)—of the most important figures; the second half goes over the same ground in Latin. Gibbons's book is a more extensive treatment of the material—the first half covering tropes, the second covering figures. Like Stirling, Gibbons also used rhymed couplets to assist his readers in memorizing the devices. A third important stylistic rhetoric is Anthony Blackwall's *Introduction to the Classics* (1718). Like the other two, this volume contains discussions of the classical figures, but it is addressed in part to a different audience—namely, gentlemen who had finished their educations but needed a refresher course so that they could continue their studies.

ELOCUTIONARY MOVEMENT

While the neoclassicists and the stylists of the century worked within the classical tradition, the third school of rhetoricians, the elocutionists, greatly expanded one of the most neglected canons of the classical tradition: delivery. Although the classical rhetoricians, especially Cicero and Quintilian, addressed questions of delivery, these treatments are "brief and the emphasis is clearly toward a natural manner of speech" (Guthrie 18). The eighteenth-century elocutionists developed elaborate systems to teach the art of delivering a speech or reading aloud a text, and these methods covered everything from gestures, facial expressions, and voice modulation and tone. While the various systems that the elocutionists developed contributed to the separation of form and content and to the assumption that rhetoric is empty bombast, the theories also made major contributions to one of the most neglected of rhetorical arts: the art of presenting a speech.

The term *elocution* is a confusing one since the Latin term for style is *elocution* while the Latin term for delivery is *declamatio*. While it is unclear where the term originated and why, it is clear that the eighteenth century became deeply concerned not only with the content of speeches but also with their delivery. This concern was especially strong concerning the clergy, who were required to deliver sermons before bored congregations. As Jonathan Swift noted in his *Letter to a Young Clergyman*, not all ministers delivered their sermons with even minimum effectiveness: "You will observe some clergymen with their head held down from the beginning to the end within an inch of the cushion to read what is hardly legible; which, beside the untoward manner, hinders them from making the best advantage of their voice: others again have a trick of popping up and down every moment from their paper to the audience, like an idle school boy on a repetition day" (qtd. in Guthrie 20). It is important to recognize, however, that the elocutionists were not only responding to an absence of good speaking. They also shared a common philosophy that G. P. Mohrmann sums up as follows: "It is fair to say that they [the elocutionists] all believed tones, looks, and gestures to be a language of emotion; that this language responded to the dictates of nature; that it was universally operative; that it was a necessary feature of true communication; and that it was essential to the progress of mankind" (118).

The importance of the elocution movement to the eighteenth century is demonstrated by the fact that it had many practitioners during the century. One of the earliest publications on the subject was *An Essay upon the Action of an Orator* (1702), an anonymous English translation of Michel Le Faucheur's 1657 *Traitté de l'action de l'orateur*. Le Faucheur's work was translated two other times during the century, and the translation of his work marks the birth of elocution in England. One of the first English contributions to the movement was John Mason's 1748 *An Essay on Elocution*. While popular, as Howell has noted it largely restated material in the Le Faucheur translations. Other, more important elocutionists were James Burgh and Thomas Sheridan. Burgh's *The Art of Speaking* (1761) presents the argument that the manner of speaking is more important than the words themselves, thus emphasizing manner over matter. The book is famous for its inventory of emotions and the gestures, tone of voice, and expressions that correspond to each. Because of his emphasis on rules for achieving elocutionary ends, Burgh, along with John Walker (*Elements of Elocution* [1781]) and others, have been placed in the "mechanical" as opposed to the "natural" school. The best representative of the latter school is Thomas Sheridan, who produced a number of books on the subject, the best known being *A Course of Lectures on Elocution* (1762). Delivered first as a set of popular lectures, this book contains Sheridan's argument for the importance of good speaking to the health of a nation. The book also continues his argument, from his *British Education* (1756), that English education should be reformed by emphasizing instruction in the vernacular. Critics have questioned the usefulness of the mechanical/natural distinction because virtually all elocutionists viewed their work as helping the orator speak naturally. Some, however, provided more rules than others to help perfect nature.

BELLETRISTIC RHETORICS

Belletristic rhetoric was the fourth tendency in eighteenth-century rhetoric. The belletristic theorists—including rhetoricians such as Edmund Burke, Adam Smith, Lord Kames, and Hugh Blair—helped reform rhetoric to make it a useful method of literary criticism, shifting the discipline from concentrating solely on the "creative act" to addressing issues of "the interpretive act" (Horner 117). They accomplished this shift by combining the study of rhetoric with the study of other disciplines of language use—including literature, history, biography, and linguistics—naming this new approach the study of rhetoric and belles lettres (Golden and Corbett 8). These theorists, therefore, helped lay the groundwork for the literary criticism that developed during the nineteenth and twentieth centuries (Horner 117). Several of the belletristic theorists held academic posts and held chairs that helped define what would become of the English department. After delivering his lectures on rhetoric in Edinburgh from 1748 to 1751, Adam Smith lectured on rhetoric and other subjects at the University of Glasgow until 1763. Hugh Blair delivered his lectures on rhetoric and belles lettres at the University of Edinburgh, where King George III appointed him in 1762 the first Regius Professor of Rhetoric.

Like the other movements in rhetoric, the belletristic tradition consisted of a loosely connected group of theorists. The belles lettres tradition was imported to England from the Continent through works such as Charles Rollin's *Traité*, which was anonymously translated into English in 1734 under the title of *The Method of Teaching and Studying the Belles Lettres.* English theorists took up the basic concepts and developed a native tradition. Although Adam Smith burned his works on rhetoric before his death, his *Lectures on Rhetoric and Belles Lettres* have come to us in the form of student lecture notes. As these notes suggest, Smith rejected many standard classical categories. While he discussed classical writers, he also discussed contemporary writers such as Swift and Shaftesbury. In addition to discussing argumentation, he also developed a system of discourse analysis that explained narrative and expository prose. Hugh Blair, by far the most influential of the belletristic theorists, expanded Smith's work in *Lectures on Rhetoric and Belles Lettres,* one of the most influential rhetorics during the nineteenth century in both England and America. Although Blair did not entirely reject classical rhetoric, he did continue the shift in theory from the production of discourse to the reading of discourse, both ancient and modern. His rejection of invention—one of the central arts of classical rhetoric—and his embrace of style as a central concern of rhetoric demonstrates his commitment to a rhetoric concerned as much with analyzing texts as with producing them.

PSYCHOLOGICAL-PHILOSOPHICAL THEORIES OF RHETORIC

The fifth tendency of thought in eighteenth-century rhetoric were the "psychological-philosophical theories" of rhetoric (Golden and Corbett 9). The theorists who fall into this category recognized the limitations of classical rhetoric and attempted to establish rhetorics based on the new principles of psychology and philosophy that contemporary theorists such as John Locke, David Hume, Francis Hutcheson, Thomas Reid, and Adam Smith—among others—developed during the century (Golden and Corbett 9). Since these philosophers created new philosophical, psychological, and aesthetic theories that redefined the human mind and its operations, innovative rhetoricians naturally attempted to use these theories as a basis for their rhetorics. Some drew on Locke's view that the mind understands the world by perceiving data through the senses and then by associating simple ideas into complex ones. Some drew on Hume's discussions of association psychology based on his argument that the mind associates ideas following the principles of resemblance, contiguity, and cause and effect; therefore, ideas in the mind become associated if they resemble each other in some way, if they are close together in time or space, or if they are related causally. Some rhetoricians drew on David Hartley's arguments that all mental activities, including reason and emotions, are based on the association of ideas that result from the physical vibrations of the muscles. Others, most notably George Campbell, also drew on the common-sense tradition of such Scottish thinkers as Thomas Reid and James Beattie who advanced the view that the mind could trust the evidence it obtained from the principles of common sense innately possessed by all minds. The common-sense position, with its acceptance of innate ideas, was in direct conflict with association psychology, which argued that all ideas result from experience and association.

Two of the best examples of rhetoricians who based their rhetorics (although in different ways) on new psychological and philosophical theories were George Campbell and Joseph Priestley. When Campbell wrote his *Philosophy of Rhetoric* (1776), he drew on the ideas of John Locke, David Hume, David Hartley, and Thomas Reid, basing his rhetoric on the human mind as understood by eighteenth-century philosophers. As Lloyd F. Bitzer has commented, as editor of George Campbell's *Philosophy of Rhetoric*, "Campbell permitted fundamental issues of metaphysics and epistemology to enter and influence his theory of rhetoric" (Campbell vii–viii). Campbell assumed that rhetoric must be based on the principles of human nature, as eighteenth-century philosophers—such as Locke, Hume, and Hartley—had delineated it. Like Locke, Campbell accepted the assumption that the human mind developed through experience, and he based his rhetoric on the principles of empiricism. He rejected syllogistic reasoning on the grounds that "in all kinds of knowledge, wherein experience is our only guide, we can proceed to general truths solely by an induction of particulars" (62–63). Rhetoric, then, must be based on empiricism with its methods of "observation and experience" (Campbell xxvi).

Campbell based his discussion of discourse types on the four mental functions—namely, understanding, imagination, emotions, and will. Discourse that is addressed to the understanding attempts either to inform or convince an audience; discourse that is addressed to the imagination, Campbell noted, attempts to exhibit "a lively and beautiful representation of a suitable object" (3); discourse that is addressed to the passions attempts to represent the "pathetic" and stimulate "love, pity, grief, terror, desire, aversion, fury, or hatred" (4); and discourse that is addressed to the will attempts to "persuade to a certain conduct" (4), the most complicated type of all.

Campbell was influenced by many Enlightenment philosophers, perhaps the most influential of whom was Hume, a fellow Scotsman with whom

Campbell corresponded. From Hume Campbell drew two central ideas. One was Hume's notion of vivacity. Like Hume, Campbell assumed that vivacity, or vividness, of ideas determined the strength of belief that the reader or listener felt. Sensations—direct perceptions of objects through the senses— provided the highest degree of vivacity and demanded the highest degree of assent. We tend to accept without question, for instance, that the paper clip on the desk before us is real. Ideas in the other two classes—ideas of memory and ideas of imagination—since they are removed from direct perception, naturally possess less vivacity and, therefore, create less assent or belief. A second notion that Campbell borrowed from Hume was the philosopher's three principles of association of ideas—that is, resemblance, contiguity, and causation. As Bitzer has written, Campbell assumed that "the mind tends to associate ideas which are similar, ideas which are contiguous in space or time, and ideas related as causes and effects" (Campbell xxxiv).

Although Campbell developed his new rhetoric within the context of the new association psychology and empiricism, he also drew some ideas from the Scottish common-sense school. When discussing the types of evidence available to the mind, he recognized that the evidence of common sense is "an original source of knowledge common to all mankind. I own, indeed, that in different persons it [common sense] prevails in different degrees of strength; but no human creature hath been found originally and totally destitute of it, who is not accounted a monster in his kind" (38–40). As Campbell noted (in a footnote on pp. 38–39), he borrowed this notion of certain innate or instinctual ideas from Reid and Beattie, the Scottish philosophers who made the arguments for the common-sense position. This influence is not surprising since Reid and Beattie along with Campbell, belonged to the Philosophical Society of Aberdeen and critiqued the essays that would become the *Philosophy* there. The purpose of the common-sense position was to avoid the extreme stance that all knowledge and mental activity had to be grounded in experience. Such notions as "the future will resemble the past," "there are other intelligent beings in the universe besides me," and "the clear representations of my memory. . . . are true" exist as part of the human mind.

It is on this point that Priestley disagreed with Campbell. When Priestley came to write his *Course of Lectures on Oratory and Criticism* (1777) (a reworking of the lectures he gave on rhetoric at the Warrington Academy), he based his rhetoric on the association psychology of Hartley. Priestley, therefore, rejected common-sense assumptions (Bevilacqua 79–80), replacing them with the view that all knowledge is grounded in experience. Priestley did not disagree that some truths were established and certain; but according to Priestley, truths were not called such because they were innately true but because they were established by the experience of many people over time or because they were based on the Scriptures. Priestley's rhetoric represents one of the most consistent applications of association psychology to rhetoric because he used it to explain invention, organization, and style in written and spoken discourse.

WOMEN'S RHETORIC

The last tendency in eighteenth-century rhetoric is women's rhetoric, the least understood and most amorphous of any category in the century. Because women were excluded from the male-dominated educational system and from the learned professions where men used rhetoric, female theorists did not produce formal rhetorical theories. Instead, they argued for more fundamental rights: the rights to speak and write in public and the right to have their discourses taken seriously. Since little research has been done to identify these rhetorics, this volume includes a sample of essays on two of the most important of the women rhetoricians of the seventeenth and eighteenth centuries, Margaret Askew Fell and Mary Wollstonecraft. Fell's 1666 *Womens Speaking Justified* argues for women's rights to speak at Quaker meetings and to preach in public. Fell based her argument largely on Scripture and Quaker doctrine when she argues that the Bible justified women's preaching and that women have the same Inner Light as men do. Wollstonecraft's discussions of rhetoric appear in her works on other subjects, such as *Thoughts on the Education of Daughters* (1787), *The Female Reader* (1789), and *A Vindication of the Rights of Woman* (1792). She felt compelled to publish *The Female Reader*, a work on the importance of elocution to a woman's education, under a male pseudonym, Mr. Cresswick. In this work Wollstonecraft argued that women are as capable as men of developing their powers of reason. Wollstonecraft also argued that society should allow women to develop qualities of intellect allowed only to males at the time. While Fell and Wollstonecraft are not the only theorists who discussed women's rhetoric, they are two of the more visible ones; and it is hoped that their inclusion in the volume will encourage more research on women rhetoricians during the period.

Although the above classification scheme implies that the rhetorics of the century neatly fit the various categories, we should remember that many of the rhetorics expressed more than a single tendency. Blair and Campbell, for instance, continued many of the traditions of classical rhetoric, while Priestley organized his system by following the major Ciceronian categories of invention, arrangement, and style, even though his handling of each category was innovative. A neoclassicist such as Lawson, although he remained largely in the classical camp, also drew on more modern ideas. But it is useful to consider these general trends of thought in the rhetoric of the period to help understand the relationships among the various rhetoricians discussed in this volume.

NOTE

1. Scholars have developed three major systems to classify the kinds of rhetoric produced in the eighteenth century, and my system borrows from all of them. The first is Wilbur Samuel Howell's, which identifies four "forms" of rhetoric: contemporary interpretations of classical rhetoric, stylistic rhetoric, elocutionists, and new rhetoric (696–98). The second system is that of James L. Golden and Edward P. J. Corbett, who have identified four schools of thought among rhetoricians of the century: the adherents of the classical school, the adherents of the elocutionary and belletristic movements, and the adherents of the "psychological-philosophical theories of public address" (7–9). The third system is that of Winifred Bryan Horner, who has identified the following traditions: neoclassical rhetoric, the old rhetoric, the elocutionists, and belletristic rhetorics (109–24).

BIBLIOGRAPHY

Bevilacqua, Vincent M. "Campbell, Priestley, and the Controversy Concerning Common Sense." *Southern Speech Journal* 30.2 (1964):79–98.

Blackwall, Anthony. *An Introduction to the Classics.* London, 1718.

Blair, Hugh. *Lectures on Rhetoric and Belles Lettres.* Reprint. Edited by Harold F. Harding. 2 vols. Carbondale: Southern Illinois University Press, 1965.

Burgh, James. *The Art of Speaking.* London, 1761.

Campbell, George. *The Philosophy of Rhetoric.* Edited by Lloyd F. Bitzer. Carbondale: Southern Illinois University Press, 1988.

An Essay upon the Action of an Orator. London, 1702.

Fell, Margaret. *Womens Speaking Justified, Proved, and Allowed by the Scriptures.* 1666. Los Angeles: Augustan Reprint Society 194, 1979.

Le Faucheur, Michel. *Traitté de l'action de l'orateur; ou, de la Prononciation et de geste.* Paris, 1657.

Gibbons, Thomas. *Rhetoric; or, a View of Its Principal Tropes and Figures.* London, 1767.

Golden, James L., and Edward P. J. Corbett. Introduction to *The Rhetoric of Blair, Campbell, and Whately,* 1–22. Rev. ed. Carbondale: Southern Illinois University Press, 1990.

Guthrie, Warren. "The Development of Rhetorical Theory in America, 1635–1850. 5. The Elocution Movement: England." *Speech Monographs* 18.1 (1951):17–30.

Holmes, John. *The Art of Rhetoric Made Easy.* London, 1739.

Horner, Winifred Bryan. "The Eighteenth Century." In *The Present State of Scholarship in Historical and Contemporary Rhetoric,* edited by Winifred Bryan Horner, 101–33. Columbia: Missouri University Press, 1983.

Howell, Wilbur Samuel. *Eighteenth-Century British Logic and Rhetoric.* Princeton: Princeton University Press, 1971.

Lawson, John. *Lectures Concerning Oratory.* Dublin, 1758. Reprint. Edited by E. Neal Claussen and Karl R. Wallace. Carbondale: Southern Illinois University Press, 1972.

Mason, John. *An Essay on Elocution.* London, 1748.

Mohrmann, G. P. "The Language of Nature and Elocutionary Theory." *Quarterly Journal of Speech* 52 (1966):116–24.

Priestley, Joseph. *A Course of Lectures on Oratory and Criticism.* 1777. Reprint. Edited by Vincent M. Bevilacqua and Richard Murphy. Carbondale: Southern Illinois University Press, 1965.

Rollin, Charles. *The Method of Teaching and Studying the Belles Lettres.* 2 vols. London, 1758.

Sheridan, Thomas. *British Education.* London, 1756.

———. *A Course of Lectures on Elocution.* London, 1762.

Smith, Adam. *Lectures on Rhetoric and Belles Lettres.* Edited and with an Introduction by John M. Lothian. Carbondale: Southern Illinois University Press, 1963.

Stirling, John. *A System of Rhetoric.* London, 1733.

Ward, John. *A System of Oratory.* 2 vols. London, 1759.

Walker, John. *Elements of Elocution.* London, 1781.

Wollstonecraft, Mary. *The Female Reader.* 1789. Reprint. Edited by Janet Todd and Marilyn Butler. New York: New York University Press, 1989.

———. *Thoughts on the Education of Daughters.* 1789. Reprint. Edited by Janet Todd and Marilyn Butler. New York: New York University Press, 1989.

———. *A Vindication of the Rights of Woman.* 1792. Reprint. Edited by Janet Todd and Marilyn Butler. New York: New York University Press, 1989.

ANONYMOUS, *AN ESSAY ON THE ACTION PROPER FOR THE PULPIT*
(1753)

Patricia B. Worrall

In 1753, the anonymous pamphlet *An Essay on the Action Proper for the Pulpit* was published by R. and J. Dodsley in London, and the question of authorship remains. The Library of Congress assigns the essay to John Mason. Wilbur Samuel Howell, in *Eighteenth-Century British Logic and Rhetoric*, has refuted Mason's authorship because the pamphlet "does not appear . . . to have been written by a clergyman" and because the author uses *action* or *manner* rather than the term *elocution* used by Mason; but Howell offers no author for the work (209). In *Elements of Pulpit Oratory in Eighteenth-Century England*, Rolf P. Lessenich has attributed the essay to the Scottish clergyman James Fordyce, and *The British Library General Catalogue* lists the 1753 essay and later editions printed in 1755 and 1815 under Fordyce. However, in the revised edition of *The Present State of Scholarship in Historical and Contemporary Rhetoric*, Winifred Bryan Horner has cited the work as anonymous (128).

Much of what the pamphlet's author said about *pulpit action*, a term he used to mean voice and gestures, is not original; nevertheless, the essay remains of interest to the study of eighteenth-century elocution. Howell's observations that the anonymous author's voice is that "of a layman or member of the congregation" (209 n. 157) and that the essay is a "superficial treatise on delivery rather than a profound discourse on rhetoric" (210) point to the pamphlet's uniqueness among eighteenth-century works on elocution. Brief and intermittent references are made to Demosthenes, Cicero, and Quintilian, but rather than depend on the authority of the ancients, the author based his discussion on familiar examples, quotations, and allusions from literature, art, drama, and theater. Two additional aspects set the essay apart from other treatises. Instead of detailed precepts and extensive instructions, the author presented general concepts followed by suggestions and illustrations; and he advised and encouraged young ministers on appropriate pulpit voice and gestures, not as a pedantic clergyman, but as an avuncular layman.

The author began by comparing two preachers that he heard on the same day. The morning preacher was of "uncommon Parts, improved by a happy Education, of fine Taste, and great Learning"; his "Composition was truly masterly," and the "Figures were bold, but natural; the Ornaments noble, but unaffected" (1–2). However, this "excellent Performance had no proportionable effect" because he "pronounced his Discourse without the least Justness, Grace or Pathos" (2). In contrast, the afternoon preacher was a "plain Man, of ordinary Capacity, little Literature, and no Refinement"; his "Method was not very judicious, nor his Style very proper," but "he *delivered* himself in so strong, so significant, and so agreeable a Manner" that the congregation was "profoundly attentive, and sensibly moved" (3). This contrast between the preachers and their "Pulpit Action" introduces the "vast importance of Just *Action* or a Right *Manner* in the Pulpit" (3).

Following the comparison, the author discussed the importance of actions because, as he remarked, "Mankind are unspeakably more influenced by their *Eyes* and their *Ears*, than by their *Understandings* alone" (4) and actions can present the "very *Picture*" of a particular sentiment or passion (5). The author used the example of the actor David Garrick to illustrate that on the stage emotions become visual through actions (16). However, he warned that "no *Action* will have effect, that carries with it the Appearance of Art" (19) and art "must be managed so finely as to appear quite *Natural*" (20). The focus then shifts to the "wide difference between that *Action* which suits the *Theatre*, and that which becomes the *Pulpit*" (23). Passions such as *Violence*, *Rage*, and *Fury*, as well as the "Low and Comic" (23), are appropriate on the stage; but in the pulpit, a "Solemnity and Sanctity of *Manner*" should always be maintained (23–24).

As with the human passions, "*Religious* Passions" can also be expressed through gestures (24); thus, members of the congregation become *Spectators*, as religion through actions takes on a visible form (25). Since prints of Raphael's "St. PAUL's Hearers at *Athens*" were readily available, the author used the painting to illustrate gestures portraying religious passions (26). He described Paul as a "Divine Orator . . . looking with such a Face of Inspiration and impetuous Ardour, and seeming to pour forth a whole Tempest of sacred Eloquence" (26). However, in an aside, he did note that the "*Apostle's* Arms [are] raised too high" in the "warm Manner of the *Italian* Preachers" (27).

In the next section two problems are identified that are related to pulpit action: young men enter the ministry "before either their *Hearts*, their *Understandings*, or their *Tastes*, are in any Measure formed" (28–29), and "Preachers, like Authors, are . . . but indifferent Judges of their own Performances" (31). To help remedy these problems, the young preacher is advised to find a friend "capable of criticizing with real Taste and Friendship" and, as Polonius advises Laertes in *Hamlet*, to "*grapple him to his Soul with Hooks [sic] of Steel* [1.3.63]" (32–33). The young man should find a model; he should not be a "Servile Imitator" but should use the model "to enrich and compleat his Native Fund" (33).

The author then concentrated on preaching, the "noblest [of] Performances" (34), his first concern being the "*Modulation* of the Voice" (35). A discourse hurriedly delivered is characterized as a "Land-flood . . . affording neither Entertainment whilst it lasts, nor advantage afterwards; whereas the same Discourse, pronounced with a proper Grace and Deliberation, might resemble some gently flowing River, which at once delights the attentive Beholder, and refreshes all the neighboring Fields" (35–36). Two advantages of "deliberate Pronunciation" are that it allows the *Speaker* time to enter into the several parts of his performance" and "the *Hearer* hath leisure to consider and to feel every thing that is said" (36). Pauses are important because they "afford equal relief to [the preacher] and to his Audience," "bring [the sermon] nearer to Life," and "add an Importance and Solemnity to the whole" (37). To illustrate the importance of variety in speaking, the author used the analogy of the "Harmony, Variety, and Power of *Numbers* in *Writing*" (45–47). According to the author, Dryden and Pope were skilled at rhyme, but Milton's blank verse afforded the ear "that high continued transport" (47). Continuing the analogy, the author said that a "Uniform cadence in Pronunciation is like constant Rhyme in Poetry, and grows Stale for the same reason" (47). In addition, there must be the "*Art of Sounds*," or, as Pope said in *An Essay on Criticism*, "*the sound must seem an Eccho to the Sense* [365]" (49). Using the divisions of the sermon, the author provided an example of the different variations of voice: "In the *Exordium* . . . Pronunciation will generally be sober, tranquil, and respectful" becoming more *animated* as the preacher moves through the discourse until he "arrives at the *Application* [when] . . . he will then give way to a superior Burst of Religious Vehemence" (51–52). The author concluded the section by cautioning the preacher "not to go beyond the Feelings of Nature, or the Limits of Decorum" (52) and reminding him that a "Theatrical Pronunciation would be inconsistent with that Seriousness which must reign throughout" the sermon (53).

The author opened the next section with the regret that "Students and Candidates for the *Ministry*, are provided with no Schools for their *Assistance*" as public speakers (53); however, since no schools were available, the author offered a self-help program. First, young men should "exercise themselves very often in reading and reciting aloud . . . in the hearing of one or more Judicious Friends . . . who wou'd correct them with all manner of candid Severity" (55–56). Second, young men should "choose some of the best Compositions of different kinds . . . but particularly some of the best Sermons on different Subjects, and sometimes *read*, sometimes *recite* those, both in the house, and in the open air" (56). And third, young men should

take care "to pronounce naturally, roundly, and easily . . . reflecting how a
Man would say such a thing who *felt* it in *real* Life" (57). The author's
advice echoes Hamlet's: "Let them . . . speak [the words] *trippingly* on the
tongue, not *mouthing* them as many do, nor dwelling on one more than
another, where the Emphasis does not require it [3.2.1–4]" (57). "Young
Performers [who] catch themselves transgressing" are instructed to "stop
immediately and . . . endeavour to correct that error" (58). If these exercises
are considered too tedious, young men are reminded of the "astonishing
pains that were taken . . . by the Ambitious Students of *Heathen* Oratory"
(59–60).

Gestures are the next topic, and the "same general Rules that are applicable to the [voice], are alike applicable to [gestures]. Nature is equally to
be followed in both" (61). For instance, "gestures are to *accompany* [a
preacher's] Words, never to come *after* them, seldom to *precede* them" (64),
and "Sense and Judgment must always be employed, to govern the Hurry
of Imagination, and to temper the Heat of *Action*" (64–65).

Rather than go into "detail of the particular Motions," the author directed the reader to Quintilian (66–67) although he did offer guidance
based on "Sense and Reflexion," such as pointing upward to "express what
is supposed to be exalted" and pointing downward to "express something
low" (67). If a preacher keeps in mind "what is *decent* and *natural*," he
will avoid improper pulpit gestures, including "shrugging of the shoulders"
and "writhing of the body" (68). As Howell has noted, some of the author's
comments echo those of Michel Le Faucheur, the French rhetorician and
author of *Traitté de l'action de l'orateur* (1657), which was translated into
English in the 1690s. One instance is when the author says "that the hands
should never be raised higher than the eyes, nor brought lower than the
edge of the Pulpit; that the *left* hand should never be employed to express
any thing by itself, but only in concurrence with the *right*" (qtd. in Howell
213). Howell has also pointed out that when the author says "that the
Speaker should move always from the *right* to the *left*, but neither much
nor quick" (68), he "gives a rule that does not appear to be authorized by
Le Faucheur" and one that "would seem anyway to be impossible to apply
in any situation" (Howell 213).

The author next turned his attention to "*the Action of the Countenance*,"
a "very Essential Part of the *Exterior* of Eloquence" (71). Using Milton's
phrase from Book III of *Paradise Lost*, he described preachers who throw
"their features into such Distortions, as quite disfigure the *Human Face
Divine* [44]" (71). He then pointed out that a preacher "whose Face *looked*
what his Words *spoke*" would be superior "to such Performers, in point of
true Execution" (72).

Some preachers may think that he has set too high a "Standard of *Pulpit
Action*" (74), but he encouraged them that even if they "should fall short
of the *Perfection* of the Art, still the Attempt is brave and honourable" (77).

As further encouragement, the author then told the young preachers that the most important qualification is a "WARM AND WORTHY HEART" (78–79), and he reassured them that the "*Action* of the *Body*. . .is the *Action* of the *Soul*, the inward Glowing of that *celestial Fire*, that must give breath, motion, and vigour to all" (79).

In the final section of the essay, the author included a sincere and personal address to his young audience: "*Gentlemen*, . . . I doubt not in the least of your succeeding, if before you Attempt to recommend Religion to *others*, You take care to cultivate [a] . . . Sense of it in *Yourselves*" (79). And the author continued: "Let what you say be but Natural; and it will. . .be pleasing and persuasive. But Men only speak *naturally*, when they speak *sincerely*, that is, what they *think* and *feel*. Take care to think and to feel the very things you would inspire" (82).

Granted, the essay is not a "profound discourse on rhetoric." But for the author's young audience, the essay provided sound principles based on nature, sincerity, and virtue; common-sense advice with familiar illustrations; and finally, encouragement for young clergymen to become "Divine Orators."

BIBLIOGRAPHY

Primary Source

An Essay on the Action Proper for the Pulpit. 1753. Reprint. New York: Garland, 1971.

Criticism

Horner, Winifred Bryan. *The Present State of Scholarship in Historical and Contemporary Rhetoric.* Rev. ed. Columbia: University of Missouri Press, 1990.

Howell, Wilbur Samuel. *Eighteenth-Century British Logic and Rhetoric*, 209–13. Princeton: Princeton University Press, 1971.

Lessenich, Rolf P. *Elements of Pulpit Oratory in Eighteenth-Century England (1660–1800).* Cologne: Böhlau-Verlag, 1972.

ANTHONY BLACKWALL
(1674–1730)

Susan Hunter

Born in 1674 at Blackwall in Derbyshire, his family's home for generations, Anthony Blackwall made his living as a grammar-school teacher and cleric and published works of classical scholarship until his death in 1730. He attended Derby School, and as a sizar, exempt from the costs of fees and of room and board, received a B.A. in 1694 and an M.A. in1698 at Emmanuel College, Cambridge. In 1698, he was appointed headmaster of Derby School and lecturer of All Saints' Church, Derby.

In 1706, while headmaster at Derby, Blackwall established his reputation as a classical scholar with an original Greek edition of *Theognidis Megarensis Sententiae Morales* and a Latin translation of it (Westby-Gibson). While teaching at Derby in 1718, he published his most influential and popular work, which was entitled *An Introduction to the Classics, containing a short discourse on their Excellencies, and Directions how to study them to advantage; with an Essay on the Nature and use of those Emphatical and beautiful figures which give strength and ornament to Writing.* During Blackwall's lifetime this two-part treatise was issued in three editions, in 1718, 1719, and 1725. After his death in 1730, *An Introduction to the Classics* was published three more times, in 1737, 1746, and 1809.

In addition to these six editions of Blackwall's treatise, the second part of his treatise was issued eight times between 1748 and 1793 as the section entitled "Rhetoric and Poetry" in the first volume of *The Preceptor* (Tedder). Distinguished by a preface and a fable entitled "The Vision of Theodore the Hermit" by Dr. Samuel Johnson, *The Preceptor* was, according to its title page, a two-volume "compendium of polite learning" intended—much as Blackwall's *Introduction* had been—to educate young scholars in grammar schools and to reeducate gentlemen who had either forgotten what they had learned in school or had been deprived of this learning (Howell 139). *The Preceptor* provided a general course of learning in twelve parts.

Robert Dodsley, a well-connected London bookseller whom Dr. Johnson credits with suggesting the idea of an English dictionary, selected the second part of Blackwall's *An Introduction to the Classics* as part five of *The Preceptor* because he found the principles of rhetoric and poetry "so concisely and sensibly handled by Mr. *Blackwell* [*sic*], in the second Part of his Introduction to the Classicks, that, despairing to get any thing better, or more to my Purpose, I prevail'd with the Proprietor of the Book, to give me leave to make such Use of it as should be thought proper" (Dodsley 405n).

In the 1748 edition, Dodsley noted that he had made some alterations to Blackwall's text, adding and exchanging "many Examples from the Poets to explain and illustrate the Rules . . . in which last Particular alone this Treatise seem'd defective" (321; qtd. in Howell 139, 141n). In 1796 Blackwall's essay was excerpted from *The Preceptor* and published in Boston for the use of Harvard students (Howell 139–40, 141n).

Appointed in 1722 as headmaster of the grammar school of Bosworth, Leicestershire, Blackwall produced in 1725 the first part and in 1727 the second part of what is considered his principal work, namely, *The Sacred Classics defended and illustrated, or an Essay humbly offered towards proving the Purity, Propriety, and True Eloquence of the Writers of the New Testament.* The second volume of this work was published posthumously in 1731 (Westby-Gibson). In his second volume Blackwall used his knowledge of the classics to justify various readings of the New Testament. While headmaster at Derby and Bosworth, Blackwall used *A New Latin Grammar, being a short, clear, and easy introduction of young Scholars to the Knowledge of the Latin Tongue, etc.* that he had composed; it was published anonymously in 1728 (Westby-Gibson).

In 1726, one of his former pupils, Sir Henry Atkins, recommended Blackwall for the living at the rectory at Clapham, Surrey. He was ordained that same year. Early in 1729 Blackwall gave up the Clapham living to become headmaster once again at Bosworth, where he died on April 8, 1730. For the first four months of 1730, it is likely that Samuel Johnson became Blackwall's usher, or assistant, at Bosworth, continuing to teach there for two and a half years after Blackwall's death (Westby-Gibson).

BLACKWALL'S RHETORICAL THEORY

A classical scholar who put his erudition to work in instructional texts for young gentlemen, Anthony Blackwall was a chief authority during the eighteenth century on what Wilbur Samuel Howell and Winifred Bryan Horner have called "stylistic rhetoric." Not only was his work excerpted and reprinted in all eight editions of Dodsley's *The Preceptor*, but John Holmes cited Blackwall as one of twenty authorities on rhetoric on the 1739 title page of *The Art of Rhetoric Made Easy* and referred to Blackwall's work in four places in that text (Howell 127, 139, 141n). In his preface to *The*

Preceptor, Dr. Johnson noted that the section on rhetoric and poetry (Blackwall's treatise) was designed to "teach the Mind some general Heads of Observation, to which the beautiful Passages of the best Writers may commonly be reduced" (xxii). This, then, was Blackwall's claim to fame: his knowledge of Latin and Greek enabled him to select passages from classical and modern texts to exemplify tropes or figures of speech that schoolmasters agreed gentlemen-scholars should learn to imitate. Indeed, his much-reprinted definition of *rhetoric*, emphasizes style: "Rhetoric is the Art or Faculty of Speaking and Writing with Elegance and Dignity, in order to instruct, persuade, and please. Grammar only teaches Plainness and Propriety: Rhetoric lays these for its Foundation, and raises upon them all the Graces of *Tropes* and *Figures*" (148–49).

Although such ideas would not be codified until later in the eighteenth century in such works as Dr. Johnson's *Dictionary* (1755) and Bishop Robert Lowth's grammar (1762), in the preface to *An Introduction to the Classics*, Blackwall was concerned with formulating a style appropriate for the literati. Blackwall asserted that extensive reading of ancient authors led to a refined sensibility and an understanding of moral virtue. Further, he believed that elegant language usage and social class were so interconnected that rhetorical style reflected a desired type of thought process or social status.

He intended his textbook to empower upper-class men of two age groups: "younger Scholars" and "Gentlemen who have for some Years neglected the Advantages of their Education and have a mind to resume those pleasant and useful Studies, in which they formerly made a handsome Progress at the Schools or Universities" (A2r). Supporting his claims with copious Greek and Latin citations, Blackwall argued in the first part of *An Introduction to the Classics* for the excellence of the classics. In the second part of the essay, he specified "the noblest Tropes and Figures, which give real Strength and Grace to Language; which heighten and improve our Notions; and are of excellent Use to persuade and please," (A5v) here offering ample English citations to illustrate them.

Although Dodsley and Holmes endorsed only Blackwall's essay on the tropes and figures, the first part of *An Introduction to the Classics* is notable because it demonstrates how many eighteenth-century writers valued Greek and Latin above "Living Languages" (2) because, unlike the English tongue, Greek and Latin were "fix'd and unalterable" (3). Blackwall first described nine ways in which classical authors excelled and that his readers would do well to emulate. When Demosthenes, Homer, Plato, Vergil, Quintilian, and Sallust composed their writings, for instance, they "took care to furnish themselves with Knowledge by close Thought, select Conversation and Reading; and to gain all the Information and *Light* that was necessary to qualify 'em to do Justice to their *Subject* . . . they took time and pains to give every part of their Discourse all possible Strength and Ornament, and to make the whole Composition uniform and beautiful"

(13). Second, Xenophon in the *Symposium* displayed "all the Politeness of a study'd Composition; and yet all the Freedom and winning Familiarity of elegant Conversation" (29). Third, upper-class men could aspire to be like Horace and Vergil who were "Persons of Quality and Fortune, Courtiers and Statesmen, great Travellers and Generals of Armies . . . Their Riches and Plenty furnish'd them with leisure and Means of Study; and their Employments improv'd them in Knowledge and Experience" (35–36). Fourth, the ancient authors were able to select the noblest meters (43) so that they could, fifth, suit sound to sense (45), and sixth, provide their readers with "a constant Succession of Pleasures" and "the Bounty and Gaiety of universal Nature" (53).

Blackwall also urged his intended audience—"*Gentlemen* of Birth and Fortune, qualify'd to manage *Public Business*, and fit as Members in the most *August Assemblies*"—to study Greek and Roman orations as "Masterpieces of clear *Reasoning* and genuine *Eloquence*" (59). Classical authors excel in an eighth way by portraying sound morals (67). Finally, in more than thirty pages of selected passages Blackwall commended the ancient authors for showing that "the *Bible* is the most excellent and useful Book in the World" and claimed that "to understand its Meaning and discover its Beauties, 'tis necessary to be conversant in the *Greek* and *Latin Classics*" (79–82). In the second chapter of this introduction, Blackwall prescribed the order in which a young scholar was supposed to read the Greek and Latin classics that Blackwall designated as canonical (116–18). His list includes as well some books of the New Testament (130–31) along with modern English and continental writers "who always have the *Ancients* in view, and write with their Spirit and Judgment" (135).

The second part of Blackwall's treatise, which Dodsley and Holmes cited and reprinted to embody rhetoric, is an essay on the use of tropes and figures, listing seven chief tropes and twenty-six chief figures of speech illustrated with examples in English. According to Blackwall, tropes such as metaphor and allegory are necessary for variety, emphasis, ornament, and decency; they should be used sparingly and cautiously, be not too remote and never convey lewd ideas (160–81). Figures, too, are used for emphasis and the expression of passion or beauty (189–272). The rhetorical question with which Blackwall closed his treatise demonstrates how taken he was with stylistic ornament: "When Numbers of [Figures] like a bright *Constellation* shed their united *Rays* upon it, how charmingly beauteous, and full of Graces, must that whole Discourse appear?" (272).

BIBLIOGRAPHY

Primary Works

Blackwall, Anthony. *An Introduction to the Classics*. London, 1718. Part 2 of this work was reprinted with revisions and additions by Robert Dodsley in *The Preceptor*. London, 1748.

————. *An Introduction to the Classics: Containing, A Short Discourse on Their Ex-cellencies; and Directions How to Study Them to Advantage: With an Essay, on the Nature and Use of those Emphatical and Beautiful Figures which Give Strength and Ornament to Writing.* 2d ed. 1719. Reprint. New York: Garland, 1971.

Dodsley, Robert. *The Preceptor.* 3d ed. Vol. 1, 405–48. London, 1758.

Biography

Tedder, Henry Richard. "Dodsley, Robert." *DNB* (1964).
Westby-Gibson, John. "Blackwall, Anthony." *DNB* (1964).

Criticism

Horner, Winifred Bryan, ed. *The Present State of Scholarship in Historical and Contemporary Rhetoric,* 125–26. Rev. ed. Columbia: University of Missouri Press, 1990.

Howell, Wilbur Samuel. *Eighteenth-Century British Logic and Rhetoric,* 128–29, 138–40. Princeton: Princeton University Press, 1971.

since terms like *literary theory* and *literature* appearing in the definition are themselves so variously defined. Influenced by French rhetoricians like Dominique Bonhours, François de Salignac de la Mothe-Fénelon, René Rapin, and Charles Rollin, British theorists regarded rhetoric as one branch of the belles lettres. Put another way, belletristic rhetoric, as David Masson wrote, conceived more broadly of rhetoric as "the science of Literature, or Literary Theory or Literary Criticism universally," which "treat[ed] the principles of Historical Writing, Poetry, and Expository Writing, as well as of Oratory" (85). In the first definition, the term *rhetoric* seems to be equated with oratory; in the second, with discourse more generally. In both cases, all the language or polite arts—including biography, drama, history, philology, poetry, oratory, and science—were believed to hold in common certain essential features whose rules could be extrapolated and taught. In studying these subjects under belletristic rhetoric's tutelage, one strove to become a successful composer and critic of both oral and written discourse. As Golden and Edward P. J. Corbett have pointed out, in constructing rhetorical theory the belletristic scholar looked not only to Aristotle's *Rhetoric* but to Aristotle's *Poetics*, Isocrates's *Antidosis*, Longinus's *On the Sublime*, and Horace's *Ars Poetica*. Although belletristic rhetoric posited that all critical principles apply equally in generating and analyzing language, as rhetoric's analytic function became more prominent—eventually obscuring its generative function—rhetoric became literary theory, or as George Saintsbury has termed it, "the Art of Literature, or in other words, Criticism" (471). By the end of the nineteenth century, the term *literature* narrowed from referring to *all* educated or polite letters to referring only to poetics; the term *belles lettres* underwent a similar narrowing. Although Blair and belletristic rhetoric are often faulted for diminishing the significance of rhetoric and enhancing the fortunes of literary criticism, under the rubric of rhetoric and belles lettres, Blair and his contemporaries studied matters now encompassed under such diverse subjects as criticism, grammar, hermeneutics, linguistics, logic, poetics, psychology, rhetoric, and semiotics (Horner and Barton 114).

Lectures on Rhetoric and Belles Lettres

In 1759 Blair began lecturing on rhetoric and belles lettres at the University of Edinburgh, in the tradition of Adam Smith, who had begun to lecture there in 1748. In 1760 the Edinburgh Town Council appointed Blair Professor of Rhetoric, and in 1762 King George III designated him the first Regius Professor of Rhetoric and Belles Lettres at the University of Edinburgh, where he taught a popular course that attracted over fifty students a session. Out of these lectures came *Lectures on Rhetoric and Belles Lettres*, a two-volume work of over a thousand pages in the 1783 London first edition. The work was published just before Blair's retirement because, as the author explains, "very defective and erroneous" editions of the lectures were circulating at the time. He was well paid for his efforts: the publishers–Strahan and Cadell in London and Creech in Edinburgh—gave him 1,500 pounds for the copyright, making him the most highly paid writer on rhetoric to date (Schmitz 94).

Blair's *Lectures* resemble those of Adam Smith, on which they are based, although Blair's are much expanded so as to outline a general philosophy of language. In the introduction, Blair discussed humans as language-using animals and defines rhetoric's domain. The lectures open with Blair commending human communicative abilities: "One of the most distinguished privileges which Providence has conferred upon mankind, is the power of communicating their thoughts to one another. Destitute of this power, Reason would be a solitary, and, in some measure, an unavailing principle. Speech is the great instrument by which man becomes beneficial to man: and it is the intercourse and transmission of thought, by means of speech, that we are chiefly indebted for the improvement of thought itself" (1:1). Writing and discourse, he concluded, must be "entitled to the highest attention," whether used for "utility or pleasure." And, indeed, in "civilized" nations, "no art has been cultivated with more care, than that of language, style, and composition," a judgment Blair supported by examining the intellectual history of Europe (1:2). Blair then argued for the "importance and advantages" of language study in education, which he saw as the foundation of all other pursuits: "The study of Rhetoric and Belles Lettres supposes and requires a proper acquaintance with the rest of the liberal arts. It embraces them all within its circle, and recommends them to the highest regard. The first care of all such as wish either to write with reputation, or to speak in public so as to command attention, must be, to extend their knowledge; to lay in a rich store of ideas relating to those subjects of which the occasions of life may call them to discourse or to write" (1:4). Like Quintilian, Blair believed that all of the liberal arts are united, and that the rhetor must possess broad knowledge. While "knowledge and science" form the substance of speech, rhetoric shapes and polishes it. Subsequent remarks reveal a richer conception of rhetoric, one that links the study of language with the study of reason itself, for as Blair put it, "When we are employed, after a proper manner, in the study of composition, *we are cultivating reason itself.* True rhetoric and sound logic are very nearly allied. The study of arranging and expressing our thoughts with propriety, *teaches us to think, as well as to speak, accurately*" (emphasis mine) (1:7).

Citing a passage from Blair, which he has compared to a selection from Isocrates's *Antidosis*, Charles W. Kneupper has discussed Blair's concern with "the social/intellectual significance" of language: "For Isocrates social institutions and 'things done with intelligence' are consequences of communication. Blair seems less explicit than Isocrates in stating that 'social reality is a rhetorical product'—to use a modern paraphrase. But Blair is quite clear in viewing reason as profoundly a social/collective activity—that the improvement of thought is rooted in the communication process" (Cohen et al. 292). And although he has admitted that it is neither developed in any full way nor a direct influence on modern thought, Kneupper has seen in Blair a "sociolinguistic/sociological aspect of rhetoric" that predates twentieth-century perspectives on language (Cohen et al. 292). He has considered Blair's insight into the sociology of language inherently rhetorical rather than philosophical or aesthetic, its adoption by other disciplines notwithstanding. What is most significant here is that Blair wished to create a philosophy of language, not just as practical guide—something that is sometimes forgotten in light of the enormous popularity that the *Lectures* enjoyed as a textbook. As Blair contended in the first lecture, "Rhetoric is not so much a practical art as a speculative science" (1:8).

Clearly, Blair did expect practical consequences to follow from this theoretical understanding, for he explained in detail the language facility required in modern society. We get here a portrait of the cultured late eighteenth-century gentleman and the requirements of his station: "We can hardly mingle in polite society without bearing some share in such discussion; studies of this kind . . . will appear to derive a part of their importance from the use to which they may be applied in furnishing materials for those fashionable topics of discourse, and thereby enabling us to support a proper rank in social life" (1:9). Although Blair's unquestioning acceptance of social and cultural mores—and his complicity in upholding class structures—has been criticized (see Berlin and Halloran), for nearly a century it seemed to be the *Lectures'* most attractive feature, for belletristic rhetoric appealed to the middle classes who longed for an education commensurate with their increasing economic power: they came to believe that an education in belletristic rhetoric would prepare them to join the cultural elite. Although usually vilified or dismissed (see Covino), Blair has a few defenders today, among them E. D. Hirsch, who has seen in Blair's union of literature and literacy a remedy to the "unnatural, uncharacteristic, and unhealthy period of disconnection from the roots of literacy" that now characterizes university English departments (16).

Taste

The concept of taste, which Blair defined as "the power of receiving pleasure from the beauties of nature and art," is seminal to Blair's rhetorical theory (1:16). Resting solidly on eighteenth-century doctrine, its foundation, Blair noted in his second lecture, is "what has been found from experience to please mankind most universally" (1:31). Thus, he attempted to discover that which transcends time and place to appeal to men of all ages and times. In developing his theory of taste, Blair took full account of prevailing ideas, both ancient and modern. Aware of the work of Aristotle and Cicero, Thomas Hobbes, John Locke, Anthony Ashley Cooper (Lord Shaftesbury), Francis Hutcheson, Edmund Burke, Alexander Gerard, David Hume, Henry Home (Lord Kames)—and, certainly, Adam Smith—Blair maintained that taste is a matter of *delicacy*, which is innate to humans, and of *correctness*, which is learned. Taste, he concluded, is neither "an internal sense" nor "an exertion of reason" (1:16–17). It cannot be reduced to an operation of reason, for a beautiful prospect or fine poem is not felt through deduction: "They sometimes strike in the same manner the philosopher and the peasant; the boy and the man" (1:16). Rather, taste is perceived through both internal sensibility *and* reason. Blair's ideas on this subject are strikingly similar to those of Kames, with whom he frequently conversed (see Schmitz 98). Although Kames's contributions to developing theories of literature are frequently acknowledged, Blair was most likely the propagator of those ideas. For both men, emotional response was paramount, a precursor of the romantic doctrines about to take hold in Britain.[4] This theory of language, in which taste figures so prominently, is the creation of the Clock-maker God. For the pleasures that result from taste we praise the "benignity of our Creator," who "by endowing us with such powers . . . hath widely enlarged the sphere of pleasures of human life" (1:45). The immutable laws of taste, then, are evidence of God's presence, power, and compassion.

To some degree, Blair argued, taste is a faculty common to all men; all men relish beauty of one kind or another, for "the principles of Taste [are] deeply founded in the human mind" (1:17). The diversity of taste among mankind does not nullify universal principles of taste, for men possess this faculty to varying degrees owing to "the different frame of their natures; to nicer organs, and finer internal powers" but still more "owing to education and culture" (1:19). To be sure, taste is an improvable faculty; experience and instruction enlighten the judgment, as when one acquires an ear for music. A range of acceptable tastes exists, but it cannot be arbitrary. An authoritarian, Blair maintained that "this admissible diversity of tastes can only have place where the objects of taste are different. Where it is with respect to the same object that men disagree, when one condemns that as ugly, which another admires as highly beautiful; then it is no longer diversity, but direct opposition of Taste that takes place; and therefore one must be in the right, and another in the wrong, unless that absurd paradox were to hold, that all tastes are equally good and bad" (1:28). Nature, Blair believed, provides the universal standard, for we always compare the imitated to the original in painting or in representing human characters and actions. Just how does one determine the standard of nature? No person possesses all the powers of nature perfectly, so as to provide an unerring standard for all men. Nor is there any other immutable standard that we can appeal to. Only human nature (through recourse to Nature) can judge standards of taste: "That which men concur in admiring, must be held to be beautiful. His taste must be esteemed just and true, which coincides with the general sentiments of men" (1:30). Over time these principles of taste can be inferred, allowing us to assign reasons for our assessments: "Taste is a sort of compound power, in which the light of the understanding always mingles, more or less, with the feelings of sentiment" (1:31). Standards of taste are negotiated publicly through "discussion and debate"—that is, they are determined rhetorically: the aim is always to discover the immutable principles at work. Blair was not referring here to the judgments of *all* men, only "men placed in such situations as are favourable to the proper exertions of Taste" (1:32). It is possible for entire countries to err in their judgment: "Accidental causes may occasionally warp the proper operations of Taste; sometimes the state of religion, sometimes the form of government, may for a while pervert it; a licentious court may introduce a taste for false ornaments, and dissolute writings" (1:33). Blair maintained, however, that in time wrong judgments are rectified, as corrupted tastes become overturned. It is in this way that the critic serves mankind well by dispelling the public's incorrect initial judgments. Finally, Blair's is a moral theory of taste, for "a good heart" as well as a "sound head" are necessary.

Style

Fifteen of Blair's forty-seven lectures deal with style, making it the canon to which Blair devoted most attention. Blair sought to develop a comprehensive philosophy of style, an endeavor that eventuated in the most complex discussion of the period. The belletristic rhetorics of the eighteenth century treated the study of content as it was revealed through style; such study would lead one to acquire the innate virtues of the text—virtues that would, in turn, manifest themselves in one's thought and behavior. Such claims are justified in a world view in which God's laws are constant and knowable, and Blair wished to account for these principles in ways that the old stylistic handbooks did not. Although interest in the vernacular had been increasing in Britain for some time, instruction in the English language was respected in Scottish schools a century earlier than it was in England. Whereas throughout the Renaissance, Greek and Latin literature had most often been used to exemplify rhetorical principles, Blair and other eighteenth-century rhetoricians included examples from the vernacular—and, in so doing, empowered the language of the people.

As Herman Cohen et al. have pointed out, Blair pushed well beyond standard eighteenth-century doctrines to develop an "individualistic perspective toward language and style" (283). "The best definition I can give of [style]," Blair maintained in the tenth lecture, "is, the peculiar manner in which a man expresses his conceptions, by means of Language" (1:183). A writer's style reveals his character—his morals, his heart, his mind—because style is intimately connected to thought. A faulty style, then, is a matter of serious concern. Detailed and lengthy analysis of particular pieces of prose and poetry is not the mere play of a dilettante, for the study of style entails the study of human nature. Accordingly, instruction in correct style and censure of barbarisms help to develop a student's character.

Not surprisingly, then, much of *Lectures on Rhetoric and Belles Lettres* is devoted to an analysis of such contemporary writers as Joseph Addison, Jonathan Swift, and Shaftesbury as well as explanations of their particular vices and virtues. Blair instructed through example, as well as through precept. Together the two—his theory and practice—have helped generations of schoolchildren to appreciate prose and poetry. Asserting that no more helpful analysis of the English language exists, classical rhetoric scholar Edward P. J. Corbett, for example, has credited Blair with teaching him how to analyze prose. To be sure, Blair's conception of style is more sophisticated than earlier conceptions, which saw language and style as the clothes for thought.

Although he championed naturalness in style and decried false ornament in the same, Blair did not see language and style as identical: style is "different from mere Language or words" (1:183); style is "the product; language the means" (Cohen et al. 282). Cohen saw this definition, and the explanation that follows it, as the most significant passage in Blair's *Lectures* "because it represents a key (perhaps *the* key) to all that Blair has to say on language and style" (Cohen et al. 282); together with taste it forms the very foundation of belletristic rhetoric (Cohen et al. 285). The passages that follow are seminal because they crystallize the dominant ideas of the lectures, which Cohen saw as "the individuality of style, its reliance on nature, and its relationship to ideas and sentiments" (Cohen et al. 285).

Elaborating on this definition, Blair declared that style "has always some reference to an author's manner of thinking. It is a picture of the ideas which arise in his mind, and of the manner in which they rise there; and, hence, when we are examining an author's composition, it is, in many cases, extremely difficult to separate the Style from the sentiment" (1:183–84). So connected are thought and style that one of Blair's two classifications of style—the one original to him—is, as Barbara Warnick put it, "in accordance with the extent and manner of expression of meaning" (Cohen et al. 301). Blair intended that his method of analyzing style would incorporate the relationship between expression and meaning, which led Blair to value precision and appropriateness above all else (Cohen et al. 301). Blair's rhetoric is frequently termed a *stylistic rhetoric*, a term intended to diminish the *Lectures'* significance. Given that Blair saw style and thought as "intimately connected," his theory of style must be reassessed accordingly—as an attempt to codify language study of the most serious kind. Clearly, Blair approached style as a subject of great importance—as the key to the essence of a text's meaning and a person's psychology. It is this critical approach to style—to literary texts—that was embraced by language theorists of the nineteenth century.

To repeat, this relationship between thought and language explains why Blair privileged the study of style. It also explains why Blair's theory of style is not simply managerial—for he almost embedded a theory of invention in his theory of style. Blair, as Warnick has asserted, "was motivated by the belief that the thoughts we have and the words in which we express them are so closely related that we can improve the quality of our thoughts by improving the quality of our expression. Blair wanted the students of his lectures and readers of his work to concentrate upon style as *a means to an end, that end being the improvement of their ability to conceive and reason about the matter at hand.* In Blair's system, then, language use had an inherently epistemological function" (emphasis mine) (Cohen et al. 301). The problem, as history has shown, is that the pedagogy Blair laid out is easily corrupted into a trifling appreciation of the surface features of language, a fate similar to that which befell the study of the classics.

Blair and Traditional Rhetoric

Blair devoted only ten lectures to "eloquence," or oratory, which had in some earlier treatises constituted the whole of rhetoric. For Blair the term *rhetoric* referred to the overarching art of discourse governing both belles lettres and eloquence. While these ten sections specifically treat the domain of public speaking—traditionally rhetoric of the bar, the assembly, and the pulpit—the other thirty-seven lectures also bear on oratory, as they do for all discourse. Although Blair had great respect for such classical rhetoricians as Aristotle, Cicero, and Quintilian—he recommended them as the starting place for all who study language and thus provided a historical account of their theories while quoting from them liberally to illustrate rhetorical principles—Blair introduced significant changes.

Well aware of the popular prejudices against rhetoric and criticism, Blair took objections head on. He acknowledged the past and potential abuses from which he wished to distance himself (for such abuses make it "a very contemptible art"), but insisted that true rhetoric and criticism do not employ these. In Blair's words:

To be truly eloquent, is to speak to the purpose. For the best definition which, I think, can be given of Eloquence, is, the Art of Speaking in such a manner as to attain the end for which we speak. Whenever a man speaks or writes, he is supposed, as a rational being, to have some end in view; either to inform, or to amuse, or to persuade, or, in some way or other, to act upon his fellow-creatures. He who speaks, or writes, in such a manner as to adapt his words most effectually to that end, is the most eloquent man. Whatever then the subject be, there is room for Eloquence; in history, or even in philosophy, as well as in orations. The definition which I have given of Eloquence, comprehends all the different kinds of it; whether calculated to instruct, to persuade, or to please. But, as the most important subject of discourse is Action, or Conduct, the power of Eloquence chiefly appears when it is employed to influence Conduct, and persuade to Action. As it is principally, with reference to this end, that it becomes the object of Art, Eloquence may, under this view of it, be defined, The Art of Persuasion. (2:3)

But like Aristotle, he insisted that an art's or science's misuse is not a sufficient argument against its proper use. To suggest that Blair was against rhetoric, as some historians have, is to ignore significant passages in the *Lectures*. True, Blair objected to the classical system of *topoi* or *loci*, which he faulted as superficial, indiscriminate, and sophistic. Given Blair's reading of classical rhetoric—and, indeed, that of the eighteenth century—Blair's rejection of *topoi* is hardly surprising. To save rhetorical studies from being mere "trifling and childish study," Blair argued that "what is truly solid and persuasive must be drawn 'ex visceribus causae,' from a thorough knowledge of the subject and a profound meditation on it."[5]

Eloquence, Blair argued, requires "solid argument, clear method, a character of probity appearing in the Speaker, joined with such graces of Style and utterance, as shall draw attention to what he says" (2:3); these qualities join to effect persuasion. Blair condemned those who would engage in "the art of varnishing weak arguments plausibly; or of speaking so as to please and tickle the ear" (2:2). But he denied the effectiveness of such tactics against the truly wise, especially since "good sense is the foundation of all. No man can be truly eloquent without it; for fools can persuade none but fools. In order to persuade a man of sense, you must first convince him; which is only to be done, by satisfying his understanding of the reasonableness of what you propose to him" (2:3). To persuade men, the rhetor must appeal to their understanding first. In insisting on the inclusion of all the cultivating faculties (see Bevilacqua), Blair attempted to broaden the narrow boundaries of classical rhetoric, as it was then understood. His eighteenth-century reading of classical rhetoric interpreted the ancients as holding a view of rhetoric as persuasion in the most narrow sense, which Blair recognized as an inadequate basis for discourse. And although different forms of discourse tend to draw on certain of the faculties (as, for instance, oratory tends to appeal to the passions), rhetoric (as the general art of discourse) appeals—at least potentially—to all of the faculties. As Eric Skopec put it, "Reason and emotion are both important in his system, but they are not presented as autonomous sources of proof" (Cohen et al. 300). Blair was thus able to reunite the arts of discourse into a general theory of language arts. Reclassifying discourse according to what scholars have called the new teleology of ends, Blair reconceived rhetoric's framework.

Blair attributed power to both art and nature. Men all have inherent abilities, he believed, but they possess them to varying degrees. Nature alone does not determine one's abilities; rather, god-given talents are enhanced or diminished by environment and training. The foundations of such talent and knowledge are always to be found in nature: "Viewed as the Art of Persuasion, it requires, in its lowest state, soundness of understanding, and considerable acquaintance with human nature; and, in its higher degrees, it requires, moreover, strong sensibility of mind, a warm and lively imagination, joined with correctness of judgment, and an extensive command of the power of Language; to which must be added, the races of Pronunciation and Delivery" (2:8). "Reason" and "good sense" were for Blair the guiding principles of rhetoric.

In short, Blair, too, defined himself in relation to classical rhetoric, insisting that such theorists as Aristotle, Demetrius, Dionysius of Harlicarnassus, Cicero, and Quintilian be read and studied. And he, like the Renaissance rhetoricians before him, quoted from classical authors to illustrate rhetorical principles. Golden and Corbett have argued that Blair, like George Campbell and Richard Whately, shared five basic premises with classical rhetorical theory:

(1) they accepted the classical communication model which focused on the speaker, the speech, and the audience; (2) they recognized that effective ethical, logical, and emotional proof are essential to persuasion; (3) they felt that a well-organized address should have interest, unity, coherence, and progression; (4) they held that style should be characterized by perspicuity and vividness; and (5) above all, they suggested that while nature endows the orator with special talents, nurture or training is needed to improve and perfect these inborn traits. (13–14)

Blair differed from classical rhetoricians in significant ways, as Corbett and Golden have also established: for Blair, the goal of rhetoric was to teach others to be effective critics of all of the arts of discourse as well as to be effective speakers. Further, rhetoric's aim was to appeal to the understanding generally, which is broader than prevailing notions of classical rhetoric that maintained that persuasion was the primary end of rhetoric. Under Blair, then, rhetoric became the study of communication broadly conceived. Significantly, he assumed that the principles he addressed apply to all language use—equally to rhetoric and to belles lettres. Finally, given his metaphysical underpinnings, Blair's supposed neglect of invention need not lead to an impoverished rhetorical theory; the Romantic belief in inspiration and genius has sustained a different but rich conception of language. Divorced from Blair's foundation, however, the neglect of invention proper is truly an impoverished rhetorical theory. Blair's *Lectures on Rhetoric and Belles Lettres* also treats such matters as the sublime and the beautiful, figurative language, sentence structure, delivery, historical and philosophical writing, poetry (including pastoral, lyric, didactic, descriptive, dramatic, and epic), tragedy, and comedy—all subjects that have received too little critical attention from twentieth-century scholars.

Blair's Influence

Belletristic rhetoric arose in Scotland in response to Europe's cultural, social, and historical circumstances. Howell has aptly characterized changes in rhetorical style between the Renaissance and the eighteenth century as "a change from the convention of imperial dress to the convention of the business suit" (*Poetics* 158); the new rhetorics of the eighteenth century developed a language theory appropriate to modern economic conditions. Elaborate tropes and schemes, appropriate for the aristocrat at court, were ill suited to the middle-class citizen's world of trade and commerce. When the monarch determines truth, the governing language theory will tend to privilege style; but when economic power—and, hence, political clout—expands beyond small aristocratic circles, as it did in late seventeenth- and eighteenth-century Britain, the governing language will promote more genuine communication and will often serve as a means of social advancement (Howell, *Poetics* 157–61). Moreover, interest shifted from oral to written discourse, this change reflecting the increasing availability and affordability of print. The public longed first for lectures and forums that discussed these works, then for formal institutional instruction. The new theory of rhetoric and belles lettres, positing a common basis for all discourse and promising guidance in discriminating among these works, had an obvious appeal to an age wishing to improve itself. Throughout England and Scotland the new reading public longed to study criticism. To accommodate the new reading public, the focus of rhetoric shifted from the one who invents (be that speaker or writer) to the one who receives (be that hearer or reader). It shifts emphasis from a generative to an analytic art. Developed accordingly, Blair's *Lectures* contained the most popular belletristic rhetoric.

Hugh Blair's *Lectures on Rhetoric and Belles Lettres* "formed the staple of instruction for half the educated English-speaking world in its day" (Schmitz 3); it also enjoyed French, German, Italian, Russian, and Spanish editions—influences that have been too little explored (see Abbott for the exception to this rule). Schmitz has listed twenty-five British and thirty-five American complete editions of the *Lectures;* but the contents of Blair's *Lectures* were also reprinted, abridged, adapted, and cited at length in a variety of publications and books—including schoolbooks and readers—throughout the eighteenth and nineteenth centuries. As Ehninger and Golden have noted, "For more than a generation following publication [of *Lectures*] no self-respecting author of a textbook in rhetoric or composition considered his work complete without one or more references to Blair's discourses" (14). In Harding's words, Blair "did more to interpret and make known the rhetorical theory of the ancients than any other British or American rhetorical writer. . . . [H]e wrote for his age the kind of book Quintilian produced for the first century AD" (vii). Although his significant influence on American and Scottish education has been well documented (Berlin;

Halloran; Johnson), his impact in England and other countries still must be traced, for we are only beginning to understand fully the shaping influence of Hugh Blair's *Lectures on Rhetoric and Belles Lettres* on English and rhetorical studies.

NOTES

1. Schmitz's *Hugh Blair* is the definitive biography and serves as the basis of much Blair scholarship, including this chapter.

2. Ehninger and Golden, "Intrinsic," 13. Elsewhere, to be sure, Ehninger and Golden, who perhaps have documented best Blair's popularity, have carefully qualified the significance of Blair's achievement and in so doing have often diminished the importance of Blair's *Lectures* (see Golden and Ehninger, "Extrinsic," 16). They have also cataloged scathing remarks by critics (see Ehninger and Golden, "Intrinsic," 14–15).

3. Ehninger, "Dominant Trends," 3–12. In 1979 Corbett distinguished four movements: the neoclassical, which contended that the Greeks and Romans provided an adequate basis for rhetorical theory; the elocutionary, based in large part on the work of Sheridan; the psychological-philosophical; and the belletristic, the rhetoric with which Blair is most identified. Howell's *Eighteenth-Century British Rhetoric and Logic*, which remains the most exhaustive and definitive account of the period, arranges the rhetorical theory of the period into somewhat different categories. The source for my discussion of belletristic rhetoric is Howell's *Eighteenth-Century British Logic and Rhetoric*.

4. See Ehninger and Golden, "Intrinsic," 19–21, for a discussion of neoclassical and romantic doctrines in Blair.

5. Corbett, "Most Significant Passage," 286, translates "ex visceribus causae" as "from the very bowels of the case" (see Cohen et al.).

BIBLIOGRAPHY

Primary Sources

Blair, Hugh. *Lectures on Rhetoric and Belles Lettres*. 1783. Reprint. Edited by Harold F. Harding. 2 vols. Carbondale: Southern Illinois University Press, 1965.

Golden, James L., and Edward P. J. Corbett. *The Rhetoric of Blair, Campbell, and Whately*. Carbondale: Southern Illinois University Press, 1990.

Biography

Finlayson, James. "A Short Account of the Life and Character of the Author." Introduction to *Sermons by Hugh Blair*. 3 vols. New York, 1802.

Hill, John. *An Account of the Life and Writings of Hugh Blair*. Edinburgh, 1807.

Schmitz, Robert Morell. *Hugh Blair*. New York: King's Crown Press, 1948.

Stephen, Leslie. "Blair, Hugh." *DNB* (1882).

Tegg, William M. "Memoirs of the Rev. Hugh Blair." Introduction to *The Beauties of Blair*. London, 1810.

Secondary Sources

Abbott, Don Paul. "The Influence of Blair's Lectures in Spain." *Rhetorica* 7.3 (1989):275–89.

Berlin, James A. *Writing Instruction in Nineteenth-Century American Colleges.* Carbondale: Southern Illinois University Press, 1984.

Bevilacqua, Vincent M. "Philosophical Assumptions Underlying Hugh Blair's Lectures on Rhetoric and Belles Lettres." *Western Speech* 31.3 (1967):150–64.

Bowers, John Waite. "A Comparative Criticism of Hugh Blair's Essay on Taste." *Quarterly Journal of Speech* 47.4 (1961):384–89.

Cohen, Herman N. "Hugh Blair on Speech Education." *Southern Speech Journal* 29.1 (1963):1–11.

———. "Hugh Blair's Theory of Taste." *Quarterly Journal of Speech* 44.3 (1958): 265–74. Reprint. In *Readings in Rhetoric*, edited by Lionel Crocker and Paul A. Carmack, 333–49. Springfield, IL: Charles C. Thomas, 1965.

Cohen, Herman, Edward P. J. Corbett, S. Michael Halloran, Charles W. Kneupper, Eric Skopec, and Barbara Warnick. "The Most Significant Passage in Hugh Blair's *Lectures on Rhetoric and Belles Lettres.*" *Rhetoric Society Quarterly* 17.3 (1987): 281–304.

Corbett, Edward P. J. "Hugh Blair as an Analyzer of English Prose Style." In *Selected Essays of Edward P. J. Corbett*, edited by Robert J. Connors, 4–13. Dallas: Southern Methodist University Press, 1989.

Covino, William A. *The Art of Wondering: A Revisionist Return to the History of Rhetoric.* Portsmouth, NH: Boynton/Cook, 1988.

Cowling, G. H. "The English Teaching of Dr. Hugh Blair." *Palaestra* 148:281–94.

Edney, Clarence W. "Hugh Blair's Theory of Dispositio." *Speech Monographs* 23.1 (1956):38–45.

Ehninger, Douglas. "Campbell, Blair, and Whately: Old Friends in a New Light." *Western Speech* 19.4 (1955):263–69.

———. "Campbell, Blair, and Whately Revisited." *Southern Speech Journal* 28.3 (1963):169–82. Reprint. In *Readings in Rhetoric*, edited by Lionel Crocker and Paul A. Carmack, 359–73. Springfield, IL: Charles C. Thomas, 1965.

———. "Dominant Trends in English Rhetorical Thought, 1750–1800." *Southern Speech Journal* 18.1 (1952):3–12. Reprint. In *Readings in Rhetoric*, edited by Lionel Crocker and Paul A. Carmack, 297–307. Springfield, IL: Charles C. Thomas, 1965.

Ehninger, Douglas, and James Golden. "The Intrinsic Sources of Blair's Popularity." *Southern Speech Journal* 21.1 (1955):12–30.

Ferguson, J. DeLancy. "Burns and Hugh Blair." *Modern Language Notes* 45.7 (1930): 440–46.

Golden, James L. "Hugh Blair: Minister of St. Giles." *Quarterly Journal of Speech* 38.2 (1952):155–60.

Golden, James L., Goodwin F. Berquist, and William E. Coleman. "Neoclassicism, the Belletristic Movement, and the Rhetoric of Hugh Blair." In *Rhetoric of Western Thought*, edited by James L. Golden, Goodwin F. Berquist, and William E. Coleman, 133–59. 4th ed. Dubuque, IA: Kendall/Hunt, 1989.

Golden, James L., and Douglas Ehninger. "The Extrinsic Sources of Blair's Popularity." *Southern Speech Journal* 22.1 (1956):16–32.

Halloran, S. Michael. "The Most Significant Passage in Hugh Blair's *Lectures on Rhetoric and Belles Lettres.*" *Rhetoric Society Quarterly* 17.3 (1987):288–90.

Harding, Harold F., ed. Introduction to *Lectures on Rhetoric and Belles Lettres*, by Hugh Blair, viii-xl. Carbondale: Southern Illinois University Press, 1965.

Hirsch, E. D., Jr. "Remarks on Composition to the Yale English Department." In *The Rhetorical Tradition and Modern Writing*, edited by James J. Murphy, 13–18. New York: Modern Language Association, 1982.

Horner, Winifred Bryan. "The Roots of Writing Instruction: Eighteenth- and Nineteenth-Century Britain." *Rhetoric Review* 8.2 (1990):322–45. Reprinted as "Writing Instruction in Great Britain: Eighteenth and Nineteenth Centuries." In *A Short History of Writing Instruction from Ancient Greece to Twentieth-Century America*, edited by James J. Murphy. Davis, CA: Hermagoras Press, 1990.

Horner, Winifred Bryan, and Kerri Morris Barton. "The Eighteenth Century." In *The Present State of Scholarship in Historical and Contemporary Rhetoric*, edited by Winifred Bryan Horner, rev. ed. 114–50. Columbia: The University of Missouri Press, 1990.

Howell, Wilbur Samuel. *Eighteenth-Century British Logic and Rhetoric*. Princeton: Princeton University Press, 1971.

———. *Poetics, Rhetoric, and Logic: Studies in the Basic Disciplines of Criticism*. Ithaca, NY: Cornell University Press, 1975.

Johnson, Nan. *Nineteenth-Century Rhetoric in North America*. Carbondale: Southern Illinois University Press, 1991.

Kitzhaber, Albert R. *Rhetoric in American Colleges, 1850–1900*. Dallas: Southern Methodist University Press, 1990.

Knowlton, E. C. "Wordsworth and Hugh Blair." *Philological Quarterly* 63 (1927): 227–81.

McDonald, James C. "Taste and the Shaping of Audience in Hugh Blair." In *Visions of Rhetoric: History, Theory and Criticism*, edited by Charles W. Kneupper, 22–29. Arlington, TX: Rhetoric Society of America, 1987.

Masson, David, ed. *The Collected Writings of Thomas De Quincey*. Vol. 10. Edinburgh: Black, 1896–1897.

Mays, Morley J. "Johnson and Blair on Addison's Prose Style." *Studies in Philology* 39.4 (1942):638–49.

Saintsbury, George. *A History of Criticism and Literary Taste in Europe from the Earliest Texts to the Present Day*. Vol. 2. New York: W. Blackwood and Sons, 1979.

Ulman, H. Lewis. *Theories of Language and Arts of Rhetoric in Eighteenth-Century Britain*. Carbondale: Southern Illinois University Press, 1993.

JAMES BURGH
(1714–1775)

Mary Hurley Moran

The son of the parish minister, James Burgh was born in 1714 at Madderty, Perthshire, in Scotland. Educated at St. Andrews, he had intended to follow his father into the ministry, but ill health caused him to go into business instead. After failing in this, he moved to London, "where he corrected the press for Bowyer, and made indexes" (Stephen 322). He eventually turned to education, working as an usher first in a school at Great Marlow and then at Enfield; and in 1747 he established his own academy at Stoke Newington, where he remained as headmaster until his retirement in 1771. He died on August 26, 1775 (Stephen 322).

Throughout his career Burgh published numerous works on varied subjects, becoming well known as a political writer with reformist sympathies. His pamphlet *Britain's Remembrancer* (1746), written in honor of the suppression of the Jacobite rebellion of 1745, went through several editions and was highly praised. Also well received was his three-volume work *Political Disquisitions* (1774, 1775), an inquiry into government defects and abuses.

As a schoolmaster, Burgh was also committed to improving education and published a handful of works propounding his views. In his book *Thoughts on Education* (1747), he argued for basing the school curriculum on subjects that would enable boys to achieve a comfortable, decent life but also would prepare them for the afterlife. Toward the latter end, Burgh asserted, pupils should receive thorough instruction in the Christian religion; and toward the former, pupils should receive a grounding in grammar, Latin, Greek, French, penmanship, music, drawing, mathematics, bookkeeping, geography, astronomy, anatomy, history, biography, and political principles. He also published a little book entitled *Youth's Friendly Monitor* (1754), intended for his own pupils upon their entrance into the world. In it he offered religious, moral, and intellectual guidance and recommended a list of books that would enlarge his pupils' ideas.

But by far the most influential of Burgh's works that were concerned with education was *The Art of Speaking* (1761), an immensely popular textbook that established the author as one of the leading voices in the elocution movement of his day. Although he had not included elocution in the ideal curriculum that he had outlined in his earlier treatise on education, by 1762 he had apparently read Thomas Sheridan's *British Education* (1756) and had become convinced of the importance of this subject. Unlike Sheridan, though, Burgh believed that the rightful place for elocutionary training was in the schools, not in the universities. His observations of the painful deficiencies of his students in public speaking and reading had no doubt convinced him of the need to begin this training early (Howell 244–46).

Although Burgh added nothing essentially new to elocutionary theory, he was instrumental in developing the so-called mechanical approach to oratorical training by providing in his textbook a list of specific rules for the expression of emotions in public speaking, as well as a series of practice recitation passages; he was therefore one of the initial forces behind the movement to include elocutionary training in the academic curriculum. The far-reaching influence of Burgh's book is reflected in the fact that it went through eighteen editions, eleven of them American, and was the first work on speech education to be published in the United States. By the 1780s *The Art of Speaking* could be found in most Ivy League and other major American university libraries; indeed, it was one of the most frequently checked out books at the Brown University library between 1788 and 1800 (Guthrie 21). Furthermore, Burgh's list of rules concerning emotional expression was adopted, both with and without acknowledgment, by numerous other elocutionists, including Sheridan (*Rhetorical Grammar* [1781]), John Walker (*Elements of Elocution* [1781]), William Scott (*Lessons in Elocution* [1779]), and several Americans.

BURGH'S RHETORICAL THEORY

In the forty-six-page "Essay" that prefaces his textbook, Burgh explained the theory and rationale underlying his approach. Like other elocutionists, he was distressed by the deplorable state of contemporary oratory, and he believed that the solution to this problem lay in giving young men intensive training in elocution before they entered the world. In the first several pages of the essay, Burgh cited the many opportunities that young men "whose station places them within the reach of polite education" (5) will have for public speaking in their eventual careers: in Parliament, at the bar, in the pulpit, at meetings of merchants, or in committees for managing public affairs. Even if a young man entered none of these professions, Burgh argued, his training would not have been wasted, for, Burgh asked, "Will he never have occasion to read, in a company of his friends, a copy of verses, a passage of a book, or news-paper? Must he never read a discourse of

Tillotson, or a chapter of the Whole Duty of Man, for the instruction of his children and servants?" (2). Thus, it was his realization of the need for such training, coupled with his awareness of the lack of available instructional materials, that motivated Burgh to write his textbook.

Like others in the elocutionary movement, Burgh was concerned solely with delivery, to the exclusion of the other parts of the rhetorical canon. Arguing that invention, composition, and style had already been copiously treated by scholars, he explained, "It is not my design to trouble the world with any thing on these branches of oratory. I shall confine myself to what the prince of orators [Cicero, presumably] pronounced to be the first, second, and third part, or all that is most important, viz. delivery, comprehending what every gentleman ought to be master of respecting gesture, looks, and command of voice" (1–2). Much of the essay supports this claim that delivery is the most important branch of rhetoric. Burgh argued that superior ideas and noble sentiments count for nothing if the speaker cannot express them effectively; for example, he pointed out: "Supposing a person to be ever so sincere and zealous a lover of virtue, and of his country; without a competent skill and address in speaking, he can only sit still, and see them wronged, without having it in his power to prevent, or redress, the evil" (2).

Although Burgh gave a passing nod to the need for a public speaker to be learned in the subject that he was expounding and for a public reader to grasp the sense of what he was reading, his real emphasis is on manner rather than matter. This is explicitly revealed in certain of his key statements, such as "What we mean does not so much depend upon the words we speak, as on our manner of speaking them" (12) and "That delivery is incomparably the most important part in public instruction, is manifest from this, that very indifferent matter well delivered will make a considerable impression. But bad utterance will defeat the whole effect of the noblest composition ever produced" (40).

Burgh seems to have been aware that in making such statements he was opening himself to the charge of advocating an artificial approach to oratory. He accordingly answered this criticism by pointing out that public speaking, like any art, does not come naturally but must be cultivated: "If nature unassisted could form the eminent speaker, where were the use of art or culture; which yet no one pretends to question? Art is but nature improved upon and refined" (6). Rationalizing his approach on the basis of the eighteenth-century theory that there exists a universal, natural language of expression ("from nature, is to be deduced the whole art of speaking properly" [12] and "nature has given to every emotion of the mind its proper outward expression, in such manner, that what suits one, cannot, by any means, be accommodated to another" [12]), Burgh described, in a thirteen-page catalog comprising the middle third of his essay and intended to serve as concrete guidelines for elocution students, "the principal passions, humours, sentiments, and intentions, which are to be expressed by speech and action" (14).

It is this inventory of the emotions that the essay is most famous for. Consisting of anywhere between 70 and 300 items (the debate over the actual number of entries arises from the confusing way in which Burgh has categorized them), in the list Burgh has described the voice tone, facial expressions, and bodily gestures that naturally accompany the various emotions. Although renowned for its detail, the list is actually curiously inconsistent in coverage, providing extensive treatment of some emotions but only scant treatment of others. Furthermore, a number of emotions that are indicated in the textbook's practice passages are not included in the catalog (pupils must consult the index at the back of the book, which refers them to a comparable emotion in the catalog). Yet another flaw is that some of the items are not emotions at all but rather physical states (e.g., intoxication, death) or actions (e.g., inquiry, fainting). Despite these defects, however, Burgh's catalog received much praise, and it was elaborated and improved upon by later textbook authors (Guthrie 26).

In the final third of the essay Burgh applied the arguments made earlier to the area of public speaking that he felt was in most need of improvement: pulpit oratory. Attributing the decline in church attendance to the ineffectualness of contemporary preaching, he urged future ministers to devote themselves more to mastering elocutionary skill than to mastering their theological studies, for without the former, "the weight of the most sacred subject, the greatest depth of critical disquisition, the most unexceptionable reasoning, the most accurate arrangement of matter, and the most striking energy of style, are all lost upon an audience; who sit unaffected, and depart unimproved" (33). Here too, then, Burgh revealed his bias in favor of delivery over substance.

Following the essay is the textbook proper, the "Lessons." These are 326 pages of readings (eighty-one in all) adapted from ancient and modern writers (among them Cicero, Shakespeare, John Milton, Alexander Pope, John Dryden, and Richard Steele), to be used by elocution students for practicing appropriate expression. In these lessons, the prescriptive nature of Burgh's approach is most fully revealed: he italicized the words that should be emphasized, noted in the margins the emotions that should be expressed, and frequently inserted footnotes with further instructions concerning voice, facial expression, and gesture. Thus, although Burgh claimed to have derived his approach from nature, and although some scholars have consequently argued that he is not truly a member of the mechanical school (e.g., Parrish, Mohrmann, and Gray), the fact remains that the real emphasis of his book is on mechanical mastery. He wanted the end result to appear natural ("Art, seen through, is execrable" [31], he warned the reader), but he essentially advocated mimicry and formulae to achieve this end. Indeed, he admonished the reader, "A correct speaker does not make a movement of limb, or feature, for which he has not a reason" (28); and he enjoined those who would be preachers to emulate the efforts of actors in attempting to master gesture and tone.

Although twentieth-century scholars have scorned Burgh's formulaic approach to oratorical training, it was influential in the late eighteenth century. His book was the first of its kind, providing the format used by most subsequent elocution textbooks (Guthrie 25). Burgh's importance to the field of rhetoric, then, was that he provided the prescriptive guidelines that formed the basis of elocutionary training in British and American secondary schools from his day down through the nineteenth century.

BIBLIOGRAPHY

Primary Source

Burgh, James. *The Art of Speaking.* London, 1761.

Biography

Stephen, Leslie. "Burgh, James." *DNB* (1917).

Criticism

Gray, Giles Wilkeson. "What Was Elocution?" *Quarterly Journal of Speech* 46.1 (1960): 1–7.

Grover, David H. "John Walker: The 'Mechanical' Man Revisited." *Southern Speech Journal* 34.4 (1969):288–97.

Guthrie, Warren. "The Development of Rhetorical Theory in America, 1635–1850. 5. The Elocution Movement: England." *Speech Monographs* 18.1 (1951):17–30.

Haberman, Frederick W. "English Sources of American Elocution." In *History of Speech Education in America: Background Studies,* edited by Karl R. Wallace, 105–26. New York: Appleton-Century-Crofts, 1954.

Hargis, Donald E. "James Burgh and *The Art of Speaking.*" *Speech Monographs* 24.4 (1957): 275–84.

Horner, Winifred Bryan, ed. *The Present State of Scholarship in Historical and Contemporary Rhetoric,* 114–17. Columbia: University of Missouri Press, 1983.

Howell, Wilbur Samuel. *Eighteenth-Century British Logic and Rhetoric,* 244–46. Princeton: Princeton University Press, 1971.

Mohrmann, G. P. "Kames and Elocution." *Speech Monographs* 32.2 (1965):198–206.

———. "The Language of Nature and Elocutionary Theory." *Quarterly Journal of Speech* 52.2 (1966): 116–24.

Murphy, Mary C. "Detection of the Burglarizing of Burgh: A Sequel." *Communication Monographs* 43.2 (1976):140–41.

Parrish, Wayland M. "The Burglarizing of Burgh, or the Case of the Purloined Passions." *Quarterly Journal of Speech* 38.4 (1952):431–34.

———. "The Concept of 'Naturalness.' " *Quarterly Journal of Speech* 37.4 (1951): 448–54.

Robb, Mary Margaret. *Oral Interpretation of Literature in American Colleges and Universities.* New York: Wilson, 1941.

Vandraegen, Daniel E. "Thomas Sheridan and the Natural School." *Speech Monographs* 20.1 (1953):58–64.

EDMUND BURKE
(1729–1797)

Stephen H. Browne

Edmund Burke's career as a writer, orator, and theorist spanned thirty years of public life. As a result, his reputation is distinguished by an ability to engage principles within the contexts of political action and advocacy. Theory and practice were thus for Burke integrated modes of activity, and we risk distorting his contributions by emphasizing one at the expense of the other. Certainly this integration is evident in *A Philosophical Enquiry into the Origin of Our Ideas of the Sublime and Beautiful*, now considered as basic to our understanding of Burke's oeuvre. After a brief biographical review, the following discussion examines the primary features of the *Enquiry*, places it within a broader field of aesthetic and rhetorical theory, and identifies its current status as a statement on the psychology of art and language.

For such a conspicuous figure in the public life of eighteenth-century England, we know rather little about Burke's private life. Enough is certain, however, to provide useful information about birth, background, and influences. Burke was born in 1729 in Dublin to a Protestant father and Catholic mother and received his early education at a nearby Quaker boarding school. The eclectic associations of Burke's childhood would be reflected in his maturity, when as a member of Parliament he fought for Catholic relief, Irish rights, and colonial demands for redress. Burke first achieved visibility during his education at Trinity College, Dublin (1744–1749), where he was instrumental in founding what is now considered the oldest university debating society in Great Britain and Ireland. In 1750 Burke moved to London and began studies for the bar at Middle Temple; he soon withdrew, however, and undertook what proved to be a fledgling literary career.

Although we do not know the specifics of these early years in London, we do know at least some of Burke's time was spent in revising an essay that he had originally written while an undergraduate at Trinity. In 1757 Burke published it as the *Enquiry*, and so announced his entrance into the intensely competitive world of English letters. The initial reviews were mixed—but, on the whole, positive—and the *Enquiry* remains, in the words of Samuel Holt Monk, "certainly one of the most important aesthetic documents that eighteenth-century England produced" (qtd. in Boulton lvi). It is, we may add, of significance to eighteenth-century rhetorical theory. The reason is suggested in the following summary.

The *Enquiry* came at a time of longstanding and widespread interest in the ideas of Beauty, Sublimity, and Taste. From the musings of Addison to the more systematic work of Alexander Gerard, Francis Hutcheson, and the Earl of Shaftesbury, writers were concerned about isolating these diffuse ideas as conceptual and critical categories. The *Enquiry* was thus situated within a complex of early aesthetic thought, and it drew into its orbit lines of inquiry stretching from Newtonian optics to association of ideas and faculty psychology. While space does not here allow for a detailed review of where Burke agreed and where he disagreed with his fellow theorists, it should be stressed that his treatise bears the marks of its precedents. In its attempt to establish the empirical basis of aesthetic response, the treatise is unmistakably a child of the eighteenth century.

BURKE'S RHETORICAL THEORY

Aesthetic Basis of Burke's Rhetorical Theory

Burke's theory of rhetoric is in the *Enquiry* implicit only: We find there no extended or fully developed set of principles on the subject. Since it is not always clear to the first-time reader how such a theory can be derived from Burke's aesthetics, the following outline may help. After identifying the author's major aims, method, and results, we should be in a better position to extrapolate a set of implications bearing on his conception of rhetoric.

The *Enquiry* is composed of five parts, with an introductory "Essay on Taste" appended to the second edition (1759). Each of these parts will be treated in greater detail below; for now, it is important to note that together they constitute a systematic and often striking examination of the psychology of aesthetic response. The "Essay on Taste" initiates the study and is characteristic of its general aims. In it, the author sought "to find whether there are any principles, on which the imagination is affected, so common to all, so grounded and certain, as to supply the means of reasoning satisfactorily about them" (13). Burke's search for the universal principles of mind relevant to aesthetic response is extended into the *Enquiry* proper. In Part One he has located the basic emotions underlying any such response, particularly pain and pleasure, in "an attempt to range and methodize some of our leading passions" (52). Part Two is concerned exclusively with those passions caused by the Sublime, one of the two primary terms of the analysis as a whole. Here Burke was explicitly interested in "the great and sublime in *nature*" (emphasis added) (57), and thus he has reminded us of the mechanistic assumptions that run throughout the treatise. Similarly in Part Three, Burke addressed the idea of Beauty, by which he meant "that quality or those qualities in bodies by which they cause love, or some passion similar to it" (91). Burke's goal of identifying the physiological relationship between external objects and their emotional apprehension is most apparent in Part Four, where he hoped to "discover what affections of the mind produce certain emotions of the body; and what distinct feelings and qualities of body shall produce certain determinate passions in the mind" (129). Finally, Part Five takes up the distinctive relationship between language and aesthetic response, and it is here where we find the author's most direct observations on the rhetorical arts.

Before turning to each section in more detail, it may prove helpful to identify the principles by which the various parts are held together. Burke was intent on extending his method to the limit, and he could at times lead the reader down peculiar paths. For this reason it is necessary to remind ourselves of the author's major assumptions, general aims, and modes of procedure.

Burke wished, first, to systematize. As he looked about the landscape of critical writings of such topics as sublimity, beauty, and taste, he noted a marked confusion and a general failure to make headway beyond the most desultory observations. The "remedy," as he stated in the preface, "could only be from a diligent examination of our passions in our own breasts; from a careful survey of the properties of things which we find by experience to influence those passions; and from a sober and attentive investigation of the laws of nature, by which those properties are capable of affecting the body, and thus of exciting our passions" (1). The results of his effort are apparent throughout the *Enquiry*, which is thoroughly systematic, if not always consistent, and is conspicuously designed to order, distinguish, and clarify.

The systematic character of the treatise alerts us to an additional assumption: aesthetic response is ultimately explicable in terms of human nature. This universalizing tendency is basic to the analysis as a whole, and permeates most of the author's specific arguments. In this, too, Burke is clearly in the company of many eighteenth-century theorists of art, language, and rhetoric. From Shaftesbury to George Campbell and beyond, the operative premise was that if the functions of mind could be accurately identified and accounted for, then its various modes of expression could be explained and improved. Among other results, such a psychology tends to dismiss the shaping influences of tradition or cultural predilection as of secondary importance. Thus, in Burke's account of the imagination, we find a typical statement: "The imagination, I conceive, can have no pleasure but what results from one or the other of these causes. And these causes operate pretty uniformly upon all men, because they operate by principles in nature, and which are not derived from any particular habits or advantages" (17).

A third and directly related premise regards the sensate basis of Burke's analysis. Whether discussing taste, sublimity, or beauty, Burke at all times assumed that qualities inhere naturally in objects, and that these qualities are immediately available to consciousness through the senses. In the *Enquiry* he was accordingly interested in examining the affective process by which objective realities solicit subjective responses. Boulton has summarized this position with considerable insight: "Sensationism with all its fallacies obviously committed Burke to a number of ludicrous and extreme statements, yet, in spite of its absurdities, it lends itself to pseudo-scientific treatment which, in turn, produces the lucidity and peculiar strength of argument so characteristic of the *Enquiry*. 'When we go but one step beyond the immediately sensible qualities of things, we go out of our depth': Burke was never in any danger of drowning" (xxxvii).

With these assumptions in place, we can now move directly into each of the five sections making up the *Enquiry*. Two prefatory points will assist our comprehension of the work as a whole: (1) we should keep in mind that Burke is attempting to expand his categories beyond the fine arts to include the fundamental basis of all aesthetic response; and (2) his conception of rhetoric is at once an extension of this plan and a departure from it. In the following discussion, each section is treated in turn.

The Passions

Burke initiated his study by systematically isolating those emotions that underlie our ideas of beauty and sublimity. The analysis is symptomatic of the whole: Burke sought the common denominators of aesthetic response, and went about his search by ordering, defining, and distinguishing categories of experience. The general goal of Part One, therefore, is to "range and methodize some of our most leading passions" (52), themselves conceived as internal states produced by objective causes. On the basis of this treatment, Burke was then in a position in Part Two to specify the nature of such stimuli.

The emotions that Burke discovered as basic to all human response and to which he would turn time and again are pain, pleasure, and indifference. He was adamant about distinguishing these emotions as clearly as possible and argued that, though these emotions are mobile states, they nevertheless are independent of each other. As Burke put it with characteristic assurance, "There is nothing which I can distinguish in my mind with more clearness than the three states, of indifference, of pleasure, and of pain. Every one of these I can perceive without any sort of idea of its relation to anything else" (33). Within the terms of Burke's calculus, moreover, he was able to delineate not only the positive qualities that mark these emotions, but the ways in which their alteration affects the mind. Thus, the cessation of pain "causes" delight, while the cessation of pleasure produces indifference, disappointment, or grief. These preliminary distinctions established, Burke moved quickly into the more substantive treatment of the sources and ends of the passions.

The leading passions are classified according to two heads: those that serve the ends of self-preservation and those that serve the ends of society, "one or the other of which all our passions are calculated to answer" (38). As to self-preservation, pain is the dominant passion; as to society, Burke cited pleasure as its leading passion. Here and throughout the *Enquiry*, Burke's treatment suggests that he was more engaged by the former than the latter; this bias, moreover, has direct implications for understanding Burke's own rhetorical practice. As a Parliamentary orator and political disputant, Burke later was to draw routinely from the stock of images associated with sublimity. In any case, Burke insisted that the emotions "which are conversant about the preservation of the individual, turn chiefly on pain and danger, and they are the most powerful of all the passions" (38). Here, too, is the source of our ideas of the sublime, to which Burke turned next.

Burke's definition of the sublime is at once clear and provocative. "Whatever is fitted in any sort to excite the ideas of pain, and danger," he writes, "that is to say, whatever is in any sort terrible, or is conversant about terrible objects, or operates in a manner analogous to terror, is a source of the sublime; that is, it is productive of the strongest emotion which the mind is capable of feeling" (39). Burke would examine the sublime in greater detail later, but here it is worth noting a few implications. The definition suggests what might be called Burke's Gothic sensibility, and it hints at a recurrent feature of the analysis: the privileging of the emotional over the rational. Together, these predilections helped to shape and direct the *Enquiry* and its legacy.

The passions that belong to society, conversely, relate directly to pain's opposite. Pleasure, whether sexual or social, is thus the ultimate source of our ideas of the beautiful; and if it is less violent and total than pain, it is nevertheless essential for the conduct of human relations. For this reason, Burke noted, "I call beauty a social quality; for where women and men, and not only they, but when other animals give us a sense of joy and pleasure in beholding them (and there are many that do so) they inspire us with sentiments of tenderness and affection towards their persons" (42–43). Burke proceeded to parse the emotions associated with society and drew special attention to sympathy, imitation, and ambition. Of these, his observations on sympathy are the richest.

Like taste, sympathy commanded the attention of some of the eighteenth century's most important thinkers, including Joseph Addison, David Hume, Adam Smith, and Thomas Reid. Burke's treatment of sympathy is not conspicuously original, but it does give evidence that he was familiar with the commonplaces associated with that concept. In sympathy Burke found a principle of community that cuts across pain and pleasure, sublimity and beauty; it therefore has direct implications for his theory of art and rhetoric. Burke defined this key passion as a process by which "we enter into the concerns of others; that we are moved as they are moved, and are never suffered to be indifferent spectators of almost anything which men can do or suffer. For sympathy must be considered as a sort of substitution, by which we are put into the place of another man, and affected in many respects as he is affected" (42).

To the extent that sympathy may be associated with sublimity as well as beauty, it is basic to all human response. Our capacity to feel with others makes it possible, even under the most terrible and alien conditions, to communicate our emotions. Sympathy thus provides an intersubjective basis for emotional response; and as Burke used the concept, sympathy renders even sublimity communicable. Indeed, this very human act is promoted and rewarded by an attending sense of pleasure. Burke explained: "As our Creator has designed we should be united by the bond of sympathy; he has strengthened that bond by a proportional delight; and there most where our sympathy is most wanted, in the distresses of others" (46).

Burke has drawn out a second implication. As a passion, sympathy is natural and necessary to the human condition; it can therefore be used to explain a variety of behaviors, including artistic response. "It is by this principle chiefly," Burke wrote, "that poetry, painting, and other affecting arts, transfuse their passions from one breast to another, and are often capable of grafting a delight on wretchedness, misery, and death itself" (44). The inference is typical of Burke's reasoning generally: moving from human nature to art, he sought to explain artistic production by the response it invokes. The result at times can be insightful. By this analysis Burke was able to account for tragic and Gothic sensibilities in often provocative ways.

Burke's is essentially a synthetic psychology, integrating observations on human nature with artistic conventions in a compelling, if not always convincing, theory of the passions. This synthetic quality is evident in the following, which serves as a useful summary of his position: "There is no spectacle we so easily pursue, as that of some uncommon and grievous calamity; so that whether the misfortune is before our eyes, or whether they are turned back to it in history, it always touches with delight. This is not an unmixed delight, but blended with no small uneasiness. The delight we have in such things, hinders us from shunning scenes of misery; and the pain we feel, prompts us to relieve ourselves in relieving those who suffer" (46).

Part Two of the *Enquiry* seeks to identify what, literally, causes the passion of self-preservation. Not surprisingly, the author turned to nature itself as the source of sublimity; and he hoped to find in nature those objective properties that may be said to stimulate a specific emotional response. The dualism here is explicit: for Burke, emotions were the effect of a natural cause. This kind of sensationism, of course, has been discredited in our time, but it led Burke to inquire directly into the functions and limits of language and art. In this section, however, these insights remain glimpses and are not developed until the final section.

Burke asked what qualities there are in nature that produce such passions as those associated with the sublime. He discovered first that those objects that are terrible are the strongest. Burke's language here is illustrative, and clearly indicates the line of reasoning throughout. "No passion," he wrote, "so effectually robs the mind of all its powers of acting and reasoning as fear. For fear being an apprehension of pain and death, it operates in a manner that resembles actual pain. Whatever therefore is terrible, with regard to sight, is sublime too" (57). This stress on the extreme, on the arational, and on pain is typical of Burke's analysis. In this section he has provided a catalog of sorts—a listing of natural properties which, if not as powerful as the terrible, at least approximate it. These properties include obscurity, power, privation, vastness, infinity, light and color, and even, Burke argued, certain sounds, animal cries, smell and taste, specific feelings, and pain.

For our purposes, Burke's analysis of sublimity is most compelling in the way it addressed the role of language. This role is given its clearest expression in Burke's discussion of obscurity as a source of the sublime. Noting that "it is one thing to make an idea clear, and another to make it affecting to the imagination," Burke argued that sublimity is seldom if ever a product of representational clarity. Rather, Burke wrote, "The proper manner of conveying the affections of the mind from one to another, is by words" because "in reality a great clearness helps but little towards affecting the passions, as it is in some sort an enemy to all enthusiasms whatsoever" (60).

Although Burke's comments are elliptical, they do suggest an important principle: that effective language works not so much by representing reality, as by communicating our apprehension of it. This nonrepresentational theory of language is succinctly captured in Burke's observation about the descriptive powers of language. Obscurity, he reasoned, is a source of the sublime; that language is best, therefore, that is able to portray this quality. Conversely, language that is merely descriptive fails in its very attempt to be clear. Indeed, Burke wrote, "to see an object distinctly, and to perceive its bounds, is one and the same thing. A clear idea is therefore another name for a little idea" (63). For evidence, Burke considered a passage from Job, and examined the relationship between the emotion invoked (terror) and the language used. Is not the passage, Burke asked, "wrapt up in the shades of its own incomprehensible darkness, more awful, more striking, more terrible, than the liveliest description, than the clearest painting could possibly represent it?" (63).

Parts Three and Four of the *Enquiry* extend the logic displayed so far.

Like the analysis of sublimity, Part Three stresses the natural origins of the emotion—love—caused by beauty. Burke was typically careful to delimit his terms and defined beauty as "that quality or those qualities in bodies by which they cause love, or some passion similar to it." This definition, he stressed, is confined "to the merely sensible qualities of things, for the sake of preserving the utmost simplicity" (91). After considering and rejecting some conventional treatments of beauty, Burke arrived at the following position. Beauty, he argued, is a function neither of proportion, nor of utility, nor even of reason. It is, rather, "some quality in bodies, acting mechanically upon the human mind by the intervention of the senses" (112). These qualities include the small and smooth, the varied, delicate, and bright. Part Four records the author's attempt to trace the effects of these natural causes—both sublime and beautiful—to their physiological origins. It thus represents the extreme limits of a sensate aesthetics, and, it must be said, led Burke to some rather implausible lines of inquiry.

All of this perhaps seems distant from our concern for Burke's rhetorical theory. The first four parts of the *Enquiry*, indeed, have little directly to say about the rhetorical functions of language. The final section, however, takes up the issue explicitly and with considerable insight. Burke remained interested in the origins of the sublime and beautiful, but recognized that language complicated the subject-object dualism driving so much of the *Enquiry*. Part Five may thus be understood as both an extension of his previous analysis and as a departure from it. As to words, Burke noted at the outset, "they seem to me to affect us in a manner very different from that in which we are affected by natural objects, or by painting or architecture; yet words have as considerable a share in exciting ideas of beauty and of the sublime as any of those, and sometimes a much greater than any of them" (163). Burke was then led to examine in some detail why and how words are able to affect such emotions independent of their direct correspondence to objects in nature.

At the heart of Burke's argument is a single claim: "In reality poetry and rhetoric do not succeed in exact description so well as painting does; their business is to affect rather by sympathy than imitation; to display rather the effects of things on the mind of the speaker, or of others, than to present a clear idea of the things themselves" (172). Around this assertion and in support of it Burke marshalled the arguments of John Locke, popular examples, and personal experience.

Words may, according to Burke (following Locke), be designated as falling into one of three categories. The first category consists of words that refer to simple ideas united by nature ("man, horse, tree, castle, & c."); Burke called these "aggregate words." "Simple abstract words" refer to single properties in nature such as colors or shapes. Finally, "compound abstract words" denote such terms as "honour, persuasion, magistrate, and the like." Burke argued that in each case, the given word functions not by calling up its direct referent in nature, but by representing their effects and the lingering emotional impact of the occasions that gave rise to them— that is, language does not depend for its effectiveness on its capacity to represent an externally conceived reality. Indeed, Burke reminded us again, "so little does poetry depend for its effect on the power of raising sensible images, that I am convinced it would lose a very considerable part of its energy, if this were the necessary result of all description" (170).

With these premises established, Burke moved to the basis of his argument. It is particularly of interest to note that he saw language functioning in ways very different from the natural forces previously identified. In fact, he noted, "we find by experience that eloquence and poetry are as capable, nay indeed much more capable of making deep and lively impressions than any other arts, and even than nature itself in very many cases" (173). There are, Burke explained, three reasons for this; for our purposes, they may be considered the most important features of Burke's theory of rhetoric. Words are particularly suited to influencing the passions because they convey not only the subject but the manner in which the speaker was affected by that subject. And as people are naturally inclined to respond to such expressions, words serve as important vehicles for human sympathy. Second, words can serve as surrogates for the nonexistent. In Burke's language, "there are many things of a very affecting nature, which can seldom occur in the reality, but the words which often represent them do" (173). Finally, words enable us to create combinations and, thus to invoke more effectively the emotions based on those combinations. In an important concluding passage, Burke drew out the implications of his theory. He was convinced that we need to distinguish between a clear expression and a strong one. This point, as we have noticed, gets hinted at in previous sections. Here Burke elaborated: "Now, as there is a moving tone of voice, an impassioned countenance, an agitated gesture, which affect independently of the things about which they are exerted, so there are words, and certain dispositions of words, which being peculiarly devoted to passionate subjects, and always used by those who are under the influence of any passion; they touch and move us more than those which far more clearly and distinctly express the subject matter. We yield to sympathy, what we refuse to description" (173).

Part Five of the *Enquiry* thus offers the richest insights about the nature and functions of language. Burke presented these observations, not as a fully developed theory, but "to shew upon what principles they [words] were capable of being the representatives of these natural things, and by what powers they were able to affect us often as strongly as the things they represent, and sometimes much more strongly" (177). A few summary points may nevertheless be identified. Burke saw language—at least emotionally effective language—as working not by invoking images from nature but by communicating the effects of nature. He thus offered the beginnings of a theory that was to have a significant influence on twentieth-century thinking about what language actually represents—and to what effect. In addition, here and throughout the treatise Burke was concerned with examining the nonrational or arational properties of human response. To that extent, he made an important contribution to the psychology of aesthetics and language. Finally, Burke's analysis of the ways in which words function provides a keen insight into the relation between language and human community. At the center of his theory can be found a principle of sympathy that unites and makes coherent the *Enquiry* as a whole.

BIBLIOGRAPHY

Primary Source

Burke, Edmund. *A Philosophical Enquiry into the Origin of our Ideas of the Sublime and Beautiful.* 1759. Reprint. Edited by James T. Boulton. Notre Dame: University of Notre Dame Press, 1968.

Biography

O'Brien, Conor Cruise. *The Great Melody: A Thematic Biography of Edmund Burke.* Chicago: University of Chicago Press, 1992.

Criticism

Boulton, James T., ed. Introduction to *A Philosophical Enquiry into the Origin of our Ideas of the Sublime and Beautiful,* by Edmund Burke, xv–cxxvii. Notre Dame: University of Notre Dame Press, 1968.

Cresap, Steven. "Sublime Politics: On the Uses of Aesthetic Terror." *Clio* 19 (1990): 111–25.

De Bruyn, Frans. "Theatre and Countertheatre in Burke's Reflections on the Revolution in France." In *Burke and the French Revolution,* edited by Steven Blakemore. Athens: University of Georgia Press, 1992.

Gould, Timothy. "Engendering Aesthetics: Sublimity, Sublimation, and Misogyny in Burke and Kant." In *Aesthetics, Politics, and Hermeneutics,* edited by Gerald Burns and Stephen Watson. Albany: SUNY Press, 1991.

Mattick, Paul, Jr. "Beautiful and Sublime: Gender Totemism in the Constitution of Art." *Journal of Aesthetics and Art Criticism* 48 (1990):293–303.

Paulson, Ronald. *Representations of Revolution (1789–1820),* 57–73. New Haven: Yale University Press, 1983.

Reid, Christopher. *Edmund Burke and the Practice of Political Writing,* 34–50. New York: St. Martin's Press, 1985.

Suleri, Sara. *The Rhetoric of English India.* Chicago: University of Chicago Press, 1992.

Wood, Neal. "The Aesthetic Dimension of Burke's Political Thought." *Journal of British Studies* 4 (1964):41–64.

GEORGE CAMPBELL
(1719–1796)

Winifred Bryan Horner and Shelley Aley

George Campbell—theologian, rhetorician, and philosopher—whose life spanned the eighteenth century, was one of the *literati* of the Scottish enlightenment. His mind was shaped by the beliefs and ideals of his time and, in turn, shaped those beliefs not only during his own time but for the following century as well. His *Philosophy of Rhetoric*, published in 1776, was widely used not only in Scotland but in England and the United States as well. Between 1800 and 1825 Campbell's *Philosophy of Rhetoric* was the second most commonly adopted textbook in American colleges, surpassed only by Hugh Blair's popular *Lectures*. During the middle of the century, it was supplanted primarily by Alexander Bain's widely used *English Composition and Rhetoric* and was finally dropped, as textbooks by American authors took the place of the Scottish rhetorics. Today there is renewed interest as modern composition theorists and historians of rhetoric look to George Campbell and his influence on twentieth-century composition.

Like so many of the rhetoricians of the eighteenth century, Campbell did not see his religious or philosophic studies as separate or distinct from his work as a rhetorician. Indeed, the bulk of his writings concerned theology. His *Dissertation on Miracles*, published in 1762, went through four editions in the eighteenth century, with a French translation in 1765, the last edition appearing in 1834. By contrast, in the eighteenth century there was only one edition of Campbell's *Philosophy of Rhetoric*, but there were numerous editions in the nineteenth century; there was also one edition in 1911 and a facsimile edition by Southern Illinois University Press (in its Landmarks in Rhetoric and Public Address Series) in 1963, reprinted with a new introduction by Lloyd F. Bitzer in 1988. The importance of George Campbell in the history of rhetoric and composition continues two centuries after his death.

Campbell was a contemporary of Thomas Reid, David Hume, Hugh Blair, and Adam Smith—all of whom were his personal friends. Born on Christmas day in 1719, Campbell lived and worked in Aberdeen for most of his seventy-seven years. He was the youngest of six children whose father was a minister. He attended Aberdeen schools, the grammar school and, later, Marischal College, enrolling in the Arts Course at the age of fifteen or sixteen, which was the custom in the northern universities. In both his early education and in the Arts Program, he studied Latin, Greek, and rhetoric, which was beginning to move toward a study of belles lettres. During his time at Marischal, the regenting or tutoring system was still in effect, before the time of professors who specialized in single subjects. In the early eighteenth century and well into the nineteenth at Aberdeen, the regents moved readily from one course to another, and each student was under one regent as a tutor during his years at the university. The atmosphere at Marischal was very different from that of Edinburgh where Campbell worked as a lawyer's apprentice and later enrolled in courses in theology at the university, where the lectures were popular and often attended by townspeople as well as students. At the University of Aberdeen, half of the students came from working-class and agricultural families (Anderson 138); and there was a constant effort to teach morals, manners, and proper London English, as well as the academic subjects. Campbell had planned to go into the law as a profession, but returned to Aberdeen after his Edinburgh apprenticeship to concentrate on theological studies. In 1748, he moved to a country village close to Aberdeen where he was installed as a minister of the gospel. It was here that he wrote the first two chapters of his *Rhetoric*. In 1757, Campbell returned to Aberdeen where he quickly became a member of the intelligentsia of that city. His reputation was firmly established with the publication of his *Dissertation on Miracles*, a refutation of an essay by David Hume on the same subject. Two years later he was appointed principal of Marischal College, and in 1771 he was elected Professor of Divinity, which added to his already heavy responsibilities as the minister at Greyfriars.

Two years after his return to Aberdeen, Campbell helped found the Aberdeen Philosophical Society, which exerted an important influence on his work. It is doubtful if the *Rhetoric* would ever have gone beyond the first two chapters, written around 1750, if it had not been for the intellectual stimulation provided by the society and its members, which, among others, included Thomas Reid, Alexander Gerard, James Beattie, and John Stewart. The *Rhetoric* was written over the years and read and discussed in the meetings (see Ulman, *Minutes*). Campbell's treatise appears to be unfinished. In Chapter 5 of Book 2, he outlined the qualities of rhetorical style as *perspicuity, vivacity, elegance, animation,* and *music*; however, the remainder of the *Rhetoric* treats only *perspicuity* and *vivacity*, albeit in great detail. H. Lewis Ulman, in *Minutes*, speculated that during the later years of Campbell's life he held three posts concurrently, and, in addition, lost the "window of opportunity provided by the meetings of the Aberdeen Philosophical Society" whose meetings ceased in 1771 (26). Campbell was not only the founder but a strong supporter of the society. He attended more meetings than any other members, except two, and presented more discourses than any other member, except Alexander Gerard, all on the subject of rhetoric (Ulman, 26). It is possible that as his duties and responsibilities increased, he may have had to withdraw his support from that group—which undoubtedly was a factor in its demise. The society had certainly served as a strong motivation and inspiration for his work in rhetoric, and he may not have continued that work after the society's lively discussions ceased to exist.

CAMPBELL'S RHETORICAL THEORY

The Philosophy of Rhetoric contains three books. After a preface that outlines the manner in which the book was written and gives due acknowledgment to the Aberdeen Philosophical Society, an introduction follows. It covers a wide range of ideas and starts with the typical eighteenth- and nineteenth-century notion of science as underlying all art: "All art is founded in science, and the science is of little value which does not serve as a foundation to some beneficial art" (lxix). Book 1, entitled "The Nature and Foundations of Eloquence," contains eleven chapters and 138 pages. The first two chapters, according to the author, are "intended as a sort of groundwork to the whole" (lxv). The remaining chapters cover *ethos, pathos,* and *logos,* the three proofs of classical rhetoric, departing from that rhetoric in their treatment of the syllogism in the now well-known Chapter 7. It is noteworthy that Campbell studiously avoided the classical terminology. Book 2, entitled "The Foundations and Essential Properties of Elocution," contains nine chapters and 146 pages and, after a discussion of language and correctness, treats the two elements of style—namely, *purity* (which is largely grammar) and *perspicuity.* The final book, called "The Discriminating Properties of Elocution," has 132 pages and is concerned with the third element of style—*vivacity.* As mentioned earlier, the last two of the five elements of rhetorical style are never covered. The book concludes with the index from the 1850 edition.

Terminology

Basic to comprehending Campbell's work is an understanding of his terminology, especially the word *eloquence*. Although the word *rhetoric* appears in his title, Campbell used *eloquence* synonymously with *rhetoric* and used *eloquence*, rather than rhetoric, quite consistently throughout the work. The 1850 index offers only a terse "see eloquence" under the term *rhetoric*. Such usage may sound strange to modern ears, but Campbell was only following the Renaissance custom of referring to *rhetoric* as *eloquence*.

Campbell defined *eloquence* a number of times, starting in his introduction where he called it "the art of speaking, in the extensive sense in which I employ the term." He added: "It is indeed the grand art of communication, not of ideas only, but of sentiments, passions, dispositions, and purposes" (lxiii). In Section 2 of Chapter 1, Book 1, he defined *eloquence* by what it is not: it is not "simply the power of moving the passions" (103) but, according to Campbell, "in its greatest latitude denotes, 'That art or talent by which the discourse is adapted to its end' " (1). He defended his definition in a footnote as that "best adapted to the subject of these papers." He then stated that the "ends of speaking" are reducible to four—namely, "to enlighten the understanding, to please the imagination, to move the passions, or to influence the will" (1). Here is evident the strong influence of faculty psychology that purported to divide the brain into separate areas serving different functions analogous to the ends that Campbell delineates. Campbell stated that discourse addressed to the understanding "proposes the *instruction* of . . . hearers" (2) while that addressed to the imagination exhibits to it "a lively and beautiful representation of a suitable object" (3). He concluded with a discussion of "the most complex of all, that kind which is calculated to influence the will, and persuade to a certain conduct" and which is "an artful mixture" of the argumentative and the pathetic (4).

In Chapter 1 of Book 2, Campbell defined *eloquence* according to its purpose—that is, "to convey our sentiments into the minds of others, in order to produce a certain effect upon them" (139). It is obvious that in his broad definitions of *eloquence* or *rhetoric*, Campbell included both speaking and thinking: "The art of speaking, then, is not less necessary to the orator than the art of thinking. Without the latter, the former could not have existed. Without the former, the latter would be ineffective" (139). He usually used speaking, writing, and oratory interchangeably, applying his rules or principles to all three. In this way, Campbell brought rhetoric into the area of modern composition studies. Occasionally, however, he differentiated between writing and speaking, with such cautions as avoiding grammatical inaccuracies for the writer, since a reader will notice them more than a hearer "however attentive he may be" (180). He also advised that brevity is more important for the speaker than the writer, since the reader has "the command of his time; he may read fast or slow, as he finds convenient; he can peruse a sentence a second time when necessary, or lay down the book and think" (338).

The words, *orator* and *oratory* are confusing in that the latter is seldom used, and the former is cross-referenced to *speaker* in the index. In his introduction, Campbell classified poetry as a branch of *oratory*:

Poetry indeed is properly no other than a particular mode or form of certain branches of oratory. . . . Suffice it to remark at present, that the direct end of the former, whether to delight the fancy as in epic, or to move the passions as in tragedy, is avowedly in part the aim, and sometimes the immediate and proposed aim, of the orator. The same medium, language, is made use of; the same general rules of composition, in narration, description, argumentation, are observed; and the same tropes and figures, either for beautifying or for invigorating the diction are employed by both. (lxxiii)

Campbell considered versification a mere "appendage" rather than a "constituent part" of poetry, which he considered a variety of eloquence rather than a different species (lxxiv).

Campbell used the term *science* throughout his book with a full explanation of the relation between art and science in his introduction. Science was the buzz word for the eighteenth and nineteenth centuries. As induction and the scientific method—after Francis Bacon—became the accepted mode of inquiry, no subject was considered legitimate unless it had the "science word" tacked on. Thus, we have the "science of rhetoric" and the "science of literature," phrases that occur time and again in eighteenth- and nineteenth-century treatises. Campbell explained the meaning of science and its relation to art in the opening section of his introduction:

All art is founded in science, and the science is of little value which does not serve as a foundation to some beneficial art. . . . Valuable knowledge, therefore, always leads to some practical skill, and is perfected in it. On the other hand, the practical skill loses much of its beauty and extensive utility, which does not originate in knowledge. There is by consequence a natural relation between the sciences and the arts, like that which subsists between the parent and the offspring. (lxix)

Campbell, like his contemporaries—and very much like Aristotle—saw art as *praxis* and saw science as the rules underlying the practice of the art. The vocabulary is different, but the concepts are similar. Following the common sense philosophy, Campbell pointed out that the arts "are founded in experience" (lxxi), and that art exists prior to the science—the formation of the rules: "As speakers existed before grammarians, and reasoners before logicians, so doubtless there were orators before there were rhetoricians, and poets before critics" (lxxiv). It is interesting that Campbell foresaw the development of criticism as he traced the steps in finding the rules underlying the art of rhetoric. Thus, the first step is "Nature," by which he meant the exploration of our own thinking processes—"the consciousness a man has of what operates on his own mind" (lxxiv). "The next step," Campbell continued, "is to observe and discriminate, by proper appellations, the different attempts, whether modes of arguing, or forms of speech, that have been employed for the purposes of explaining, convincing, pleasing, moving, and persuading" (lxxiv). And he added, "Here we have the beginnings of the critical science" (lxxiv). It was at this time that the move from rhetoric as the study of the creative act to rhetoric as the study of the interpretive act took place. In the eighteenth- and nineteenth-century study of literature and belles lettres, the terms associated with rhetoric were regularly used.

Metaphor, irony, and *simile* were all concepts from the old rhetoric. As criticism moved into the twentieth century, the emphasis shifted from the creative act of the writer to the interpretative act of the reader, and the old terminology was augmented by the new. In his discussion in *Philosophy of Rhetoric,* Campbell traced the beginning of what he called the "science of criticism."

Certainly no discussion of Campbell's terminology would be complete without some notice of his use of the word *philosophy* in the title. There is only one index entry of the term with the cryptic reference "nonsense in, 271–2." In that reference, Campbell had little good to say about philosophy and logic: "This art [logic], it must be owned, observed a wonderful impartiality in regard to truth and error, or rather the most absolute indifference to both. Such an art as this could at bottom be no other than a mere playing with words, used indeed grammatically, and according to certain rules established in the schools, but quite insignificant, and therefore incapable of conveying knowledge. 'Vain wisdom all, and false philosophy' " (271). Undoubtedly, the reason for the use of the word *philosophy* in Campbell's title is directly related to his reliance on the philosophies of his day. The heavy influence of Bacon is apparent throughout Campbell's discussion of induction and the scientific method, his rejection of Aristotle's topics and the syllogism, and his antipathy to the old logic (as evidenced in the preceding quotation). The influence of David Hume is evident in Campbell's reliance on empiricism, which stressed truth as based solely on observation through the senses. The common-sense philosophy as articulated by Thomas Reid was a corrective to this narrow view: "Let scholastic sophisters entangle themselves in their own cobwebs; I am resolved to take my own existence, and the existence of other things, upon trust: and to believe that snow is cold, and honey sweet, whatever they may say to the contrary" (qtd. in Horner 29). Thomas Reid, with his common-sense philosophy, and others of the Scottish school obviously had a profound effect on Campbell's rhetoric. The Scottish school of philosophy proceeded on the assumptions that we can study the human mind by observation of our own consciousness and that we can know the workings of our own minds through our own experience and through the experiences of others—and that this knowledge is communicated through language. In Book 1, Part 3, Chapter 5, titled "Common Sense," Campbell acknowledged the work of Thomas Reid and James Beattie, who were fellow members of the Aberdeen Philosophical Society (and to whom he read this part of his book) and whose discourses were also subjects of discussion in the meetings of that society. Following these philosophies and psychologies, Campbell based his logic on "the conformity of our conceptions to their archetypes in the nature of things" (35). He then evidenced his reliance on the doctrine of the association of ideas, whereby we gain knowledge through sensory experience as we relate it to other knowledge that we already have. This position is an extension of Francis Bacon's inductive reasoning. Obviously the philosophy that Campbell referred to in his title and that shaped his theory of rhetoric was that of the Scottish school, based ultimately on Descartes, Bacon, Locke, Hume, and Reid. The signposts all pointed forward to a new rhetoric rather than back to the old.

Logos, Pathos, and Ethos

Although Campbell never mentioned the classical terms, he followed the organization of traditional rhetoric in treating the three rhetorical proofs from the credibility of the speaker, the formation of good arguments, and the appeal to the hearer. In establishing the relationship among the three, he saw logic as serving rhetoric:

The sole and ultimate end of logic is the eviction of truth; one important end of eloquence, although, as appears from the first chapter, neither the sole, nor always the ultimate, is the conviction of the hearers. Pure logic regards only the subject. . . . Eloquence not only considers the subject, but also the speaker and the hearers, and both the subject and the speaker for the sake of the hearers, or rather for the sake of the effect intended to be produced in them. (33)

Campbell's logic is based on two sources of evidence: intuitive and deductive—the latter of which he also termed scientific evidence. In his discussion of intuitive evidence, he included mathematical axioms, consciousness, and common sense. Here is where the philosophies of his time are clearly represented. Under *consciousness*, he echoed Descartes when he asserted that he was sure of his own existence from his own consciousness, but he was further assured "that he exists . . . that he thinks, that he feels, that he sees, that he hears and the like" (37). The third source of intuitive evidence is common sense, "an original source of knowledge common to all mankind" (39). Scientific evidence is derived from the properties or associations between general ideas, while moral evidence "is founded on the principles we have from consciousness and common sense" and from our experience in judging the future from the past and the unknown from the familiar (43). He devoted the last part of this chapter to the superiority of scientific evidence by reason of the fallibility of our own faculties.

Campbell's Chapter 6 is well known to scholars for its attack on the syllogism and what Campbell called the school logic. Campbell quoted the authority of Locke, who said that the syllogistic art "serves more to display the ingenuity of the inventor, than to assist the diligent inquirer in his researches after truth" (62). Campbell continued by asserting that the syllogism "bears the manifest indications of an artificial and ostentatious parade of learning, calculated for giving the appearance of great profundity to what in fact is very shallow" (62). Campbell went on to argue that the syllogism is useless in its application to matters that we can know only through experience, since in moving from individual instances to generalizations, from the species to the genus, there is increasingly less certainty. In the syllogism the natural movement from the particular to the general in induction is reversed and, consequently, is far less reliable, just as the general is less reliable than the particular instance. He supported his argument with a number of examples of syllogisms.

The next two chapters deal with consideration of the hearers, as men in general and men in particular.[1] Under the first heading, Campbell considered understanding, imagination, memory, and the passions. He spent a large portion of the chapter on a discussion of the passions—the circumstances that arouse the passions—and concluded with "How an Unfavorable Passion must be calmed" (93).

The final chapters in Book 1 are primarily concerned with ways in which the speaker can gain the good opinion of the hearers. Campbell divided the different kinds of public speaking into orations for the bar, the senate, and the pulpit, and then looked at these discourses from the stance of the person speaking, the persons addressed, the subject, the occasion, and the end in view. Campbell's discussion here seems to concern verbal discourse rather than writing and follows a familiar pattern.

The final chapter in this book contains Campbell's criticism of the views of pity and pain suffered in viewing tragedy put forth by Abbe de Bos, Fontenelles, David Hume, and Mallarme—none of which satisfied him. His own hypothesis rests on the association of the passions, no one of which appears in isolation. Thus, the pleasure felt in pity comes from "its own nature, or from the nature of those passions of which it is compounded" (134), a clear reflection of the Scottish philosophy, which followed from his own view of consciousness as the source of evidence.

Language

In the titles of his second and third books, Campbell used the word *elocution*, a term that was common in the eighteenth century but was used with a different meaning in Campbell's *Rhetoric*. Both *eloquence* and *elocution* are English words derived from the Latin *elocutio*, the third canon of classical rhetoric, style. During the Renaissance, rhetoric had become reduced to a study of the figures and tropes; hence, the term *eloquence*—which was derived from *elocutio*, meaning "style"—was an appropriate name for the truncated Renaissance rhetoric. During the eighteenth century the study of gestures and pronunciation, called "elocution," was another reductive form of rhetoric that was much in vogue. No one seems quite sure why the movement was called "elocution," since gestures and pronunciation were properly a part of the fifth canon of rhetoric, delivery. It was a misnomer and Campbell was using the anglicized term *elocution* in its proper meaning of "style." He wisely ignored the "elocution" of his own period.

Nowhere does Campbell sound more modern than in his discussion of the nature of language and grammar in the first four chapters of Book 2. Following another definition of *eloquence* that stressed its close connection with language, Campbell defined grammar: "It is not the business of grammar . . . to give law to the fashions that regulate our speech. On the contrary, from its conformity to these, and from that alone, it derives all its authority and value" (140). He then defined grammar as "a collection of general observations" about language. The eighteenth century was a period when "correctness" in language, sometimes called "purity," was much in vogue; and Robert Lowth, who wrote one of the most popular grammars of the period (*A Short Introduction to English Grammar* [1762]), was praised by one of his admirers for showing "the grammatic inaccuracies" of English. Before embarking on his discussion of grammar, which he called "purity," Campbell delineated what constituted "purity" in language. He based his grammar on usage, which in turn was based on three elements: reputable, national (as opposed to provincial or foreign), and present use. He used an elaborate metaphor to explain the basis for his discussion of the "offenses against purity": "Thus I have attempted to explain what that *use* is, which is the sole mistress of language, and to ascertain the precise import and extent of these her essential attributes, *reputable, national,* and *present,* and to give the directions proper to be observed in searching for the laws of this empress. In truth, grammar and criticism are but her ministers" (151). Campbell then described the role of the grammarian who determines the laws of the language based on these criteria and the role of the critic who notices and calls the offenses. Campbell, himself, then proceeded to take on the role of the grammarian by determining the criteria for "purity" when use is divided. Again his modernity and good sense are evident. He preferred analogy, harmony, simplicity, ancient usage, brevity etymology, and clarity in disputed matters; and he warned against using words that are barbarisms, obsolete, or too newly coined. After concluding his discussion of "purity," a "quality purely grammatical," he moved to the rhetorical qualities of style, the "simple and original qualities of style, considered as an object to the understanding, the imagination, the passions, and the ear" (216).

The first quality is "perspicuity," which includes "grammatical purity" but which further necessitates the avoidance of a number of faults such as the "affectation of excellence" and other matters that obscure the meaning of words. Campbell insisted first on clarity: "But whatever be the ultimate intention of the orator, to inform, to convince, to please, to move, or to persuade, still he must speak so as to be understood, or he speaks to no purpose" (216). Campbell concluded this section with a discussion on effective and ineffective sentences and a short chapter on the possibility that certain styles may have to reconcile "perspicuity" with the force and vivacity required by some kinds of composition.

Book 3 begins with a discussion of "vivacity," the third quality of rhetorical style after "purity" and "perspicuity": "Having discussed the subject of perspicuity, by which the discourse is fitted to inform the understanding, I come now to those qualities of style by which it is adapted to please the imagination, and consequently to awake and fix the attention" (286). "Vivacity" depends on the choice of words, their number, and their arrangement. Campbell devoted most of the chapter to familiar figures of speech such as metaphor, metonymy, personification, and alliteration, avoiding almost entirely the classical appellations. The next chapter is concerned largely with brevity and ways to avoid repetition and verbosity. The remaining two chapters in the book treat the arrangement of words into sentences and, lastly, connectives. In the introduction to Book 3, Campbell indicated that his book would treat two qualities of rhetorical style, although he treated only one and omitted any mention of animation and music. He concluded abruptly and, clearly, did not finish the book. Thus, he has left us an incomplete philosophy of rhetoric.

SUMMARY

George Campbell worked within part of the framework established by traditional rhetoric, carefully avoiding its terminology but adopting some of its ideas and coloring them with his own philosophic cast. For example, he treated carefully the three arguments of Aristotle's *Rhetoric*—ethos, logos, and pathos—while calling them the "considerations" that the speaker should have of himself and of the hearers. When he spoke of the hearers, however, he borrowed from Hartley, Locke, and Hume, who considered all men to be endowed with imagination, understanding, memory, and passions. In his consideration of logic, which Campbell felt should be included in a rhetoric, he roundly rejected the old "school logic" and drew from Reid's philosophy of common sense. In his treatment of style, he stayed within the classical boundaries but managed to range freely within those confines. Within "perspicuity" and "vivacity," he gave extensive treatment to figurative language without using the usual terminology, and his treatment of grammatical propriety, which he termed "purity" was very modern in contrast to the prevailing thought of his day.

Campbell departed drastically from traditional rhetoric in other areas. He abandoned memory and delivery, probably as inappropriate to written language, and firmly rejected deductive reasoning and syllogism. He finally enlarged the scope of rhetoric to include written as well as spoken language and informative discourse as well as judicial, demonstrative, and epideictic rhetoric. In these areas alone, he changed the nature of rhetoric.

Without ever quite abandoning the traditional framework, Campbell introduced a new rhetoric. To the twentieth-century reader, he sounds modern in many ways. He turned, not to the ancient philosophers, but to the philosophers of his own time in the Scottish enlightenment, many of whom were his friends and acquaintances. Nor did he turn to the rhetoricians of his own day, but boldly struck out on his own into new territory. It is hard to believe that the traditional rhetorics so popular in his own day, that for the most part are restatements of the classical canon, were published only two decades earlier. It is also difficult to believe that he belonged to the same century as the popular elocutionary movement championed by such notables as Thomas Sheridan and John Walker. Nor did he join the growing belletristic movement so fashionable in the southern Scottish universities or embrace the "doctrine of correctness" espoused by Bishop Lowth and others of the eighteenth century. George Campbell was, indeed, far ahead of his day, as evidenced by the editions of his book, only one in the eighteenth century and over twenty in the nineteenth century. While Hugh Blair's *Lectures* continued to hold some interest for English literature scholars, George Campbell's work dropped from view in the early twentieth century. Campbell scholarship in this century was dormant before the thirties, when speech- and English-department researchers in the history of rhetoric rediscovered him and realized that the best of today's rhetorics reflect his ideas. He is a key figure in the history of rhetoric, and is the true progenitor of North American composition theory and *praxis*.

NOTE

The bibliography that follows was prepared by Shelley Aley.

1. I find myself increasingly annoyed with Campbell's use of the generic *man* and *he*, when he is so modern in so many other ways. It is necessary, however, to remember that the generic *he* was the convention of the time and that his rhetoric is written primarily for persons who would pursue careers in law and the church, occupations closed to women. In addition, pursuing a university degree was not a choice for women in the eighteenth century.

BIBLIOGRAPHY

Primary Sources

Campbell, George. "The Character of a Minister of the Gospel as a Teacher and Pattern." A sermon preached before the Synod of Aberdeen, April 7, 1752.
———. *A Dissertation on Miracles*. 2 vols. 3d ed. Edinburgh, 1797.
———. *Lectures on Systematic Theology and Pulpit Eloquence*. Boston, 1832.
———. *The Philosophy of Rhetoric*. Edited by Lloyd F. Bitzer. 1963. Reprint. Carbondale: Southern Illinois University Press, 1988.

Biography

Bitzer, Lloyd F., ed. Introduction to *The Philosophy of Rhetoric*, by George Campbell. Carbondale: Southern Illinois University Press, 1988.

Bizzell, Patricia, and Bruce Herzberg, eds. "George Campbell." In *The Rhetorical Tradition: Readings from Classical Times to the Present*. Boston: Bedford, 1990.

Golden, James L., and Edward P. J. Corbett. "George Campbell." In *The Rhetoric of Blair, Campbell, and Whately*. Carbondale: Southern Illinois University Press, 1990.

Stephen, Leslie. "Campbell, George." *DNB*. London, 1882.

Secondary Sources

Anderson, R. D. *The Student Community at Aberdeen, 1860–1939*. Aberdeen: University of Aberdeen Press, 1988.

Bevilacqua, Vincent M. "Campbell, Priestly, and the Controversy Concerning Common Sense." *Southern Speech Journal* 30.2 (1964):79–98.

———. "Campbell, Vico, and the Rhetorical Science of Human Nature." *Philosophy and Rhetoric* 18.1 (1985):23–30.

———. "Philosophical Origins of George Campbell's Philosophy of Rhetoric." *Speech Monographs* 32.1 (1965):1–12.

Bitzer, Lloyd F. " 'All Art Is Founded in Science.' " *Rhetoric Society Quarterly* 13.1 (1983):13–14.

———. "Hume's Philosophy in George Campbell's Philosophy of Rhetoric." *Philosophy and Rhetoric* 2.3 (1969):139–66.

———. "The Lively Idea: A Study of Hume's Influence on George Campbell's *Philosophy of Rhetoric*." Ph.D. diss., University of Iowa, 1962.

———. "A Re-Evaluation of Campbell's Doctrine of Evidence." *Quarterly Journal of Speech* 46.2 (1960): 135–40.

Bormann, Dennis R. "George Campbell's *Cura Prima* on Eloquence, 1758." *Quarterly Journal of Speech* 74.1 (1988):35–51.

———. "Some 'Common-Sense' about Campbell, Hume, and Reid: The Extrinsic Evidence." *Quarterly Journal of Speech* 71.4 (1985):395–421.

———. "Two Faculty Psychologists on the 'Ends' of Speaking: George Campbell and Johann Sulzer." *Central States Speech Journal* 33.1 (1982):299–309.

Burwick, Frederick. "Associationist Rhetoric and Scottish Prose Style." *Speech Monographs* 34.1 (1964):21–34.

Cohen, Herman. "The Faculties and the Ends of Discourse." *Rhetoric Society Quarterly* 13.1 (1983):19–20.

———. "William Leechman's Anticipation of Campbell." *Western Speech* 32.2 (1968):92–99.

Crawford, John. "The Rhetoric of George Campbell." Ph.D. diss., Northwestern University, 1947.

Dillman, Richard. "[E. D.] Hirsch and [George] Campbell." *Rhetoric Society Quarterly* 9.2 (1979):92–96.

Dolph, Phil. "Taste and *The Philosophy of Rhetoric*." *Western Speech* 32.2 (1968): 104–13.

Edney, Clarence W. "George Campbell's Theory of Public Address." Ph.D. Diss., University of Iowa, 1946.

———. "Campbell's Theory of Logical Truth." *Speech Monographs* 15.1 (1948): 19–32.

————. "Campbell's Lectures on Pulpit Eloquence." *Speech Monographs* 19.1 (1952):1–10.

Ehninger, Douglas. "Campbell, Blair, and Whately: Old Friends in a New Light." *Western Speech* 19.4 (1955):263–69.

————. "George Campbell and the Revolution in Inventional Theory." *Southern Speech Journal* 15.4 (1950): 270–76.

Ettlich, Ernest, et al. "Symposium: The Rhetorical Theory of George Campbell." *Western Speech* 32.2 (1968):84–113.

Golden, James L., Goodwin F. Berquist, and William E. Coleman. "The Rhetorics of Campbell and Whately." In *The Rhetoric of Western Thought*, 186–216. 4th ed. Dubuque, IA: 1989.

Hagaman, John. "George Campbell and the Creative Management of Audience." *Rhetoric Society Quarterly* 13.1 (1983):21–24.

————. "On Campbell's Philosophy of Rhetoric and Its Relevance to Contemporary Invention." *Rhetoric Society Quarterly* 11.3 (1981):145–54.

Hall, Alta. "George Campbell's *Philosophy of Rhetoric*." Ph.D. diss., Cornell University, 1934.

Holcomb, Kathleen. "Wit, Humour, and Ridicule: George Campbell's First Discourse for the Aberdeen Philosophical Society." In *Aberdeen and the Enlightenment*, edited by Jennifer J. Carter and Joan H. Pittock, 282–90. Aberdeen: University of Aberdeen, 1987.

Horner, Winifred Bryan. *Nineteenth-Century Scottish Rhetoric: The American Connection*. Carbondale: Southern Illinois University Press, 1993.

Howell, Wilbur Samuel. "George Campbell and the Philosophical Rhetoric of the New Learning." *Eighteenth-Century British Logic and Rhetoric*, 577–612. Princeton: Princeton University Press, 1971.

LaRusso, Dominick. "Root or Branch? A Re-examination of Campbell's 'Rhetoric.' " *Western Speech* 32.2 (1968):85–91.

McDermott, Douglas. "George Campbell and the Classical Tradition." *Quarterly Journal of Speech* 49.4 (1963):403–9.

McKerrow, Ray E. "Campbell, Whately on the Utility of Syllogistic Logic." *Western Speech Communication* 40.1 (1976): 3–13.

Mohrmann, G. P. "George Campbell: The Psychological Background." *Western Speech* 32.2 (1968):99–104.

Rasmussen, Karen. "Inconsistency in Campbell's Rhetoric." *Quarterly Journal of Speech* 60.2 (1974):190–200.

Ulman, H. Lewis, ed. *The Minutes of the Aberdeen Philosophical Society, 1758–1771*. Aberdeen: Aberdeen University Press, 1990.

————. "The Most Significant Passage in Campbell's Rhetoric: The Handmaids of Reason." *Rhetoric Society Quarterly* 13.1 (1983):25–27.

————. "Thought and Language is George Campbell's *The Philosophy of Rhetoric*." Ph.D. diss., Pennsylvania State University, 1985.

Warnick, Barbara. "Charles Rollin's Traité and the Rhetorical Theories of Smith, Campbell, and Blair." *Rhetorica* 3.1 (1985):45–65.

WILLIAM ENFIELD
(1741–1797)

John S. Gentile

William Enfield was born on March 29, 1741, in Sudbury, Suffolk, and received his early education under the guidance of the Reverend William Hextall, a dissenting minister whose influence in Enfield's life was felt not only in Enfield's choice of the ministry as a career but also in his lifelong love of literature. At seventeen, Enfield attended the Daventry Academy; and upon the completion of his studies, he was offered the office of Minister to the Congregation of Protestant Dissenters at Benn's Garden in Liverpool, where he was ordained in November 1763. He held this position for seven years, during which time he married Mary Holland (the daughter of a Liverpool draper), entered Liverpool society, and began his literary career with the publication of his two-volume *Sermons for the Use of Families* (1768–1770).

In 1770, Enfield accepted an invitation for two positions at the academy at Warrington. The first position, that of tutor of belles lettres, suited Enfield well; the second, *Rector Academiae* (i.e., director of the academy) did not. The rectorship brought Enfield great distress; he tried to free himself from that portion of his duty to Warrington, but difficulty in securing a successor ultimately led to his holding both positions until the dissolution of the academy from various causes in 1783 (Aikin ix–x; Wakefield 214–16).

While Enfield's tenure at Warrington may not have been tranquil, it was his most prolific period. Enfield secured his professional reputation by producing in quick succession many volumes of collected sermons and hymns. An estimation of Enfield's publications during these years is offered by John Aikin in his 1798 memoir: "Several of them belong to the humble but useful class of compilations; yet in them he found occasion to display the elegance of his taste, and the soundness of his judgment" (x). Both Enfield's taste and his judgment are apparent in his elocution textbook *The Speaker; or, Miscellaneous Pieces, from the Best English Writers, and Disposed under Proper Heads, with a View to Facilitate the Improvement of Youth in Reading and*

Speaking. First published in 1774, the same year the University of Edinburgh conferred upon its author an LL.D. degree, the book was reprinted
numerous times in Britain over the next decades and printed in an American edition in 1798. *The Speaker* was one of the most popular elocution
textbooks of the late eighteenth century, along with William Scott's *Lessons
in Elocution*, to which it has been compared (Robb 42). In 1781, Enfield
compiled *Exercises in Elocution*; its subtitle, *A Sequel to The Speaker*, demonstrates the earlier book's popularity. For two years following the dissolution of the academy, Enfield remained in Warrington, occupied as a tutor
to private pupils, some of whom he took in as boarders. He also continued
the pastoral care of the Cairo Street Presbyterian congregation, which he
had originally begun upon his arrival in Warrington in 1770; and he did
not resign until 1785, when he accepted an invitation to serve as minister
at the octagon-dissenting congregation at Norwich.

John Aikin characterized the last decade of Enfield's life as "tranquil and
serene" (xxiv) following Enfield's recovery from the trauma of the death of
his eldest son (of five children) from a fever. Enfield's writings continued
to be published; he contributed regularly to the *Monthly*, a literary magazine,
and completed "the most laborious of his literary tasks" (Aikin xxii), an
abridgment of *Brucker's History of Philosophy*, which appeared in two volumes in 1791.

ENFIELD'S RHETORICAL THEORY

Enfield's position in the history of rhetoric and elocution rests, not on
the originality of his rhetorical theory—which reflects principles described
by Quintilian and by the eighteenth-century elocutionists of the Natural
School—but on his contribution to pedagogy. Enfield's *Speaker*, as stated
earlier, was widely popular in Great Britain and was printed in the United
States. Originally intended to help his own students at Warrington acquire
"a just and graceful Elocution" (iii), Enfield's *Speaker* helped shape a generation of public speakers and was still being used in the early nineteenth
century. Enfield's "Essay on Elocution" in *The Speaker* clarifies his philosophy and methods of elocution. He declared: "Follow Nature, is certainly
the fundamental law of Oratory, without a regard to which, all other rules
will only produce affected declamation, not just elocution" (vi). Having
urged the student-orator to "follow nature," Enfield then offered assistance
beyond merely emphasizing observation. He qualified his earlier declaration
and proceeded to methodize nature through a series of rules. He resolved
the nature-rule contradiction by arguing: "What are rules or lessons for
acquiring this or any other art, but the observations of others, collected into
a narrow compass, and digested in a natural order, for the direction of the
unexperienced and unpracticed learner?" (vii).

Enfield then proceeded to introduce his eight rules, accompanying them with suggested methods of practice. In condensed form, these rules are the following:

Rule 1: Let Your Articulation Be Distinct and Deliberate. Faults of articulation may be corrected either by reading sentences so contrived as often to repeat the faulty sounds or by guarding against them in familiar conversation. Read aloud passages chosen for that purpose, such as those that abound with long and unusual words or with many short syllables together. Aim at nothing higher until you can read distinctly and deliberately.

Rule 2: Let Your Pronunciation Be Bold and Forcible. Draw in as much air as your lungs can contain with ease, and expel the air with vehemence while uttering those sounds that require an emphatical pronunciation. Read aloud in the open air and with all the exertion you can command. Preserve your body in an erect attitude while you are speaking.

Rule 3: Acquire a Compass and Variety in the Height of Your Voice. To acquire the power of changing the key in which you speak at pleasure, accustom yourself to pitch your voice in different keys, from the lowest to the highest notes you can command. Read, as exercises on this rule, such compositions as have a variety of speakers or such as relate dialogues, observing the height of voice that is proper to each key and endeavoring to change it as nature directs.

Rule 4: Pronounce Your Words with Propriety and Elegance. Look for this standard among those individuals who are both men of learning and of the world. An attention to such models and a free intercourse with the polite world are the best guards against the peculiarities and vulgarisms of provincial dialects.

Rule 5: Pronounce Every Word Consisting of More Than One Syllable with its Proper Accent. In accenting words, the general custom and a good ear are the best guides.

Rule 6: In Every Sentence, Distinguish the More Significant Words by a Natural, Forcible, and Varied Emphasis. For this purpose it is necessary that the reader should be perfectly acquainted with the exact construction and full meaning of every sentence that is recited. It is another office of emphasis to express opposition between the several parts of a sentence where the style is pointed and antithetical. Pope's "Essay on Man," "Moral Essays," and "Proverbs of Solomon" will furnish many proper exercises in this species of speaking. Study the construction, meaning, and spirit of every sentence and adhere as nearly as possible to the manner in which we distinguish one word from another in conversation.

Rule 7: Acquire a Just Variety of Pause and Cadence. The tones and heights at the close of a sentence ought to be infinitely diversified, according to the general nature of the discourse and the particular construction and meaning of the sentence. Narrative, argumentative, interrogative, and pathetic pieces require different use of tone, pause, and cadence. The best method of correcting a uniform cadence is frequently to read (a) select sentences in which the style is pointed and frequent antitheses are introduced and (b) argumentative pieces, or such as abound with interrogatives.

Rule 8: Accompany the Emotions and Passions That Your Words Express by Corresponding Tones, Looks, and Gestures. Nature is always the same, and every judicious imitation of it will always be pleasing. All endeavors, therefore, to make men orators by describing to them in words the manner in which their voice, countenance, and hands are to be employed in expressing the passions must be weak and ineffectual. Observe in what manner the several emotions or passions are expressed in real life or by those who have with great labor and taste acquired a power of imitating nature.

In performing these exercises, Enfield encouraged daily reading aloud but favored memorized recitation. Recitation has several advantages as a method of elocutionary study: "It obliges the speaker to dwell upon the ideas which he is to express, enables him to discern their particular meaning and force, and gives him a previous knowledge of the several inflections, emphases, and tones. And by taking off his eye from the book, it gives him greater liberty to attempt the expression of the countenance and gesture" (xxvii).

Arranged in order of complexity, the literary selections in *The Speaker* and its sequel reflect and promote the taste and cultural values of a British gentleman of the eighteenth century. While featuring heavily the works of Shakespeare and of major British writers of the seventeenth and eighteenth centuries, Enfield betrayed his "Presbyterian predilection for obscure Scottish poets" (Hargis 229) by including several selections by minor Scottish writers of his day. Enfield apparently chose his selections not only for their literary merit but for their potential assistance in the moral edification of young men. Enfield followed Quintilian in teaching young orators not only what is eloquent but what is morally good. Enfield's morality is made even more explicit in his "Counsels to Young Men" (an essay appended to the 1794 edition of *Exercises in Elocution*), which offers moral education in the form of a father's letter to his son.

Accepting as self-evident that "the importance of a good elocution is sufficiently obvious" (v), Enfield nevertheless concluded his "Essay on Elocution" with a warning on the misuse of accomplished elocution. Young orators ought not view their cultivated eloquence as an end unto itself but as a service to their professions. Thus, he cautioned: "Always employ your powers of elocution with caution and modesty; remembering that though it be desirable to be admired as an eminent Orator, it is of much more importance to be respected, as a wise Statesman, an able Lawyer, or a useful Preacher" (xxix).

When accessing Enfield's contribution to the elocutionary movement, it is difficult not to agree with Donald E. Hargis's comment that "*The Speaker* provides only a bare outline of selected theoretical and practical principles, not a developed system of elocution" (230). We may, however, temper this harsh critique by emphasizing that Enfield was writing for an audience of young, novice orators as well as by remembering the enduring popularity of *The Speaker*—which points to the conclusion that many instructors in Britain and America found the book useful and effective in their classrooms.

While *The Speaker* provides us with an understanding of Enfield's work as a teacher of elocution, we know little of him as an orator himself. Enfield has been characterized as an amiable, learned, and accomplished man by both Gilbert Wakefield and John Aikin, but we have only a brief description of his platform style. Aikin has assisted us in understanding why Enfield's contribution to rhetoric, however influential, remains limited; he has reminded us that Enfield's true vocation was not that of an elocutionist but that of a preacher. Aikin has written of Enfield:

His manner of delivery was grave and impressive, affecting rather a tenor of uniform dignity than a variety of expression, for which his voice was not well calculated. It was entirely free from what is called *tone*, and though not highly animated, was by no means dull, and never careless or indifferent. As to his matter, it was almost exclusively that of a *moral preacher*. Religion was to him rather a principle than a sentiment; and he was more solicitous to deduce from it *a rule of life*, enforced by its peculiar sanctions, than to elevate it into a source of sublime feeling (xiv).

BIBLIOGRAPHY

Primary Sources

The majority of Enfield's writings are outside the field of rhetoric. For a more complete bibliography, see John Aikin's memoir, listed below.

Enfield, William. *Exercises in Elocution; Selected from Various Authors, and Arranged under Proper Heads: Intended as a Sequel to a Work Entitled "The Speaker."* London, 1780.

———. *The Speaker; or, Miscellaneous Pieces, Selected from the Best English Writers, and Disposed under Proper Heads, with a View to Facilitate the Improvement of Youth in Reading and Speaking.* London, 1774.

Biography and Criticism

Aikin, John. "Memoir of the Author." In *Sermons on Practical Subjects*, by William Enfield, iii–xxvii. London: J. Johnson, 1798.

Hargis, Donald E. "Enfield and Elocution." *Western Speech* 25.4 (1961):222–31.

Robb, Mary Margaret. *Oral Interpretation of Literature in American Colleges and Universities: A Historical Study of Teaching Methods.* New York: Johnson Reprint, 1968.

Wakefield, Gilbert. *Memoirs of the Life of Gilbert Wakefield.* vol. 1, 211–26. London, 1804.

MICHEL LE FAUCHEUR
(1585–1657)

Lynée Lewis Gaillet

Few biographical details are known about Michel Le Faucheur, the seventeenth-century Protestant minister credited with being the most influential Continental authority behind the doctrines of the eighteenth-century English elocutionists. Le Faucheur was born in Geneva in 1585. As a clergyman serving at Montpellier, Charenton, and Paris, he was admired for his learning and oratorical ability and earned the respect of French Catholics for his honest speech and conduct. It has been noted in the *Biographie Universelle* that after hearing Le Faucheur deliver a sermon on dueling, a high-ranking French military officer declared that he would refuse all future dueling challenges. When a rule forbidding foreigners to preach in France threatened his career, Le Faucheur considered but did not accept a position as professor of theology at Lausanne. During his lifetime, Le Faucheur published several religious tracts and sermons. However, his most famous work *Traitté de l'action de l'orateur; ou, de la Prononciation et de geste* was not published until shortly after his death on April 1, 1657, by his friend and fellow clergyman Valentin Conrart, known as the father of the French Academy. Le Faucheur is not acknowledged as the author on the title page of the 1657 edition of the *Traitté,* and in later editions the work is attributed to Conrart, who was long considered to be the author of the treatise. By the end of the seventeenth century, Le Faucheur's *Traitté* had gone through at least seven editions in French (Paris, 1657; Paris, 1667; Paris, 1676; Lyon, 1676; Paris, 1686; Leyden, 1686; and Amsterdam, 1697), and had been translated into Latin (under Conrart's name) by Melchior Schmidt, theology professor at Helmstadt (1690). Le Faucheur's *Traitté,* which lays out specific rules for the beginning lawyer and minister to follow in order to ensure effective oratorical delivery, gave authority to and greatly influenced the early elocutionary movement in eighteenth-century England (Howell 162–63; Nicolas; Philbert).

LE FAUCHEUR'S RHETORICAL THEORY

Wilbur Samuel Howell has claimed that "Le Faucheur's *Traitté* is one of the most respectable works of scholarship in the whole history of the elocutionary movement and one of the leading treatises on delivery in the history of rhetorical theory" (168). With slight qualification, this praise can be extended to the English translations as well. The French *Traitté* was translated into at least three English versions in the eighteenth century: *An Essay upon the Action of an Orator* (1702?), *The Art of Speaking in Publick* (1727), and *An Essay upon Pronunciation and Gesture* (1750). Apart from the titles, the second and third English translations vary little from the first, and none of the three English translations attributes the work to Le Faucheur. The data of publication of the first translation is often recognized as the birth of the English elocutionary movement. Unfortunately, the first translation is neither signed nor dated. Howell has disputed the accepted date of publication—around 1680—and makes a convincing case that the first English translation was published early in the eighteenth century, probably in 1702 (165). The first translator tried to maintain an exact equivalent rendering of Le Faucheur's French text into English. However, on three occasions the translator used the word *elocution* as a term for vocal utterance, when the French text did not authorize him to do so (Howell 180). The primary difference between the English translation and Le Faucheur's *Traitté* lies in the emphasis on the importance of delivery. The English translator suggested in his preface that delivery is the main end of rhetoric, when in fact in *An Essay upon the Action* Le Faucheur stated that delivery is not the primary goal of classical rhetoric at all but rather the "Fourth Part: That is, Action; which consists of Speaking and Gesture" (2). Le Faucheur viewed delivery as a member of the hierarchy of oratorical arts and not as the sole end of rhetoric.

In *An Essay upon the Action* Le Faucheur addressed his work to "young Gentlemen, who have not yet got an ill habit of Speaking" and to "those that are bred up to Divinity or the Law" (16). He claimed that the study of delivery is neither indecent nor irreverent and warned that "if honest Men should deny themselves these Arts of Persuasion in a Good Cause, others yet would make use of them in a Bad One" (32). Initially led to write upon this part of classical rhetoric to fill a void, Le Faucheur explained that the great classical rhetoricians insisted on the importance of effective delivery but that only Quintilian offered any specific advice on this subject, advice which subsequently became outdated (9–10). At the urging of his friends, Le Faucheur wrote his *Traitté* because he believed that effective delivery made up for deficiencies in invention, arrangement, and style (2). At one point in *An Essay upon the Action,* Le Faucheur has instructed the lawyer and minister to ignore the rules of delivery while in the process of pleading a case or delivering a sermon "for the very Thought of Rules and the Care of observing them would mightily distract and amuse. Besides that it would take off the Warmth and Spirit of his Discourse, perplex his Head, and disturb his Memory." While speaking, according to Le Faucheur, the orator should use only those gestures "which arise naturally from the Subject of his Discourse, from the Place where he speaks, and the Presence of the Person, to whom he addresses himself" (209). Le Faucheur believed that it was a trivial waste of time to memorize gestures before delivering a speech; instead, the orator should focus on the message of his speech. Unfortunately, many of Le Faucheur's translators and later imitators did not adopt his comprehensive conception of classical rhetoric. This disregard of his view of rhetoric is most clearly illustrated in the work of Thomas Sheridan, the best-known figure of the elocutionary movement. Sheridan reduced classical rhetoric to nothing more than delivery, even when quoting the ancients who disagreed with his position.

Within the fourteen chapters of his *Traitté*, Le Faucheur devoted eight chapters to the variations of the voice. He laid down specific rules for the orator to follow so that the audience can hear and understand with ease, pleasure, and satisfaction. In *An Essay upon the Action* Le Faucheur instructed the orator how to vary the voice not only in regard to volume, tone, and speed of delivery but also according to the "Figures of Rhetoric" (128). In addition, Le Faucheur offered advice for adapting the delivery to the various types of discourse, particular occasions, and the passions of the audience. In this section of the *Traitté*, Le Faucheur indirectly defined many of the terms from the other parts of classical rhetoric; he listed the figures of rhetoric, the six parts of the formal oratorical discourse, the kinds of rhetorical subjects, and stylistic variations.

The second half of Le Faucheur's *Essay upon the Action* comprises first a general discussion of gestures and then the particular rules concerning posture and the positioning of the head, eyes, eyebrows, mouth, lips, shoulders, face, and hands. Le Faucheur warned that some gestures are indecent and exhorted his readers not to "thrust out the Belly, and throw back the Head" (194), not to bite or lick the lips (193), and not to shrug the shoulders (193). He believed that the hands "are the chief Instruments of Action" and gave seventeen prescriptive rules for their use (194). He concluded by offering instructions for "putting all the above-mention'd Precepts in Practice" (207) and encouraged young orators to memorize select passages and practice delivering them often "in the Presence of a Friend" until they master the rules of delivery (207).

During the eighteenth century, Le Faucheur's *Traitté* was widely incorporated, though rarely acknowledged, into the works of the English elocutionists. Although Le Faucheur indicated in the title of his work that he intended for it to be used only by the pulpit and the bar, the English translators widened the scope of the audience to include the senate, the theater, and the court. The theater adopted the *Traitté* to lend authority to the art of acting. In *The Life of Mr. Thomas Betterton,* a work applying the rules of oratorical delivery to the conduct of an actor, the author Charles Gildon admitted that he borrowed from a French source; yet he never directly acknowledged either Le Faucheur's *Traitté* or the English translations. Howell has noted at least twelve passages in Gildon's work, such as the following one, that borrow nearly verbatim from Le Faucheur's translators (187): "There are, in short, two things to make the Speaker heard and understood without Difficulty; first, a very distinct and articulate Voice, and next a very strong and vigorous Pronunciation" (Gildon 101). Compare this Gildon quotation to the following quotation from *An Essay upon the Action*: "First, there are two things requisite to qualify a Man for this Work: That is, a very Distinct and Articulate Voyce, and a very Strong and Vigorous Pronunciation" (64–65).

Echoes of Le Faucheur's *Traitté* also can be found in a short pamphlet that greatly influenced the elocutionary movement. Depending almost entirely upon the first English translation of Le Faucheur's *Traitté*, the unsigned *Some Rules for Speaking and Action; To Be observed At the Bar, in the Pulpit, and the Senate, and by every one that Speaks in Publick. In a Letter to a Friend* (1715) went through five editions by 1750. John Henley, the most prominent of the early elocutionists, was greatly influenced by the popularity of *Some Rules for Speaking and Action* and by the English translations of Le Faucheur's *Traitté* (Howell 194). *Some Rules for Speaking and Action* was later cited by John Ward in his lectures on rhetoric at Gresham College and also by John Mason in his popular work *An Essay on Elocution; or, Pronunciation*. In addition, Mason borrowed often from the first and second translations of Le Faucheur's *Traitté* without acknowledging those sources, as seen in the following passages concerning gestures of the head (Howell 207): "It [the head] should always be on the same Side with the Action of the Hands and Body, except when we express an Abhorrence, or a Refusal of anything, which is done by rejecting it with the Right-hand, and turning away the Head to the Left" (Mason 39). Compare this Mason quotation to the following quotation from *An Essay upon the Action*: "To this I must add that the Head ought always to be turn'd on the same side with the other Actions of the Body, save only when they are exerted upon things we refuse . . . or upon things we detest and abhorr" (181).

The English translations of Le Faucheur's French *Traitté* clearly influenced the early elocutionary movement of the eighteenth century. The adoption of Le Faucheur's treatment of the fourth part of classical rhetoric gave authority to the doctrines of the English elocutionists. However, in a native English contribution, the later elocutionists isolated delivery from the classical rhetorical program supported by Le Faucheur and applied the term *elocution* to vocal utterance. Eventually, the word *elocution* became the term for the entire art of rhetoric. The English elocutionary movement gave rise to the common belief that rhetoric meant empty and insincere speaking

divorced from thought and emotion. The early signs of this trend are seen in the English translations and interpretations of Le Faucheur's *Traitté*.

BIBLIOGRAPHY

Primary Sources

Le Faucheur, Michel. *An Essay upon the Action of an Orator, As to his Pronunciation and Gesture, Useful both for Divines and Lawyers, and necessary for all Young Gentlemen, that study how to speak well in Publick*. London, 1702.
———. *The Art of Speaking in Publick; or, an Essay on the Action of an Orator, As to his Pronunciation and Gesture. Useful in the Senate or Theatre, the Court, the Camp, as well as the Bar and Pulpit. The Second Edition Corrected. With an Introduction relating to the Famous Mr. Henley's present Oratory*. London, 1727.
———. *An Essay upon Pronunciation and Gesture, Founded upon the Best Rules and Authorities of the Ancients, Ecclesiastical and Civil, and Adorned with the finest Rules of Elocution*. London, 1750.
———. *Traitté de l'action de l'orateur; ou, de la Prononciation et de geste*. Paris, 1657.
Gildon, Charles. *The Life of Mr. Thomas Betterton, The Late Eminent Tragedian*. London, 1710.
Mason, John. *An Essay on Elocution*. London, 1748. Reprint. English Linguistics 1500–1800 Facsimile Reprints, 1967.

Biography

Nicolas, Michel. "Michel Le Faucheur." *Nouvelle Biographie Générale* (1852–1866).
Philbert. "Michel Le Faucheur." *Biographie Universelle* (1843–1865).

Criticism

Howell, Wilbur Samuel. *Eighteenth-Century British Logic and Rhetoric*. Princeton: Princeton University Press, 1971.

MARGARET ASKEW FELL
(1614–1702)

Susan Seyfarth

Margaret Fell was born Margaret Askew in 1614 at Marsh Grange in Lancashire. There is little certainty about her ancestry, but it is thought that she was reared and educated in the manner typical for female children of gentle birth in seventeenth-century England. As a girl, she sometimes wrote in the rather wordy and involved style of her time, but usually she expressed concisely and fully her high ideals. In 1631 she married Thomas Fell (later, Judge) of Swarthmoor Hall near Ulverston; she bore him eight daughters and one son, all but one surviving into adulthood. In 1652 George Fox, a Quaker founder, visited Swarthmoor Hall several times; and in July, Margaret Fell converted to Quakerism. Although Judge Fell never converted, he was an avid supporter of Fox and the Friends; and his home became a center for Quaker activities. Judge Fell died in October 1658; and from that time to the end of her life, Margaret Fell dedicated herself to Quaker causes. She wrote letters and called on national leaders such as Cromwell, Charles II, James II, and William on behalf of persecuted and imprisoned Friends. She also traveled throughout England visiting Friends' Meetings. In 1659 she spearheaded a petition to the Rump Parliament against persecuting Quakers for nonpayment of tithes. The petition was signed extensively by women, marking the first unified effort of Quaker women for action against the British government's policies of intolerance (Irwin 179–80; Latt iv; Ross 5, 42). From February 1664 to June 1668, Margaret Fell was imprisoned with George Fox at Lancaster Castle for refusing to take an oath of allegiance to England and the Anglican Church and for holding unlawful Friends' Meetings. This was the first of Fell's troubles with the courts in her defense of the Quakers; she was sentenced or imprisoned on at least two more occasions in her lifetime.

George Fox and Margaret Fell married on October 27, 1669. Fox was dedicated to the idea of equality in marriage; for example, he matched each of his wife's gifts to him. The marriage was a strong spiritual union in which the two endured much physical separation owing to their different preaching itineraries and their frequent imprisonment (Bacon 16). Fox died in January 1691; Fell survived him by twelve years, dying at Swarthmoor Hall on April 23, 1702.

While Fox is known as the founding father of Quakerism, Margaret Fell is the "Nursing Mother of Quakerism" (Bacon 15). Fell was the first of many Quaker women to establish herself as a writer. The Fell opus comprises letters, pamphlets, and books. Although many of Fell's letters were not preserved and those that remain were edited inaccurately by well-meaning friends, Fell's writings are important because they exhibit in an authoritative style her keen understanding of the Quaker doctrine of Inner Light and her eagerness to impart that understanding to others (Hobby 240; Ross 33). However, when she attempted to teach these doctrines, Fell discovered opposition from within the Quaker sect to women's preaching publicly. In was this opposition from her male contemporaries that prompted her to write her most important work in rhetoric, *Womens Speaking Justified* (1666), which addressed women's rights to speak in church.

FELL'S RHETORIC

Fell's contributions to seventeenth-century rhetoric are rooted firmly in the traditions of rhetoric performed for social good and in pulpit oratory. She was a practitioner, not a theorist. Before taking an active part in the Quaker ministry, she wrote letters to judges and kings in defense of persecuted Quakers, and her language was strong but usually tactful. *A Brief Collection* contains a letter that she wrote to Parliament, in which she addressed "every particular member of the Body," to draw in her entire audience, and asked each member to be "sensible of the Hardships and Sufferings of others" (Fell 58). To be sensible of is to be keenly aware and cognizant of; so in making this request, Fell attributed rational and logical capabilities to her audience. The phrase "Hardships and Sufferings" evokes pity. Thus, Fell combined logos and pathos in her appeal to Parliament. In another letter, she abandoned tact for harsher, more Juvenalian language: she called a Justice of the Peace a caterpillar (Ross 40). Her pamphlets focus on the Quaker doctrine of Inner Light, which relies on the spirit and not solely on the Bible. Following Judge Fell's death, she assumed a more prominent role in the Society of Friends.

As the Quakers' most influential female preacher, she joined the ensuing debate over women's rights to preach and teach with the publication of her *Womens Speaking Justified*. Here, Fell dealt with a basic tenet of Quakerism, gender equality. She explained that we are God's prophets because we all contain the Indwelling Spirit. Since women possess Inner Light, they might speak God's word just as well as men. Women can and should preach, and Fell used biblical authority to justify this right. Added to her strategy of repeated Scriptural references, Fell clearly articulated her purposes. For example, she promised to explain God's word on women's speaking: "We shall *shew* clearly . . . But first let me *lay down how God* . . . " (3). She often addressed her readers harshly as haters of women and as resisters of the messages that God sends through women. These haters and resisters are the "blind priests" (16). Fell argued that women carry God's word; Christ at Sumaria said he was the Messiah, and he said it to women. She employed imagery freely, often creating positive pictures of God's Light and God's preservation of those who recognize that light. According to Fell, there are also negative images of those who deny women's rights to speak: "But all this opposing and gainsaying of Women Speaking, hath risen out of the Bottomless Pit, and Spirit of Darkness that hath spoken for these many hundred years together in this night of Apostasy" (10). In her most extreme images, Fell referred to the murders and killings of those who are not "joyn with one another" (10), that is, those who debate and reject the doctrine of companionability or gender equality.

The main objections to women's preaching were based on Paul's letters to the Corinthians and the books of Timothy and Genesis. These Scriptures provided the standard argument that Eve was tempted and fell, resulting in women's subsequent corruption and intellectual limitations. The clergy and others believed women to be unworthy preachers meddling in God's work (3). Fell's argument began with her title page's scriptural verses that proclaim the doctrine of equality. From John 6:45, she found evidence that all people are God's messengers: "It is written in the Prophets, they shall be all taught of God, saith Christ"; in Acts and Joel she found direct references to women's preaching: "Your sons and daughters shall prophesie" (Acts 2: 27; Joel 2:28). Fell argued that God made males and females alike. It is men who see them as different. Both are made in God's image, and they are equally weak. Only God is strong; and according to 1 Corinthians 12: 9, his "strength is made manifest in weakness" (3). In Matthew, Christ said that God's definition of marriage is that man and woman become one in the flesh (5); they are the same. Therefore, Fell concluded that it was appropriate for weak men and women to spread God's word. She also acknowledged the serpent's tempting of Eve, but claimed that Eve's fall did not make women inferior because Adam was tempted, too: "They were both tempted into transgression and disobedience" (4). Furthermore, God put enmity between the seed of the serpent and woman, so "it is manifest that those that speak against the woman and her Seeds Speaking, speak out of the enmity of the old Serpents Seed" (4). After aligning her opponents with the snake, Fell pointed out that God, in fact, called his church "Woman." After citing several passages from Psalms, Jeremiah, and Revelation, she stated that "thus much may prove that the Church of Christ is a woman, and those that speak against the womans speaking, speak against the Church of Christ and the Seed of the Woman, which Seed is Christ" (5).

Fell claimed that women of the Bible were singled out by Christ. For example, John said that Christ spoke to Martha first of his resurrection, and Luke narrated the story of a female sinner washing Christ's feet. Thus, "Jesus owned the Love and Grace that appeared to Women" (6), such as Mary Magdalene, Joanna, and Mary, the mother of James—all of whom were told of Christ's rising and who delivered the news to the Apostles. Women, therefore, were chosen to speak for God, and men believed their messages (6–7).

Next, Fell interpreted the Apostle Paul's instructions that women should maintain silence in church. Paul, she said, attempted to bring order to services in which men and women from the general congregation spoke out of turn or in different languages. Not only did he silence the women, but he also forbade any men to speak in an unknown tongue. Fell believed the Scriptures referred to women who had not found their Inner Light and that similar verses focused on silence in marriage, not the church. For example, she explained that when Paul said that women must learn from their husbands at home, he was addressing those women who "were in strife, confusion and malice in their speaking" (9) and women who did not cover their heads but adorned their plaited hair with jewels. Disorderly, improperly attired women were to subject themselves to their husbands. Furthermore, the appearance of indecent women in church was, for Fell, no reason for decent ones to be silent (9–10), and she proved that the misapplication of such passages were based on historical ignorance. In addition, Fell countered the argument that Paul wanted women silenced by asking why he had his fellows help the women who "labored with him in the Gospel" (10). Why did the Apostles pray with these women? And why did Jesus refer to his church as feminine—as "the Bride, the Lamb's Wife" (11) if they were less worthy Christians than men? She moved toward the end of *Womens Speaking Justified* with positive examples of biblical women's speaking, such as Mary, Elizabeth, Rachel, and Leah, whose words have been incorporated into men's prayers. She cited Judith, who spoke to the elders of Israel, who praised Judith for her words (14–16). However, it is clear that Fell denied the rights of women to speak if they represented the false church, "the great Whore . . . that denies Revelation and Prophesie" (16–17). It is also clear that she condemned the "blind Priests" (16), those men who would incorporate women's words into their sermons and still speak against their rights to preach. And finally, nowhere did Margaret Fell find the Apostles claiming that women should not preach.

Womens Speaking Justified closes with a postscript of Old Testament passages further supporting Fell's notion that women have preached successfully. She left us with the story of a husband and wife to whom God appeared. The husband responded by saying that death was imminent because they had seen God. The wife disagreed, explaining that God meant them to see him, to hear his words, and to live. For Fell, this was a persuasive example of "a woman who taught" (18–19).

Womens Speaking Justified, then, is Margaret Fell's most important work because after the Reformation she was the first woman to fully state the case that justified theologically and historically women's speaking, preaching, and holding meetings. Through Scripture, strategies of classical argumentation (such as anticipating her opponents' arguments and appealing to logic and emotion), and stylistic devices (such as exaggerated imagery), she focused steadily on women inspired by God—and, hence, his messengers—and she demonstrated that women were not unimportant in the history of Christian texts and theology. The book has been and remains a milestone in the history of women and their rights to speak (Bacon 16; Campbell 218).

BIBLIOGRAPHY

Primary Sources

Fell, Margaret. *Womens Speaking Justified, Proved, and Allowed by the Scriptures.* 1666. Reprint. Los Angeles: University of California, 1979.
———. *A Brief Collection of Remarkable Passages.* London, 1710.

Biography

Bickley, Augustus Charles. "Fell, Margaret." *DNB* (1921–1922).
Ross, Isabel. *Margaret Fell: Mother of Quakerism.* 2d ed. York, Eng.: Ebor Press, 1984.

History and Criticism

Bacon, Margaret Hope. *Mothers of Feminism: The Story of Quaker Women in America.* San Francisco: Harper & Row, 1986.
Bainton, Roland. *What Christianity Says about Love, Sex, and Marriage.* New York: Association Press, 1957.
Blain, Virginia, Patricia Clemens, and Isobel Grundy. "Fell, Margaret." In *The Feminist Companion to Literature: Women Writers from the Middle Ages to the Present,* edited by Virginia Blain, Patricia Clemens, and Isobel Grundy. New Haven: Yale University Press, 1990.
Barbour, Hugh. *The Quakers in Puritan England.* New Haven: Yale University Press, 1964.
Campbell, Carolyn Kohrs. "The Sound of Women's Voices." *Quarterly Journal of Speech* 75.2 (1989): 212–20.
Hobby, Elaine. "Fell, Margaret." In *British Women Writers: A Critical Reference Guide,* edited by Janet Todd, 239–41. New York: Continuum, 1989.
Irwin, Joyce L. "Margaret Asket [*sic*] Fell." *Womanhood in Radical Protestantism, 1525–1675,* 179–80. New York: Edwin Mellen, 1979.
Latt, David J. Introduction to *Womens Speaking Justified, Proved, and Allowed by the Scriptures,* by Margaret Fell. Los Angeles: William Andrews Clark Memorial Library, 1979.

FRANÇOIS DE SALIGNAC DE LA MOTHE-FÉNELON
(1651–1715)

Kathy M. Houff

François de Salignac de la Mothe-Fénelon was born in 1651, to a noble family that had suffered financial reverses. Educated at home because of his delicate health, Fénelon studied both Greek and Latin as a youth (Barnard vii). In this early regard for the classics, Fénelon's education resembled that of the prominent English rhetoricians of the period. Like many of these rhetoricians, Fénelon also had strong connections to the Church. According to Charles Butler, "as soon as his years permitted, [Fénelon] embraced the ecclesiastical state" (12). In 1666 Fénelon enrolled in the College du Plessis; and during 1672 or 1673 he began his formal training for the priesthood at the seminary of Saint-Sulpice, where he was ordained in 1674 or 1675 and served for three years as a priest. However, Fénelon's devotional career was not without incident. His connection to a religious scandal during the late 1680s and 1690s, because of his growing interest in mysticism and the sect of Quietism, resulted in both a papal dismissal of his *Explanation of the Maxims of the Saints* and his exile by Louis XIV to Cambrai, where Fénelon served as Archbishop for many years. Despite these difficulties, Fénelon was, by all accounts, deeply religious. His religious career spanned almost forty years, and his death may well have been hastened by an injury sustained while performing his pastoral duties.

Known primarily as a religious figure and as an educator, Fénelon's most famous student was the Duke of Burgandy, grandson of Louis XIV, for whom Fénelon wrote his most famous pedagogical work *Télémaque*. A heroic poem in the Homeric tradition, the *Télémaque* was designed to instruct a young prince in all suitable lessons. In it Fénelon displayed both his love of classical models and his belief that education should be pleasurable. His other influential works in the field of education include *The Education of Girls, Fables,* and *The Dialogues of the Dead. The Education of Girls* has the distinction of being one of the few works that Fénelon actively sought to publish. However, feminist scholars will note with dismay his unenlightened view of young women whom he associated, in this text, with vanity, passion and artifice. *The Education of Girls* displays, as does Fénelon's rhetorical works, a pronounced antipathy toward the artificial (Davis 44). Fénelon's *Fables* are significant because through them the author attempted to make learning more enjoyable to children, while his *Dialogues of the Dead* further illustrates his application and appreciation of models from antiquity. The form he used in these dialogues can be traced to the Greek satirist, Lucian (64).

Fénelon's influence in the field of education extended well beyond the seventeenth and early eighteenth century (Barnard xliii). In his pedagogical works, Fénelon advocated a method of indirect instruction and the use of the dialogue as a teaching device. More importantly, these works, along with his *Dialogues on Eloquence,* illustrate Fénelon's high regard for the natural and his distrust of the artificial (Davis 96). In his educational practices as in his rhetorical views, Fénelon stressed simplicity. Despite his enduring reputation in several fields, during his lifetime he was a simple man who wrote primarily for pragmatic reasons, not with the hope of attaining a literary reputation (35). Since he was not very interested in seeing his work published, the publication of his writings was usually done at the behest of someone else. Neither of his major rhetorical works, for example, were published until after his death.

Despite being written over thirty years apart, Fénelon's major rhetorical statements, *Dialogues on Eloquence* and *Letter to the French Academy,* are remarkably of a piece. Both of his rhetorical works champion antiquity; and, as Howell has stated in his introduction to Fénelon's *Dialogues on Eloquence,* both works turn back from "elevated, unusual style and a profusion of ornament" (Howell 21) typical of the Ramistic rhetoric that preceeded them. Both rhetorical works advocate a more natural, more conversational rhetorical style. The differences between the two works result primarily from the different purposes for which they were written. The primary purpose of *Dialogues on Eloquence* was to instruct future pulpit orators while the *Letter* served chiefly as a defense of classical rhetorical ideals.

Fénelon's *Dialogues on Eloquence* was written as early as 1678, although some scholars suggest that this work was written as late as 1685. The *Dialogues* was published in 1717 or 1718 and was first translated into English in 1722 by the Reverend William Stevenson, who also translated a substantial part of the *Letter.* According to Wilbur Samuel Howell, however, Stevenson "took so many liberties with the French text that his work can hardly be accepted as an accurate version" (50). In 1750 this translation of the *Dialogues,* including the excerpt from the *Letter,* was published in Glasgow, making Fénelon's work available to an English-speaking audience by mid-century. The *Dialogues* was translated again in 1847, 1897, and most recently in 1951.

The *Letter to the French Academy* was published, at the insistence of the academy, in 1716. However, despite its reputation and significance, no English version of the *Letter,* other than Stevenson's translated excerpt, was available until 1984, when Barbara Warnick translated it. Fénelon wrote this piece in 1713 at the request of the French Academy, of which Fénelon had been a member since 1693. In this request the academy asked members "what projects should be undertaken after the Dictionary, which the Academy had been compiling for the preceding seventy years, was complete" (qtd. in Warnick 1). In his *Letter,* Fénelon outlined the need for a grammar, a rhetoric that "would be far more valuable than a grammar" (59), a poetic, and a history. The scope of the *Letter* was obviously much greater than that of the *Dialogues.* And although both the *Dialogues* and the *Letter* display an awareness of the conflicts between classical attitudes regarding eloquence and more modern attitudes, in the *Letter* this awareness is made explicit.

Fénelon's *Letter* has "often been accepted as a better statement of his literary philosophy than are the *Dialogues*" (Howell 45). However, "the *Dialogues* are undisputably the best statement we have of his rhetorical theory" (46). Both Fénelon's literary philosophy and the rhetorical theory advocate knowledge, simplicity, and naturalness. Mannered and highly stylized writing or oratory call attention to themselves and shift the focus away from the subject. For Fénelon careful observation or study of the subject about which one was writing or speaking was far more important than laborious attention to form (5). In his *Dialogues* Fénelon suggested that artists should "imitate nature and see what she does when one lets her act in her own way and when art does not constrain her" (100).

Fénelon's *Letter* also anticipated some of the eighteenth-century linguistic concern by advocating a language that was clear but flexible and suited to a variety of uses (Warnick 20). Unlike some of the eighteenth-century English rhetoricians who argued against the expansion of the English language, Fénelon favored the expansion of French. In his *Letter* Fénelon remarked, "I would like to admit any pleasant sounding word which we lack, so long as using it does not cause ambiguity" (57). As Howell has observed in his introduction to the *Dialogues,* stylistic and linguistic changes were necessary during Fénelon's lifetime because trope- and figure-laden language, the legacy of Peter Ramus, no longer served all men equally well; the scientists of the period were especially limited and encumbered by such a language (25). The rhetorical ideas of Fénelon—with their turn away from ornamentation toward a classical emphasis on clarity, naturalness, simplicity, and a combined logical and emotional appeal—were better suited not only to the eighteenth-century rhetor but also to the eighteenth-century scientist.

Fénelon's work was well thought of by the English rhetoricians of the eighteenth century. Hugh Blair commented in his *Lectures on Rhetoric and Belle Lettres* that Fénelon's major rhetorical works were most honorable and just (136). In *A System of Oratory,* John Ward echoed Fénelon's recommendation that students of eloquence study the masters of antiquity (Warnick 41). The ideals that Fénelon set forth in his *Dialogues on Eloquence* and his *Letter to the French Academy* are, for the most part, most compatible with the ideas held by the English rhetoricians early in the eighteenth century. Fénelon's rejection of ornament, his return to naturalness, his focus on substance, and his concern with the clarity and flexibility of language are important issues in the works of John Lawson, Adam Smith, and Hugh Blair. Just as Lawson's work served as a primary transitional work in English rhetoric by restating the best of ancient rhetorical theory, so too did Fénelon's work serve a similar function in France.

Fénelon contributed to the eighteenth century most significantly by providing a clear, eloquent, and impassioned restatement of the best of ancient theory. He also functioned as a rhetorical diplomat by helping to heal the rift between rhetoric and logic that had been widened by the work of Peter Ramus and by negotiating critical disputes concerning the use of the ancients that arose in late seventeenth-century France. Another important contribution he made was in the realm of pulpit oratory where he advocated, as elsewhere, classical ideals of naturalness.

FÉNELON'S RHETORICAL THEORY

Fénelon's thorough knowledge and love of the classics is readily apparent in his *Dialogues on Eloquence* and his *Letter to the French Academy*. Most of his examples of excellence in eloquence come from the ancients; however, he favored the Greeks, especially Demosthenes. The oratory of Demosthenes was clear, passionate and unaffected (Warnick 20) and exemplified a Greek simplicity that Fénelon admired and chose to emulate (Butler 172). This profound regard for the simplicity and naturalness found in the best of ancient models is perhaps Fénelon's greatest contribution to the rhetoric of the eighteenth century.

As Howell has pointed out in his introduction to Fénelon's *Dialogues,* at a time when "the notion of rhetoric as the theory of verbal ingenuity and ornament" (22) threatened to prevail, Fénelon, in addition to valuing the ancients' simplicity, upheld the classical idea that rhetoric be used for persuasion. In early eighteenth-century France, radically shifting attitudes challenged classical criticism and questioned the role of rhetoric. But Fénelon, in his *Dialogues,* persuasively argued that rhetoric and eloquence are integral to communication and are not mere sophistry. His diplomatic *Letter* helped to ensure the continued use of classical models by effectively illustrating their value. As more modern criticism validated work for its entertainment value and focused increasingly on audience and on pleasure, Fénelon upheld classical ideals of sublimity. He believed no work could be considered worthy if it did not appeal to that which is good in humans. He clearly suggested what eloquence should do in this passage from his *Letter*: "We must not think of eloquence as a frivolous art which an orator uses to impress the multitude's weak imagination and to traffic in words. It is a very serious art destined to instruct, curb the passions, reform customs, sustain laws, influence public deliberations, and make man good and happy" (66). He further suggested that there was a decline in the quality of oratory because oratory was no longer as vital to the state as it was in antiquity. Speaking of the Greeks he said, "Eloquence was more cultivated among them than it can be in our nation. Among [them] everything depended on the people, and they depended on the spoken word . . . eloquence was the great activity in peace and war" (60). Although the role of rhetoric was less vital in the seventeenth and eighteenth centuries, Fénelon believed that in the realms of religious instruction and pedagogy the art was important and should adhere to classical ideals. In his *Letter,* Fénelon stated that the model of a perfect rhetoric would include "only the best works of purest antiquity, [and] would [thereby] produce a brief, exquisite, and delightful work" (59). In his *Dialogues on Eloquence,* Fénelon adopted these principles; and while they may not fully merit the description "exquisite and delightful," a modern reader should find them readable and pleasant. In his *Letter* and *Dialogues,* Fénelon clearly restated major components of classical rhetorical theory and argued for their continued application.

Fénelon also contributed to the development of eighteenth-century rhetorical thought by acting as rhetorical 'peacemaker'. He did this in two ways. First, Fénelon sought to reclaim rhetoric and redeem eloquence, by suggesting that logic and eloquence are inextricably bound and by suggesting that logic alone doesn't have the power to move or persuade listeners. The division between logic and rhetoric—which arose, in part, because of the writings of Peter Ramus and Audomarus Talaeus in the late sixteenth century—helped to create the highly ornamented rhetoric that Fénelon rejected. According to Howell, in his Introduction to the *Dialogues,* Antoine Arnauld, in his *Port Royal Logic,* began reevaluating the relationship between logic and rhetoric but was still somewhat suspicious of the appeal to the emotions (6–36). The proper relation between reason and passion was a point much debated in the eighteenth century, particularly in the work of John Lawson. Fénelon's work is significant because Fénelon accepted the necessity of both logical and emotional appeal in eloquent oratory. In his *Dialogues,* in particular, he considered the relation between logic and eloquence. For Fénelon these two elements, far from being separate pursuits, were inextricably bound. They were "so closely connected that the obligation to prove by logic" was "part of the problem of achieving eloquence" (42). His second contribution as peacemaker was related to his love of the classical. During critical debates in the French Academy during the late seventeenth century, classical critics, such as Fénelon, were largely appalled by the modern writer's lack of standards. The more modern critics of the period, such as Charles Perrault and Bernard le Bovier de Fontenelle, favored a more subjective critical stance in which entertainment value was the chief measure of a work's success (Warnick 4). Fénelon graciously remarked in his *Letter* that "I begin by wishing that the moderns would surpass the ancients" (100), and used his letter as a brilliant piece of arbitration between the disputing critical factions within the French Academy. Although he clearly favored a more classical view regarding the purpose of eloquence, oratory and writing throughout the *Letter,* tolerance and a talent for arbitration typify his work. George Saintsbury has suggested that Fénelon's primary strengths as a literary critic stemmed from his open-mindedness (306). Fénelon managed to champion ideals of antiquity without offending more modern sensibilities.

Although he had no great quarrel with contemporary writers, within the body of his *Dialogues* and his *Letter* Fénelon's other examples come not from contemporary works but from the Scriptures and the Church Fathers. His belief, expressed in the *Dialogues,* that "the end of eloquence is to instruct mankind and make men better" (57) helps explain his use of such examples. Moreover, if the purpose of eloquence or rhetoric is to improve men morally, a particularly appropriate forum for eloquence is the pulpit.

The development of pulpit oratory was significant in the eighteenth century; and many of the key rhetoricians of this period, like Fénelon, were religious men. Although Howell, in his introduction, has rightly remarked that the *Dialogues* is not merely a treatise on preaching but is "designed to be a complete theory of communication" (2), in them Fénelon addressed the practical problems of the pulpit orator who had also to minister to his flock. In this regard Fénelon's *Dialogues,* like John Lawson's *Lectures on Oratory,* can be seen both as a general statement on rhetoric and eloquence and as a course of study for those who intend to make preaching their profession. Consequently, the Stevenson translation of the work found its way into *The Young Preacher's Manual; or, Treatises on Preaching,* compiled by Ebenezer Porter and published in 1819 in Boston.

Fénelon's work advocates a return to a more simplified preaching style, a style that stresses communicating powerful ideas as clearly as possible. Comparisons can be drawn between his *Dialogues* and Lawson's *Lectures Concerning Oratory;* and, indeed, anyone reading the two works would not be surprised to discover that Lawson had a copy of Fénelon's *Dialogues* in his library. Both men felt that the best way to teach or to study eloquence was to refer to the best models of antiquity, and both their works are replete with examples. Lawson was more suspicious of the emotions and of emotional appeal than Fénelon was. But both men encouraged a naturalness and simplicity, especially regarding delivery; and both eschewed the somewhat corrupt uses that eloquence had been put to in their societies. Certainly, a major part of Fénelon's importance lay in his influence on people like Lawson and John Ward.

Fénelon's advice to aspiring preachers included remarks on what to preach about, how to organize a sermon, and how to deliver one. Regarding an appropriate topic for a sermon, Fénelon, in his *Dialogues,* suggested that a preacher "ought not to search for subtleties" (149). According to Fénelon, the subjects best suited for sermons are "those truths that are most important and best suited to the needs of the people" (149). Although Fénelon agreed that order is necessary, he disagreed with Lawson, who advocated, in his *Lectures on Oratory,* the use of divisions in sermons. Fénelon claimed that "one ought not to have in the discourse any clearly marked partitioning" (113), for such divisions make the work stilted and artificial. The delivery of sermons should be impassioned; and he remarked, as did Lawson and other English rhetoricians, that "it is necessary to feel passion in order to paint it well" (105); however, Fénelon agreed that the gestures and vocal inflections of the effective orator should not be forced or exaggerated.

Fénelon illustrated his dismay at empty oratory and pointed out one of its problems by asking, "What would you say of a man who persuaded you without proof? Such a one would not be a true orator" (88). He decried the highly ornamented eloquence of his age and suggested that those examples of eloquence were "very fragile beauties indeed" (58). In their place he prefered an eloquence grounded in thorough knowledge of a subject that would produce "discourse with more body and less spirit" (58).

However, in his pursuit of a more logical, more subject-oriented rhetoric, Fénelon did not neglect the importance of appealing to the emotions. In accordance with his belief that "the aim of eloquence is to move the passions" (84), he suggested that "in eloquence everything consists in adding to solid proof the means of interesting the listener and of using his passions for the purpose one has in mind" (90). The rhetor evokes these passions through the use of "the lively portraiture of things" (94); and, comparing orators to painters, he suggested that "we must be able to paint them [those things we would speak of] well with their various objects and effects" (84). Fénelon praised thorough general knowledge and recalled the advice of Plato who "would have the speaker commence with the study of man in general" (82) in support of this.

In both *Letter* and *Dialogues* Fénelon cautioned against the abuse of the pulpit and sharply criticized those who used pulpit oratory for their own gain. In his *Letter* he remarked: "The more an orator tries to dazzle me with the marvels of his discourse, the more I am shocked by his vanity" (66). He suggested that the prevalence of frivolous, ornamented eloquence could be attributed, at least in part, to the uses to which it was put by self-serving preachers and lawyers (60–61).

In the introduction to her 1984 translation of Fénelon's *Letter,* Barbara Warnick has suggested that *Letter* is a "key work in the transition from seventeenth century classicism to eighteenth-century Enlightenment" (ix). In his introduction Howell has suggested that *The Dialogues on Eloquence* are "the earliest statement we have of what may be said to have become the

dominant modern attitude toward rhetoric" (46). Clearly the work of Fénelon occupies a unique position in rhetorical thought and acts as a bridge
between classical and more modern rhetoric. Fénelon accomplished this by
restating the most enduring concepts from antiquity and by showing how
these concepts might have modern application (45). By doing so he helped
clear the way for the rhetoricians who would follow.

In the introduction to his *Lectures on Rhetoric and Belles Lettres,* Hugh
Blair suggested that the value of his own work consisted in its "endeavour
to explode false ornament, to direct attention more towards substance than
show, to recommend good sense as the foundation of all good composition,
and simplicity as essential to all true ornament" (31). These are exactly the
rhetorical values of Fénelon, and the restatement of these values by Blair
illustrates the importance of Fénelon's contribution to the development of
eighteenth-century rhetorical thought.

BIBLIOGRAPHY

Primary Sources

Fénelon, François de Salignac de la Mothe-. *Dialogues on Eloquence.* Translated by
    Wilbur Samuel Howell. Princeton: Princeton University Press, 1951.
————. *Dialogues concerning Eloquence in General; and particularly that Kind which
    is fit for the Pulpit: By the late Archbishop of Cambrai, with his letter to the
    French Academy, concerning Rhetoric, Poetic, History, and a Comparison be-
    twixt the Ancients and Moderns.* Translated by William Stevenson. 1722. Re-
    print. Glasgow: R. and A. Foulis, 1760.
————. *Fénelon's Letter to the French Academy.* Translated by Barbara Warnick. Lan-
    ham, MD: University Press of America, 1984.
Porter, Ebenezer, ed. *The Young Preacher's Manual.* Boston, 1819.

Biography

Butler, Charles. *The Life of Fénelon.* Baltimore, 1811.
Davis, James Herbert, Jr. *Fénelon.* Boston: Twayne Publishers, 1979.
Lear, H. L. Sidney. *Fénelon: Archbishop of Cambrai.* London: Longmans, Green and
    Co., 1907.

Criticism

Barnard, H. C. *Fénelon on Education.* vii-xlix. Cambridge: Cambridge University
    Press, 1966.
Blair, Hugh. *Lectures on Rhetoric and Belles Lettres.* Reprinted in *The Rhetoric of
    Blair, Campbell, and Whately,* edited by James L. Golden and Edward P. J.
    Corbett. Carbondale: Southern Illinois University Press, 1990.
Howell, Wilbur Samuel. *Eighteenth-Century British Logic and Rhetoric.* Princeton:
    Princeton University Press, 1971.
————. Introduction to *Dialogues on Eloquence,* by François de Salignac de la Mothe-
    Fénelon, 1-53. Princeton: Princeton University Press, 1951.

Saintsbury, George. *A History of Criticism and Literary Taste in Europe.* Vol. 2.
    London: William Blackwood and Sons Ltd., 1902.
Warnick, Barbara. Introduction to *Fénelon's Letter to the French Academy,* by François
    de Salignac de la Mothe-Fénelon. Lanham, MD: University Press of America,
    1984.

ALEXANDER GERARD
(1728–1795)

Elizabeth K. Larsen

Alexander Gerard was born on February 22, 1728, in Aberdeenshire; and he died on the same day in 1795 at age sixty-seven. The eldest son of a minister, he entered Marischal College at twelve and received his M.A. four years later. He studied theology at both Aberdeen and Edinburgh; and in 1750, at Marischal, he was appointed interim professor of philosophy, a chair that he kept on a permanent basis. His duties as professor of philosophy included instructing a group of students through an entire course of study, including logic, ontology and pneumatology, morals, politics, and natural science. In 1755 he published a "Plan of Education in the Marischal College and University of Aberdeen." The plan, which was put into practice, altered the traditional pedagogical order of study whereby students began with logic and concluded with more concrete subjects such as politics and natural science; Gerard believed, instead, that students should begin their study with classics, history, and mathematics and conclude with the more abstract metaphysics and logic.

Gerard was a member of the Select Society of Edinburgh, formed in 1754 for the purpose of providing Scottish intellectuals with weekly discussions. In 1755 the society decided to award prizes in two annually chosen subject areas, one in "polite letters" and one in science. Gerard received the 1756 prize for his *Essay on Taste*, published in 1759 in both London and Edinburgh. It went through four editions; the first two (1759 and 1764) included brief discussions of taste entitled "Three Dissertations on Taste by Mr. De Voltaire [François-Marie Arouet], Mr. De Montesquieu [Charles-Louis Secondate, Baron de Montesquieu], and Mr. D'Alembert [Jean Lerond D'Alembert]," translated from the *Encyclopédie; ou, Dictionnaire raisonné des sciences, des arts et des métiers* (1757). Gerard made major changes to the second edition (see Hipple xxiii–xxiv); and to the third edition (1780) he added Part 4, "Of the Standard of Taste," and an appendix,

"Concerning the Question, Whether Poetry be properly an Imitative Art? and if it be, In what sense is it Imitative?," incorporating some of his growing interest in genius. French and German translations appeared in 1766; the American edition (1804) reprinted the first edition but included only the selection by Montesquieu.

Another study group that provided inspiration for Gerard (Fabian xii) was the Philosophical Society of Aberdeen (1758–1773), which included in its membership George Campbell, Thomas Reid, and James Beattie. For some of the meetings of the society, Gerard selected topics on imitation and genius (in 1768 and 1769). Records of the society, as well as Gerard's assertions in the preface to *An Essay on Genius* (that he had completed Part 1 of the essay and was working on Part 2 by 1758), suggest that Gerard, like others, read his work to the society as it was written. *An Essay on Genius* was published in 1774.

Gerard's two essays, *Genius* and *Taste,* are his primary writings. In addition to them, Gerard published *Dissertations on Subjects Relating to the Genius and Evidences of Christianity* (1766); *The Pastoral Care* (1799); and *Compendious View of the Evidences of Natural and Revealed Religion,* completed for publication by Gerard's son, Gilbert, in 1828. Among his other writings is "The Influence of the Pastoral Office on the Character Examined; with a View, especially, to Mr. Hume's Representation of the Spirit of that Office," preached before the Synod of Aberdeen in 1760 (Hipple ix). The *Dictionary of National Biography* also credits him with "Liberty: A Cloak of Maliciousness, both in the American Rebellion and in the Manners of the Times" (1778).

Alexander Gerard became professor of divinity at Marischal and minister of Greyfriars Church of Aberdeen in 1760. In 1771 he left those posts to become professor of divinity at King's College, Aberdeen, where he remained until his death (in 1795).

Relatively unknown to historians of rhetoric (neither of his essays appears in the primary source listing of eighteenth-century texts in Winifred Bryan Horner's *The Present State of Scholarship in Historical and Contemporary Rhetoric* [1983]), Gerard has a secure place in the history of aesthetics. Bernard Fabian, editor of the 1966 edition of *An Essay on Genius* (which was selected as the first in a planned series of reprints from eighteenth-century English aesthetics), has noted that *An Essay on Taste* soon after publication became "established as one of those valuable contributions to the 'science of human nature' " (ix–x). The *Essay on Genius* he has called "the sum and substance of what, about 1770, could be said on the vexing question of the nature of genius;. . . certainly the best-considered and most carefully wrought contribution to the literature on a subject which engaged the attention of practically the whole period from 1750–1800" (xi).

The lack of attention from rhetoricians is due to the fact that taste and genius have not been considered as instrumental concepts in the development of eighteenth-century rhetorical theory. However, the century's ideas about the nature of invention and taste did affect rhetoric; and, therefore, Gerard, who synthesized ideas on both invention and taste, has relevance.

Like his fellow Scots, Gerard studied the work of David Hume and John Locke; and it was Hume's ideas that he developed, giving readers one of the best accounts of the way invention actually was understood in the late eighteenth century. *An Essay on Genius* is, in fact, a study of invention because for Gerard genius was "the faculty of invention" (8). The "invention" to which he referred is the first act in a composing process, and he saw it as critical to the production of truth in science and the production of beauty in art. His goal in *Genius* was to make the process of genius understandable. Further, *Genius* is not solely about extraordinary individuals; rather, the generative act as Gerard described it is embedded in a normal human mental continuum and is explained through associationism's common process. Thus, although Gerard took pains to note that genius, as he defined it, is not to be confused with "mere capacity" (7), the text itself does more than describe how "great" works might be created. For instance, the category "genius" is permeable and not only includes improvements on (17), additions to (26–27), and imitations of the works of others (129), but also suggests degrees of genius (29, 128, 184). More importantly, for readers interested in rhetoric, imagination—the basic quality of genius for Gerard—is available to all persons. In short, Gerard believed that the mind of a genius works like that of a lesser mortal—through general principles of associationism.

In *An Essay on Genius,* Gerard studied invention in its generic sense as a mental capacity and built a model that can be applied to the composing of informative, persuasive, scientific, or poetic discourse as well as to any other kind of creative activity. This conceptualization includes the following features of interest to historians of rhetoric:

1. Invention is a normal human mental process, by definition part of any associationist approach to rhetoric.

2. Memory or recollection is only one—*not* the essential—factor in the complex of "powers" that compose invention.

3. Continuous revisioning is part of composing. Judgment, essential to invention, negotiates constantly with imagination, which is the necessary ground of invention.

4. The pedagogy for the new invention is provided by the principles revealed by the study of the human mind as it discovers/invents knowledge. Invention, as described by Gerard, emphasizes the particular and individual and uses induction as its method: explanation will provide a path that leads back to experience—a path that can be followed by others.

The text, then, is concerned with a theory of invention that lies within the associationist framework and that was available to the Scottish realists.

In this way, Gerard's work extended traditional assumptions and suggests that the period did exhibit interest in process and recursivity—a focus more completely worked out in late twentieth-century composition scholarship.

In *An Essay on Taste,* Gerard applied associationism to the idea of taste, providing a detailed discussion of a topic primary to belles lettres, wherein taste frequently explains general critical preference, as in Hugh Blair's *Lectures.* Gerard's thoughts on the subject are significant not only because they suggest that, in the eighteenth century, taste (appropriate reception of an object such as a written text) was by no means clearly understood but also because Blair shows his knowledge of Gerard's text in his *Lectures.*

While Gerard showed that the principles of "good taste" might be definitive, he also showed that knowledge about how critics (or students) should arrive at or apply those principles to any specific work is not clear: He noted that "the general qualities which gratify taste" will one day be known but believed the understanding that compares "the taste of one man with that of another" is less easily "resolved" (197–98). Finally, he did not explain the process of developing standards of taste satisfactorily, although his solution is consistent with his associationist principles. His suggestion is that when humans reflect upon their various feelings, they will be able to judge, with reason, between works. Thus, to improve taste, individuals must reflect, analyze, and judge, supporting judgment with reason (147). On the other hand, "[to] those who are destitute of taste, general principles and rules, however just, will not supply the want of it." These individuals must learn by observing and applying principles of taste (268).

For Gerard, the study of the human mind provided not only structure for criticism and education but insight into the way people distinguish among works of art, poetry, and science. Unable to attribute taste to a single quality or function of the mind, he saw taste as interactive. While his interest in interaction represents primarily an interest in mental components—"internal senses" (73), judgment, sensibility, and refinement—Gerard also engaged outer components, such as "external organs" (201) and "dissimilar modes of exercise and culture" (204). He also saw all of these as being different among different people. His description of taste is an attempt to show the receiver's mind, and it reveals a possible awareness that judgments causing one piece of written discourse—whether speech or essay—to be defined as better than another are both subjective and communal. His work in taste reveals that there was a sense in the eighteenth century that what appeared to be common-sense judgments about beauty and truth were in fact negotiated agreements.

BIBLIOGRAPHY

Primary Sources

Gerard, Alexander. *An Essay on Genius.* 1774. Reprint. Edited by Bernard Fabian. Munich: William Fink Verlag, 1966.

————. *An Essay on Taste*. 1780. Reprint. Edited by Walter J. Hipple, Jr. Gainesville, FL: Scholars' Facsimilies and Reprints, 1963.

Biography

Blaikie, William Garden. "Alexander Gerard." *DNB* (1963).

Chambers, Robert. *Bibliographical Dictionary of Eminent Scotsmen*. London: Blackie, 1875.

McCosh, James. *The Scottish Philosophy: Biographical, Expository, Critical, from Hutcheson to Hamilton*. Hildesheim: George Olms, 1966.

Criticism

Fabian, Bernard, ed. Introduction to *An Essay on Genius*, by Alexander Gerard, ix-xlvii. Munich: William Fink Verlag, 1966.

Grene, Marjorie. "Gerard's *Essay on Taste*." *Modern Philology* 41.1 (1943): 45–58.

Hipple, Walter J., Jr. *Beautiful, Sublime, and Picturesque in Eighteenth-Century British Aesthetic Theory*, 120, 122, 305-18. Carbondale: Southern Illinois University Press, 1957.

————, ed. Introduction to *An Essay on Taste*, by Alexander Gerard, v-xxviii. Gainesville, FL: Scholars' Facsimilies and Reprints, 1963.

Horner, Theodore. "A Note on the Probable Source of Provost Smith's Famous Curriculum for the College of Philadelphia." *Pennsylvania Magazine of History and Biography* 58(1934): 370–77.

Kivy, Peter. *The Seventh Sense: A Study of Francis Hutcheson's Aesthetics and Its Influence in Eighteenth-Century Britain*, 178-87. New York: Burt Franklin and Co., Inc., 1976.

Larsen, Elizabeth. "Re-Inventing Intention: Alexander Gerard and *An Essay on Genius*." *Rhetorica: A Journal of the History of Rhetoric* 11.2 (1993): 181–97.

Miller, Thomas. "The Formation of College English." *Rhetoric Society Quarterly* 20.3 (1990): 261–86.

THOMAS GIBBONS
(1720–1785)

Maureen Byrnes Hardegree

Thomas Gibbons was born in 1720 in Reak, Swaffham Prior, Cambridge-shire, England. Like his father, also Thomas, who served as a dissenting minister of congregations in Olney, Buckinghamshire, and in Royston, Hertfordshire, Gibbons entered the clergy, first serving as an assistant to Presbyterian Reverend Thomas Bures. A year later, Gibbons, then twenty-three, headed his own independent congregation of Haberdasher's Hall. Besides serving in the clergy, Gibbons tutored at Mile End Academy, a school for independent ministers, from 1754 until his death, teaching logic, metaphysics, ethics, and rhetoric. In 1759, he began lecturing publicly at the Monkwell-Street meeting house, which chose him as its Sunday evening lecturer. Other honors included two university degrees. The College of New Jersey awarded him an M.A. in 1760, and in 1764 Gibbons received a D.D. from the University of Aberdeen (Cannan 1144). In 1767, Gibbons published his treatise on tropes and figures entitled *Rhetoric; or, A View of Its Principal Tropes and Figures,* which was a departure from his usual publications. For the most part, Gibbons wrote elegies and sermons about disasters like fires and earthquakes, historical events such as the Seven Years War and the oppression of Protestants in France, and occasions such as the death of friends and others whom he considered pious. He usually "tagged [to these sermons] a hymn to be sung by those who chose to read" them (Sanders 2:203). Such work was fodder for the pen of Robert Sanders, a hack writer. He believed that Gibbons's effort was "rubbish" that could only have been "of considerable service to the cheese-mongers and tobac-conists" (203). In 1774, Sanders satirized the Mile End Academy and its tutors in *The Lucubrations of Gaffer Graybeard.* In one part of the work, Sanders portrayed Gibbons as more concerned with whether the crimes of attending a play and visiting a "bawdy-house" are "of a damnable nature" than if the student being expelled is guilty (2:80). Although Sanders could not be counted among them, Gibbons had many friends and acquaintances who respected him. One was Dr. Samuel Johnson, whom Gibbons met in 1781 and with whom he occasionally dined (Boswell 3:224, 350).

Although scholars like Winifred Bryan Horner have rightly described Gibbons's work as typical of other stylistics written in the eighteenth century (199–200), scholars of the period should not overlook his *Rhetoric*. By stressing the importance of tropes and schemes while others, especially John Locke, were seeking to discredit them, Gibbons helped keep one part of classical rhetoric alive. Gibbons's *Rhetoric* is also important because it was a practical and thorough text written to meet the needs of young men preparing for careers in law, the clergy, and Parliament. It merits additional attention as one of several stylistics that contributed to the breach between style and the other parts of rhetoric, which began in the Renaissance and continued during the eighteenth century.

GIBBONS'S RHETORICAL THEORY

Although Gibbons never felt the need to explain his view of rhetoric in his text, his work certainly follows in the tradition of classical rhetoric. In defining and providing rules for the different tropes and figures, Gibbons borrowed heavily from the tenets set down by Cicero and Quintilian and, before them, Aristotle. When explaining the parameters of a trope, Gibbons, in his *Rhetoric*, quoted Quintilian's definition that "it may extend farther than a word and make up a sentence" (2) and quoted Aristotle's suggestion that "tropes . . . are to be taken from those things which are agreeable, whether in sound, or touch, or sight, or any other sense" (18). He also, as he termed it in his preface, *harvested* the work of neoclassicists Anthony Blackwall and John Ward, who also worked on tropes and figures in *An Introduction to the Classics* (1719) and *A System of Oratory* (1759), respectively. For example, Gibbons borrowed Blackwall's example of *enanthiosis* (261) and quoted Blackwall's sentiments about *prosopopeia* (397). Gibbons borrowed from Ward when he cited Ward's definition of *metalapsis* (69).

Gibbons's methodology also reveals classical influence. Knowing the rules, imitating excellent models, and practicing speaking and writing were, in Gibbons's opinion, the way to become eloquent. Classical rhetoricians called these learning processes "memorization" and "imitation." The first half of *Rhetoric* defines and provides rules that students and professionals of his day could memorize and examples of well- and poorly executed tropes (those that were well done could be imitated). The second part of the text covers figures in the same depth. Gibbons also concluded each major section of the text with a short, versified statement of the material that he hoped would help the reader memorize the Latin terms (vii). For synecdoche, he rhymed,

SYNECDOCHE our stile diversifies,
And at her call a thousand beauties rise.

The whole intends a part. To quench the flames
Of raging thirst we drank the silver *Thames.*
A part denotes the whole. At *Blenheim's* field,
How did great MARLBOROUGH *Britain's* thunder wield,
Sweep down the *Gallic* ranks, and fill the plain
With purple currents, and with heaps of slain! (113)

Gibbons most likely borrowed this mnemonic device from Nicholas Burton's *Figurae Grammaticae and Rhetoricae Latino Carmino Donatae,* which
was quite similar in subject matter, the difference being that Burton's verse
was in Latin. John Holmes, in his 1766 edition of *The Art of Rhetoric Made
Easy,* included Burton's verse without translating it into English (Howell
140–41). This text was undoubtedly the biggest competitor of Gibbons's
Rhetoric.

Gibbons's emphasis on style, however, was not entirely classical. Like the
practitioners of the new rhetoric that advocated a plain writing style devoid
of heavy ornament, Gibbons did not discuss the different types of Ciceronian
style: plain, middle, and high. Gibbons emphasized plain style, which uses
ornament to keep the attention of readers and listeners. He was careful to
warn his readers against creating an overornate—or high—style by over-
using tropes and figures. For example, when discussing parabole, or comparison, Gibbons warned that "it is possible we may be excessive in the use
of Parabole and rather debase than adorn our discourses by redundance"
(458).

Besides stressing the importance of style, Gibbons contributed thoroughness to the study of tropes and figures. As an educator and lecturer, Gibbons
understood the value of discussing tropes and figures in depth and not only
included a number of explanations of a particular trope or figure but also
provided numerous examples from classical and modern authors such as
Aristotle, Horace, and Longinus, on the one hand, and Fénelon, Joseph
Addison, and Alexander Pope, on the other. Undoubtedly, Gibbons owed
some of his concern for thoroughness to Ward, who in his treatise *A System
of Oratory* was extremely thorough in his discussion of four tenets of classical
rhetoric. In fact, it seems that Gibbons attempted to outdo Ward—at least
when it came to tropes and figures—by providing even more classical and
modern examples.

Part of the text's thoroughness also lies in the way Gibbons provided his
readers with examples of what not to do. Rather than just tell his readers
how to avoid infelicities, Gibbons showed them how to avoid errors, often
in a humorous way. When advising his readers not to use "ridiculous"
tropes, Gibbons asked, "Who would think that 'Nature's confectioner
whose suckets are moist alchemy,' should be the description of a bee gath-
ering honey?" (15). To illustrate another kind of problem, Gibbons pre-

sented an inaccurate, or mixed, metaphor often used from the pulpit by preachers who urged their congregations to "cast anchor" upon the "rock of salvation" (Jesus Christ) when in the midst of a storm (29). Gibbons carefully explained to his readers that "were it attempted by a vessel in a storm, [it] would end in [the vessel's] destruction" (29), which was not the point that the ministers wanted to convey about Christ.

Part of what made Gibbons's treatment of tropes and figures so thorough was the way in which he anticipated his readers' needs. Gibbons recognized that his readers needed reassurance that even though they would make mistakes, they could with practice learn to write eloquently. He told his readers that "the materials out of which our Tropes are formed lie within the reach of every person's understanding" (13). Furthermore, Gibbons demonstrated to his audience that even famous authors like Cicero and Addison made mistakes at times (36). In order not to offend the living authors singled out, Gibbons followed the offending metaphors with examples of the same authors' "charming" ones so that he would "not seem to take a pleasure in detecting their faults" (40).

Although Gibbons's work on tropes and figures should be commended and studied for its thoroughness, it should also be examined (by those interested in eighteenth-century rhetoric) for a more dubious distinction—namely, the role that Gibbons's work played in divorcing style from the rest of the rhetorical process (Horner 112). This narrowness of focus began during the Renaissance and contributed to a view that rhetoric should deal only with tropes and figures. Gibbons—like his predecessor Thomas Farnaby (who published *Troposchematologia* [1648]) and his contemporaries John Stirling (*A System of Rhetoric* [1733]) and John Holmes (*The Art of Rhetoric Made Easy* [1738])—did not address the other four *processes* of rhetoric: invention, arrangement, memorization, and delivery. Wilbur Samuel Howell, in *Eighteenth-Century British Logic and Rhetoric,* has attributed this shortsightedness, at least in the case of Stirling and Holmes, to the way these rhetoricians looked at "elocution as if the part were in reality the whole, and as if the tropes and the figures of style were in fact the whole of rhetoric" (142). As evidence of the narrowed view of these rhetoricians, Howell has pointed to the disparity between the broad titles and the limited content of their works (142). Gibbons should be included among these rhetoricians since he is guilty of the same limited focus.

Although Thomas Gibbons's *Rhetoric* was not a major work of the era and did not develop new theories, his treatise still merits our consideration for what it is—a thorough treatment of classical tropes and figures clearly presented for a well-defined audience of future members of the clergy, bar, and Parliament. And Gibbons would agree. Gibbons dedicated his *Rhetoric* to the Duke of Newcastle (who was also the Chancellor of Cambridge University), stating, "Eloquence is of so much Importance in the Senate, in the

Pulpit, and at the Bar, that every Attempt to facilitate and extend the knowledge of its Principles and Powers, not only needs no Apology, but may hope for some Degree of Commendation" (i).

BIBLIOGRAPHY

Primary Source

Gibbons, Thomas. *Rhetoric; or, A View of Its Principle Tropes and Figures.* Reprint. Edited by R. C. Alston. Menston, Eng.: The Scolar Press, 1969.

Biography

Boswell, James. *The Life of Samuel Johnson.* Edited by Edward G. Fletcher. 3 vols. New York: Heritage Press, 1963.
Cannan, Edwin. "Gibbons, Thomas." *DNB* (1963).
Sanders, Robert. *The Lucubrations of Gaffer Graybeard.* 4 vols. London, 1774.

Criticism

Horner, Winifred Bryan. "The Eighteenth Century." In *The Present State of Scholarship in Historical and Contemporary Rhetoric,* edited by Winifred Bryan Horner, 101-26. Columbia: University of Missouri Press, 1983.
Howell, Wilbur Samuel. *Eighteenth-Century British Logic and Rhetoric.* Princeton: Princeton University Press, 1971.

CHARLES GILDON
(1665–1724)

Rochelle S. Glenn

Charles Gildon was born at Gillingham, near Dorsetshire. His father was a member of Gray's Inn and had suffered on the Royalist side in the civil war. Gildon's family was Roman Catholic; and at age twelve, Gildon was sent to Douay to study for the priesthood. At about age nineteen, Gildon returned to Gillingham. He inherited his father's property, which he spent in a short time. He married at the age of twenty-three. Afterward, he led the life of an author. He wrote on various subjects—including poetry, Deism, the Restoration stage, and Defoe—and, therefore, was often referred to as a miscellaneous writer. After studying religion for seven years, Gildon abandoned Catholicism for Deism. In 1695 Gildon's *Miscellaneous Works of the Deist, Charles Blount (1654–1693)* was published, in whose preface Gildon defended the practice of suicide. Gildon then renounced his Deism after reading Charles Leslie's *Short and Easy Method* (1697). In 1705, Gildon's *Deist's Manual* was published, in which Gildon defended the orthodox creed, with a letter from Leslie appended. He afterward came into conflict with Alexander Pope, attacking the poet in the 1714 *New Rehearsal; or, Bays the Younger, containing an examen of Mr. Rowe's plays and a word or two on Mr. Pope's "Rape of the Lock"* (Stephen 1226).

Gildon was best known as a dramatic critic. By 1694, among his miscellaneous works, Gildon had contributed considerably to the evolution of a critical approach to the stage. In 1699 Gildon went on to rewrite Shakespeare's *Measure for Measure*, as an attempt to improve it.

GILDON'S RHETORICAL THEORY

Gildon's greatest contribution to eighteenth-century rhetorical theory is contained in *The Life of Mr. Thomas Betterton*, published in 1710. The first part of the title indicates that the work is a biography of a distinguished actor; however, as Wilbur Samuel Howell has noted, its main purpose is to apply rules for oratorical delivery to acting (182). The full title reads as follows:

The Life of Mr. Thomas Betterton, The Late Eminent Tragedian. Wherein The Action and Utterance of the Stage, Bar, and Pulpit, are distinctly consider'd. With The Judgement of the late Ingenious Monsieur de St. Evremond, upon the Italian and French Music and Opera's; in a Letter to the Duke of Buckingham. To which is added, The Amorous Widow, or the Wanton Wife. A Comedy. Written by Mr. Betterton. Now first printed from the Original Copy. London: Printed for Robert Gosling, at the Mitre, near the Inner-Temple in Fleetstreet. 1710.

Although the author of the work is not identified on this title page, Howell has argued that Gildon is the author because his name appears on the letter dedicating the book to Richard Steele (182).

The work itself contains a miscellany of items and, therefore, is misrepresented by the first six words of the title. *The Life of Betterton* begins with a dedicatory epistle, followed by a preface and some verses written by Nicholas Rowe and spoken by Mrs. Barry at a performance on April 7, 1709, for the benefit of Betterton. In addition, the work contains a collection of documents that are loosely associated with the great actor's career. The collection consists of a biography of Betterton; critical observations on dancing, music, and opera; a list of plays in which Betterton acted; and Betterton's play, *The Amorous Widow*. These sections supplement the main information, which covers the rules for being a good actor, useful also for lawyers and ministers.

The third and fourth sections of the book follow a format similar to that of Cicero's *De Oratore*. In these sections, Betterton engages in a dialogue with two friends who have come to visit him. This dialogue is said to have taken place the year before Betterton's death, at his country house in Reading. The conversation focuses on famous actors and actresses and on the characteristics of good acting and speaking. In the dialogue, Betterton's friends encourage him to go into detail on the latter subject, so that they can "form a System of Acting, which might be a Rule to future Players, and teach them to excel not only themselves, but those who have gone before them" (17). Betterton replies by suggesting that he is not equipped to deliver such sentiments owing to his "Ignorance of the learned Tongues" (17) but agrees to refer to a manuscript on the topic of action and speaking written by another one of his friends. He makes it clear that he has contributed all that he knew on the subject to his friend's manuscript. Betterton assures his two friends that if the rules of the manuscript are followed, "our Stage would rise and not fall in Reputation" (18). At this point in the text, one of Betterton's friends recognizes the handwriting of the manuscript as that of Betterton himself.

The manuscript—which is concerned with movement and utterance in oratory and acting—contains two shorter papers. In the first of these papers, the focus is on the various natural gestures, and in the second the discussion is about several natural defects of voice. Betterton reads both shorter papers on acting aloud and afterward discusses a manuscript on rules for dancing, singing, and opera with his friends. The dialogue ceases after the reading of this paper, and Betterton's friends leave on their journey back to London.

In the introduction to *Betterton,* Gildon justified using Thomas Betterton as an example of a man who practiced the proper conduct of an actor. Gildon identified Betterton as "the last of our Tragedians" (1) and expressed a desire to preserve the type of excellence in acting that Betterton exemplified. Gildon and a friend visited Betterton a year before his death; after Betterton's death, Gildon did not want Betterton's method of acting to die with him. Gildon gave the following reason for using Betterton's career as the focal point of the book: "To give our English Actor yet the Preeminence, I shall here by writing his Life make him convey to others such Instructions, that if they are perfectly understood, and justly practised, will add such Beauties to their Performances, as may render his Loss of less Consequence to the Stage" (2–3).

The bulk of *Betterton* is devoted to rules for the stage that can also be applied to the bar and the pulpit. Gildon stated that these rules are only meant for those who have a genius for speaking and acting because those without such genius would not be able to understand them. The rules are divided into two categories: action and speaking. Action refers to the movements that speakers should employ to enhance the effect of their words. Speaking consists in using the voice in a manner appropriate to the subject. A mastery in these two categories is what makes a complete actor.

For a speech to be effective, the actor must support it with action and gesture. Gildon argued that "the best Speaking, destitute of Action and Gesture (the Life of all Speaking) proves but a heavy, dull, and dead Discourse" (51). On the contrary, at the bar and in the pulpit, reason and proof are most important; therefore, the primary effect is achieved by the discourse itself. On the stage, the actor must also express passions through facial expressions and gestures.

The action of various body parts is crucial to being a good actor. The movements of the eyes, head, arms, hands, or feet, must appear purely natural, as genuinely deriving from the things expressed and the passions that move one to speak. The art of gesture is more difficult to accomplish than the art of speaking because speakers can hear and judge their own voices but cannot see their faces or gestures. To alleviate the latter difficulty, Gildon recommended that the actor follow Demosthenes, who watched himself in a mirror to judge the effectiveness of his expressions and gestures to correct errors. Gildon also recommended using a friend who is an expert on appropriate gestures and motions.

The first concern of a speaker should be to consider the nature of the thing that is to be spoken of and allow the mind to get a deep impression of it, so that the speaker may be touched by it and able to convey the same passion to others. The speaker ought to be heard and understood with ease and pleasure, using a voice that can be heard by every member of the audience. This type of voice comes naturally for some speakers; however, others attain it through practice and exercise. Pronunciation should be appropriate to nature and to the subject being spoken about. The voice should not be too low or too loud; the level of volume should be determined by the playhouse and the audience. Nature should guide the player in speaking, as in action, so that the player neither over- nor underacts the part.

Gildon used Demosthenes as an example of an orator who was originally defective in speaking, action, and gesture but who, through daily exercise, was able to strengthen his delivery. However, Gildon did not condone allowing anyone with a speech defect to act: "For if a Man's voice be good for nothing, by Reason of any Indisposition of the Organs, as the Tongue, Throat, Breast, or Lung; if he have any considerable lisping, hesitation, or stammering, he is not proper for the Stage, the Pulpit, or the Bar" (99).

To avoid defective pronunciation, Gildon, following Quintilian, advised speakers to employ the following qualities: (1) purity, (2) perspicuity, (3) ornament, and (4) hability, or aptitude. *Purity* is defined as a certain healthfulness of voice, which has in it nothing vicious. *Perspicuity* consists of articulately observing the proper points and stops. *Ornament* is more naturally derived from a voice that is easy, great, happy, flexible, firm, sweet, durable, clear, pure, penetrating, high, and adorned. *Hability,* or *aptitude,* refers to a pleasing variety of pronunciation, which is determined largely by the diversity of the subject. The ability to vary the voice, according to the nature of the ideas it delivers, enlivens the hearers and refreshes the speaker. This quality is contrary to monotony, perpetually speaking in the same unvaried tone, which makes the discourse tiresome for the speaker and the hearers.

To be a complete actor, according to the system of acting espoused by Gildon in *Betterton,* the actor should be concerned about the fitness of his mind and body, should understand moral philosophy and rhetoric, should be highly knowledgeable about painting and sculpture, and should be a good critic of the stage. However, the most necessary quality that an actor should possess is "to know what is fit and to express it" (139), using a body that is neither too tall nor too short but of a moderate size; and an actor should not be fat or extremely thin. An actor's body should be active, pliant, and compact, qualities that can be developed by learning to dance, fence, and vault.

Gildon believed that the instructions for speaking well on the stage could, and should, be applied to the bar and the pulpit. To achieve perfection Gildon recommended that all speakers employ the rules of action and speaking contained in the book.

Gildon's *Betterton* made a significant contribution to eighteenth-century rhetorical theory by providing a unique and almost unprecedented handbook of theatrical methodology and by contributing greatly to a critical approach to the stage. It also demonstrates that the elocutionary movement in England was concerned not only with pulpit or political oratory but also with dramatic delivery.

BIBLIOGRAPHY

Primary Source

Gildon, Charles. *The Life of Mr. Thomas Betterton, The Late Eminent Tragedian.* London, 1710.

Biography

Lowe, Robert W. *Thomas Betterton.* New York: AMS Press, 1972.
Stephen, Leslie. "Gildon, Charles." *DNB* (1917).

Criticism

Horner, Winifred Bryan, ed. Introduction to *The Present State of Scholarship in Historical and Contemporary Rhetoric*, 101-26. Columbia: University of Missouri Press, 1983.
Howell, Wilbur Samuel. *Eighteenth-Century British Logic and Rhetoric*, 182-89. Princeton: Princeton University Press, 1971.

JOHN HENLEY
(1692–1756)

Jo Allen Bradham

Born August 3, 1692, at Melton-Mowbray, son and grandson of its vicars, John Henley attended the grammar schools of Melton and Oakham and graduated from St. John's College, Cambridge, with a B.A. in 1712 and an M.A. in 1716. He began his career in letters, scholarship, and theology early and practically simultaneously, publishing his four-part poem *Esther, Queen of Persia* in 1714, issuing the first installment of his ten-part treatise on languages *The Compleat [sic] Linguist* in 1719, and taking up his duties as assistant curate at Melton-Mowbray, where he was also headmaster of the grammar school, in 1716. Frustrated, seemingly by the lack of opportunity in the parish where his father found great satisfaction—and certainly by his distance from the presses that printed his *Compleat Linguist*—Henley moved to London in 1720 as assistant preacher in the chapels of Ormond Street and Bloomsbury. Offered in 1723 the rectory of Chelmondiston in Suffolk, he resigned it in 1725 rather than submit to the residence that the appointment required. On July 3, 1726, Henley established The Oratory, the institution that would occupy him for the rest of his life, give him his name—Orator Henley—and accord him the reputation that bedeviled him. The Oratory—a place not only in which Henley hoped to purify the services of the Anglican Church by returning to what he called a primitive liturgy but also in which he intended to offer secular classes on a wide range of subjects so that any man might have an education—had two locations, first in Newport Market (1726-1729), second in Lincoln's Inn Fields (1729–1756). Henley was careful to register under the terms of the Toleration Act, but he was constantly under siege for his theology, his style of preaching, and his charging of admission. He disputed with all who challenged him and actively invited any man who would question the wisdom of his endeavors to "fix his Time for a Disputation himself," as he stated in *Oratory Transactions* (18). His wife Mary Philips, by whom he had no children, predeceased him in 1737; his family in effect disowned him; he died October 13, 1756. His primary memorials remain Pope's scathing portrait in and Warburton's notes for *The Dunciad* (A ii 2, 338, iii 195; B 112, 370, iii 199) and Hogarth's prints "The Christening of the Child" and "The Oratory."

In his long career, Henley published as poet, translator, editor, periodical essayist, apologist for Whig causes, and preacher. His published works—excluding notices, advertisements, and other short pieces in newspapers—exceed fifty. But for all his writing and his attention to rhetoric in many genres, Henley enunciated a theory of rhetoric only in passing. He sought to find a means to enliven preaching and teaching and in the process championed rhetorical performance. The explanation of his endeavor, set out in his *Plan of the Oratory* (1726), clarified the name of the institution and the relative value of oratory—in the sense of effective delivery—in that institution. Having defined other terms basic to his project, Henley declared: "we come next to the word Oratory: This is taken in a variety of senses; it either means a place, where devotions, or orations, or both are us'd; or the persons that join and assist in them; or it implies the art of rhetoric, or of speaking well. It is here taken for the place and persons of this assembly" (49). In an oratory as a place of religious observance, Henley viewed rhetoric as a means of moving soul and mind; moreover, the way in which Henley introduced his discussion of rhetoric into works original with him shows that his concern with effective and appropriate delivery was part of a much larger whole. How fleetingly he actually addressed rhetoric is not apparent by surveying a list of Henley's corpus. Some of his titles mislead by insinuating a focus on rhetoric when in fact the works do not support that content; other works were only translations; one work has been erroneously linked with Henley because of prefatory comments about his practices.

In the first of these categories is his ambitious collection for attaining fluency in a variety of languages: *The Compleat Linguist; or, an Universal Grammar*. Dissatisfied with the method of teaching language in the schools and universities, Henley prepared, with the assistance of others, ten separate guides, the first appearing in August 1719, the last in 1726. After an introduction affirming the necessity of a knowledge of many tongues, Henley's work begins with Spanish, the easiest to learn, and proceeds through Italian, French, Greek, Latin, Hebrew, Aramaic, Arabic, Syriac, and Saxon, in that order, Henley noting in his opening remarks any similarity between the language he has just outlined and the one that he will next develop. The concluding title "An Introduction to an English Grammar" suggests that it might be of some help in understanding English rhetoric. But the long preface gives a history of the Saxon language, and the whole amounts to a prototextbook for the study of Old English. Useful in the history of language and comparative linguistics, the sixty-one-page explanation illuminates nothing about rhetoric.

In the second category, translation, one title dominates: Jean Pierre de Crousaz's *La Logique,* translated into English by Henley in 1724 as *A New Treatise of the Art of Thinking.* Henley supported himself, in part, by translation; and his efforts with Crousaz appear to have been entirely financial.

In the third category comes Michel Le Faucheur's *Traitté de l'action de l'orateur,* first printed about 1657 in Paris. The 1727 translation into English, as *The Art of Speaking in Public,* by an unidentified hand, carries in the subtitle the note: "With an INTRODUCTION relating to the famous Mr. Henly's [*sic*] present Oratory." Because the *Dictionary of National Biography* and the many biographical notes derived from it incorrectly attribute the translation to Henley himself—and because the coversheet for filming in the British and Continental Rhetoric series preserves the error—the translation has been wrongly assigned to Henley. Since *Henley* is the only proper name on the title page (other than that of the printer N. Cox), perhaps the false attribution is understandable; but the front matter "relating to the . . . present Oratory" makes clear that its author was an enemy of Henley, not the habitually self-lauding Orator himself (i.e., Henley). In the prefatory comments to this translation, Henley's performances are dismissed as "*Comical Fopperies* and *Buffonery*" (xx) and his gestures as "not conformable to the Precepts he lays down" (xxiv).

HENLEY'S RHETORICAL THEORY

After discounting the works that at first glance would assign Henley a more conspicuous place in rhetorical theory, we can more accurately define his own position. A member of the movement to improve the quality of preaching (an effort that Joseph Addison and Jonathan Swift shared) and an early representative of the elocutionary school that Thomas Sheridan and John Walker climaxed, John Henley promulgated—but failed to practice convincingly—a fairly elaborate system of decorum: a decorum of speaker, subject, and audience—all interacting. His theory, as it appears on the page only, sounds high and flawless. Late in his career and in defense of his life and methods, Henley wrote in *Informer's Winding-Sheet*:

A *Calvinist-Preacher,* a *Church-Divine,* or the like, have *their Principles, their Decorum*: An Orator is essentially more Free, for Rhetoric is speaking on all Subjects, occasionally, in all Shapes, serious, or entertaining, grave or pleasant; they [the Calvinist or the church-divine] may not make Use of Ridicule, or Secular Matters, in Discourse, because it is not their System, nor Practice; it would not be relish'd by their People: But if any Man of a different Principle hears an Orator, he is to consider him as such, his Discourses are more unlimited, and the Hearer is not to be shock'd at his using all the Figures of Rhetoric, Modes of Argument, Questions, Themes, and Topicks, in the Universe; as the Point, the Time, or Circumstance demands, or his Genius dictates. (32)

Having established that an orator has the obligation to match stylistic elements and delivery with subject and occasion, Henley in the same essay went on to equate speaking with oratory and to grant freedom to each speaker to conduct his lectures in a way appropriate to his own particular place (24). Henley's commitment to decorum in point, time, and circumstance was so thoroughgoing that he equated "*False Speaking*" with "Expressions [that] are not agreeable to the Meaning and Duty of the Speaker" as well as with those expressions inaccurate about the "Truth of Things" (32).

These definitions and emphases, made in 1748 when Henley was fifty-six, restated those that he set forth in opening The Oratory. In 1728 Henley began printing, under the collective title *Oratory Transactions,* explanations of his project. The section titled "A Narrative" and attributed to a Mr. Welstede—but almost certainly written by Henley himself—is a biographical account. After summing up Henley's early life, his academic success, and his need to give up his parish so that he might preach more effectively, the narrative focuses on the naturalness as well as the effectiveness of Henley's public utterance, "his Sermons and Orations are more Rhetorical and Persuasive; his Speaking is peculiar to himself, and natural" (17). Section Four, Number 1 of *Oratory Transactions* identifies the course of study that will be available during the week at The Oratory. Rhetoric, as both written and oral craft, was part of Henley's curriculum. Henley, or the Orator, promised to teach those who enroll with him, as Item 10, "To make a Theme, which is the Foundation of all Beautiful Prose-Discourses" (49); as Item 14, "To invent and plan happily a Subject, and compose well an Oration, Lecture, Sermon, Declamation, Dissertation, Epistle, Dialogue, Thesis: Or any Work in Prose, in the serious Vein, or in that of Ridicule, Humour, Wit and Fancy" (49–50); and as Item 15, "To get off, and speak well, any Work for the Publick" (50). Later in his list, Henley identified rhetoric, as he would teach it at The Oratory, as an aspect of the "Practical Life," and he equated rhetoric with "addressing the Passions" (51). In 1728, he issued a list of "Academical, or Weekday Subjects of The Oratory, from July 6, in the First Week 1726, to August 31, 1728." Many of the titles for lectures had to do with rhetoric: for example, July 6: "The General Principles of Speaking"; July 10: "The General Principles of Action"; September 20: "The Action of the Hands in Publick Speaking"; October 12: "Rhetorick, or the History and Principles of Eloquence." The full lectures do not appear to have been printed, but many Henley writings exist in manuscript (see Midgley's appendix for list and locations).

This focus in the weekday curriculum was the secular counterpart to the Orator's "sacred eloquence," as Henley called the way he preached and the way he believed all truly devout servants of God should deliver their messages. Incorporated in a work so ponderously titled as *The Primitive Liturgy for the Use of the Oratory. Part I. Being a Form of Morning and Evening*

Prayer, not impos'd as necessary, but propos'd, as expedient; as full, regular and compendious, as the usual Method will admit; taken entirely from Scripture, and the primitive Writers, but especially the most antient and authentick Liturgy of the Apostolical Constitutions are references to Henley's theory of "sacred eloquence." Henley, as the Orator, proclaimed: "Let the Reading of the Liturgy be always perform'd according to the Laws of Speaking and Action, established in the Oratory, founded on a just Impression in the Mind and Heart of the Reader, and a ready Command and Memory of the whole Service. The Voice and Gesture varying, as the Thing requires . . . Let the Lectures and Readings be read with distinctness and propriety in the speaking and address" (9).

The directive that delivery be "perform'd according to the Laws of Speaking and Action established in the Oratory" would have made sense to Henley's contemporaries because the year before, in 1725, the Orator had printed a sermon, or an expanded version of a sermon, which the title page claims he preached in the church of St. George the Martyr, London, on Sunday, November 15, 1724. The title conveys the inseparable nature of the divine word and its appropriate delivery: *The History and Advantages of divine Revelation, with the Honour, that is due to the Word of GOD; especially in regard to the most Perfect Manner of delivering it, form'd on the antient Laws of Speaking and Action: Being an ESSAY to restore them.* In this work, Henley began by tracing the way God spoke in early times, through the prophets and leaders whose words and actions the Old Testament records, then through Christ, "the only-begotten of the father, full of grace and truth" (7) and the "holy train of apostles" (7), followed in turn by "evangelists, pastors, and teachers, to support the same work, and raise the present and eternal happiness of men" (7–8). For these evangelists, pastors, and teachers—in order to witness properly—Henley insisted that each be qualified in nature and education and that each be ready with "a well weigh'd composition, or, a discourse in the mind" (14). Having taken care of the matter that a man of God would present, Henley turned to the style of "sacred eloquence." By its standards, a minister was to deliver "the truths of God, in the most just, forcible, and compleat manner" (14), a technique that "takes in all the powers of the whole man" (15). According to Henley, proper delivery or performance "demands a right management of the utterance, and of the behaviour . . . otherwise it must be imperfect and deficient" (15). He who preaches must manifest the qualities of the "natural, easy, lively, graceful, harmonious, and solemn" (15). To achieve these qualities, the minister must manage each gesture and control each intonation that is selected for its evocative power. Furthermore, the minister must studiously avoid reading the text and making any gesture that leads to misinterpretation. A well-trained minister has an image of himself and can, in effect, choose the right techniques from his experience, training, and personal sense of what is fitting. In working out this rhetorical principle, Henley was restating the old ideas of decorum, that manner of presentation must suit and transmit the matter presented:

In proper speaking and gesture, the nature of the thing spoken, strongly imprinted on the mind, and the present feeling of the orator, is the only guidance; and as things are, in their own nature, various, they necessarily require a variation of the voice, and of the deportment, that is conformable to each of them: and the precise fitness of one certain sound and movement of the whole person, even to a line of the countenance, to one certain thing, most properly and perfectly express'd, and the consequent unfitness of any other, to it, are as demonstrable, as any proposition in the Mathematics. (15–16)

Henley would break down a discourse to talk about delivery of different parts; and he emphasized that the close "ought to be spoken with the greatest force, not, as the method is, by lowering the voice, to the end of it, which indeed makes a conclusion, strongly utter'd, seem to break off abruptly before the usual doxology" (16). Henley advocated a rising and ringing conclusion, reminiscent of a peroration that moves the heart and leaves an audience caught up in the grandeur of both delivery and thesis. For correct declarations of God's truth, "a true discourse must be suppos'd to grow it self stronger, towards the conclusion of it, and to end with a kind of triumph; and as the last impression ought to be very forcible" (16).

According to Henley, each condition of the soul and each part of the religious service requires a particular tone and facial expression:

The passions require a language and address, different among themselves, as well as from other things; according to their several kinds, degrees, mixtures, and circumstances; all objects vary in proportion, the good or bad qualities of Men, the prosperous or unhappy events of life; the several ways of addressing God, in confession, petition, thanksgiving and the like. These, and all other subjects, claim a diversity of pronunciation, and of the conduct, agreeable to the distinct and true nature and merits of them. And this should be carefully study'd, in the reading of the offices of our church, as well as in our discourses. (16–17)

To anchor these generalizations about appropriateness in familiar examples, Henley explained that it would "be very absurd, to mention the pains of hell with a gay aspect; to press the fear of God with an air of negligence; or to exhort and persuade in the posture of forbidding, and of rebuke" (17).

All of Henley's suggestions about choice and control in matching matter and manner had a common purpose: achieving a pastoral oratory that "awakens, draws, and fastens the attention" (17) as "it renders the utmost honour to God, and service to mankind" (17). Failure to attain a decorum of speech "flattens, palls, and fatigues the hearer, and is apt to make the truths of religion appear less considerable, than matters of a far inferior concern" (17).

Echoing these principles enunciated in the early sermon are the tenets that Henley set forth in his 1726 *Plan of the Oratory*. There, the still young, ambitious, and sincere-sounding Henley insisted "on a study and practice of the proper natural rules of speaking and action, as the most perfect manner of enforcing the word of God; and we think a preacher oblig'd in conscience to use the most perfect manner of delivering it" (62).

Henley, never hesitant to reuse and reissue, incorporated the 1725 *History and Advantages of divine Revelation* in both *The Appeal of the Oratory* (1727) and *Oratory Transactions,* Number 2 (1729). In *Transactions,* the sermon takes the heading "A Discourse on Action in the Pulpit." This recycling suggests that Henley felt the piece summed up and showed off his theory of sacred eloquence. Consistent with the statements that he made elsewhere, the thrice-printed explanation not only sums up his ideas but also shows off his style. It allows the reader to reconstruct Henley preaching.

As a practitioner of rhetoric, Henley seems to have combined a traditional approach with oratorical flourish—at least when he was at his best. In *History and Advantages of divine Revelation,* he began with the Scripture that he would explicate, then set up the three points that he would treat. He specified that each point was "to give the text all the light possible" (3). Having enumerated his three points, he developed each in order, indicating, as he began each one, what the new emphasis was and making a transition from the part that he had concluded. In the development, he supplied many examples and followed a procedure of step-by-step reasoning with his audience. When he reached his conclusion, he built its phrases and balanced its diction so that the impassioned delivery he felt essential for the conclusion of a sermon grew from the text:

Let us be induc'd to set a proper value upon the divine word, which is so nobly calculated for our present and eternal welfare; that we may prevent the removal of this lamp from us, that we many escape the curse, that we may inherit all the blessings which are display'd to our view, in the book of God.

So shall we rise from lower privilege of this distant converse with him, like that of Israel with Moses, behind a veil, to the joy of seeing him, as he is, face to face, in the happy regions of eternity face to face. (20)

According to Henley, the power of pulpit oratory resided in the three-part build of the "that we may" constructions; in the force of the verbs (*prevent, escape, inherit, rise*); in the evocation of visual images in lamps, veils, and book; and in the series of short phrases that would allow the voice to modulate from the strong ("So shall we rise from the lower privilege of this distant converse with him") to a kind of parenthetical fall ("Like that of Israel with Moses") and then mount and crescendo for the awe-inspiring peroration: "In the happy regions of eternity face to face." The pulpit orator should end on sharp, clear sounds—a strategy that would enhance his delivery by allowing him a vocal climax. The repetition of "face to face" in the final sentence Henley caught before the reprinting in *The Appeal of the Oratory,* in which *eternity,* as the concluding word, reinforces the *e* sounds of *regions* for an even stronger oral appeal than the original carried.

If Orator Henley had simply written his theory of the decorum of sacred eloquence, we might remember him as another in a long line of rhetoricians who championed the unassailable principle of appropriateness and as a minister who insisted that the voice of man be a credit to the word of God. Henley, however, lived and preached, taught, disputed, wrangled, and sneered in addition to writing. The off-the-page reality compromised the sanity of his stated theory of rhetoric. By 1735, an anonymous *Art of Preaching,* printed for Robert Dodsley, summed up the unsavory reputation of Henley:

> So the great H——ley hires for Half a Crown,
> A quack Advertisement to tell the Town
> Of some strange Point to be disputed on:
> Where all who love the Science of Debate,
> May hear Themselves, or other Coxcombs prate.

When Alexander Pope dismissed Henley as "preacher at once and zany of his age," he intended to damn him to artistic and cultural hell; ironically, the balanced terms explain Henley well and set up the tension of opposites that any serious consideration of the man and his work demands. Pope's term *preacher* glanced at the training, profession, and ordination of Henley, but the term may refer as well to the seriousness and commitment that the man voiced on many occasions. *Zany* was Pope's summary for the buffoonish figure who distorted educational and religious ideas and promulgated them in wild gestures and money-making schemes. "Preacher . . . zany" echoes the dichotomies of Dryden's "mature in Dullness" or "confirmed in full stupidity"; and like MacFlecknoe, whom these fusions of magnification and diminution immortalize, Henley evidenced heights, ability, and promise but undermined them with folly, meanness, and an irascibility.

Henley is Ancient and Modern simultaneously. Well trained in Greek, Latin, and Hebrew, he distinguished himself in preparatory school and at Cambridge. Ordained as an Anglican and seeking a traditional purity in that church, Henley appears able to meet even Swift's standards for an Ancient. On the other hand, his separation from the church and his setting up of a private religious enterprise in which he preached from a tub throws him into the Modern camp of hacks and dissenters. He earned at least part of his living from the Grub Street press and even hacked for Edmund Curll. Henley was not a bad real-life version of Martinus Scriblerus, the misguided pedant and projector created as the satiric object by Swift, Gay, Pope, Parnell, and Arbuthnot during the Scriblerus Club days of 1713. Like Martinus, the Orator "dipped into all the arts and sciences but injudiciously into each." But *Modern* with Henley goes beyond the connotations Swift and his circle held. Henley was modern in the contemporary sense: for him the medium became the message. He believed in and attempted to practice a style of preaching that would symbolize the God he claimed and that would give memorable reality to the word of that God; rather, his reputation hangs on the strangeness and distortion of his medium, into which his original message is now subsumed. Furthermore, he appears to be a prototype of a modern evangelist who, while claiming to purify the faith and preach it with fervor, puts excessive emphasis on money, operates—at least on occasion—in legal imbroglio, and suffers the scorn of the general public.

BIBLIOGRAPHY

Primary Sources

Henley was extremely prolific, but no work has been reprinted. For a complete bibliography of Henley's writing, see Graham Midgley's biography, listed below.
Henley, John. *The Academical, or Weekday Subjects of The Oratory.* London, 1728.
———. *The History and Advantages of divine Revelation.* London, 1725.
———. *The Informer's Winding-Sheet; or, Nine Oaths for a Shilling.* Dublin and London, 1748.
———. *Oratory Transactions.* No. 1 London, 1728.
———. *The Plan of The Oratory.* London, 1726.
———. *The Primitive Liturgy for the Use of the Oratory.* London, 1726.

Biography

Henderson, T. F. "Henley, John." *DNB* (1964).
Midgley, Graham. *The Life of Orator Henley.* Oxford: Clarendon Press, 1973.
[Henley, John.] "A Narrative." In *Oratory Transactions,* Number 1, by John Henley. London, 1728.

Criticism

The Art of Speaking in Publick. London, 1727.
D'Israeli, Isaac. "Disappointed Genius." In *Calamities of Authors.* Vol. 1. 1812. Reprint. New York: Johnson, 1971.
Howell, Wilbur Samuel. *Eighteenth-Century British Logic and Rhetoric,* 193–203. Princeton: Princeton University Press, 1971.

JOHN HERRIES
(?–1781?)

Melissa L. King

The record of the life of John Herries is limited to a few vague details. He may have been a Scot: a reviewer in 1773 described Herries' work *The Elements of Speech* as "a bold attempt in a North-Briton to erect . . . the standard of the true pronunciation of the English language" (qtd. in Kemp 136). He was probably a relatively young man in 1773 when he published *Elements*, for in his concluding chapter he promised a more complete and detailed description of his theory in the future; and he admitted that "it cannot be supposed that at my early time of life, an undertaking of this kind should be executed with that accuracy and precision which may be expected from a person of more years and experience" (251). The promised second theoretical work never appeared, perhaps because of Herries' apparently early death. An obituary column in the June 2, 1781, issue of the *Gentleman's Magazine*, mentioning "a decline of the Rev. Jn. Herries A.M.," suggests that Herries may have died of consumption (Kemp 136). Unfortunately, little else of Herries' personal life is ascertainable.

Although Herries wrote only on the theory and practice of speaking, he attempted through a series of lectures to further interest in elocution among adults and university students. A pamphlet in the Bodleian Library at Oxford outlines a course of seven lectures that Herries had delivered previously in London, Dublin, Glasgow, and Edinburgh. Herries also delivered these lectures at the Mitre in Oxford in 1773, following the publication in the same year of *Elements* (Howell 247). His Oxford lectures addressed the same topics covered in *Elements*, though in less detail; and he referred his audience to the written work for a more minute description of his theories (Howell 247).

Herries' work is in the tradition of the elocutionists, who limited their discussion of rhetoric to voice and gesture (Howell 145–46). In confining their attention to a single part of the total rhetorical program, the elocutionists implied that other parts of rhetoric were unimportant; their exaggerated emphasis of delivery encouraged practices that "inevitably led to declamation without sincere conviction and earnest feeling" (Howell 145). Herries was typical of the elocutionists in that he limited his rhetorical theory to an analysis of delivery. But he was less typical in focusing solely on the voice; and *Elements* contains none of the detailed discussion of gesture and movement that marked the work of major elocutionists, such as Thomas Sheridan.

In focusing solely on vocal delivery, however, Herries limited the use of his theories; hence, his role in eighteenth-century rhetorical theory is a minor one. He should be praised, however, for encouraging speakers to make the fullest possible use of the vocal instrument and to develop an expressive vocal delivery. Furthermore, his detailed emphasis of the physical aspect of speech production makes him a particularly interesting figure in the history of phonetics (Laver 6).

HERRIES' RHETORICAL THEORY

Herries' theory in *Elements* was devoted entirely to correcting what he saw as "the neglect of cultivating the voice in our younger years" (4), which he felt had caused the decline of eloquence. He believed that "almost the whole effect of publick speaking results from the skilful use of this one faculty" (4); thus, the orator who did not focus on cultivating a "command of utterance" and "a propriety and expression of tone" would find the other tools of elocution—the "theatrical pomp of action, a studied grimace of features, violent gestures, varied attitudes, or any other superficial tricks of oratory"—a vain substitute (4–5). Herries intended *Elements* to establish vocal delivery's central focus in rhetoric and proposed to "throw some new light on this curious and important study" of the human voice (9).

Herries felt that an orator must have full knowledge of his voice, and he devoted the first half of *Elements* to a thorough explanation of vocal production. Herries described the process of respiration and its connection to the voice—and is, interestingly, the only elocutionist to stress the importance of proper breathing (Kemp 138). His description of the organs of speech was based on the work of the physiologist Albrecht von Haller (Kemp 137). Like von Haller, Herries detailed the organs of sound production (the lungs, windpipe, larynx, glottis, epiglottis) and of articulation (the tongue, jaw, uvula, nostrils, palate, lips, and teeth), as well as their function in speech production.

Because Herries felt that an orator's command of the voice must be accompanied by a thorough knowledge of the pronunciation of his language, he devoted an extensive part of *Elements* to a detailed plan of all the articulate sounds of the English language. On a fold-out folio leaf he listed and numbered all the articulate sounds of English—nine vowels, nine half-vowels, five aspirates, and six mutes—and paired each sound with examples of their use in English words. He admonished speakers to be precise in their pronunciation and to speak a "pure standard" English, free of deviations found in provincial dialects (26). Because of the "imperfection of our mode of spelling" (40), Herries recommended that speakers study his list of all the possible pronunciations of each letter of the alphabet.

Like Sheridan, Herries believed in the need for educational reform and advocated a strong emphasis on training in elocution. For Herries this meant teaching children the importance of correct pronunciation and encouraging its cultivation through distinct and slow pronunciation of sounds and careful attention to word spellings. Children should also be encouraged to speak loudly and fully and to learn to exert great energy when they speak. Herries also suggested specific techniques for overcoming common speech impediments in children and adults; he suggested that most speech defects could be cured through careful attention to articulation, citing as examples the work of Thomas Braidwood and Johann Amman who taught deaf persons to speak. He also advocated teaching the natural origins of the "simple sounds" (80) that are the basis of articulate speech, and he stressed the importance of mastering proper articulation of language in order to give "energy and gracefulness to the tones of nature" (91).

Herries devoted the second half of *Elements* to specific advice for the orator's cultivation of articulate speech, beginning with practical hints for encouraging proper breathing and strengthening the voice. The orator should stand erect and take deep breaths, should always keep his throat and nostrils clear and open, and should practice retaining his breath as long as possible. Herries recommended vigorous exercise to strengthen the lungs and nostrils and praised the classical practice of repeating long sentences while running uphill. He recommended imitating the technique of Demosthenes, "who, to remove the weakness and hesitation of his voice, loudly declaimed on the sea shore, while the waves were dashing against the rocks" (117). According to Herries, careful development of the lungs and vocal chords and the "eager and unremitting practice" of speaking loudly and fully (109) are essential for the orator, and his first object should be "the manliness and spirit of his pronunciation, independent of harmony or sweetness" (117).

But a powerful voice must also be agreeable, and Herries offered practical advice for maintaining both grace and power in speech. The orator should use a round and open tone, should make smooth transitions between sounds, and should vary the emphasis and duration of syllables. He should use emphatic pauses and vary his level of exertion; this "oeconomy of the voice" (163) would not only give his speech drama and variety but would help prevent fatigue. Varying the pitch of his voice would help him avoid monotony; but the orator should always maintain a command of the "medium" (149), which Herries defined as the comfortable range of tones that a speaker uses in normal conversation.

Once a speaker has mastered the cultivation of his voice, his next step would be to focus on other aspects of proper vocal delivery. Herries stressed the importance of the "harmony of speech" (168), which arises from a skillful combination of "sound and sense" (169). A discourse should not only "please the ear" but "inform the judgment" and "move the passions" as well (168). Despite his brief mention of other aspects of rhetoric, Herries discussed only how an orator can make his vocal delivery pleasing in sound, which a speaker can achieve through attention to the rhythm of speech and the modulation of tone. Herries also stressed that an orator must be familiar with the cadences of speech—iambic, trochaic, dactylic, and anapestic meters—and he suggests beating out the cadences of speeches during practice. Vocal modulation—"an agreeable mode of raising or sinking the tone" (188)—should be used to stress words or phrases, and a speaker can also vary his modulation to convey different moods. The orator who uses a skillful combination of rhythm and modulation can make full use of the "obscure melody" of language (189).

Although the chief emphasis of *Elements* is the effective management of the voice, Herries did not overlook the importance of conveying meaning. "The chief purpose of language," he said, "is to convey to others our ideas and feelings" (203). He stressed that vocal modulations, rhythmic accents, and emphatic pauses must be designed not only to please the ear but to "illustrate the sense" (199). Herries' discussion of this "sense" is limited to the passion an orator conveys. The speaker should "be animated with the spirit of the passions" (227) and should always understand and believe in what he is saying, for he "will affect his audience according to the degree in which he is affected himself" (248). An orator should use discretion, however, in displaying passion, so as not "to curb the impetuosity of nature, but only to direct it properly" (154). The speaker who uses a controlled display of passion, Herries argued, convicts an audience; but a "bouncing, frantic declaimer" is "pathetic" and "truly tragical" (208), and his audience will either "pity his weakness, or laugh at his absurdity" (208). As important as a speaker's sincerity and moderation is his "love for virtue and mankind" (255), which Herries felt was essential for an orator. He argued that rhetoric should always be used for noble purposes, and concluded that an orator "cannot be truly great, unless he is truly good" (255).

The Elements of Speech offers practical advice to the orator who wishes to polish his vocal delivery. As Alan Kemp has remarked, Herries and the other eighteenth-century elocutionists helped draw public attention to the importance of the study of speech; Herries was also the first to make the work of Amman and Haller available in English (144). His emphasis on correct pronunciation helped provincials Anglicize their speech so that they could participate more fully in English society. His clear presentation of ideas is easy to read; and though *Elements* is a minor work, it has perhaps been unfairly overlooked. Although the elocutionists' isolation of delivery may have tended to trivialize the topic, the work of theorists such as Herries was an important effort to encourage development of the voice and thus improve public speaking in eighteenth-century England.

BIBLIOGRAPHY

Primary Source

Herries, John. *The Elements of Speech.* London, 1773. Reprint. Edited by R. C. Alston. Menston, England: Scolar, 1968.

Criticism

Howell, Wilbur Samuel. *Eighteenth-Century British Logic and Rhetoric,* 144–248. Princeton: Princeton University Press, 1971.
Kemp, Alan. "Elocution and General Phonetic Theory: John Herries." *Histoire Epistemologie Language* 7 (1985): 133–47.
Laver, John. "The Concept of Articulatory Settings: An Historical Survey." *Historiographia Linguistica* 5.1(1978): 1–14.

JOHN HOLMES
(1703–1759)

Larry Ferrario

Although many historians of rhetoric have mentioned John Holmes and his *Art of Rhetoric Made Easy* (1739), hardly any have discussed Holmes's work or his life. In fact, very little is known about John Holmes. Judging by the advertisements for his other books in the back of the first edition of his *Art of Rhetoric,* Holmes was already a prolific author by the time he published *The Art of Rhetoric Made Easy* in 1739. By this date, he was also master of the public grammar school in Holt, Norfolk, a post that he held for many years, as evidenced by an advertisement in the 1755 edition of his *Art of Rhetoric,* which says that the school was kept by John Holmes "and Proper Assistance."

Holmes wrote textbooks for the school boys in his grammar school; but as the complete title to his history of England suggests, he also aimed at a wider audience: *The History of England Being a Compendium to the Capacities and Memories of Youth at School and Likewise Useful for all Others who have weak Memories and would willingly retain what they read in the English History* (1737). In addition to this work, Holmes published Latin (1732) and Greek (1735) grammars, a book on rhetoric (1739), a key to the Latin and Greek grammars (1739), a grammarian's arithmetic, a French grammar, and *The Grammarian's Geography and Astronomy* (1751). Perhaps the most curious of his published works was a letter-sized copy of an engraved copper plate that sold for nine pence called "Rhetorick Epitomiz'd" (1738), which depicted rhetoric as a tree with the canons as its branches. This single sheet purported to teach its purchaser the rudiments of rhetoric in an hour.

Holmes's Latin and Greek grammars went through many editions, as did his *Art of Rhetoric Made Easy.* In its original form, the rhetoric was reprinted in London in 1755 and again in 1766. However, the most enduring incarnation of Holmes's rhetoric was the edition that coupled it with John Stirling's *System of Rhetoric.* Featuring a truncated version of Holmes's work presented in a question-and-answer format, this combined edition first came out in 1786 and was reprinted as late as 1864 (Howell 137n).

Judging by the number of editions of Holmes's *Rhetoric* and some of his grammars, many of Holmes's books were widely used. Holmes's main purpose throughout was to make learning less painful and more interesting than the existing works available to students. Typical is his statement in the preface to his 1743 edition of his Greek grammar, where he said that he wanted to make Greek grammar "plain, easy, and delightful. For it is certainly a great Mistake in Education, to vex and torture the Minds of Youth with dry, insipid, grave and perplexing Trifles" (i).

In his book on rhetoric, Holmes offered eighteenth-century youth a distillation of classical rhetoric intended "for the Compleating of YOUTH in their Grammatical Knowledge and their further Instruction in the Excellent Art of SPEAKING WELL and WRITING ELEGANTLY, in their own or either of the Learned LANGUAGES" ("Preface" to *The Art of Rhetoric Made Easy*). Although Holmes admitted that there were many rhetorics on the market already, he saw none written expressly for schoolboys in grammar school—a void he hoped that his volume would fill.

HOLMES'S RHETORICAL THEORY

Holmes's *Art of Rhetoric* was to appeal to youth by simplifying concepts from the "glorious and extensive Plan of the Ancients," following their method entirely but eliminating the "Copious Parts" of their works (Preface to *The Art of Rhetoric Made Easy*). In addition, to make his book on rhetoric more accessible to grammar-school students, Holmes employed three unusual devices: (1) he began each of his sections with a series of questions that schoolboys might ask about that canon of rhetoric; (2) he reduced Ciceronian rhetoric to twenty-four principles for schoolboys to memorize; and (3) he created verses—often heroic couplets—as mnemonic devices for the students.

Holmes began each part of his discussion of rhetoric with questions that he thought schoolboys would need to answer. For example, under disposition he asked: "What is disposition? How many Parts are there in an Oration, and in what Order should they Stand? 1-What is the Business of an Exordium? What is the Narration? What doth the Proposition? What is the Confirmation? What doth the Refutation? What doth the Peroration? Give an example of an Oration or Declamation from the Classics" (15). By way of answering the questions that he posed, Holmes offered crucial maxims for commitment to memory. He identified these maxims with a capital letter, as in the following example: "L. DIGNITY is that which adorns Language with sublime Thoughts, and Rhetorical Flowers, such as noble Tropes, moving Figures, and beautiful Turns. TROPES affect only single Words; but FIGURES whole Sentences" (28). The rest of Holmes's text consists of annotations in English, Greek, and Latin, which elaborate on or explain the maxims. In this fashion, Holmes could quote and refer to the works of many rhetoricians, both ancient and modern. Some of the ancients that he constantly referred to are Cicero, Aristotle, and Quintilian; while Fénelon, Peter Ramus, and Anthony Blackwall are among the moderns that he cited.

Another unusual feature of *The Art of Rhetoric Made Easy* is Holmes's extensive use of rhymes to help students memorize the important elements of rhetoric. For example, when Holmes discussed pronunciation (or delivery), he explained the importance of the voice (Maxim 10) through these verses:

> Vary your Tone just as your Subjects go,
> Cant not, nor pitch your Voice too high or low,
> Strain not, nor speak your words too fast or slow. (74)

The Art of Rhetoric Made Easy consists of two parts. Except for the major omission of memory as a rhetorical canon, Part One is a short (ninety-six pages) and fairly straightforward Ciceronian rhetoric; while Part Two presents a digest of Longinus's *On the Sublime,* along with an abstract of Longinus's life in nine letters written by Holmes to an anonymous correspondent. Holmes included Longinus in Part Two "To point out to the young Student The Height and Excellency of good Writings. To perform which, I humbly conceive Nothing could be more properly introduced than the Substance of the Celebrated LONGINUS on the Sublime" (From the Preface to *The Art of Rhetoric Made Easy*).

In Part One, Holmes began by defining rhetoric as "the Art of Speaking or Writing well on any Subject. It's [*sic*] Principal End is to Influence, Persuade, and Please. It's [*sic*] Chief Office is to seek what may be most conducive to Persuasion. The Subject it treats on is any Thing whatever; whether it be moral, philosophical, or Divine" (1).

Next Holmes divided rhetoric into the four classical canons of *invention, disposition* (arrangement), *elocution* (style), and *pronunciation* (delivery), but omitting *memory* because "Ramus argued that it was a common factor in many arts, and that it did not belong in particular to the speaker" (Howell 25). Holmes quoted Ramus on this, and Ramus cited Cicero as his authority because Cicero, in his *Orator,* said that memory did not belong to rhetoric but was common to many arts. Of course, as both Ramus and Holmes knew, elsewhere Cicero insisted that memory was one of the five parts of rhetoric (Howell 25n).

In delineating the four rhetorical canons, Holmes presented a standard classical rendering—albeit brief—of rhetoric. Except for his omission of *memory,* he provided a fairly mundane rehashing of the major elements of classical rhetoric; this was, after all, a rhetoric for grammar-school students.

Unfortunately, too often in his book on rhetoric he simply listed elements to be memorized. Like other eighteenth-century Ciceronians, Holmes privileged elocution (Howell 142). To a lesser extent, he also emphasized *pronunciation* over *invention* and *disposition*. Indeed, in the preface to his *Art of Rhetoric* he stressed figures, tropes, repetitions, and pronunciation but never mentioned invention and disposition.

The structure of the text itself further reveals Holmes's bias toward *elocution* and *pronunciation*. He devoted only ten pages to *invention,* wherein he discussed such elements as (1) deliberative, judicial, and demonstrative arguments; (2) arguments derived from reason, morals, and the emotions; and (3) the topics. The eight pages devoted to *disposition* consist entirely of the six parts to an oration and the seven parts of a theme. *Pronunciation* focuses on voice and action; and while the pronouncements themselves are succinct, Holmes provided many pages of examples in English, Greek, and Latin for the student to practice. However, *elocution* occupies the majority of Holmes's attention and space; a lengthy forty-eight pages, elocution makes up half of *The Art of Rhetoric Made Easy*. In the process it covers over 250 figures and tropes, which Holmes bragged was "indeed many more than all that are treated of in any other One Book" (Preface, *The Art of Rhetoric Made Easy*). Holmes may have been pleased to offer so many figures in one volume, but other prominent eighteenth-century rhetoricians did not share his zeal. For example, in his lectures on rhetoric and the belles lettres given at the University of Edinburgh between 1748–1751, Adam Smith inveighed against this system, calling books that divided and subdivided figures "silly and not at all instructive" (23).

Besides making the system of tropes, figures, and turns the major element in his rhetoric, Holmes linked this stylistic rhetoric with his digest of Longinus's work in the 1739 edition of *The Art of Rhetoric Made Easy*. And after Holmes's death his work was coupled with Stirling's one-dimensional style guide. Consequently, all editions of Holmes's rhetoric offer the reader a disproportionate amount of style. Even in his "Rhetoric Epitomiz'd," Holmes devoted two-thirds of the single sheet to style.

Although Holmes claimed to imitate classical theory, in his book on rhetoric he showed little interest in invention and arrangement. He emphasized only two offices of rhetoric—namely, style and delivery. In fact, in the last words of *The Art of Rhetoric Made Easy* Holmes exhorted his readers to concentrate solely on these two parts of the classical system: "Z—TO CONCLUDE. Upon the Whole, if you design or hope for any Success in your Arguments, or would render yourselves acceptable Orators—Adorn with TROPES and FIGURES your Oration, By VOICE and ACTION grace Pronunciation" (74–75). "Rhetoric Epitomiz'd" also prominently displays this same heroic couplet, and the version of *The Art of Rhetoric Made Easy,* combined with John Stirling's rhetoric, ends with it.

In many ways, John Holmes summarized classical notions of rhetoric and helped to keep that tradition alive in the eighteenth century. At first glance, Holmes, like Cicero, seems to have been concerned with the idea of rhetoric as one great art consisting of a number of lesser arts; but ultimately, Holmes presented a very limited view of the classical system. Mostly, he wrote a technical rhetoric marked by the use of prescriptive language; sometimes it seems little more than a formulaic handbook of rhetoric for grammar-school boys. Furthermore, by emphasizing style, *The Art of Rhetoric Made Easy* joins an earlier and continuing trend toward a narrow interpretation of classical rhetoric. Nevertheless, there are also elements in Holmes's work that may indicate other developments in eighteenth-century British rhetoric as well. For example, Holmes's extensive use of James Thomson's "The Seasons" to illustrate aspects of the sublime in his section on Longinus suggests the association of rhetoric and belles lettres—a connection that later theorists, such as Adam Smith and Hugh Blair, were to develop. Finally, by elevating pronunciation along with style, Holmes also reflected the emphasis on delivery advocated by the new elocutionary movement, which began in Great Britain in the early eighteenth century (Howell 145–46).

BIBLIOGRAPHY

Primary Sources

Holmes, John. "Rhetorick Epitomiz'd." London, 1738.
———. *The Art of Rhetoric Made Easy*. London, 1739.
Stirling, John, and John Holmes. *A System of Rhetoric To which is added The Art of Rhetoric Made Easy*. New York, 1788.

Criticism

Howell, Wilbur Samuel. *Eighteenth-Century British Logic and Rhetoric*, 125-42. Princeton: Princeton University Press, 1971.
Smith, Adam. *Lectures on Rhetoric and Belles Lettres Delivered in the University of Glasgow*. Carbondale: Southern Illinois University Press, 1971.
Winterowd, W. Ross. *Rhetoric: A Synthesis*. New York: Holt, Rinehart and Winston, 1967.

DAVID HUME
(1711–1776)

Adam Potkay

The younger son of a Scottish laird, David Hume was born in 1711 in Edinburgh. In "My Own Life," an autobiographical essay that Hume wrote shortly before his death in 1776, he recalled of his youth: "My studious disposition, my sobriety, and my industry, gave my family a notion that the law was the proper profession for me; but I found an unsurmountable aversion to every thing but the pursuits of philosophy and general learning" (xxxiii). After attending Edinburgh University and briefly working at a Bristol merchant's office, Hume spent the years 1734–1737 in France, where he wrote his major philosophical work *A Treatise of Human Nature*. Published in three volumes between 1739 and 1740, the *Treatise*, by Hume's own account (see *Essays*), "fell dead-born from the press"; and he attributed its "want of success . . . more [to] the manner than the matter" of the work (xxxiv–xxxv). His subsequent efforts in a more popular essay form met with a far better reception: *Essays: Moral and Political* (1741–1742) were widely read and praised, as were the *Political Discourses* (1752). Hume's commercial success as a man of letters rested largely on his essays, as well as on his six-volume *History of England* (1754–1761). The corpus of his essays, which he continually supplemented and revised, reached its final form with the posthumous edition of *Essays: Moral, Political and Literary* (1777). In his own era, he acquired rather more notoriety than esteem in his roles as skeptical metaphysician (in Book 1 of the *Treatise* and its recasting as *An Enquiry Concerning Human Understanding* [1748] and as critic of religion (in "Of Miracles," Section 10 of the *Enquiry*, in *The Natural History of Religion* [1757]; and in the *Dialogues concerning Natural Religion* [1779]). His works of moral philosophy (Books 2 and 3 of the *Treatise* and the related *Enquiry Concerning the Principles of Morals* [1751] were indifferently received by the public at large, but proved quite congenial to the good number of Hume's philosophically inclined contemporaries who shared his assumptions of natural benevolence and social sympathy.

Although Hume never contributed to the practical study of oratory, he nonetheless had a considerable influence on eighteenth-century rhetorical theory. His influence has two distinct aspects. First, Hume's essay "Of Eloquence" (1742) popularized a Longinian taste for sublime political oratory in the manner of Demosthenes. British interest in Demosthenes had already been revived by political writers who opposed the allegedly "tyrannic" ministry of Sir Robert Walpole (1721–1742); Hume's own achievement was, without denying the ideological importance of Demosthenes' speeches, to elevate appreciation of them above narrowly partisan aims.

The second aspect of Hume's influence on rhetoric is more narrowly theoretical, but no less significant. In his writings on the nature of knowledge and belief, Hume advanced a psychological vocabulary well suited to describing the dynamics of persuasion. Thus, the theory of belief that Hume advanced in Book 1 of the *Treatise* helped to shape George Campbell's theory of what constitutes effective speaking. And thus the mechanics of mental association propounded in the *Treatise* supplied a number of rhetoricians, including Adam Smith, with a rationale for insisting on an articulated continuity of narration. Following Hume, Smith and others contended that an orderly and connected style of narration, in orations as elsewhere, conforms to our orderly association of ideas—and, hence, naturally pleases an audience that is "in a healthful state of association," to borrow a phrase from Wordsworth's "Preface to Lyrical Ballads."

HUME'S RHETORICAL THEORY

Hume's "Of Eloquence"

Hume's essay "Of Eloquence" calls for the revival of ancient eloquence in eighteenth-century Britain—specifically, for the revival of deliberative eloquence of an Athenian variety. Hume conceded that any attempt at judicial eloquence in the high style is discouraged by "the multiplicity and intricacy of laws" in modern times: first, because "the study of the laws [is now] a laborious occupation, requiring the drudgery of a whole life to finish it, and incompatible with every other study or profession"—that is, with general learning; and second, because the modern lawyer is obliged to "draw his arguments from strict laws, statutes, and precedents," rather than appeal, as was anciently done, "to the equity and common sense of the judges." However, Hume contended (see *Essays*) that even if "this circumstance" did "banish oratory from Westminister-Hall"—that is, from the courts of law—it would not preclude it "from either house of parliament" (102–3). Hume continued by observing the aptness of an Athenian model for the modern deliberative orator:

Among the Athenians, the Areopagites [members of the highest judicial court] expressly forbad all allurements of eloquence; and some have pretended that in the

Greek orations, written in the *judiciary* form, there is not so bold and rhetorical a style, as appears in the Roman. But to what a pitch did the Athenians carry their eloquence in the *deliberative* kind, when affairs of state were canvassed, and the liberty, happiness, and honour of the republic were the subject of debate? Disputes of this nature elevate the genius above all others, and give the fullest scope to eloquence; and such disputes are very frequent in [the British] nation. (103)

Hume went on to deplore the modern state of parliamentary eloquence, and expressly yearned for something more than mere "good sense, delivered in proper expression" (104). For Hume, modern eloquence, "calm, elegant, and subtle" (108), paled in comparison to the sublime and pathetic eloquence of the great classical orators:

Even a person, unacquainted with the noble remains of ancient orators, may judge, from a few strokes, that the style or species of their eloquence was infinitely more sublime than that which modern orators aspire to. How absurd it would appear, in our temperate and calm speakers, to make use of an *Apostrophe,* like that noble one of Demosthenes, so much celebrated by Quintilian and Longinus, when justifying the unsuccessful battle of Chaeronea, he breaks out, "No, my Fellow-Citizens, No: You have not erred. I swear by the *manes* of those heroes, who fought for the same cause in the plains of Marathon and Plataea." . . . What noble art and sublime talents are requisite to arrive, by just degrees, at a sentiment so bold and excessive: To inflame the audience, so as to make them accompany the speaker in such violent passions, and such elevated conceptions: And to conceal, under a torrent of eloquence, the artifice, by which all this is effectuated! (100–101)

In this passage, and indeed throughout his essay, Hume borrowed his terms as well as his aesthetics from Longinus, who in *On the Sublime* called Demosthenes' apostrophe from *On the Crown* "a passage of transcending sublimity" and praised the art by which the orator concealed his art: "In much the same way as dim lights vanish in the radiance of the sun, so does the all-pervading effluence of grandeur utterly obscure the artifices of rhetoric" (Chs. 16-17). Adopting Longinus's metaphor, Hume concluded his comparison of ancient and modern oratory in this way: "When compared with Demosthenes and Cicero," modern eloquence is "eclipsed like a taper when set in the rays of a meridian sun" (108).

In the same essay ("Of Eloquence"), Hume also included a comparison of Demosthenes and Cicero and awarded the palm to the former: in his preference for the Athenian orator, and in his very phrasing, Hume was following the example of Fénelon's *Dialogues sur l'éloquence* (1717). Hume wrote,

Could [Demosthenes' manner] be coupled, its success would be infallible over a modern assembly. It is rapid harmony, exactly adjusted to the sense: It is vehement reasoning, without any appearance of art: It is disdain, anger, boldness, freedom, involved in a continuous stream of argument: And of all human productions, the orations of Demosthenes present to us the models, which approach the nearest to perfection. (105–6)

Hume intensely admired Demosthenes' vehemence of thought and expression, his appeal to the common passions as well as the common sense of his audience (107). He approved even the ancient orators' violent "action," noting that "the *supplosio pedis,* or stamping of the foot, was one of the most usual and moderate gestures they made use of" (101).

In our own day, Hume's tribute to Demosthenic eloquence has raised the eyebrows of the historian of rhetoric, Wilbur Samuel Howell, who has surveyed eighteenth-century rhetoric in strict progressivist terms and has called Hume's essay "curiously static, curiously unhistorical, and curiously antiquarian" (616). I would contend, however, that Hume's essay simply reveals the extent to which eighteenth-century rhetoric was, all in all, a retrospective as well as a forward-looking technology. It is, moreover, crucial to recognize—as Howell has not—that the British nostalgia for ancient eloquence was never merely a stylistic concern but, rather, reflected some degree of yearning for the sense of *political* affiliation presumably enjoyed by the ancients. "Eloquence" was, in eighteenth-century parlance, a political as well as a stylistic ideal.

True eloquence aligns with civic virtue: this assumption, at least as old as Quintilian, was revived in the 1720s and 1730s by the political Opposition to the prime minister Robert Walpole. Walpole's chief antagonists, Lord Bolingbroke and his circle, maintained that only the good citizen could be a good speaker, and they rigorously defined the good citizen by the classical political virtues: love of justice; civic participation; and, above all, a preference for the public—as opposed to any merely private—good. In the years leading up to Hume's "Of Eloquence," the members of Bolingbroke's party filled their writings with references to and quotations from Demosthenes, the orator who evoked an Athenian esprit de corps even as he opposed any compromise with the tyrannic Philip. Demosthenes' noble cause, along with his fabled action and his fiery figures of speech, seized the political imagination of British patriots who sought a talisman to unify their interests and avert the putative threat of ministerial tyranny in Georgian England. It is in keeping with this Opposition commonplace that Hume in "Of Eloquence" asked, "It would be easy to find a Philip in modern times; but where shall we find a Demosthenes?" (106). And indeed, Hume partially answered this question later in his essay: "Lord Bolingbroke's productions contain a force and energy that our orators scarcely ever aim at" (108). Hume's comments here reveal that his vision of ancient eloquence was indeed rooted in eighteenth-century Opposition politics (as well as in Fénelon). His achievement, however, was to help preserve this vision long after the particular agenda of Bolingbroke's Opposition to Walpole had been forgotten.

That Demosthenes' eloquence continued to be equated with civic virtue, praised for its sublimity, and preferred to Cicero's more artificial style was owing, at least in part, to Hume's considerable influence among his contemporaries. Adam Smith developed a number of Hume's observations in his *Lectures on Rhetoric and Belles-Lettres* (nos. 25-30); and Hugh Blair derived his own verdict on Demosthenes directly from "Of Eloquence":

Were Demosthenes' Philippics spoken in a British assembly, in a similar conjuncture of affairs, they would convince and persuade at this day. The rapid style, the vehement reasoning, the disdain, anger, boldness, freedom, which perpetually animate them, would render their success infallible over any modern assembly. I question whether the same can be said of Cicero's orations. . . . [Note:] In this judgment I concur with Mr. David Hume, in his Essay on Eloquence. (2:32)

The Influence of Hume's Epistemology on the Philosophy of Rhetoric

This influence has two distinct aspects, which I will treat successively.

1. Hume's Influence on George Campbell's *Philosophy of Rhetoric*. Campbell based his psychological analysis of effective speaking on terms and concepts that he derived from the theory of belief presented in Hume's *Treatise of Human Nature*.

Hume's theory of belief is properly a psychology of belief, although Hume did not use the term (it was introduced into English by David Hartley). According to Hume, all belief is essentially irrational: it derives simply from the "vivacity" with which a given perception strikes the mind. Hume wrote: "Thus it appears, that the *belief* or *assent*, which always attends the memory and senses, is nothing but the vivacity of those perceptions they present; and this alone distinguishes them from the imagination. To believe is in this case to feel an immediate impression on the senses, or a repetition of that impression on the memory" (86). We believe in our impressions, as we feel or remember them, because of their "superior force and vivacity" compared to the "mere fictions of the imagination" (85).

Yet while we always believe in our impressions, we only sometimes believe in our "ideas." As Hume defined them, ideas originate as the fainter representations of our original perceptions. Accordingly, "Impressions always actuate the soul, and that in the highest degree; but 'tis not every idea which has the same effect" (118). An idea is vivified, or made to approximate the force of an impression, either by a trick of nature or by a device of art. Chief among naturally induced beliefs is our inclination to associate causes and effects; chief among the artificial means of procuring belief are the methods of oratory. Having stated that "belief must please the imagination by means of the force and vivacity which attends it," Hume conversely argued "that a belief not only gives vigour to the imagination, but that a vigorous and strong imagination is of all the talents the most proper to procure belief and authority. 'Tis difficult for us to withhold our assent from what is painted out to us in all the colours of eloquence; and the vivacity produc'd by the fancy is in many cases greater than that which arises from custom and experience" (122–23). Hume proceeded to assert that a speaker's "fire and genius," or simply "a blaze of poetical figures and images," would suffice to allow "any shadow of argument" to procure our "full conviction" (123).

Lloyd Bitzer has noted that the notion of "vivacity," in particular, "establishes the historical link between Hume and Campbell" and that "vivacity, or the liveliness of ideas—according to Hume the essential quality of belief—became in Campbell's theory the essential quality in effective rhetorical discourse: the success of nearly every instance of discourse hinges upon the creation of 'lively and glowing ideas' " (4–5). Campbell followed Hume in holding that sense, memory, and imagination possess decreasing amounts of vivacity; accordingly, the orator's task is to find ways to enliven the ideas raised in the imagination to such a degree that they resemble the perceptions of the senses and the transcripts of the memory. As Campbell phrased it, the orator must "make the ideas he summons up in the imagination of his hearers, resemble, in lustre and steadiness, those of sensation and remembrance" (81). Particularly "conducive to vivacity" are the tropes of synecdoche, metaphor, metonymy and personification—the last of which, Campbell remarked, makes such a strong impression on the mind that it "hath [itself] come to be termed vivacity, or liveliness of style" (299–310).

As Vincent Bevilacqua has pointed out, Campbell's concept of vivacity is not entirely indebted to Hume, but "rests also on principles in the tradition of Longinus that by the mid-eighteenth century were commonplace in English aesthetic theory" (11). I would add that neither is Hume's concept of vivacity entirely or even chiefly his own, but rests squarely within that same rhetorical tradition. Indeed, as I argue in *Of Eloquence,* perceptions that "strike" the mind in the *Treatise* do so with the same "force" and "vivacity" that classical and neoclassical rhetoricians attributed to the sublime orator. Thus, the reason that Campbell could easily incorporate the main concepts of Hume's epistemology into his *Philosophy of Rhetoric* is that, as he was doubtlessly aware, those concepts originate in the discourse of rhetoric. By (re-) applying Hume's terms to the powers of persuasive speech, Campbell effectively uncovered the theory of oratory that informed Hume's science of mind.

2. Hume's Influence on Associationist Theories of Effective Narration. In the *Treatise,* Hume believed that he had found psychological equivalents to Newton's physical laws of gravitation in the three "principles of association"—resemblance, contiguity, and causation. In his "Abstract" of the *Treatise,* Hume declared:

There is a secret tie or union among particular ideas, which causes the mind to conjoin them more frequently together, and makes the one, upon its appearance, introduce the other. Hence arises what we call the *apropos* of discourse: hence the connection of writing: and hence that thread, or chain of thought, which a man naturally supports even in the loosest *reverie.* These principles of association are reduced to three, viz. *Resemblance*; a picture naturally makes us think of the man it was drawn for. *Contiguity*, when St. Dennis is mentioned, the idea of Paris naturally occurs. *Causation*; when we think of the son, we are apt to carry our attention to the father. 'Twill be easy to conceive of what vast consequence these principles must be in the science of human nature, if we consider, that so far as regards the mind, these are the only links that bind the parts of the universe together, or connect us with any person or object exterior to ourselves. For as it is by means of thought only that any thing operates upon our passions, and as these are the only ties of our thoughts, they are really *to us* the cement of the universe. (662)

Hume thus established the "association of ideas" as a normative principle of psychology. (Locke, by contrast, addressed only the associative principle of contiguity, which he regarded chiefly as the basis of irrational fears and aversions.)

Moreover, Hume gave mental association a rhetorical equivalent: "the *apropos* of discourse . . . the connection of writing." He developed this implicit link between orderly narration and the natural association of our ideas in Section 3 of his *Enquiry Concerning Human Understanding*: "In narrative compositions the events or actions which the writer relates must be connected together by some bond or tie . . . [T]he most usual species of connection among the different events which enter into any narrative composition is that of cause and effect" (33–34). Hume demonstrated how the associative principle of causation governs proper narration in history, biography, epic and dramatic poetry; furthermore, he suggested that any deviation from this principle is apt to occasion "a breach or vacuity in the course of [our] passions, by means of this breach in the connection of ideas" (37). Thus, narrative digression, or any other violation of a neoclassical "unity of action," disrupts our natural tendency to associate in an orderly manner. Hume employed his psychology of association to vindicate his aesthetic taste for continuity and connection (not surprisingly, Hume preferred Racine to Shakespeare). We may observe both a similar taste—and, implicitly, an appeal to the same associative principle of causation—in his conclusion to "Of Eloquence":

I shall conclude this subject with observing, that, even though our modern orators should not elevate their style or aspire to a rivalship with the ancient; yet is there, in most of their speeches, a material defect, which they might correct, without departing from that composed air of argument and reasoning, to which they limit their ambition. Their great affectation of extempory discourse has made them reject all order and method. . . . But it is easy . . . to observe a method, and make that method conspicuous to the hearers, who will be infinitely pleased to see the arguments rise naturally from one another, and will retain a more thorough persuasion, than can arise from the strongest reasons, which are thrown together in confusion. (110)

As Martin Kallich has amply demonstrated, Hume's conflation of "nature and associationism and neoclassicism" (87) proved very influential among both rhetoricians and aesthetic theorists of the later eighteenth century. Adam Smith, Alexander Gerard, Lord Kames, and Archibald Alison all concurred with Hume that transition and connection in writing and oratory please us because they conform to the natural train of our associations. As Kallich has remarked, "Associationism was in the air; and men of genius were able to revise old conceptions by means of the new psychology" (94); the new psychological critics did not aim "to subvert Aristotelean order and structure and the rules for judging and creating regular works of art, but to ground critical theory anew upon Hume's 'discoveries' in the philosophy of human nature" (133).

Although not a rhetorician himself, Hume is a figure of signal importance in the history of eighteenth-century rhetorical theory. His essay "Of Eloquence" advanced the stylistic and political ideal of Demosthenic eloquence—an ideal that Blair would disseminate still more widely. And his epistemology influenced the ways in which many of his contemporaries—among them, Adam Smith and George Campbell—thought about how language and the mind act and how they interact with each other.

BIBLIOGRAPHY

Primary Sources

Blair, Hugh. *Lectures on Rhetoric and Belles-Lettres.* 2 vols. Edited by Harold F. Harding. Carbondale: Southern Illinois University Press, 1965.
Campbell, George. *The Philosophy of Rhetoric.* Edited by Lloyd F. Bitzer. Carbondale: Southern Illinois University Press, 1988.
Hume, David. *A Treatise of Human Nature.* Edited by L. A. Selby-Bigge, and revised by P. H. Nidditch. Oxford: Clarendon, 1978.
———. *An Enquiry Concerning Human Understanding.* Edited by Charles Hendel. Indianapolis: Bobbs-Merrill, 1955.
———. *Essays: Moral, Political and Literary.* Edited by Eugene F. Miller. Indianapolis: Liberty Classics, 1985.

Biography

Mossner, Ernest Campbell. *The Life of David Hume.* Austin: University of Texas Press, 1954.

Criticism

Bevilacqua, Vincent. "Philosophical Origins of George Campbell's *Philosophy of Rhetoric.*" *Speech Monographs* 32 (1965): 1–12.
Bitzer, Lloyd F. "Hume's Philosophy in Campbell." *Philosophy and Rhetoric* 2 (1969): 139–66.
Howell, Wilbur Samuel. *Eighteenth-Century British Logic and Rhetoric.* Princeton: Princeton University Press, 1971.

Kallich, Martin. *The Association of Ideas and Critical Theory in Eighteenth-Century England*. The Hague: Mouton, 1970.

Potkay, Adam. "Classical Eloquence and Polite Style in the Age of Hume." *Eighteenth-Century Studies* 25.1 (1991): 31–56.

———. *Of Eloquence: Literature and Politics in the Age of Hume*. Book manuscript.

Richetti, John. "Hume." Chap. 4 in *Philosophical Writing*. Cambridge: Harvard University Press, 1983.

Sitter, John. "Hume's Stylistic Emergence." Chap. 1 in *Literary Loneliness in Mid-Eighteenth-Century England*. Ithaca: Cornell University Press, 1982.

Smith, Adam. *Lectures on Rhetoric and Belles-Lettres*. Edited J. C. Bryce. Indianapolis: Liberty Classics, 1985.

Wordsworth, William. "Preface to Lyrical Ballads." In *Romantic Criticism, 1800–1850*, edited by R. A. Foakes. Columbia: University of South Carolina Press, 1970.

HENRY HOME, LORD KAMES
(1696–1782)

Christy Desmet

Henry Home, later Lord Kames, was born in 1696 on the Kames estate in Berwickshire, Scotland. He was the son of Agnes Walkinshaw and George Home. Kames's early education took place at home, where his tutor beat him regularly but taught him little. Because his father was poor, Henry was not sent to a university. Instead, he was indentured to a Writer of the Signet in Edinburgh to study law. Kames considered the standard training he received there—copying statutes, summonses, and charters by rote without ever discussing principles of law—to be unsatisfactory. When his indenture was completed, he therefore hired another tutor to teach him Latin, Greek, mathematics, and philosophy. He also studied civil law at the University of Edinburgh. During the next twenty-five years, Kames passed the bar examination, married, and inherited his family's estate, which he renovated and made the site of agricultural experiments. His continuing interest in gardening and agriculture produced several publications.

In 1752, Kames was made a judge. He became known not only for his acute understanding of law but also for his severity and his irregular behavior on the bench. Ross, in his book *Lord Kames,* has said that when a man with whom Kames played chess was found guilty of attempting to murder his pregnant mistress with arsenic, Kames reportedly cried out, "That's checkmate to you, Matthew!" (311). Kames was also a respected legal scholar: both John Quincy Adams and Thomas Jefferson, for instance, owned copies of his *Historical Law-Tracts* (1758). Kames continued in his capacity as judge until his death at the age of eighty-six. Ross, in his book, has informed us that when Kames was leaving his courtroom for the last time, he was said to have turned to his colleagues and said, "Fare ye a'weel, ye bitches" (370). Six days later he died.

Although an advocate by profession, Lord Kames participated enthusiastically in the intellectual life of the Scottish Enlightenment. He was prominent enough that James Boswell, who was an acquaintance, considered writing his biography. Kames was also intimate with David Hume, who for a time treated him as a mentor. The relationship was mutual, for the philosophy behind Kames's own rhetorical and aesthetic writings was influenced by Hume. Kames's *Essays on the Principles of Morality and Natural Religion* (1751), a response to Hume's *Treatise of Human Nature* (1739), earned him a reputation as a skeptic because he dismissed free will as a delusion. Kames was accused of heresy before the Edinburgh presbytery a few years later, but the charges were dismissed. Later in his life Kames met and corresponded with Benjamin Franklin, another self-made man who shared Kames's interest in moral education, theology, and practical inventions (Barker; Randall 1–22; Bevilacqua, *Theory* 13–37; Ross, *Kames* 197–201).

In some ways, Lord Kames contributed more directly to the history of rhetoric as a patron than as an author. It was Kames who convinced Adam Smith to deliver his first lectures on rhetoric and literature at the University of Edinburgh, an event that led to the creation of the Regius Professorship of Rhetoric and Belles-Lettres. Its first occupant was Hugh Blair, whose *Lectures on Rhetoric and Belles-Lettres* (1783) was published with Kames's help. In his own era, however, Kames was well known as an author. The *Elements of Criticism* (1762), his principal work on rhetoric, was highly regarded and widely read. Between 1762 and 1823 the book went through eight English editions and four American editions; it was also translated into German. The influence of Kames's *Elements* can be detected in the work of Hugh Blair and Joseph Priestley and perhaps in George Campbell's *Philosophy of Rhetoric*. Kames's work was also popular in America, where it influenced textbooks of rhetoric and composition (Barker; McGuinness 25; Bevilacqua, *Theory* 186–99; Randall 69–88; Ross, *Kames* 283–91). Although commentators disagree about the intrinsic merits of Kames's *Elements,* his philosophic inquiry into the principles of art, based on a systematic theory of human nature, epitomizes the "rational criticism" of the Scottish Enlightenment.

LORD KAMES'S RHETORICAL THEORY

Lord Kames's importance to the history of rhetoric rests largely on his account of the psychology of persuasion. Kames's rhetoric has been called "Newtonian" because it sought a general principle that would unify language use as the principle of gravity had unified the physical world (Randall 23–27). In the *Elements,* the association of ideas provided that unifying principle. As a general account of aesthetic response rather than a theory of persuasion, Kames's *Elements* nevertheless privileges verbal art over other arts because language unfolds in time and, therefore, imitates the succession of ideas more accurately than other art forms do (1:97). In this way, the book's theory of art implies a theory of persuasion that was reinforced by Kames's study of belief and human reason in other works.

Lord Kames's interest in the association of ideas led him simultaneously in two directions: toward an examination of invention and toward an account of pathos, or audience response. As stated in the *Elements*, while awake a man "is conscious of a continued train of perceptions and ideas passing in his mind. It requires no activity on his part to carry on the train: nor can he at will add any idea to the train" (1:17). Although ideas originate in sense perceptions, they succeed one another in a logical way: "There is implanted in the breast of every man a principle of order, which governs the arrangement of his perceptions, of his ideas, and of his actions" (1:22). For Kames as for Hume, ideas were governed by a few simple relations: cause and effect, contiguity in time or in place, high and low, prior and posterior, resemblance and contrast. Kames implied that these basic relations were utilized intuitively in thought and perhaps in discourse, but in the *Elements* he emphasized the importance of analyzing trains of ideas when criticizing art: Virgil's *Georgics*, for instance, could be faulted for interrupting the natural course of ideas with digressions and authorial intrusions (1: 28–29).

The *Elements* has nothing more to say about invention. But in his *Sketches of the History of Man* (1774), Kames explored further the notion of using the association of ideas as a heuristic device. Although concerned more with logic than with rhetoric, the *Sketches* develops Kames's ideas on invention by considering how the quest for truth is satisfied and thwarted. Like most practitioners of the new rhetoric after John Locke, Kames considered "truth" to be a matter of factual accuracy rather than of logical consistency. Kames therefore disliked the logic of Aristotle, which, as he stated in *Sketches*, had "kept the reasoning faculty in chains more than two thousand years" (2:132). Kames implied that the Aristotelian syllogism was a circular argument, proving what was intuitively obvious or readily apparent from everyday experience, and was no more than an "enchanted castle" where "phantoms pass for realities" (2:132). For Kames, Aristotle's whole logical system, became like the Egyptian pyramids or Babylon's beautiful hanging gardens, "absolutely useless unless for raising wonder" (2:181).

Dismissing Aristotelian logic as fit only for academic disputation, Kames, in his *Sketches*, described human reasoning as a process governed by the association of ideas. For Kames, reasoning involved two mental powers: the power of invention, which allows us to discover propositions; and the power of perceiving relations between those propositions (2:118). According to Kames, much reasoning, based on simple relations such as cause and effect and analogy, is intuitive. But in matters of opinion where probability rather than certainty can be attained, we must be more attentive to the connections between propositions.

Like Kames's earlier work, *Sketches* expresses optimism about the power of the human mind to circumvent misinformation. Kames was confident that truth could be achieved because he believed man had an innate moral sense and that the external and "internal" senses governing reason would correct one another's errors. To a jaundiced eye everything may look yellow; but Kames believed that God had erected "in the mind a tribunal, to which there lies an appeal from the rash impressions of sense" (2:127). Simple perception, on the other hand, assures us that summer is warm and that the sun will rise tomorrow. Perhaps more important, evidence of the senses combats the pernicious effects of rhetorical eloquence.

In *Sketches,* Kames also examined the sources of false reasoning. In his *Essays on the Principles of Morality and Natural Religion,* Kames had taken issue with Hume's idea that beliefs derive from sense impressions by arguing that a belief is a feeling (227–29). By contrast, in the *Sketches* he attributed belief less to feeling than to proper logical method. Kames identified three sources of false belief. Errors caused by the "imbecility" of reason in so-called primitive cultures included etiological myths explaining the origins of natural phenomena: Kames cited a Scandinavian fable explaining the alternation of day and night. He also discussed errors due to natural bias. To exemplify the natural though erroneous preference for external appearances over hidden intentions in his own field of expertise, he discussed a Dutch law that made a criminal's confession essential to capital punishment. If a confession were not forthcoming, the suspect would be tortured until he did confess, as if "sounds merely were sufficient, without will or intention" (2:154). English law, however, was no less absurd. Although in England the accused was not required to confess, he had to plead either innocent or guilty: "But what if he stand mute? He is pressed down by weights till he plead; and if he continue mute, he is pressed till he give up the ghost" (2:155). Finally, to illustrate errors created by learned prejudice, Kames recounted the historical dispute over the sun's relation to the earth. Aristarchus, teaching that the earth moved around the sun, was persecuted by heathen priests for "troubling the repose of their household-gods." Copernicus, "for the same doctrine, was accused by Christian priests" of contradicting Scripture (2:174). And Galileo, following Copernicus, was imprisoned and forced to recant by the Church. Thus, under different religious systems the same scientific error replicated itself through learned prejudice.

Examining the principles that govern thought helps man uncover factual truth and resist prejudice. In the *Elements* Kames also used the association of ideas to explain art's moral effect. In this way Kames complemented his investigation of invention with a more fully developed account of audience response. *Sketches* links the development of taste in Western culture to the development of the moral sense. *Elements* rationalizes this conflation of aesthetics and morality. Every work of art that conforms to "the natural course of our ideas" is agreeable and every work that violates that order is disagreeable (1:27). The association of ideas produces not only aesthetic pleasure but also sympathy, the emotion that makes art ethical. Taking issue with Locke on the subject of "Our Attachment to Objects of Distress" in his early *Essays,* Kames denied that pleasure and pain govern all human actions. To the contrary, nature makes us social beings by encouraging an identification with our fellow creatures: "We have a strong sympathy with them; we partake of their afflictions; we grieve with them and for them; and, in many instances, their misfortunes affect us equally with our own" (16). It is this sympathy that accounts for the power of tragic drama. In his discussion of Aristotle's *Poetics,* Kames in *Elements* attributed pity directly to the "social affections" and fear to a "selfish" desire to avoid the hero's misfortune that is still rooted in identification rather than in mere self-interest (2: 376–77).

In some cases sympathy involves simple identification with representations of emotion. For instance, as discussed in *Elements,* a display of courage makes the spectator feel courageous (1:62). Emotions resemble their cause, sometimes in a mechanistic way:

Sluggish motion, for example, causeth a languid unpleasant feeling; slow uniform motion, a feeling calm and pleasant; and brisk motion, a lively feeling that arouses the spirits and promotes activity. A fall of water through rocks, raises in the mind a tumultuous confused agitation, extremely similar to its cause. When force is exerted with any effort, the spectator feels a similar effort, as of force exerted within his mind. A large object swells the heart. An elevated object makes the spectator stand erect. (1:178)

More often in Kames's economy of emotion, sympathy depends on lively images and the orderly succession of ideas—that is, on the quality of an artistic representation. In this way Kames diminished the direct connection between subject matter and audience response.

In *Elements,* Kames reinforced the point that emotions raised by art are moral rather than merely mechanical with an optimistic account of art's final cause. Agreeable objects such as a rich field of grain exist to "excite our industry" (1:183). On the other hand, disagreeable objects such as rotten carcasses, dirty marshes, and barren heaths accomplish the same end by arousing in us an aversion to them (1:183). Unlike his romantic successors, who found the relationship between artful illusion and dangerous delusion more complicated, Kames argued in *Elements* that aesthetic experience was inevitably wholesome and benign. He also defined cautiously what Samuel Taylor Coleridge would later call the "willing suspension of disbelief." Kames described the epistemological status of art by the term *ideal presence,* a state somewhere between "real presence" and mere "remembrance." Unlike remembrance, the state of ideal presence is intuitive rather than reflective, transforming past memory into present spectacle. Unlike "real presence," on the other hand, ideal presence, as stated in *Elements*, "may properly be termed *a waking dream*; because, like a dream, it vanisheth the moment we reflect upon our present situation" (1:91). In this way art achieves the vividness necessary for arousing emotion but does not degenerate into delusion.

For Kames, Lockean psychology explained both the loss of rational control that characterizes pathos and the self-consciousness that aids invention and criticism. The effect of the association of ideas is, therefore, paradoxical. The problematic nature of a rhetorical machine that both enhances and effaces human reason becomes particularly apparent in Kames's use of the association of ideas to distinguish wit (which joins things by "distant and fanciful relations") from judgment (which attends only to "substantial and permanent" relations). A person of unintentional wit such as Shakespeare's Mistress Quickly, who cannot distinguish slight from solid connections between ideas, risks falling into nonsense. A man of judgment, by contrast, cannot have a great flow of ideas; for this reason, as stated in *Elements*, accurate judgment "is not friendly to declamation or copious eloquence" (1:20–22). Wit without judgment is thoughtless; judgment without wit lacks passion. In his introduction to the *Elements*, Kames recommended the "science of rational criticism" as an exercise to improve both the heart and the understanding (1:9). His reliance on a mechanist psychology legitimated but also complicated the process by which heart and head are reconciled to one another.

Kames never articulated a theory of rhetorical arrangement, either in the *Elements* or elsewhere. However, in scattered comments and through his own practice he suggested that forms of argument that follow most closely the succession of ideas—analogy, cause and effect, analysis (moving from particulars to generalizations) and synthesis (moving from generalizations to particulars)—are most effective. In works of literature, neoclassic principles such as simplicity, variety, contrast, and novelty produce lively impressions by properly ordering the succession of ideas. In poetry, arrangement sometimes mimics passion directly. In *Elements*, Kames praised Hamlet's soliloquy—"Oh, that this too too solid flesh would melt"—for accurately representing the broken and interrupted language of violent passion (1:506–7). Kames also seemed uninterested in delivery, which is not surprising in a work dedicated primarily to criticism of the arts rather than to oratory. Nevertheless his account of the "language of passion" does link the *Elements* tenuously to the elocutionary rhetoric of the eighteenth century. Assuming that human nature is uniform, Kames concluded in *Elements* that a universal and logically precise language of passionate gesture exists: joy, a "chearful elevation of mind," is expressed by an "elevation of body"; and grief, which, according to Kames, "depress[es] the mind," is expressed by a similar depression of the body (1:429).

Besides his account of the psychology of persuasion, Kames's greatest contribution to the history of rhetoric is his application of associationist psychology to style. In this way he provided a new foundation for the stylistic rhetorics of classical authors such as Demetrius of Helicarnassus and Longinus. Much of Kames's advice on style was traditional. In *Elements,* he suggested that because "language is the dress of thought," it should be clear, natural, and appropriate to the sentiments expressed (2:24). Proceeding from smaller to larger units, Kames defined beautiful language as a system of sounds, syntax, and significations; he then examined relations among those units. He also included a discussion of versification and its relation to passion.

More original but also more problematic is Kames's anatomy of literary effects and rhetorical ornament. Like many stylistic rhetorics of the period, Kames's *Elements* is ambivalent about the relationship between passion (which involves feeling subjects) and poetic representation (which involves objects). In this way Kames addressed what contemporary literary theory labels the subject-object dialectic. In an exploration of "The Idea of Self and Personal Identity" from his early *Essays,* Kames had healed the Cartesian split between thinking subjects and the objective world by appealing to man's feeling, or "consciousness of self, carried through all the different stages of life, and all the variety of action, which is the foundation of *personal identity*" (233). A vaguely defined but innate feeling, akin to the moral sense of other common-sense philosophers, articulates a stable relationship between subject and object by assuring us that the self is not fragmented by time and succession. The self is created by sense impressions from the world but has an integrity and consistency that, in the later *Elements,* allowed Kames to assume that subjective feeling colors and shapes external objects. Subject and object exist in balanced harmony.

When Kames focused on the mechanics of literary language, subject-object relations became less clear. In his discussion of literary effects, Kames emphasized the power of language to arouse passion (which privileges the perceiving subject, both author and reader). But he also established a relationship between emotion and subject matter (which privileges the aesthetic object). Beauty, for instance, may be either "intrinsic" or "relative." Intrinsic beauty, which can be discovered in a single object, depends on a subjective response: thus, we read in *Elements* that "to perceive the beauty of a spreading oak or of a flowing river, no more is required but singly an act of vision" (1:198). Relative beauty, which depends on relations between objects, arises from a more neutral "reflection" on the object's use or function (1:198). In a complex philosophical move, Kames suggested that while "intrinsic" beauty appears to belong to the object, the appearance of beauty depends completely on the subject's emotional response. In cases of relative beauty, by contrast, we consciously transfer the quality of an effect to its cause. Thus, in *Elements* we read that "an old Gothic tower, that has no beauty in itself, appears beautiful" because it offers a defense against enemies

(1:198). Paradoxically, as noted by Ross in *Lord Kames*, the thinking subject's understanding of beauty in this instance suggests that there may be objective standards for beauty (270).

In his discussion of the sublime, Kames was less successful in manipulating the paradox of subject-object relations. The term *sublimity* also describes both objects and the emotions that they arouse. Because the sublime is simultaneously subjective and objective, Kames's description (in *Elements*) of its effect risks descending into bathos: "A great object makes the spectator endeavor to enlarge his bulk; which is remarkable in plain people who give way to nature without reserve; in describing a great object, they naturally expand themselves by drawing in air with all their force. An elevated object produces a different expression: it makes the spectator stretch upward, and stand a-tiptoe" (1:211). Uniting artist and audience in a mutual gesture of expansion, Kames made the effect of the sublime correspond mathematically to the magnitude of the object being represented. As a result, man's erect and aspiring mind, the final cause of sublimity, seems to stand "a-tiptoe" in a ridiculously literal way (1:210).

In his discussions of tropes, Kames was equally ambivalent about the relationships among artist, audience, and objects of representation. He described figuration as the result of passion but also attributed to it an epistemological function. As stated in *Elements*, when a man is "cool and sedate," he "is not disposed to poetical flights." But when he is "elevated or animated by passion," he "is disposed to elevate or animate all his objects: he avoids familiar names, exalts objects by circumlocution and metaphor, and gives even life and voluntary action to inanimate beings" (2:204). Assuming that artist and audience are moved by comparable passions, Kames offered a subjectivist account of figuration. To explain that transfer of emotion, however, he also had to assume a congruity between poetic figures and their objects that makes aesthetic experience universal. Underlying and subverting Kames's description of pathos as a transaction between subjects is a neoclassic theory of mimesis based on poetic decorum. Kames's definition of personification in *Elements*, for instance, is psychologically subtle. The mind, "agitated by certain passions, is prone to bestow sensibility upon things inanimate" (2:228). But by distinguishing personification's affective from its heuristic function when he contrasted "passionate" with "descriptive" personifications, Kames raised once again the question of whether figuration originates in the subject or in the objective world. A descriptive personification—one that identifies the ground as "thirsty" or represents a dart as "furious"—probably derives not from heightened emotion but from a simple need to make abstract ideas concrete (2:236, 240). A similar confusion characterizes the definition of hyperbole. "An object of an uncommon size," either large or very small, "strikes us with surprise; and this emotion produces a momentary conviction that the object is greater or less than it is in reality" (2:259). From Kames's account of the trope, it is unclear whether the impetus toward hyperbole inheres in the spectator or in the object of uncommon size. Still, Kames's definitions surpass classical discussions of the tropes. Rooting figuration in human emotion, *Elements of Criticism* suggests a psychological rationale for rhetorical ornamentation.

The paradoxes of Kames's rhetoric are its strengths as well as its weaknesses. For in striving to articulate relationships between rhetoric's speaking subjects and its external objects, Kames effected a tentative synthesis between the concerns of classical rhetoric and an eighteenth-century psychology of human nature. For this reason the influence of his *Elements of Criticism* was extensive and enduring.

BIBLIOGRAPHY

Primary Sources

Kames, Henry Home, Lord. *Elements of Criticism.* 6th ed. 2 vols. 1762. Reprint. New York: Garland, 1972.
————. *Essays on the Principles of Morality and Natural Religion.* 1751. Reprint. New York: Garland, 1976.
————. *Sketches of the History of Man.* 3d ed. 2 vols. Dublin, 1779.

Biography

Barker, George Fisher Russell. "Home, Henry, Lord Kames." *DNB* (1963).
Ross, Ian Simpson. *Lord Kames and the Scotland of his Day.* Oxford: Clarendon, 1972.

Criticism

Bevilacqua, Vincent Michael. "The Rhetorical Theory of Henry Home, Lord Kames." Ph.D. diss., University of Illinois, 1961.
————. "Rhetoric and Human Nature in Kames's *Elements of Criticism.*" *Quarterly Journal of Speech* 48.1 (1962): 46-50.
————. "Lord Kames's Theory of Rhetoric." *Speech Monographs* 30.4 (1963): 309–27.
Bushnell, Nelson S. "Lord Kames and Eighteenth-Century Scotland." *Studies in Scottish Literature* 10 (1973): 241–54.
Grobman, Neil R. "Lord Kames and the Study of Comparative Mythology." *Folklore* 92.1 (1981): 91–103.
Horn, András. "Kames and the Anthropological Approach to Criticism." *Philological Quarterly* 44.2 (1965): 211–33.
Howell, Wilbur Samuel. *Eighteenth-Century British Logic and Rhetoric,* 393-97. Princeton: Princeton University Press, 1971.
Irish, Loomis Caryl. "Human Nature and the Arts: The Aesthetic Theory of Henry Home, Lord Kames." Ph.D. diss., Columbia University, 1961.
Lehmann, William C. *Henry Home, Lord Kames and the Scottish Enlightenment: A Study in National Character and in the History of Ideas.* The Hague: Martinus Nijoff, 1971.
McGuinness, Arthur E. *Henry Home, Lord Kames.* New York: Twayne, 1970.

McKenzie, Gordon. "Lord Kames and the Mechanist Tradition." *University of California Publications in English* 14 (1943): 93–121.

Randall, Helen Whitcomb. "The Critical Theory of Lord Kames." *Smith College Studies in Modern Languages* 22, nos. 1–4 (1940–1941).

Ross, Ian. "Scots Law and Scots Criticism: The Case of Lord Kames." *Philological Quarterly* 45.3 (1966): 614–23.

Thomson, Ian. "Rhetoric and the Passions, 1760–1800." In *Rhetoric Revalued: Papers from the International Society for the History of Rhetoric,* edited by Brian Vickers, 143-48. Binghamton, NY: Medieval and Renaissance Texts and Studies, 1982.

JOHN LAWSON
(1709–1759)

Michael G. Moran

John Lawson was born in 1709 in Magherafelt, County Derry, in Ireland, the son of Alexander Lawson, an Anglican clergyman. Young Lawson chose to follow his father into the church and matriculated at Trinity College in Dublin on June 1, 1727. However, since his father had died in 1718 and since his family was not wealthy, Lawson entered Trinity as a sizer, which exempted him from the costs of fees and of room and board. He developed an impressive career as a student and teacher at the college, receiving his B.A. in 1731, his M.A. in 1734, and his D.D. in 1745. He was Archbishop King's Lecturer in Divinity in 1746 and also served as the school's first librarian. In 1753 he won appointment as a lecturer in oratory and history on the foundation of Erasmus Smith, a seventeenth-century London businessman who left an endowment to educate the Irish children on his estates in that nation. The fund was later expanded to endow two sets of lectures at Trinity, one in experimental philosophy, the other in oratory and history. When Lawson assumed the professorship in oratory and history, one of his duties was to deliver public lectures, which he was required to submit to the board of governors for approval before publication. Of the many people holding the Smith lectureships over the years, only Lawson and one other person, Thomas Leland, actually met the publication requirement of their positions. The title of Lawson's volume was *Lectures Concerning Oratory*, which appeared in November 1758, only three months before his death in January of the following year (Claussen and Wallace ix–xvi; Howell 616–17; Godwin).

While Lawson studied, taught, and wrote his *Lectures* there, Trinity was an important center of rhetorical study in the British Isles. The Erasmus Smith lectures on oratory were one of the oldest supports for this subject in Ireland. While a student, Lawson himself probably attended lectures on oratory by his predecessor, Robert Shawe. Lawson probably knew Edmund

Burke, who, in 1750, founded at Trinity the Academy of Belles Lettres, the first debating society in Great Britain (Claussen and Wallace xix). Since many of Trinity's students planned to become Anglican clergy, they too were interested in oratory, especially the oratory of sermons, and Lawson designed his *Lectures* to meet the needs of this group.

While not as innovative as the rhetorics of George Campbell and Hugh Blair, *Lectures Concerning Oratory* was still important. Lawson was the first member of his generation to publish his lectures on oratory, which encouraged other teachers of the period, including Blair, Campbell, and Joseph Priestley, to do likewise. As one of the best examples of neoclassical rhetoric of the period, the lectures restated classical theory, drawing particularly on the work of Plato, Aristotle, Cicero, and Quintilian, thereby stimulating interest in ancient rhetoric at a time when many theorists questioned its value. But far from simply restating previous theory, Lawson's work also addressed many of the important issues of eighteenth-century rhetoric, including the basis of argumentation and persuasion in faculty psychology; the importance of natural rather than artificial methods of delivery; and the application of rhetorical theory to pulpit oratory.

LAWSON'S RHETORICAL THEORY

Lawson's commitment to classical rhetoric was deep. He looked to classical rhetoric and its practitioners for models of the function that rhetoric could perform in eighteenth-century England. He noted that rhetoric for the ancients performed social good, as when Demosthenes warned Athenians against falling into indolence and corruption and Cicero pled for Caius Ligarius' life before Ceasar. He also believed that the study of the art could encourage rhetors to work for the social good. Lawson argued that the speaker "who employeth his Talent aright, is one of the most useful Members of the Community, infusing Principles of Religion, Humanity, and virtuous Industry in all who hear him, contributing to preserve Peace, Justice, and Harmony among Men" (9). To encourage the development of a useful rhetoric in England, Lawson presented an excellent summary of classical theory, concentrating on the works of Aristotle, Cicero, and Quintilian throughout his *Lectures*. He also devoted an entire section, Lecture 18, to a summary of Plato's *Phaedrus*, in which he emphasized the speaker's need to understand thoroughly the subject at hand in order to (1) speak to all audiences, not just the uneducated; (2) dispose of all parts of the subject in their proper places in the discourse; and (3) define the main ideas of the subject and divide it into its proper parts. Lawson accepted Plato's argument that rhetoricians must first understand the truth and then speak it as if they were talking to the gods—and that thereby rhetoricians would "speak truly and sincerely" (333). Lawson devoted the whole of Lecture 4 to an allegory about the "Palace of Eloquence" (61), where the forgotten tenets of classical rhetoric are locked away from modern speakers and writers.

Lawson believed that to rediscover ancient eloquence, moderns must turn to one of the most important methods of classical education, imitation. Using this method, the modern student would first study the works of genius of the ancients and, thereby, "transform" himself into a more eloquent speaker through practice. This borrowing from other writers is common to all writing traditions. Latin writers such as Cicero, Virgil, and Horace, Lawson noted, imitated the Greeks. All progress in the arts, including eloquence, comes not from the innovation of an isolated genius but from the imitation of earlier writers.

But to view Lawson as only restating classical theory is misleading because he modernized many of the ancient tenets by discussing them in the context of eighteenth-century philosophy and psychology. Although he organized much of his rhetoric according to four of Cicero's five arts (invention, arrangement, style, memory, and delivery), he modernized his discussions of each by placing these arts in the context of eighteenth-century thought. He noted, for instance, the importance of Aristotle's topics of invention, and he referred favorably to Bacon's call for a set of modern topics; but he did not provide an extensive list of his own. Instead, he argued the more modern position that the speaker should know the subject thoroughly through wide reading and careful examination of all sides of the issue.

When discussing arrangement, he rejected the set order of the classical speech and argued for the geometric methods of analysis and synthesis that many other eighteenth-century rhetoricians—such as Smith, Campbell, and Priestley—also advocated. The first method begins with simple elements and leads to remote truths (similar to induction); the second begins with general principles and moves to particular truths (similar to deduction). Both help the speaker avoid digressions and offer "Clearness, Strength, and Precision" of thought (132). However, Lawson also recognized the contingent nature of rhetoric, which deals with possibilities rather than absolutes. Therefore, he told his students that most of their topics would not allow full demonstration of every step. He also told them that their audiences would not be able to follow long chains of reasoning of the type that geometricians use because "the Hearer [would] not be able to bear in Mind, or recollect them" all (132). He also allowed the use of other methods of arrangement, such as short historical narrations, to break up long passages of close reasoning and refutations to attack opposing positions.

Lawson's discussion of style is also modern in that he largely rejected the classical emphasis on tropes and schemes. Like many other eighteenth-century rhetoricians, he argued that style should be simple and clear enough to "communicate our Sentiments for the Instruction or Perswasion of other Men" (187). He attacked the Asiatic style with its wordiness and preferred the Attic, which he described as "pure, terse, and properly concise" (189).

However, while the plain style may be suitable for instruction, Lawson recognized that the orator must also "*please* and *move*. He must, to Perspicuity, add Ornament" (191), which would capture and keep an audience's attention. To engage the audience's passions, the orator must also use figures of speech, which Lawson viewed not as artificial ornaments but as natural ones that communicate strong passions that the orators must feel themselves before communicating. To learn how figures appeal to the imagination and the passions, in Lectures 16 and 17 Lawson recommended that orators read poetry. But figures must be used sparingly in oratory, Lawson warned, for overuse of tropes quickly tires the audience, destroys the speaker's credibility, and obfuscates the discourse. Lawson's final pronouncement on style was that it results not from artificial tropes but from the content of the discourse: "If the Sentiments be [clear], they will quickly form to themselves a suitable Stile, clear, easy, and unaffected; preserving throughout a certain Air of Seriousness, and Sincerity, or Plainness and Probity" (409).

Lawson's discussion of delivery—which included pronunciation, gestures, and expressions—is historically important because he rejected the artificial systems of such elocutionists as James Burgh. An advocate of the natural method of delivery, Lawson grounded his discussion of this art in "*Nature*" (413). He rejected all "mechanical" theories of pronunciation which attempted to mark tones of speech similar to the way musicians mark notes of a musical score on the grounds that such a system was too hard to learn and, therefore, took time away from more important studies that created knowledge. Rather than rely on such artificial systems, the orator should learn to speak in ways that are appropriate to the rhetorical situation. To do this, Lawson recommended that students observe a variety of speakers and learn to speak extempore, as if engaged "in an animated Conversation" (418). The best way to improve speaking skills, Lawson advised, is to ask a friend to critique one's pronunciation and delivery.

One of the more modern elements of Lawson's theory is his interpretation of rhetoric in the context of eighteenth-century faculty psychology. In general, he was suspicious of systems that created faculties to explain all mental phenomena, and he rejected the argument that taste is a faculty of the mind. But he did accept other faculties. Being an Anglican minister, he argued that all the faculties—the understanding, the passions, the judgment, the memory, and the imagination—are not separate but are different operations of "the whole Soul which acts in every Case, that judges, imagines, remembers; that every Mode of Apprehension from simple Sensation up to the most abstract Reasoning, many of which we distinguish by the Names of several Faculties, are only Actions of the same Faculty of the Understanding; or more properly of the Soul exercising this Faculty" (154). Despite this philosophical distinction, Lawson based much of his explanation of rhetorical appeals on the various faculties, each of which plays a role in convincing and persuading an audience. The primary purpose of eloquence is to address the understanding because rhetoric is "the Handmaid of Truth" (127) whose primary purpose is to convince. However, given human nature, conviction is not enough to galvanize people to action; consequently, the orator must also appeal to a second faculty, the passions. All passions, according to Lawson, are based on two primal ones, desire and aversion, or love of happiness and hatred of misery. Without passions, humans would degenerate into sloth and "languish in total Inaction" (157). To cause an audience to act, the orator must engage passions by showing which actions will lead to happiness and which to misery. Passions, however primal, are subject to a third faculty, the will, which allows humans to restrain their emotions; and this restraint, according to Lawson, is the basis of all "human Liberty, and principal Source of human Virtue" (158). If human nature were perfect, the orator would only have to convince an audience by appealing to its understanding; but, human nature being imperfect, orators must often, especially when addressing an uneducated audience, appeal to the passions in order to persuade as well as convince.

One of Lawson's most important contributions to eighteenth-century rhetoric was his discussion of pulpit oratory, a significant topic for his divinity students. Lawson considered this one of the most necessary sections of his book because the ancients had not addressed this kind of discourse and because little had been written on it in English. He clearly considered the sermon one of the most important forms of discourse, as his statement about the ends of preaching suggests: "the Advancement of Piety and Virtue, by laying before Men their Duty, and engaging them in the Practice thereof" (364). To help his students prepare themselves to achieve these ends, Lawson discussed in detail the necessary preparation of ministers, on the one hand, and strategies for composing and delivering sermons on the other.

To prepare themselves for the ministry, Lawson advised, students must first master the qualities essential to preachers. They must first become virtuous because the minister's character determines how the congregation responds to the message. A person with no firm belief in religion cannot argue convincingly about the subject. Furthermore, since they must teach religious principles, preachers must be highly educated about religious matters. They must be widely read in religion, in philosophy and ethics, in polite literature, and in mathematics and geometry (to learn close reasoning). They must know not only Latin and Greek but also their native tongue, since they will address their congregations in English. Lawson viewed the ethical character of religious orators as central to their ability to communicate effectively; this reminder was important at a time when Anglican preferments were too often political rather than religious.

Lawson's comments on sermons demonstrate his assumptions that this kind of discourse should be practical and useful rather than abstract and intellectual. Ministers should not strive to be innovative because innovations lead to what Lawson considered the "extraordinary Doctrines" of many modern theologians (388). At the heart of his advice was his assumption that the congregation preached to is likely to be "illiterate" rather than "learned," or a mixture of the two. The illiterate audience, he warned, cannot follow complicated chains of reasoning, so the orator should use arguments that are "plain, consisting of few Steps, drawn from Authority, common Sense, and Experience" (393). The preacher should avoid "hazardous Conjectures, or attempting to qualify an unbounded, often presumptuous Curiosity" (369) and should emphasize, instead, plain explanations of doctrine so as not to confuse the parishioners. He should avoid discussing debated points of doctrine and emphasize, instead, the application of doctrine to behavior. As Lawson argued: "Few, if any there are, who seriously doubt, whether they ought to be temperate and just: But wherein consist these Duties; what Advantages they lead to; how we may be induced to practise them; what Motives there are to encourage, what Precepts to direct, what Temptations to avoid:—These are Articles intelligible and useful, not involved with Subtilties [*sic*], and affecting all Mankind" (319). Lawson considered such anti-intellectualism necessary for audiences that needed encouragement to act virtuously. He did not, however, assume that an illiterate audience was easy to persuade because such people, though untrained and childlike, also possess "a Fund of natural Reason . . . which enables them, so far as their Knowledge extends, to judge rightly" (31).

To speak effectively, Lawson argued, ministers must strive to achieve two goals. First, they must be clear. They must, for instance, choose a text for the sermon that is neither too long nor too difficult. The sermon growing from this text should address one subject to give it "Unity of Design" (378) and should be divided into clear heads, each of which should receive adequate explanation and proof. Lawson advised his students to state all the heads—no fewer than three and no more than five—at the beginning of the sermon, prove each head with a few carefully selected arguments in the body, remove objections by refuting other positions on the doctrine under discussion, and then restate the main points and deduce important consequences that follow from them at the end of the discourse, all the while speaking in language that is plain and clear.

The second goal is to be persuasive. Although the major appeal should be to the congregation's understanding, ministers must also rally pathetic appeals, especially when attempting to persuade their audiences to choose moral behavior. "Here it is," Lawson argued, "that you are to unfurl all the Sails, or to raise the Metaphor, that you are to pour forth the whole Storm of your Eloquence; to move, to exhort, to comfort, to terrify, to inflame, to melt. Your Thoughts, your Language, your Voice, your whole Form should be animated" (403). Such fulminations are appropriate because of the importance of the cause: saving souls from damnation by encouraging proper belief and moral behavior. By painting vice vividly, by drawing the eternal torments of hell vividly, the minister can use eloquence to save souls.

Despite his detailed advice to his theology students, Lawson did not believe that oratory was an easy art for all students to master. The reason for this difficulty was found in his concept of genius, which he defined as the natural talents that all persons possess. These talents are God-given, and each student has to discover those areas in which his genius lies. For some students genius lies in eloquence, and these few will be able to develop into excellent speakers and writers. For those devoid of genius in this area, speaking will always be difficult. But Lawson also recognized a second principle, hard work or "Application," which can help all speakers develop eloquence by reading the works of the great speakers in history and practicing what they learn from them. Nevertheless, natural ability still must exist in order for a speaker to become more than adequate.

Lawson should be viewed as an important transition figure in eighteenth-century rhetoric. By emphasizing the positive contributions of classical theory and practice, he demonstrated the importance of rhetorical theory to his own culture. He also brought classical systems to the attention of eighteenth-century rhetoricians and, thereby, encouraged them to see the limitations of those methods. But Lawson did not merely summarize classical theory; he also suggested some more modern directions for contemporary rhetoric to take: Consequently, Lawson pointed the way for the more important work of the period. Finally, by publishing his lectures, he undoubtedly encouraged other professors of rhetoric—including Campbell, Blair, and Priestley—to do the same. While not a major theorist himself, he encouraged major theorists to write and publish their more significant work.

BIBLIOGRAPHY

Primary Source

Lawson, John. *Lectures Concerning Oratory*. Dublin, 1758. Reprint. Edited by E. Neal Claussen and Karl R. Wallace. Carbondale: Southern Illinois University Press, 1972.

Biography

Godwin, Gordon. "Lawson, John." *DNB* (1986).

Criticism

Claussen, E. Neal, and Karl R. Wallace, eds. "Editors' Introduction." *Lectures Concerning Oratory*, ix–liii. Carbondale: Southern Illinois University Press, 1972.

Howell, Wilbur Samuel. *Eighteenth-Century British Logic and Rhetoric*, 616–31. Princeton: Princeton University Press, 1971.

Keesey, Ray E. "John Lawson's *Lectures Concerning Oratory.*" *Speech Monographs* 20.1 (1953): 49–57.

Warnick, Barbara. "The Bolevian Sublime in Eighteenth-Century British Rhetorical Theory." *Rhetorica* 8.4 (1990): 349–69.

THOMAS LELAND
(1722–1785)

Mae Miller

Born in Dublin in 1722, Thomas Leland received his early education from Dr. Thomas Sheridan, father of the well-known elocutionist Thomas Sheridan and grandfather of Richard Sheridan, the dramatist. Dr. Sheridan was a respected teacher, whom Jonathan Swift called "doubtless the best instructor of youth in these kingdoms, or perhaps in Europe" (216). He wrote of Sheridan's students: "Among the gentlemen of this kingdom who have any share of education, the scholars of Dr. Sheridan infinitely excel, in number and knowledge, all their brethren sent from other schools" (216–17). With this strong classical education as a foundation, Leland entered Trinity College, Dublin, in 1737. He graduated with a B.A. in 1741 and was elected a fellow in 1746.

Leland's first published work reflects his roots in the classics as he collaborated with Dr. John Stokes in a Latin translation of *The Philippic Orations of Demosthenes*, published in 1754. He reissued an English translation of this work in a complete edition in 1770, and it was frequently reprinted thereafter. In 1758, he published *The History of Philip, King of Macedon*, a two-volume work. Three years afterward, Leland was elected to the important post of Erasmus Smith Professor of Oratory and History at Trinity College. This position, inaugurated in 1724, was intended for the instruction of students in "such parts of Oratory as conduce to . . . improvement in elocution" (qtd. in Claussen xix). Thus, it was one of the first professorships with the specific goal of the instruction of university students in oratory (Claussen xviii).

Leland's appointment indicates his success in the academic world and represents his inclusion in an elite group of scholars, authors, and educators working in Dublin at this time. These educated men were greatly concerned about the role of oratory in a changing age. They expressed wide varieties of opinions, especially regarding oratory in education. In his public lectures on elocution and throughout his writings, Thomas Sheridan, for example, emphasized the importance of elocutionary skills in public speaking and writing; while John Lawson, a previous Erasmus Smith Professor of Oratory and the author of *Lectures Concerning Oratory*, disliked "any system that purported to create art by mechanical and simplistic means while ignoring nature and genius" (Claussen xxxi). All of these educators, scholars, and writers shared a similar grounding in the classics, but most were questioning the role of the classical authors in a changing world. Thomas Leland was an important member of this group as an eminent professor, minister, and writer with an established reputation as a classical scholar.

The Erasmus Smith professorship included several requirements for the furtherance of oratory in education. As specified in Trinity College documents containing details of this appointment, Leland was required to present four public lectures a year; and if approved, two of these lectures were intended for publication (Claussen xviii). He fulfilled this obligation with *A Dissertation on the Principles of Human Eloquence* (1764), a work that assumed a dual role. Leland wrote in the Advertisement for the *Dissertation* that the work was "intended originally for Young Hearers; to whom . . . they were at first addressed in another form merely to fulfill the duties of an *Academical Office*, and without intention of farther publication." On the title page, the work is described as "The substance of several Lectures read in the Oratory-School of Trinity-College, Dublin." Therefore, Leland obviously considered the work primarily to be the fulfillment of one of his duties as the professor of oratory, an academic exercise intended to instruct his students as an example of oratory. At the same time, the treatise was written as a scholarly response to an essay by William Warburton, Bishop of Gloucester, entitled *Doctrine of Grace* (1762), which considered eloquence in the inspired scriptural writings, long a subject of controversy among divines and scholars. In response to Leland's *Dissertation*, Bishop Hurd, an advocate of Warburton, published his *Letter to the Rev. Dr. Thomas Leland* (1764), which in turn prompted Leland's reply, *An Answer to a Letter to the Reverend Doctor Thomas Leland* (1765).

By his own account, Leland never intended his *Dissertation on Human Eloquence* and *Answer to a Letter* to be rhetorical handbooks for students. Indeed, in his dissertation on English rhetorical theory, Harold Harding wrote that the essays by Warburton, Hurd, and Leland "represent a chapter in the history of controversial ecclesiastical writing and in spite of a promising title do not add greatly to the body of rhetorical theory" (81). Certainly, by his two works on rhetoric, Leland did not achieve the stature as rhetorician of John Lawson, who previously occupied the Erasmus Smith chair and published *Lectures*. However, Harding continued, these works should not be neglected because of the main points of the quarrel: "First, the writers are at one in regarding rhetoric as principally a matter of style, and secondly, the learned documentation of their arguments reveals the genuine interest of the more scholarly eighteenth-century church dignitaries in the study of literary theory and criticism" (81). The conflicting discussions of rhetoric and eloquence by Leland and Warburton exemplify the varied views of eighteenth-century scholars on the proper use of these qualities in speech and writing.

LELAND'S RHETORICAL THEORY

In the essay that began the controversy, Warburton's *Doctrine of Grace*, the Bishop responded to a statement made by Dr. Conyers Middleton in his *Essay on the Gift of Tongues* (1755) that the inspired language of the Scriptures should be

pure, clear, noble, and affecting, even beyond the force of common speech, since nothing can come from God, but what is pefect in its kind. In short, the purity of Plato, and the eloquence of Cicero. Now. . .if we try the apostolic language by this rule, we shall be so far from ascribing it to God that we shall scarce think it worthy of man. . .it being utterly rude and barbarous, and abounding with every fault that can possibly deform a language. (qtd. in Warburton 1:54)

Middleton's statement led to dangerous questions about the veracity of the Scriptures. Therefore, Warburton's purpose was to refute the claim that the scriptural writings could not have come from God since they did not conform to the classical models.

The Bishop claimed that Middleton's position was founded on two false propositions: First, an inspired language must be a language of perfect eloquence; second, eloquence is "congenial and essential to human speech" (Warburton 1:55). The Bishop continued his argument by saying that "eloquence is not congenial or essential to human speech, nor is there any Archetype in nature to which that quality refers. It is accidental and arbitrary, and depends on custom and fashion. It is a mode of human communication which varys with the varying climates of the Earth; and is as inconstant as the genius, temper and manners of it's [*sic*] much diversified inhabitants" (Warburton 1:70). Thus, Warburton stated that eloquence was not a necessary quality of the Scriptures because it was not a necessary quality in any effective writing or speaking. It varied with differing conditions, making the search for a model of eloquence in the classical writers a futile quest.

Leland, on the other hand, clearly believed in an archetypal eloquence, the reflection of a higher, natural order. Certainly, he saw language as a means of establishing political and spiritual order in a changing society. In his *Dissertation on Eloquence*, he stated that the best reflection of this order was "perfect Eloquence," with words signifying clearness and truth, determined by settled rules and principles apart from fashion or custom (69). The ideal of "genuine, natural Eloquence" was determined by the man of judgment, reason, and experience, who "distinguishes between external pomp, and intrinsic greatness; . . . which stands the shock of time; prevails over all accidental changes of manners; nor is impaired by the alteration of language; but however, and whenever it is proposed to those who are qualified for judging, must always be approved and admired" (50). In Leland's view, the task of the educated man was to strive toward this "perfect Eloquence" as a way to impose order.

Leland believed that the writer and speaker should seek the highest form of eloquence, but he also insisted that eloquence was found naturally in human speech:

If then, passions and affections are naturally excited in the human breast, and have the principal influence on human actions; if they have their peculiar modes of speech, not invented for the purpose of pleasing, but arising from necessity . . . such modes as are generally called eloquent, cannot be deemed the artificial abuse of words, but are really congenial and essential to human speech. (7–8)

Used correctly, then, eloquence is the natural result of human passions and emotions. If speakers and writers feel an emotion themselves, they will naturally impart it to their hearers in the pursuit of truth. Therefore, eloquence is not accidental or arbitrary, as the Bishop claimed. It is a necessary part of speech.

Leland clearly distinguished eloquence from his definition of "rhetoric." *Eloquence* he defined simply as "that mode of speech which signifies emotion or passion in the speaker, and tends to excite them in the Hearer" (35). The word *rhetoric*, on the other hand, had mixed connotations for Leland, since he restricted it almost completely to ornaments in language. Most often, Leland attributed these ornaments to "art," which is subject to abuse and "artifice." However, used clearly and naturally, rhetorical art has its place in persuading an audience. He included an example from the Bishop's work in which rhetorical art is used effectively to convince the reader (19–20). Leland summed up the differences between eloquence and rhetoric in this way: "There is a real distinction between this natural and genuine Eloquence, the effect of exalted and enlightened thoughts, noble passions, and generous principles; and the rhetorical ornaments of style, the result of artifice and imitation" (104). For Leland, eloquence was essential to language, and "Perfect Eloquence" represented the highest form of language.

Leland's reply to Bishop Warburton's *Doctrine of Grace* is respectful and scholarly. However, the controversy got nastier with the publications of Hurd's essay and Leland's subsequent reply. Leland's barely civil answer to Hurd is entertaining, but it offers very little material different from his original *Dissertation*. Much of the document is devoted to a discussion of whether inspiration was given to apostolical writers in single terms or idiom. In *Answer* he reiterated his distinction between perfect eloquence, which he called "chaste," and "rhetorical art," which he claimed "has not the least share in our debate" (42).

Although these works show the interest of eighteenth-century scholars in rhetorical studies, Leland's failure to publish a true rhetoric diminished his contribution to the study of oratory in his time, nor have these essays had much influence on later studies. His best offering to literary history is widely acknowledged to be the publication of the *History of Ireland* in three volumes quarto in 1773. This work was criticized at the time but later gained more respect, becoming a classic history of the country. Leland also contributed greatly to Irish history in his purchase of the very important medieval Irish manuscript, the *Annals of Loch Ce*, which he donated to the library at Trinity College. In his long career, Leland was a leader in many fields of literature. Therefore, although his rhetorical contribution is not extensive, his works deserve consideration.

BIBLIOGRAPHY

Primary Sources

Leland, Thomas. *A Dissertation on the Principles of Human Eloquence*. London, 1764.
————. *An Answer to a Letter to the Reverend Doctor Thomas Leland*. London, 1765.
————. *The History of Ireland*. Dublin, 1773.
————. *The History of the Life and Reign of Philip, King of Macedon*. London, 1806.
————. *Orations of Demosthenes*. New York: Colonial Press, 1900.
————. *Sermons on Various Subjects*. Dublin, 1788.

Biography

"Leland, Thomas." *Allibone's Dictionary of Authors*. Edited by S. Austin Allibone. Vol. 1. Philadelphia: J. P. Lippincott, 1897.
Moore, Norman. "Leland, Thomas." *DNB* (1964).

Criticism

Claussen, E. Neal, and Karl R. Wallace, eds. "Foreword." *Lectures Concerning Oratory*. By John Lawson, ix–liii. Carbondale: Southern Illinois University Press, 1972.
Disraeli, Isaac. *Quarrels of Authors*. Vol. I. London, 1814.
Harding, Harold F. "English Rhetorical Theory, 1750–1800." Ph.D. diss., Cornell University, 1937.
Hurd, Richard. *The Works of Richard Hurd, D.D.* Vol. 8. New York: AMS Press, 1967.
Nichols, John, ed. *Literary Anecdotes of the Eighteenth Century*. Vol. 8. New York: AMS Press, 1966.
Swift, Jonathan. *Miscellaneous and Autobiographical Pieces, Fragments and Marginalia*. Vol. 5 of *The Works of Jonathan Swift*. Edited by Herbert Davis. Oxford: Basil Blackwell, 1962.
Warburton, William. *The Doctrine of Grace*. Vol. 1. London, 1763.

JOHN LOCKE
(1632–1704)

William Walker

John Locke was born at Wrington, Somerset, and raised at Belluton house, near the village of Pensford. He was the first son of the Puritans John Locke, an attorney and clerk to the Justices of Peace, and Agnes Keene, a tanner's daughter who was ten years older than her husband. When Locke was fifteen years old, Colonel Alexander Popham, under whom Locke's father had served in the Parliamentarian army as captain, nominated him to Westminster School, whose Master was the great Royalist pedagogue, Richard Busby. Locke was admitted and spent the next five years there mainly reading the classics (the last three years as a King's Scholar). In the spring of 1652, he was elected to a studentship at Christ Church, Oxford; he took his B.A. in 1656 and, upon receiving his M.A. in 1658, was elected Senior Student of Christ Church. After the Restoration, he held the positions of Lecturer in Greek, Lecturer in Rhetoric, and Senior Censor; but he also pursued studies in science and medicine at both the university and the house of the chemist, Robert Boyle. This stay at Oxford was broken by a brief diplomatic mission to Cleves in 1665. On his return, Locke continued his scientific studies in Oxford in collaboration with both Boyle and the accomplished physician, Thomas Sydenham. He also happened to meet Lord Anthony Ashley Cooper (afterward First Earl of Shaftesbury) and, by the spring of 1667, was residing with him in London as his personal physician.

In London, Locke became involved in several of Shaftesbury's financial and colonial schemes, wrote drafts of what became *An Essay concerning Human Understanding*, and began to suffer from the respiratory problems that bothered him the rest of his life. After receiving a bachelor's degree in medicine from Oxford in 1675, he left for France and did not return until 1679 when London was embroiled in the Popish plot, which Shaftesbury was shaping into the exclusion crisis. Locke served Shaftesbury in the affair, and it is highly probable that he wrote *Two Treatises of Government* on this occasion, rather than on the occasion of the Glorious Revolution. As an ally of Shaftesbury, Locke was at risk when the scheme to exclude Charles's Catholic brother James from the succession failed and Shaftesbury, after being charged with high treason and acquitted, had, late in 1682 fled to Holland, where he died early in 1683—Locke himself fled to Holland later that year. During his five years in Holland, Locke revised the *Essay*, wrote the *Epistola de Tolerantia*, and composed letters to his friend Edward Clarke, which in 1693 were published in a revised form as *Some Thoughts concerning Education*. Having been deprived of his studentship at Oxford by Charles and named as a traitor under James, Locke spent some of this time in hiding and under a false name, "Dr. van der Linden." He returned to England, fifty-six years old, with Queen Mary early in 1689, the year in which *Two Treatises of Government*, the *Epistola de Tolerantia*, and *A Letter concerning Toleration* (William Popple's English translation of the *Epistola*) were anonymously published.

He spent two years in London before moving in with Sir Francis and Lady Masham at Oates in Essex, Lady Masham being the daughter of the Cambridge Platonist, Ralph Cudworth, and a woman with whom Locke had formed a brief romantic attachment ten years earlier. Up until 1700, Locke divided his working hours between his administrative duties (he was Commissioner of Appeals and Commissioner of Trade) and his writing. Besides maintaining correspondence with his friends, revising *An Essay concerning Human Understanding* (the first edition of which was published in 1690), and publishing an old manuscript on interest rates and money in 1691, Locke publicly defended his views: he published several extensive responses to Edward Stillingfleet, Bishop of Worcester's criticism of the *Essay*, Jonas Proast's criticism of *A Letter concerning Toleration*, and John Edwards' criticism of *The Reasonableness of Christianity*, which Locke had published anonymously in 1695. In his final years, he wrote and prepared for publication an extensive commentary on the epistles of Paul, which was published in 1705–1707, two years after his death. A frugal man who invested in several trading companies and the Bank of England, Locke had amassed an estate worth close to £20,000, most of which he bequeathed to the Masham's son, Francis, and his cousin, Peter King, though he also remembered his friends, his servants, and the poor.

LOCKE'S RHETORICAL THEORY

Locke may seem out of place in a volume on rhetoric, given that his best known statement on the subject is the following passage from *An Essay concerning Human Understanding*:

Since Wit and Fancy finds easier entertainment in the World, than dry Truth and real Knowledge, *figurative Speeches*, and allusion in Language, will hardly be admitted, as *an* imperfection or *abuse* of it. I confess, in Discourses, where we seek rather Pleasure and Delight, than information and Improvement, such Ornaments as are borrowed from them, can scarce pass for Faults. But yet, if we would speak of things as they are, we must allow, that all the Art of Rhetorick, besides Order and Clearness, all the artificial and figurative application of Words Eloquence hath invented, are for nothing else but to insinuate wrong *Ideas*, move the Passions, and thereby mislead the Judgment; and so indeed are perfect cheat: And therefore however laudable or allowable Oratory may render them in Harangues and popular Addresses, they are certainly, in all Discourses that pretend to inform or instruct, wholly to be avoided; and where Truth and Knowledge are concerned, cannot but be thought a great fault, either of the Languge or Person that makes use of them. What, and how various they are, will be superfluous here to take notice; the Books of Rhetorick which abound in the world, will instruct those, who want to be informed: Only I cannot but observe, how little the preservation and improvement of Truth and Knowledge, is the Care and Concern of Mankind; since the Arts of Fallacy are endow'd and preferred. 'Tis evident how much Men love to deceive, and be deceived, since Rhetorick, that powerful instrument of Error and Deceit, has its established Professors, is publickly taught, and has always been had in great Reputation: And, I doubt not, but it will be thought great boldness, if not brutality in me, to have said thus much against it. *Eloquence*, like the fair Sex, has too prevailing Beauties in it, to suffer it self ever to be spoken against. And 'tis in vain to find fault with those Arts of Deceiving, wherein Men find pleasure to be Deceived. (508)

Locke's statement on rhetoric is, however, much more complex than this passage has generally led historians of rhetoric and literature to believe. For in describing several mental activities in the *Essay*, Locke described the structure of specific tropes. Consider, for example, his account of perception:

We are farther to consider concerning Perception, that the *Ideas we receive by sensation, are often* in grown People *alter'd by the Judgment*, without our taking notice of it. When we set before our Eyes a round Globe, of any uniform colour, *v.g.* [*sic*] Gold, Alabaster, or Jet, 'tis certain, that the *Idea* thereby imprinted in our Mind, is of a flat Circle variously shadow'd, with several degrees of Light and Brightness coming to our Eyes. But we having by use been accustomed to perceive, what kind of appearance convex Bodies are wont to make in us; what alterations are made in the reflections of Light, by the difference of the sensible Figures of Bodies, the Judgment presently, by an habitual custom, alters the Appearances into their Causes: So that from that, which truly is variety of shadow or colour, collecting the Figure, it makes it pass for a mark of figure, and frames to it self the perception of a convex Figure, and an uniform Colour; when the *Idea* we receive from thence, is only a Plain variously colour'd, as is evident in Painting. (145)

Locke was here describing a form of substitution: the idea of a sphere, an idea of judgment, takes the place of the idea of a circle, an idea of sensation. And since, according to Locke, the sphere is the cause of the circle, the cause of what appears as a circle, an idea of a cause is being substituted for

an idea of an effect of that cause. Now, if the substitution of the *name* of
a cause for the *name* of an effect is a metonymy, it follows that the structure
of the substitution of *ideas* here described by Locke is that of metonymy.
That is to say, Locke identified as a metonymy, in all but name, the substitution of ideas that can occur in the act of perception. Leibniz, in his treatment of this passage in *Nouveaux essais sur l'entendement humain*, his great
commentary on the *Essay*, simply added the name: in the case of the painting
mentioned by Locke that makes us think we see directly that which causes
the image, Leibniz's spokesman Théophile claims, "There is, at the same
time, a metonymy and a metaphor in our judgments" (Leibniz 134–35).

Locke continued to describe the structures of substitution that define
specific tropes in his account of both other mental *actions*, such as the association of ideas, and the formation of specific *concepts*, such as substance,
space, time, and infinity. His account of the idea of infinity, for example, is
essentially an account of an imperfect synecdoche: the ideas that the mind
takes to be its idea of infinity are only ideas of finite parts of a whole that
is intimated through the idea of the mind's power to repeat and conjoin its
ideas. And his account of substance is clearly an account of a kind of metonymy: the mind takes a set of ideas that it observes to constantly cluster
together to be the effect of a cause (substance); the mind's postulation of
this cause is only the effect of its having those ideas. The reason that there
can be this major, but not explicitly announced, analogy in the *Essay* between structures of ideational substitution and such structures of linguistic
substitution as metonymy and metaphor is that Locke understood ideas to
be not only the meanings of words but also *signs*. Because Locke saw both
ideas and words as signs, his descriptions of their substitutions appear to
correspond in important respects to the accounts in rhetorical tradition of
substitution of words. Although he condemned as instruments of deceit the
substitutions that define tropes, Locke was continually describing them in
his account of how the mind thinks and of the specific concepts that it
produces. As Locke explained in his *Essay*, the trope is not simply something
that men use to deceive men; it is a model for the various substitutions of
ideas that are involved in various kinds of mental actions and productions.
As such, it is the model of error, since most of the tropological substitutions
of ideas described by Locke result in bogus concepts, such as the ideas of
infinity and substance, and epistemologically pernicious processes, such as
the association of ideas and sensory perception infected by judgment
(though Locke also suggested that there was some pragmatic value to this
infection). But as a model for this kind of error, the trope is not an *instrument* of deceit; it is simply the *analogue* for certain kinds of mental errors.

Besides offering instruments of deceit and models of mental errors, rhetoric also offers a means of transmitting knowledge. This is evident even in
Locke's condemnation of rhetoric in his *Essay*, where he claimed that "all
the Art of Rhetorick, *besides Order and Clearness*, all the artificial and fig-

urative application of Words Eloquence hath invented" is for nothing else but to deceive (508). Order and clearness—cardinal Enlightenment virtues of style—are here placed alongside the figurative application of words as accomplishments *within* the art of rhetoric (as they are in the rhetorical manuals of Aristotle, Cicero, and Quintilian). Although men may use the art of rhetoric to deceive other men, they may also use it to achieve order and clarity in what they are saying—and, thus, instruct others. Moreover, the figurative application of words itself may serve this purpose, as Locke explains in the following passage from the opening chapter of Book 3 of his *Essay*:

It may also lead us a little towards the Original of all our Notions and Knowledge, if we remark, how great a dependance our *Words* have on common sensible *Ideas*; and how those, which are made use of to stand for Actions and Notions quite re-moved from sense, *have their rise from thence, and from obvious sensible* Ideas *are transferred to more abstruse significations*, and made to stand for *Ideas* that come not under the cognizance of our senses; *v.g.* [*sic*] to *Imagine, Apprehend, Comprehend, Adhere, Conceive, Instill, Disgust, Disturbance, Tranquillity*, etc. are all Words taken from the Operations of sensible Things, and applied to certain Modes of Thinking. *Spirit*, in its primary signification, is Breath; *Angel*, a Messenger: And I doubt not, but if we could trace them to their sources, we should find, in all Languages, the names which stand for Things that fall not under our Senses, to have had their first rise from sensible *Ideas*. By which we may give some kind of guess, what kind of Notions they were, and whence derived, which filled their minds, who were the first Beginners of Languages; and how Nature, even in the naming of Things, unawares suggested to Men the Originals and Principles of all their Knowledge: whilst, to give names, that might make known to others any Operations they felt in themselves, or any other *Ideas*, that came not under their Senses, they were fain to borrow Words from ordinary known *Ideas* of Sensation, by that means to make others the more easily to conceive those Operations they experimented in themselves, which made no outward sensible appearances; and then when they had got known and agreed Names, to signify those internal operations of their own Minds, they were sufficiently fur-nished to make known by Words, all their other *Ideas*; since they could consist of nothing, but either of outward sensible Perceptions, or of the inward Operations of their Minds about them; we having, as has been proved, no *Ideas* at all, but what originally come either from sensible objects without, or what we feel within our selves, from the inward Workings of our own Spirits, which we are conscious to our selves of within. (403–4)

This passage is fruitfully understood as the empiricist elaboration of Ci-cero's general claim, in the third book of *The Making of an Orator*, that when man first began to use language, the lack of terms necessitated met-aphorical usage. For Locke here asserted that many words that were origi-nally used to stand for ideas derived from the sensation of outward objects were and still are used for representing ideas derived from the mind's per-ception of its own operations (what he elsewhere in the *Essay* called "ideas of reflection"). That is to say, many terms have been *transferred* from a sensible idea to an abstruse idea, *taken from* a sensible idea and *applied to* an idea of a mode of thinking, *borrowed from* a sensible idea and used to stand for an idea of a mental operation. And these transfers and borrowings seem to have been necessary because the first terms were for ideas of sensation and there were no spare terms that might be used to designate ideas of reflection. Since tropes are defined in terms of this kind of borrowing and transference, it is reasonable to say that Locke was here simply claiming that all terms that stand for ideas of reflection are—or, at least, were originally—tropes. And, again, though Locke did not use technical rhetorical terminology to describe these linguistic borrowings and transfers, Leibniz recognized that tropes were what Locke was discussing: in *Nouveaux essais*, Théophile considers prepositions, all of which are "taken from place, distance, and movement, and then transferred to all sorts of changes, orders, inferences [*suites*], differences, and situations [*convenances*]." This kind of transference, he adds, is an example of the "analogy between sensible and insensible things which has served as the foundation of tropes" (277). "Metaphors, synecdoches, and metonymies," he observes a few pages later, "transferred [*ont fait passer*] words from one signification to another, in such a way that the route of this transference can not always be traced" (283).

It is important to observe here that Locke did not cite the tropological nature and history of all terms for ideas of reflection as grounds for condemning them; on the contrary, he claimed that these borrowings and transfers (1) helped "make known to others" ideas of reflection, (2) made "others the more easily to conceive" the speakers' perceptions of their own minds, and (3) made "known by Words" ideas other than those derived from sensation (403–4). That is to say, Locke was here granting a positive epistemological function to at least some of those borrowings that, even though *he* did not, the rhetoricians and Leibniz named tropes. In short, he was claiming, as Aristotle did in his *Rhetoric*, that some tropes *instruct*. Besides (1) identifying the figurative application of words as things that persons use to please, deceive, and arouse the passions of others and (2) implicitly invoking words as models of mental errors and careless linguistic usage, Locke tacitly affirmed the value of words in relation to what he identified as the principal function of language: the communication of thoughts (405).

Like his treatment of figures and tropes, Locke's treatment of persuasion in his *Essay* is complex and somewhat misleading. The term *persuasion* is firmly established in this work as one of the names for *belief* of varying strengths, which Locke explicitly identified as a different kind of thing than *knowledge*. This explicit differentiation in *kind*, however, is challenged by explicit statements such as the following: "*Probabilities* [sometimes] rise so near to *Certainty*, that they govern our Thoughts as absolutely, and influence all our Actions as fully, as the most evident demonstration: and in what concerns us, we make little or no difference between them and certain Knowledge: our Belief thus grounded, rises to *Assurance*" (662). The *Essay*'s pervasive representation of ideas and words as material objects that strike the mind with different amounts of force and which compel or correspond with varying amounts of belief reinforces this conception of the difference between belief and knowledge as a difference in degree or amount: knowledge, as a mental state, is simply a high degree, a great amount of belief. If *persuasion* is the proper term for all degrees and strengths of belief, and if knowledge, as a mental state, is simply one degree or amount of belief (a strong belief, a relatively large amount of belief), then *persuasion* is the proper term for both belief and knowledge. And though Locke did not in this work provide instructions concerning how to praise or change other people's beliefs, or get them to do certain things, he did describe how the visible connection of ideas, the force of words, and the force of ideas, custom, desire, passion, and fashion govern the persuasions of the mind, which range from the weakest belief to the certainty that defines knowledge. Because Locke's epistemological writing identifies belief and knowledge as persuasion and gives an account of what governs it, that writing is reasonably understood as a theory of persuasion.

The complex attitude toward rhetoric that Locke articulated in his *Essay* is also evident in his educational writings. In *Some Thoughts concerning Education* (1693), Locke ranked learning, including rhetoric and grammar, behind virtue, wisdom, and breeding in his list of the four things a gentleman's son should have. He was evasive concerning whether or not all gentlemen need to be taught grammar and rhetoric and claimed to have said so little of rhetoric and logic "because of the little advantage young People receive by them. For I have seldom or never observed any one to get the Skill of reasoning well, or speaking handsomly by studying those rules, which pretend to teach it" (296). In keeping with this criticism of the rules of logic and rhetoric, in particular and his rejection of rules in favor of *example*, in general, Locke condemned the practice of teaching rhetoric, "as if the Names of the Figures, that embellish'd the discourses of those who understood the Art of Speaking, were the very Art and Skill of Speaking well. This, as all other things of Practice, is to be learn'd, not by a few, or a great many Rules given; But by Exercise and Application according to good rules, or rather Patterns, till Habits are got, and a facility of doing it well" (298). He later asked, "Would it not be very unreasonable to require of a learned Country School-Master (who has all the Tropes and Figures in *Farnaby's Rhetorick* at his Fingers' ends) to teach his Scholar to express himself handsomly in *English*, when it appears to be so little his Business or Thought, that the Boy's Mother (despised, 'tis like, as illiterate for not having read a system of *Logick* and *Rhetorick*) out-does him in it?" (299–300). Locke's refusal in his *Essay* to name the substitutions he described as tropes here finds its complement, and perhaps rationale, in an explicit scorn of those names and the books that cataloged them.

Yet Locke also claimed in this work that "there can scarce be a greater Defect in a Gentleman, than not to express himself well either in Writing or Speaking" (297–98). What Locke meant by speaking and writing well was not speaking and writing literally but speaking and writing in accordance with the Ciceronian ideal of eloquence. To prevent this defect of poor expression, Locke advised, "Let him [your son] be conversant in *Tully*, to give him the true *Idea* of *Eloquence*, and let him read those things that are well writ in *English*, to perfect his Style in the purity of our Language" (296). He later specified that a child is taught to speak well by first being taught to tell tales:

The Fables of *Aesop*, the only Book almost that I know fit for children, may afford them Matter for this Exercise of writing *English*, as well as for reading and translating to enter them in the *Latin* Tongue. When they are got past the Faults of Grammar, and can joyn in a continued coherent discourse the several parts of a Story, without Bald and Unhandsom [*sic*] forms of Transition (as is usual) often repeated, he that desires to perfect them yet farther in this, which is the first step to speaking well, and needs no invention, may have recourse to *Tully*, and by putting in Practice those Rules which that Master of Eloquence gives in his First Book *De Inventione*, p 20. make them know wherein the Skill and Graces of an handsom [*sic*] Narrative, according to the several Subjects and Designs of it, lie. (298)

After having achieved "a tolerable Narrative Stile," children should be taught to write letters: "When they are perfect in this [telling tales], they may, to raise their Thoughts, have set before them the Example of *Voitures* for the entertainment of their Friends at a distance with Letters of Complement, Mirth, Raylery or Diversion; and *Tully's Epistles* as the best Pattern, whether for Business or Conversation" (299).

Given this firm recommendation of not only Cicero's letters and his works on rhetoric but also the work in which he entrenched eloquence in civic duty, *On Duties* (294), it can hardly be said that Locke condemned rhetoric and eloquence in his educational writings. Just as Cicero in this latter work affirmed and claimed for himself "what is proper to an orator, that [he] speak suitably, clearly and elegantly" (2), Locke strongly asserted the importance of speaking and writing well, where this consisted in speaking "clearly and perswasively in any Business," speaking with "facility, clearness, and elegancy," and, in the case of letters, writing "without any incoherence, confusion or roughness" (299–301). In making this assertion, Locke was not calling for a strictly literal, nonfigurative linguistic usage, but one whose figurative application of words would be, like Cicero's, answerable to the demands of elegance, clarity, and persuasiveness. What Locke was condemning was the Ciceronian view of how to teach a gentleman's son to

speak and write well—namely, the view that speaking and writing well could
be taught simply by giving someone rules and a rhetorical handbook that
named and defined the tropes and figures. That is to say, Locke condemned
the books of rhetoric, not because he thought they were about a useless and
pernicious practice, but because he thought they were ineffective educational
tools. Although providing rules, such as those set forth by Cicero in *De
Inventione*, may be of some help, it was primarily by providing examples of
good speaking and writing and by having the gentleman's son imitate them
that one taught him how to speak and write well, that is, how to speak and
write like Cicero.

In addition to teaching the gentleman's son by providing him examples
for imitation, his tutor and parents could instruct him through a practice
that may well be described in terms of the three means of persuasion that
Aristotle identified in his *Rhetoric: logos, ethos,* and *pathos.* "A gentle Perswasion [*sic*] in Reasoning" would, according to Locke, in most cases do
much better in instructing and setting the will right than the interposition
of authority and command. This persuasion through reasoning, he claimed,
"must be suited to the Child's Capacity and Apprehension"; children must
be "convinced . . . by such *Reasons* as their Age and Understanding are capable of, and those proposed always *in* very *few and plain Words*"; "the
Reasons that move them must be *obvious*, and level to their Thoughts, and
such as may (if I may so say) be felt, and touched" (180–81). In giving
such advice, Locke might well have cited Aristotle's account of *logos* early
in the latter's *Rhetoric*. For in explaining the value of rhetoric as the art of
persuasion, Aristotle claimed that "even if our speaker had the most accurate
scientific information, still there are persons whom he could not readily
persuade with scientific arguments. True instruction, by the method of logic,
is here impossible; the speaker must frame his proofs and arguments with
the help of common knowledge and accepted opinions" (6). Besides using
what Aristotle would call *logos* to instruct the child—reason framed with the
help of what a child may be expected to know—the parents and tutors of
a gentleman's son, according to Locke, could also use some tactics that
Aristotle considered under the rubric of *ethos*. In speaking to children, Locke
advised, "you should make them sensible by the Mildness of your Carriage,
and the Composure even in your Correction of them, that what you do is
reasonable in you, and useful and necessary for them: And that it is not out
of *Caprichio*, Passion, or Fancy, that you command or forbid them any
Thing" (181). That is to say, by representing himself or herself as a certain
kind of person (one who is reasonable, mild, composed) the teacher can
convince children of various things. Finally, Locke identified the appeal to
the passions, what Aristotle called *pathos*, as a means of educating a gentleman's son. The pride that children have in being treated as rational creatures
"should be cherished in them, and as much as can be, made the greatest
instrument to turn them by" (181). Besides pride, love and fear, implanted

in a boy though a combination of severity and tenderness towards him, could be addressed in order to educate him: "*Reverence*, which is always afterwards carefully to be continued, and maintained in both Parts of it, *Love*, and *Fear*, [is] the great Principle, whereby you will always have hold upon him, to turn his Mind to the Ways of Vertue, and Honour" (205). The tutor and parents of a boy could, by addressing themselves in speech, among other ways, to the love and fear that they have implanted in him, instruct him and mould his character and action. Thus, though Locke emphasized example, he also quietly recommended persuasion as a means of education (for Aristotle, example itself fell under *logos* as a means of persuasion). Speaking in a way that appeals to the child's reason, speaking in a way that reveals one's character to be one of probity, and speaking in a way that appeals to the child's passions were recommended by Locke as efficient means of instruction. The pedagogy recommended by *Some Thoughts concerning Education* is, in part, the practice of persuasion as *logos*, *ethos*, and *pathos*.

This pedagogical sanctioning of rhetoric is evident in *Of the Conduct of the Understanding*, a long piece that Locke wrote in the late 1690s as an additional chapter to the *Essay*. He failed to include it in the fourth edition of 1700, however, and it was first published in the posthumous works of 1706. Here again we find explicit criticism of rhetoric, where rhetoric is the practice of arguing on both sides of a question by drawing arguments from the topics of argument listed by Aristotle and Cicero (38), using similes and metaphors to explain things to ourselves (72–73), and using "deceitful ornaments of speech" (93). But the ability of arguing on both sides of a question seems to be affirmed by Locke when he said that, in cases that are not capable of demonstration, all the arguments on both sides must be "examined and brought to a balance" (40). And the criticism directed against simile under the heading "Simile" is highly unstable. For it seems that similes, metaphors, and allegories are useful in teaching and instructing others: similes "may be a good way and useful in the explaining our thoughts to others" (72). Later in this section, he claimed, "Figured and metaphorical expressions do well to illustrate more abstruse and unfamiliar ideas which the mind is not yet thoroughly accustomed to but then they must be made use of to illustrate ideas that we already have, not to paint to us those which we yet have not. Such borrowed and allusive ideas may follow real and solid truth, to set it off when found, but must by no means be set in its place and taken for it" (73). As in his *Essay* where he used the term *abstruse* to refer to those ideas of reflection that are communicated to others by means of a term borrowed from an idea of sensation, so here Locke used *abstruse* to describe those ideas that the mind illustrates to itself and others by means of figured and metaphorical expressions. Although he identified the rhetorical figures as things that might be used to deceive others and as ways of speaking that cannot help us attain new ideas and knowledge, Locke also claimed that they might be used to explain and illustrate our ideas both to ourselves and others. He was thus restating Thomas Sprat who, in his *History of the Royal Society*, wrote that the "Ornaments of speaking" were "at first" used by wise men "to represent *Truth*, cloth'd with Bodies; and to bring *Knowledg* back again to our very senses, from whence [*sic*] it was at first deriv'd to our understandings" (112). Both were making Aristotle's point concerning good and useful things, such as strength, health, wealth, military skill, *and* rhetoric: "Rightly employed, they work the greatest blessings; and wrongly employed, they work the utmost harm" (6).

Locke affirmed rhetoric more directly in one of his principal political writings, *A Letter concerning Toleration*. In considering the relation between religious belief (faith) and the magistrate's force, Locke invoked the concept of persuasion as belief of varying strengths expressed in his *Essay*. Locke here identified religious belief and faith as forms of persuasion (perhaps alluding to Romans 14:5, "Let every man be fully persuaded in his own mind"): "All the Life and Power of true Religion consists in the inward and full perswasion of the mind; and Faith is not Faith without believing" (26). And, again: "True and saving Religion consists in the inward perswasion of the Mind, without which nothing can be acceptable to God" (27). But the identification of religious belief as persuasion in *Toleration* led Locke to make a move which he did not make in his *Essay*:

Oh that our Ecclesiastical Orators, of every Sect, would apply themselves with all the strength of Arguments that they are able, to the confounding of mens Errors! But let them spare their Persons. Let them not supply their want of Reasons with the Instruments of Force, which belong to another Jurisdiction, and do ill become a Churchman's Hands. Let them not call in the Magistrate's Authority to the aid of their Eloquence, or Learning; lest, perhaps, whilst they pretend only Love for the Truth, this their intemperate Zeal, breathing nothing but Fire and Sword, betray their Ambition, and shew that what they desire is Temporal dominion. (34–35)

Here, and elsewhere in the *Letter*, Locke explicitly affirmed oratory and eloquence, as distinct from material force, as proper means of addressing religious belief—belief as persuasion is properly addressed by persuasion as eloquence. This claim that belief as persuasion is legitimately addressed by eloquence is not without a noteworthy implication when conjoined with the implicit claim of his *Essay* that both belief and knowledge are forms of persuasion: it is that eloquence legitimately addresses knowledge, that eloquence is sanctioned even "where Truth and Knowledge are concerned." In his *Letter*, Locke explicitly affirmed eloquence as a means of addressing inner persuasion; and, in conjunction with the categorization, in his *Essay*, of belief and knowledge as different strengths of inner persuasion, he sanctioned "all the artificial and figurative application of Words Eloquence hath invented" in epistemological discourse.

These observations demonstrate how mistaken it is to claim, as many have, that Locke's statement on rhetoric is an uncompromising negation and that, more generally, a central dimension of Restoration culture is defined by this negation. It is true that Locke condemned rhetoric in many ways throughout his writings: he condemned the tropes and figures for being instruments of error and deceit, he condemned the practice of teaching the topics of argument as an inefficient means of teaching how to find the truth, and he condemned the practice of making students read rhetorical handbooks as an inefficient way of teaching them how to write and speak well. But these condemnations do not amount to a condemnation of rhetoric in toto. Even in his most celebrated attack on rhetoric, he conceded that in discourses that aspire to be beautiful and to give pleasure and delight, figurative speeches are no fault. More importantly, he parenthetically noted that the art of rhetoric can be called upon to achieve order and clarity—the stylistic desiderata of discourses where truth and knowledge are concerned. Elsewhere in his *Essay*, Locke presented a critique of some concepts, mental operations, and linguistic usages—a critique that may reasonably be said to be rhetorical in that Locke described the things critiqued as tropological substitutions: although Locke did not explicitly recognize this, Leibniz and other eighteenth-century commentators did. In addition, his epistemology may reasonably be described as a theory of persuasion since it ultimately identifies both belief and knowledge as forms of persuasion, where, on the one hand, persuasion is any degree, amount, or quantity of belief, and, on the other, the determinants of persuasion are passion, interest, fashion, habit, words, and ideas. Moreover, in both his *Essay* and his political and educational writings, Locke affirmed the figurative application of words as a means of communicating thoughts, of instructing, and of educating. Finally, he recommended rhetoric—in the form of a particular practice of persuasion—in the context of both educating the sons of gentlemen and addressing religious beliefs that are thought to be mistaken. Locke's condemnation of the figurative use of words and the practice of persuasion, then, is deeply qualified by the often implicit ways in which he affirmed them (these observations concerning what Locke said *about* rhetoric should be supplemented by observations, made by John Richetti and others, concerning Locke's practice of persuasion and his extensive use of the tropes and figures in his own writing).

Locke's influence on eighteenth-century thinking about trope and persuasion is powerful and complex. Because those works that Locke explicitly identified as works on rhetoric were written within the context of a general theory of ideas and a faculty psychology, Locke, as one of the major proponents of this theory and psychology, must be seen as a foundational figure for these works: he set the terms within which much of what explicitly identifies itself as rhetorical theory proceeds. In addition, many of his positions on more specific issues have been precedents for the writings of those who have explicitly identified themselves as students of rhetoric. Locke's condemnation of figurative language, for example, was a clear precedent for the condemnation of figurative language that was a staple of many eighteenth-century rhetoricians, though their grounds for condemning figurative language were often not epistemological but aesthetic—Adam Smith, Joseph Priestley, and David Hume, for example, were critical of figurative language, not so much because it was epistemologically pernicious, but because it was vulgar and ugly. Moreover, as Wilbur Samuel Howell has observed, the authority of Locke was called upon by the "new rhetoricians," such as Smith, Hugh Blair, and George Campbell, when they condemned the topics of argument and the syllogism, gave more attention to nonartistic proofs, called for a plain style, and made instruction (besides persuasion) the subject of rhetorical study.

But in gauging Locke's influence on eighteenth-century writing on tropes and persuasion, it is crucial to understand that much of this writing presented itself not as rhetorical theory but as aesthetics (belles lettres), philosophy, psychology, and etymology. If rhetorical studies are taken to include the study of tropes in certain texts and the various effects they have, then a significant portion of eighteenth-century epistemological writing may be said to be a form of rhetorical study, since one of its preoccupations was with metaphor, more specifically, metaphor in the text of philosophy. Leibniz, Thomas Reid, and Dugald Stewart, for example, all made Locke's point (a point made from Plato onwards) concerning the epistemological dangers of figurative language, but they also observed that Locke's own epistemological discourse was pervasively figurative and that his account of knowledge was, therefore, defective. This procedure of observing the master metaphors of Locke's text and the ways in which they govern (and corrupt) his account of knowledge has, in fact, been a principal mode of not just eighteenth-century writers on Locke but nineteenth-century commentators on him, such as T. H. Green, as well as twentieth-century historians of philosophy, such as Gilbert Ryle and Richard Rorty. A principal mode of the entire philosophical commentary on Locke may thus reasonably be said to be rhetorical in that it has focused on metaphor and its implications in Locke's epistemological text. A second way in which eighteenth-century philosophical commentary is implicitly a mode of rhetorical investigation is, as Harold Bloom has observed, in its elaboration of Locke's account of the association of ideas. For the eighteenth-century men of letters, such as David Hume and David Hartley, who wrote on associationism under the auspices of philosophy, followed Locke in observing that the structures of the substitution of ideas in mental processes, such as association, are the same as the structure of specific tropes. Eighteenth-century epistemology and philosophical writing on associationist psychology were powerfully influenced by Locke's account of the association of ideas in a chapter that he added to the fourth edition of his *Essay*: both are forms of rhetorical study.

Aesthetics and etymology are two further eighteenth-century sites of thinking about tropes and persuasion. Association was extensively discussed in writings that authors identified as works on the beautiful, the sublime, criticism, imitation, and genius (what was called "aesthetics" during the eighteenth century). In these discussions, Locke's presence is strong, and the rhetorical dimension of association is much more explicitly articulated. As Martin Kallich has observed, tropes and figures of speech were discussed with respect to the association of ideas by Francis Hutcheson, Richard Hurd, John Baillie, George Turnbull, Hugh Blair, and Joseph Priestley. In connection with eighteenth-century aesthetics, it should also be observed that, besides Locke's statement on association, his account of the distinction between primary and secondary qualities and the distinction between wit and judgment became virtually axiomatic. These doctrines significantly mark the eighteenth-century discussion of tropes and figures as dimensions of the literary text. Eighteenth-century etymology was a site of rhetorical study in the 1700s because the study of tropes was part of rhetorical study and the goal of this etymology was to identify and catalog the tropes that constituted abstract discourse (the discourse of theology, metaphysics, and epistemology). Locke again seems to have exercised considerable authority over this mode of rhetorical study since, as Hans Aarsleff has put it, the passage from Locke's *Essay*, quoted above, concerning the tropological origins of all terms for ideas of reflection "became the unquestioned rationale for all etymological searching for the history of thought" (31). That is to say, Locke's implicit description of tropes functioned as an authorization in the work of not only Étienne Bonnot de Condillac, Anne Robert, Jacques Turgot, and Charles de Brosse, but also the wild English etymologist, John Horne Tooke, at the end of the century.

BIBLIOGRAPHY

Primary Sources

Hardback editions of all of Locke's major texts and his complete correspondence have recently been published by Oxford University Press. Their edition of *An Essay concerning Human Understanding* is also available as an electronic text on floppy disk. The following is a list of the more readily available and less expensive editions referred to in this chapter.

Aristotle. *The Rhetoric of Aristotle.* Translated by Lane Cooper. 1932. Reprint. Englewood Cliffs, NJ: Prentice-Hall, 1960.

Cicero. *On Duties.* Translated by E. M. Atkins, and edited by M. T. Griffin and E. M. Atkins. Cambridge: Cambridge University Press, 1991.

Locke, John. *An Essay concerning Human Understanding.* Edited by Peter Nidditch. Oxford: Clarendon Press, 1975.

———. *A Letter concerning Toleration.* Translated by William Popple, and edited by James Tully. Indianapolis: Hackett Publishing, 1983.

———. *Some Thoughts concerning Education.* London, 1693.

———. *Two Treatises of Government.* Edited by Peter Laslett. New York: Mentor, 1965.

————. *Educational Writings*. Edited by James Axtell. Cambridge: Cambridge University Press, 1971.

————. *Of the Conduct of the Understanding*. Edited by Thomas Fowler. New York: Lenox Hill, 1971.

Biography

Cranston, Maurice. *John Locke: A Biography*. 1957. Reprint. Oxford: Oxford University Press, 1985.

Dewhurst, Kenneth. *John Locke, Physician and Philosopher*. London: Wellcome Historical Medical Library, 1963.

Fox Bourne, H. R. *The Life of John Locke*. London: Henry King, 1876.

Criticism

Aarsleff, Hans. *The Study of Language in England, 1780–1860*. Minneapolis: University of Minnesota Press, 1983.

Bloom, Harold. "Poetic Crossing: Rhetoric and Psychology." *Georgia Review* 30.3 (1976): 495–524.

De Man, Paul. "The Epistemology of Metaphor." *Critical Inquiry* 5.1 (1978): 13–30.

Howell, W. S. *Eighteenth-Century British Logic and Rhetoric*. Princeton: Princeton University Press, 1971.

Kallich, Martin. *The Association of Ideas and Critical Theory in Eighteenth-Century England: A History of a Psychological Method in English Criticism*. The Hague: Mouton, 1970.

Kroll, Richard. *The Material Word: Literate Culture in the Restoration and Early Eighteenth Century*. Baltimore: Johns Hopkins University Press, 1991.

Leibniz, Gottfried Wilhelm. *Nouveaux essais sur l'entendement*. Sämtliche Schriften und Briefe, vol. 6, no. 6. Berlin: Akademie-Verlag, 1962.

MacLean, Kenneth. *John Locke and English Literature of the Eighteenth Century*. New Haven: Yale University Press, 1936.

Miller, Perry. "Edwards, Locke, and the Rhetoric of Sensation." In *Perspectives of Criticism*, edited by H. Levin. New York: Russell and Russell, 1950.

Richetti, John. *Philosophical Writing*. Cambridge: Harvard University Press, 1983.

Tuveson, Ernest. *The Imagination as a Means of Grace: Locke and the Aesthetics of Romanticism*. Berkeley: University of California Press, 1960.

Weedon, Jerry. "Locke on Rhetoric and Rational Man." *Quarterly Journal of Speech* 56.4 (1970): 378–87.

JOHN MASON
(1706–1763)

Brenda H. Cox

John Mason, the son of an independent minister, was born in Dunmow, Essex, in 1706. Destined to follow in both his father's and his grandfather's footsteps, he trained for the ministry under John (David) Jennings and served as tutor and chaplain for the family of Governor Feaks near Hatfield, Hertfordshire. He was appointed to the Presbyterian pulpit in 1729 at Dorking, Surrey, and in 1746 at Carbuckle Street, Chestnut. Thus, he became known as "Reverend John Mason, the nonconformist minister of Chestnut." He received his M.A. from Edinburgh University, presumably between April 1746 and December 1749 (his name does not appear on any of the rosters of Edinburgh's graduates—names were not recorded during that period). Mason also trained students for the ministry, thereby developing an intense interest in the eighteenth-century concept of elocution—the art of pronunciation, or oral delivery. From 1740 until his death in 1763, he published sermons, lectures, and rhetorical treatises. His religious and rhetorical ideas were more influential than original; but his works achieved wide popularity, as evidenced by their publication in multiple editions both during his own time and long after his death. From 1794 to 1796, numerous selections from his sermons were published in *Protestant Dissenter's Magazine*, and his name appears in religious histories and collections as late as 1884 (see Geikie and Howell).

An Essay on the Power of Numbers and *An Essay on the Power and Harmony of Prosaic Numbers*, both published in 1749 and later reprinted together as *Essays in Poetical and Prosaic Numbers* in 1761, remain the primary works on eighteenth-century prosody, along with Daniel Webb's *Observations on the Correspondence Between Poetry and Music*, published later in 1769. However, Mason's primary contribution to eighteenth-century rhetoric is his authorship of one of the earliest and most influential treatises in the elocutionary movement, *An Essay on Elocution*, published originally in 1748 and reprinted in four editions until 1761.

MASON'S RHETORICAL THEORY

Several historians of rhetoric regard highly the contribution of Mason's *Essay* to eighteenth-century rhetoric. W. M. Parrish has considered Mason to be the "originator of the elocution movement in England" (2), and Warren Guthrie has described Mason's *Essay* as one of "the great works on elocution" (21). Douglas Ehninger has regarded Mason's pamphlet as one of the first important elocutionary manuals published in England (297).

However, in *Eighteenth-Century British Logic and Rhetoric*, Wilbur Samuel Howell has claimed that Mason "occupies a modest position" in the elocutionary movement in England despite the popularity of his *Essay* over four decades (191). He has found Mason's *Essay* to be "not even remotely original in its approach to the fifth part of rhetoric" (204). His low opinion of Mason's contribution to the period rests on Mason's own admission that he had taken his ideas on emphasis in pronunciation from the anonymous pamphlet *Some Rules for Speaking and Action*, first published in 1715, which itself was based on the English version of Michel Le Faucheur's *Traitté de l'action de l'orateur; ou, de la Prononciation et de geste* (204). Howell has also found Mason's interpretation of the ancient rhetorical tradition of *elocutio* to be "cloudy" and riddled with "inexcusable laxities" in its conflation of the concepts of ancient eloquence with the more modern concepts of pronunciation and delivery (208). In addition, Mason has been both praised and criticized by historians of rhetoric as an elocutionist who helped to keep the study of rhetoric alive during the eighteenth century but whose emphasis on pronunciation and action also helped to reduce the popular conception of rhetoric to oral delivery.

However, Mason's liberties in adopting the term elocution for the classical concept of pronunciation and action (or delivery) was not without precedent. John Wilkins had already established the new use of "Eloquution," the word that he used to refer to oral presentation in his *Ecclesiastes; or, A Discourse Concerning the Gift of Preaching*, published in 1646. Since Mason and his father and grandfather were all ministers concerned with pulpit oratory, they were probably familiar with the concept of elocution explained in Wilkins's popular work and accustomed to using it to help young ministers deliver more effective sermons. In addition to Wilkins's *Ecclesiastes*, Mason knew *Some Rules for Speaking and Action* and would almost surely have been familiar with at least one of the several translations of Le Faucheur's *Traitté* published in 1657; as Howell has indicated in "Elocutionary Movement," the authors of both of these works had abandoned the neo-Ciceronian use of "elocution" to indicate style and, instead, employed it to mean delivery (Howell 142–48). However, Mason had found himself in the mid-eighteenth century operating within a culture that was intensely concerned with eloquent oratory delivered in good taste, usually in the reading of sermons, the recitation of poetry, or parliamentary debates. Thus, as he explained in his *Essay on Elocution*, he used "elocution" not to refer to the classical concept of *elocutio* but to refer to the eighteenth-century concept of eloquence (2–5).

Mason deserves credit as one of the major early figures of the English elocutionary movement who, through his influential *Essay*, helped to revive interest in the neglected art of rhetorical delivery—and, consequently, in the classical treatises of Longinus, Cicero, and Quintilian, which appeared in multiple printings between 1739 and 1800 (see "Note" in *Essay on Elocution*).

An Essay on Elocution

To the eighteenth-century orator, Mason's *Essay on Elocution*, offers practical advice on "the Art of managing the Voice, and Gesture in speaking" (4). He based his instruction on the teachings of Cicero and Quintilian as well as the ideas expressed in the anonymous pamphlet *Some Rules for Speaking and Action*. He addressed primarily preachers and advised them about the "manner of reading" texts, especially sermons and books of devotion (10–11). For Mason, a good pronunciation was marked by the speaker's sincerity, a value ensuring an effective ethos and forging a strong bond of trust between speakers and their audiences. He asserted his purpose for advocating greater attention to the oral delivery of discourse: "The Great Design and End of a good Pronunciation is, to make the Ideas come from the Heart; and then they will not fail to excite the Attention and Affections of them that hear us" (5).

His advice on delivering a good pronunciation began with a description of a bad one. According to Mason, a bad pronunciation is delivered in a voice that is mumbling, uneven, thick, monotonous, "unnatural"-sounding, too loud or too low, too quick or too slow. He continually stressed the importance of accommodating the expectations of an audience of persons of "Delicacy and Judgment" whose good taste would serve as the standard of excellence to which the speaker would aspire in a public reading. Above all, the speaker should strive to attain "Earnestness, Life and Solemnity," qualities that Mason believed were those that would "never fail to move an Audience" (13–15).

Although his suggestions ranged from obvious and general advice to often minutely detailed instruction about the calibration of the voice, Mason consistently relied on practical, commonsense methods to "avoid" a "bad" pronunciation in reading. For example, he suggested training a low voice to grow louder through conversations with the deaf, or tempering a loud voice by conversing regularly with those who speak in low voices. In offering advice on correcting a bad pronunciation, Mason consistently advocated imitating the natural conversation among people of taste and recommended reading "those Books that are writ in a familiar Stile, that comes nearest to that of Common Conversation; such as the *Pilgrim's Progress*, the *Family Instructor*, or some innocent *Novel*" (18–19).

Imitation was not the only means by which a speaker attained the "natural, easy, and graceful Variation of the Voice, suitable to the Nature and Importance of the Sentiments we deliver" (20). Mason believed in the importance of natural ability in those persons "of a quick Apprehension, and a brisk Flow of animal spirits (setting aside all Impediments of the Organs)" (20). Although Mason thought that these persons had "generally a more lively, just, and natural Elocution than Persons of a slow Perception and a flegmatick Craft," he also thought that anyone who diligently applied himself to "Rule, Imitation, and Practice" would acquire a good pronunciation (20, 33). Thus, he offered specific instruction ranging from the length and types of pauses required at each type of punctuation mark, to the kind of emphasis needed to invoke different passions, to the use of "Cadence" or dropping to a lower tone (19–28). He also believed in the importance of the public reader's immersion in the "Sense and Spirit" of an author's text and the "study of Nature," or observation of one's own "natural Disposition" and "affections" as well as those of others for insights into good elocution (28–31).

Mason also offered practical advice on "Action—or the expression on the face, movement of the head, movement of the eyes and hands, and posture of the body (34–39). Again, he called for the greatest dignity and eloquence in movement, which, in adhering to the model established by the ancients, required the speaker to "follow Nature, and avoid Affectation" (38). He explained that "the Action of the Body, and the several Parts of it, must correspond with Pronunciation, as that does with the Stile, and the Stile with the Subject. A perfect Harmony of all which compleats the Orator" (39).

To the purist historian of rhetoric, Mason was guilty of appropriating the term *eloquence* and should be considered as one of the culprits who elevated the art of delivery to a position of singular importance among the elements of rhetoric. The popular conception of rhetoric in England and America would eventually be reduced to the art of delivery, but this happened as a result of cultural forces far beyond the control of any single elocutionist. Although not entirely original in his ideas or practice, Mason deserves to be remembered as an important contributor to eighteenth-century British rhetoric. His influential and immensely popular *Essay* served to revive interest in the all-but-forgotten art of oral delivery and stressed the importance of natural eloquence in public discourse.

BIBLIOGRAPHY

Primary Sources

Mason, John. *An Essay on Elocution*. London, 1748. Reprint. English Linguistics 1500–1800 Facsimile Reprints, 1967.

Biography

Geikie, Archibald. "John Mason." *DNB* (1921).

Criticism

Ehninger, Douglas. "Dominant Trends in English Rhetorical Thought: 1750–1800." In *Readings in Rhetoric*, edited by Lionel Crocker and Paul A. Carmack, 297–307. Springfield, IL: Charles C. Thomas Publishers, 1965.

Guthrie, Warren. "The Development of Rhetorical Theory in America, 1635–1850. 5: The Elocution Movement—England." *Speech Monographs* 18.1 (1951): 17–30.

Howell, Wilbur Samuel. "The British Elocutionary Movement: 1702–1806." In *Eighteenth-Century British Logic and Rhetoric*, 204–8. Princeton: Princeton University Press, 1971.

———. "Sources of the Elocutionary Movement in England, 1700–1748." In *Historical Studies of Rhetoric and Rhetoricians*, edited by Raymond F. Howes, 139–58. Ithaca, NY: Cornell University Press, 1961.

Parrish, W. M. "Elocution—A Definition and a Challenge." *Quarterly Journal of Speech* 43.1 (1957): 1–11.

JOSEPH PRIESTLEY
(1733–1804)

Michael G. Moran

The son of a cloth-dresser, Joseph Priestley was born on March 13, 1733, in England at Fieldhead, near Leeds in Yorkshire; he died in America on February 6, 1804, in Northumberland, Pennsylvania. During his long life, he wrote on many subjects, including religion, education, politics, electricity, chemistry, grammar, and rhetoric. His scientific work was particularly important. After meeting Benjamin Franklin and other intellectuals interested in natural philosophy (experimental science) in London in 1766, Priestley became intrigued by this new field; he soon wrote a book on the history of research into electricity (which also contained discussions of some of his own experiments) (see Bazerman), and he later advanced knowledge in chemistry by isolating oxygen through a series of important experiments. Becoming a fellow of the Royal Society in 1766, he received its prestigious Copley Medal for his work on impregnating water with carbon dioxide to create soda water.

Although Priestley is now probably most famous for his work in science, he was during his life known as an important dissenting clergyman and as a radical political thinker. As a clergyman, he held positions in several Dissenting (or Nonconformist) churches in the Midlands and wrote numerous discourses on religious controversies, which he advocated approaching by means of reason rather than by faith alone. Thinking his way through these controversies, Priestley gradually rejected many religious mysteries, such as the Trinity and atonement, and eventually embraced Unitarianism, a sect that he helped found in America. A great advocate of individualism and a supporter of the rights of man (Crowther 176–77), Priestley actively participated in many of the political discussions of his day, usually voicing radical opinions. Such opinions became suspect following the French Revolution, which threatened the English status quo with the possibility of revolution being exported across the Channel. The fact that Priestley's Unitarian meeting house and personal residence, along with his extensive library and scientific equipment, were burned in Birmingham in 1791 by a mob with conservative views suggests how unpopular Priestley's liberal views on politics and religion had become among right-wing circles. Because of the hostile climate in the Midlands for radical thinkers, Priestley left Birmingham for London and eventually followed his sons to Pennsylvania in 1794, where he lived his last years.

When young, Priestley had shown a facility for learning, and his maternal aunt, with whom he lived after his mother's death, therefore financed his early education. According to his *Memoirs*, he first attended local schools and, by the age of twelve or thirteen, mastered Latin and the basics of Greek. During the holidays, he studied Hebrew under a local minister. Suffering from ill health due to the cold and damp climate of England, he thought that he would have to move to a warmer climate, so he taught himself French, Italian, and High Dutch (70) in the hope of making a career as a merchant in a Mediterranean region. He also studied two days a week under a George Haggerstone, who taught him mathematics and helped him read natural philosophy, Watt's *Logic*, and Locke's *Essay concerning Human Understanding* (72). His health improved, however, and his aunt sent him to the academy at Daventry, which was run by Dr. Caleb Ashworth (70). This school was one of England's foremost Dissenting academies (schools designed to teach religious Nonconformists) and was based on the liberal theological principles of Philip Doddridge, the important Dissenting educator. Studying there from 1752–1755, Priestley experienced the joys of debating controversial issues and the excitement of independent thought. As Priestley commented in his *Memoirs*, the school allowed considerable "free inquiry" (76); consequently, students discussed those questions that Priestley considered central to the human condition: "Liberty and Necessity, the sleep of the soul, and all the articles of theological orthodoxy and heresy" (75). Since some of the older students were already well educated, Priestley noted, the lectures had "the air of friendly conversations" (76) rather than formal presentations. As Hoecker and Fruchtman (*Apocalyptic*) have noted, while studying at the academy Priestley imbibed a strong belief in the perfectibility of human nature, an assumption that colored much of his later political and educational thought; and he read David Hartley's *Observations on Man*, a book that influenced his later reflections on rhetoric (Alexander and Hartog 360). At the end of his studies, Priestley left Daventry with a strong sense of the importance of unfettered inquiry and a belief that he should question orthodox opinions.

Although he was not ordained as a Dissenting minister until 1762, Priestley, after leaving Daventry, accepted positions at Dissenting congregations. He went first to Needham Market (1755) and later to Nantwich (1758). Although Priestley always considered his clerical duties to be his primary responsibilities, like many Dissenting clergy he spent many years teaching. He opened small schools in both towns, but his most important teaching took place at the Warrington Academy, where he taught languages and belles lettres from 1761 to 1767. Since he had become interested in scientific experimentation at Nantwich—where he taught his students to conduct experiments publicly—he had hoped to teach this subject at Warrington. However, this position went to John Holt; therefore, Priestley accepted the position as the tutor of languages, grammar, literature, and rhetoric.

Warrington was one of the most important of the eighteenth-century Dissenting academies. Like other such schools, it served the needs of various students, especially the children of religious Dissenters. Unlike most denominational schools, however, it opened its doors to all sects. One of the school's primary functions was to train Dissenting ministers, but Warrington also prepared students for other professions. While Oxford and Cambridge trained Anglicans for traditional roles as ministers, lawyers, and politicians, Dissenters were not allowed to matriculate, so academies for Dissenters arose to prepare the children of Nonconformists to enter other professions, including business, industry, and trade.

Priestley thought deeply about education and advocated various reforms. In his most important statement on educational theory and practice, "Essay on a Course of Liberal Education for Civil and Active Life" (1765), written while teaching at Warrington, Priestley argued for a new emphasis on the practical in English education. The problem with the system then in place was that it offered no systematic education for gentlemen entering what Priestley called "the active life," which included professions in law, governance, industry, trade, and the military. Since men in these professions "will considerably affect the liberty and property of [their] countrymen, and the riches, strength and security of [their] country" (83), Priestley believed that educators had an obligation to prepare young gentlemen for their future stations. Such preparation was historically necessary given the beginnings of England's development into a world power poised to dominate much of the known world. According to Priestley, the necessary preparation for this great responsibility included the study of ancient and modern history, constitutional law, foreign tongues, language, grammar, and rhetoric. As the instructor of belles lettres at Warrington, Priestley delivered lectures on many of these subjects, including rhetoric.

In 1777, ten years after leaving Warrington, Priestley published *A Course of Lectures on Oratory and Criticism*, which consisted of little more than his reworked lecture notes. Priestley did not attempt to deal systematically with all issues that the rhetoric raises—and, therefore, the book appears to be unfinished. Even with this weakness, however, it is one of the most important rhetorical statements of the century for two related reasons. First, it represents the most thorough attempt to base a rhetoric on the association philosophy of John Locke and David Hartley, both of whom Priestley read as a student. Second, because Priestley attempted to demonstrate the connection between rhetorical theory and the operation of the human mind, the book stands as one of the best examples in the century of a psychological rhetoric.

PRIESTLEY'S RHETORICAL THEORY

As the title of the book suggests, Priestley conceived of his rhetoric in two general parts: oratory (rhetoric) and criticism (style). (He then divided oratory into two sections: invention and arrangement. Criticism, or style, stood as a third, independent section.) Each part, he made clear in his preface, was influenced by a different theorist. John Ward's *A System of Oratory* (1759), the most thorough restatement of classical theory in the century, influenced the first part, which consists of the two sections on oratory, and provided the system that connected criticism with the other two sections. Because Ward was one of the foremost interpreters of classical rhetoric during the century, this influence had a conservative effect on Priestley's work. While rhetoricians such as Adam Smith, George Campbell, and Hugh Blair rejected or modified much of the classical model, Priestley kept its outline, organizing his rhetoric along Ciceronian lines, his rhetoric including discussions of invention, arrangement, and style. Although Priestley generally followed the Ciceronian divisions of rhetoric, he gave each modern names, so that invention became "recollection," arrangement became "method," and style became "criticism." Priestley mentioned in his first lecture (5) that he had planned to include a section on *elocution*, the eighteenth-century term for delivery, but he never wrote it; he did note, however, that he spent class time teaching the more practical elements of delivering a speech. He did not include a separate section on memory, either, although he did conflate invention and memory in his category of recollection. The lack of emphasis on methods for memorizing speeches, however, suggests that, despite the term *oratory* in his title, Priestley considered his rhetoric at least as appropriate to the writer as to the speaker.

The second major influence on Priestley's rhetoric was Lord Kames's *Elements of Criticism*, which forms much of the basis of the second part mentioned in the work's title: criticism, or style. Kames's discussion of style was more innovative than Ward's discussion of rhetoric because it attempted to use the principles of the new psychology to explain the effects that literary texts have on the human mind. In part because of this influence, in his discussions of style, Priestley used literary examples, especially from poetry and drama, to teach his Warrington students to write and speak well. Priestley assumed that the study of poetic figures would help students write better prose, and the term *criticism* in his title suggests that he recognized an important connection between reading literature and communicating effectively. This interest points to a link between Priestley's work and that of theorists in the belles lettres tradition, such as Adam Smith and Hugh Blair.

It also indicates that Priestley was aware of the work on style by the Scottish Enlightenment rhetoricians, who included George Campbell in addition to Kames, Smith, and Blair.

While Priestley was familiar with the work of the Scottish rhetoricians, and while *Lectures* reflect their influence, his rhetoric is based largely on assumptions different from theirs. He based his rhetoric on association psychology, a system that largely rejected the existence of innate ideas and assumed that all knowledge rested ultimately on experience. While many of the Scottish rhetoricians were influenced by the common-sense philosophy of Thomas Reid and James Beattie—which assumed that the human mind possessed certain innate, or instinctual, ideas—Priestley rejected this theory because it did not explain whence such ideas originated (see Bevilacqua). In place of the common-sense position, Priestley argued (following Hartley) that all ideas arise ultimately from experience. In *Observations on Man*, a work that Priestley knew well, Hartley had developed the principles of association to explain all human knowledge. As John Locke had argued, the basis of all knowledge begins with simple ideas introduced to the human mind through the senses. All complex ideas result from the combining of simple ones. What this means, of course, is that all ideas that the mind possesses result from experience. Hartley's contribution to Lockean psychology was to assert a physiological basis for associationism, which he explained by the vibration of nerves. Following Locke and Hartley, therefore, Priestley attempted a consistent explanation of rhetorical action and effect based on the model of association psychology. Such an approach was consistent not only with the new epistemology but also with the new empirical science that Priestley himself practiced.

While Priestley was deeply committed to association psychology, he also believed that the human mind consisted of mental faculties (Bevilacqua and Murphy xxv). This view of psychology assumed that the mind possessed certain distinct powers, including memory, reason, judgment, passion, and imagination. Although discrete, the faculties functioned together through the unifying operations of association. The faculties were important to *Oratory and Criticism* because Priestley used them as one of the systems to organize his rhetoric by identifying each rhetorical art with a mental faculty. He associated invention with memory, method with reason, and style with judgment, passion, and imagination.

Invention or Recollection

Although the first two parts of *Oratory and Criticism* covering oratory followed Ciceronian order, Priestley's treatment of them was innovative. By replacing *invention* with *recollection*, Priestley changed invention from a search for knowledge to a matter of remembering what one already knew. He therefore limited rhetoric to the art of helping the rhetor communicate the findings of systematic researches into particular subjects. Thus, Priestley assumed that knowledge resulted, not from dialectic within social contexts, but from more field-specific investigations into areas of specialized knowledge through reading and empirical exploration. Rhetoric, then, does not provide knowledge, only the ability to manage that knowledge once discovered. As Priestley commented, "Whatever subject, therefore, any person intends to write or speak upon, he must, by applying the proper sources, acquire a perfect knowledge of it, before he can expect any assistance from the art of oratory" (3). Once the person's researches stock the mind with information, the art of oratory can "assist him in the habit of *recollection*" to find arguments and material to "confirm or illustrate" them (5). Invention can help rhetors only by speeding up the processes of recollection and selection. Priestley, therefore, demoted invention from a process of discovery to a process of memory. He further diminished it by arguing that it can help produce only one of the two types of discourse—namely, argumentation. The other type—narration—can benefit only from the third part of rhetoric, style.

Despite his diminution of invention, Priestley provided a list of topics based on those of Cicero: definition, adjuncts, antecedents, consequents, means, analogy, contrariety, example, and authority—all of which would help one find material for arguments. He justified providing topics in two ways. First, he argued that topics, which merely establish associative connections between two ideas, assist the thinker in associating ideas—which is the basis of all recollection. The advantage of topics, then, is that they offer thinkers a systematic method to probe their memories. These topics are in some sense natural activities of the human mind, for persons who have never heard of topics unknowingly use them (22). Second, he noted that the writings of the ancients, especially those of Cicero and Quintilian, suggest that the ancients used topics extensively. But, Priestley insisted, despite their use in classical times, topics have limited usefulness. They can be useful to those persons, especially ministers, who must frequently compose "*moral essays* and *sermons*" (23) that need not be original because "their chief business is merely to *recollect*, and *digest* the most valuable materials upon each subject" (23). Being a minister himself, Priestley appreciated topics as a kind of shorthand way to produce a sermon by making connections among traditionally accepted bits of information. But topics cannot help the thinker make original discoveries, and Priestley's final evaluation of topics leaves them with little strength:

I am very ready, however, to acknowledge, that rhetorical topics are more useful in the composition of *set declamation on trite subjects*, and to *young persons*, than in the communication of original matter, to persons much used to composition. Original thoughts cannot but suggest themselves, so that all the assistance any person can want in this case, is a proper manner of *arranging* them. And a person much used

to composition will have acquired a habit of recollection, without any express attention to topics; just as a person used to the harpsichord, or any other instrument of
music, will be able to perform without an *express attention* to rules, or even to the
manner of placing his fingers. (24–25)

Just as harpsichordists had come, through practice and experience, to associate closely finger movement and sound, so that they played the music
without conscious thought, the experienced writer could move from idea to
idea, following chains of associated thought, without conscious application
of the topics. Only the young and inexperienced needed them.

Arrangement or Method

The second section of oratory, which Priestley called "method," also
draws on association psychology. "Method" concerns the ways in which the
rhetor could organize discourse; and Priestley recognized two general strategies: narration and argumentation. Priestley's discussion of narration is inadequate, because he assumed that narration was purely factual and required
no invention and little reflection on how to organize the information (6).
According to Priestley, the writer of natural or civil history or travels need
only start at the beginning and end at the end. Since the mode is based
either on personal experience (travels, for instance), on direct observation
(natural history, for instance), or on reading (civil history), the writer need
take no pains to invent material or to organize it in ways other than simple
chronology. Priestley's second division of discourse, the one he explored in
more detail, is argumentation, which he divided into two methods: synthesis
and analysis. Both of these forms of argument concern themselves with proving propositions, and both are connected closely to invention because they
offer ways for writers to explore debatable issues. Both terms have long
histories in mathematics and logic. Many other rhetoricians of the century
discussed them, so the concepts are not new. But Priestley contributed to
rhetoric a discussion of methods that clarified their rhetorical usefulness as
ways to organize arguments.

The two methods mirror each other. Synthesis begins with an established
proposition or theorem; the writer then proceeds with a "kind of *demonstration*" (45), which makes up the bulk of the discourse. Like Descartes,
who viewed effective thought as having a mathematical certainty, Priestley
based his theory of synthesis on Euclid's geometric method. Such demon-
strations begin, Priestley argued, either with axioms, which are self-evident
truths (based ultimately on human experience), or propositions logically derived from either axioms or "matters of revelation" (46). The rhetor also
must define all key terms so that the audience understands all the words in
the axiom. These definitions must remain constant throughout the discourse. The rhetor then moves by means of deduction from axioms to other

propositions. Priestley called this method "the *very touchstone of truth*" (46) because any propositions logically inconsistent with the axiom must be false (47). Synthesis, Priestley noted, is the method best used "to explain a system of science to others" (42); the method, therefore, was appropriate for textbooks. In fact, he commented, "we find very few treatises drawn up in this method, except *elementary* ones, for use of students, and particularly in pure mathematics and philosophy" (55). One of the most notable examples of synthetic discourse is Hartley's *Observations on Man*.

Analysis, on the other hand, is the opposite of synthesis because it is the method employed to investigate truth by testing hypotheses. With analysis, the discourse begins, not with an axiomatic or established truth, but with a proposition to be proved or disproved. The writer then traces in prose the process of testing the proposition using a loose series of steps that include discovering the evidence through research and thought; comparing the results of the exploration with the original proposition; noting the differences between the findings and the original proposition; developing a new proposition, if necessary, and repeating the procedure (see Moran; Lawson). Analysis—the method of investigating uncertain truths—was the method of science; and Priestley used it in his scientific discourse (see Moran). According to Priestley, analysis was also the method that rhetors should use to argue about any uncertain subject because the method carries considerable rhetorical power. This power comes from the readers' being shown not only the investigation's conclusion but also the processes used to arrive at the conclusion. The reader who understands the process of discovery will be likely to accept the truth of the proposition.

Style or Criticism

The first two sections of oratory, recollection and method, are based on the faculties of memory and reason, respectively. Priestley's third part, criticism, finds its basis largely in the faculties of passion, judgment, and imagination. Priestley argued that for audiences interested in the subject matter of a discourse, it is enough that orators recall appropriate content and logically organize that content to make it easily understandable. However, in cases where the audience lacks inherent interest in the topic, the orator must either engage the audience's passions, their judgment, or their more "delicate sensations," which Priestley, following Addison, called "the pleasures of the imagination." Although Priestley framed his discussion of style with the assumptions of faculty psychology, his purpose was to demonstrate how the associationism that he borrowed from Locke and Hartley explained the effects of stylistic devices.

For Priestley, the passions played an important role in rhetoric. When an audience's passions are engaged, that audience becomes interested in the topic; and the intensity of this interest is in direct relationship to the vividness of the ideas that excite the passions. Rhetorically, the purpose of the passions is to rouse people to action without the intervention of reason. One of the best ways to engage the passions is to present as many sensible images as possible, because humans experience life as a series of particulars rather than generalities. To stimulate anger at an enemy, for instance, it is most effective to list a series of specific harmful deeds that this enemy has committed. Strong passions also generate belief. Since external objects and circumstances of reality excite the passions, people come to associate strong emotions and vivid ideas with the reality that excites them. Consequently, when, in connection with their argument, orators raise a passion in an audience, the audience will be inclined to associate the passion with what is real and true—and will, therefore, tend to accept the argument as valid. This acceptance—and the passion itself—can be transferred (again, by association) to related ideas.

Priestley pointed to the audience's faculty of judgment to explain how the orator can gain his audience's assent or belief. He argued that rhetors are convincing when they appear to believe strongly in their argument, when they know their subjects thoroughly, when they possess a "redundancy of proof," and when they appear to be candid and unprejudiced. All of these qualities are effective rhetorically because the audience, owing to its past experience, associates them with qualities such as truth and honesty. In other words, the audience judges that the two ideas are consistent and hence part of the same complex. For instance, listeners associate a strong conviction with truth, so they tend to believe orators who demonstrate a deep commitment to their positions. For the same reason, listeners also tend to believe speakers who appear candid and impartial.

In the bulk of his discussion of style, Priestley explored the importance of the "pleasures of the imagination," those figures of speech and thought that appeal to intellectual pleasures that people in cultivated societies learn from experiencing the fine arts. Educated people develop a sense of taste that allows them to appreciate these finer pleasures. Taste is, however, not an innate quality but the result of experience and learning, which for Priestley was due to the development of complex associations. He gave as an example the uneducated shoemaker who, when seeing a statue, could judge the quality of its sandals but not the quality of the statue itself. The shoemaker understood the craft of making sandals but lacked a taste refined enough to appreciate the fine art of sculpting.

These intellectual and refined pleasures Priestley attributed to two mental operations. First, people experience intellectual pleasure when they exercise their mental faculties moderately. Readers, therefore, enjoy figures of speech because these figures require them to reflect on the meaning of the language more than unadorned discourse requires them to do. It is pleasing, for instance, to puzzle out a passage of figurative prose as long as the puzzle is not too frustrating. If the prose is too dense or obscure, pleasure turns to pain because the faculties are overtaxed, and the prose loses rhetorical effect. Second, the pleasures of the imagination grow from the transferring of qualities from one object or idea to another. This process results directly from association; for when two objects or ideas are associated, their qualities are commingled. For instance, when a writer uses a metaphor such as "John is a lion in debate," some of the qualities of the lion—such as strength, courage, and power—become transferred to John the debater. The figures of speech discussed by Priestley owe their effectiveness to a combination of these mental operations, although some figures gain their power primarily from one or the other. The figure of novelty, for instance, gives pleasure because it stimulates "perceptive and active powers" (146) of the mind, but it achieves its rhetorical power from association because part of its effect results from the mind's comparing the surprising idea with less novel ideas that came before it. Metonymy, the simple transference of the meaning of one word to another, on the other hand, owes its effect primarily to impressions that are "variously mixed, combined, and transferred from one object to another, by [association]" (228). This process of association, of course, also pleasantly exercises the faculties.

While Priestley's contributions to rhetoric were not as lasting as those of Blair and Campbell, he should be recognized for his consistent use of association psychology to explain rhetorical effects. By rejecting the common-sense assumptions of many of the Scottish rhetoricians, Priestley founded rhetoric on experience, thereby making rhetoric consistent with Lockean and Hartlean assumptions about the mind's operation by means of the association of ideas. Since experience became the foundation of his rhetoric, he reinterpreted many of the basic ideas of eighteenth-century aesthetics, including taste and sublimity, and explained these concepts in terms of human experience rather than innate mental powers. While the book consists of little more than lecture notes not fully fleshed out, it is one of the most important statements of rhetoric based on association psychology in the century.

BIBLIOGRAPHY

Primary Sources

Priestley, Joseph. *A Course of Lectures on Oratory and Criticism.* Edited by Vincent M. Bevilacqua and Richard Murphy. Carbondale: Southern Illinois University Press, 1965.
———. "An Essay on a Course of Liberal Education for Civil and Active Life." In *Joseph Priestley: Selections from His Writings*, edited by Ira V. Brown, 79–100. University Park: Pennsylvania State University Press, 1962.

Biographies

Aykroyd, W. R. *Three Philosophers (Lavoisier, Priestley and Cavendish).* London: Heinemann, 1935.

Crowther, J. G. "Joseph Priestley." In *Scientists of the Industrial Revolution*, 175–70. London: Cressett, 1962.

Gibbs, F. W. *Joseph Priestley: Adventurer in Science and Champion of Truth*. London: Nelson, 1965.

Gordon, Alexander, and P. J. Hartog. "Joseph Priestley." *DNB* (1964).

Holt, Anne. *A Life of Joseph Priestley*. London: Oxford University Press, 1931.

Lindsay, Jack. Introduction to *Autobiography of Joseph Priestley*, 11–66 Bath, Eng.: Adams and Dart, 1970.

Priestley, Joseph. *Memoirs of Dr. Joseph Priestley (Written by Himself) with a Journal of His Travels*. In *Autobiography of Joseph Priestley*, edited by Jack Lindsay, 69–144. Bath, Eng.: Adams and Dart, 1970.

Criticism

Bazerman, Charles. "How Natural Philosophers Can Cooperate: The Literary Technology of Coordinated Investigation in Joseph Priestley's History and Present State of Electricity (1767)." In *Textual Dynamics of the Professions: Historical and Contemporary Studies of Writing in Professional Communities*, edited by Charles Bazerman and James Paradis, 13–44. Madison: University of Wisconsin Press, 1991.

Bevilacqua, Vincent M. "Campbell, Priestley, and the Controversy Concerning Common Sense." *Southern Speech Journal* 30.2 (1964): 79–98.

Bevilacqua, Vincent M., and Richard Murphy, eds. Introduction to *A Course of Lectures on Oratory and Criticism*, by Joseph Priestley. Carbondale: Southern Illinois University Press, 1965.

Burwick, Frederick. "Associationist Rhetoric and Scottish Prose Style." *Speech Monographs* 34.1 (1967): 21–34.

Eakins, Barbara, and R. Gene Eakins. "Comparison: Proof or Ornament." *Central States Speech Journal*, 26.1 (1975): 99–106.

Fruchtman, Jack, Jr. *The Apocalyptic Politics of Richard Price and Joseph Priestley: A Study in Late Eighteenth-Century English Republican Millenialism*. Philadelphia: American Philosophical Society, 1983.

———. "Joseph Priestley on Rhetoric and the Power of Political Discourse." *Eighteenth-Century Life* 7.3 (1982): 37–47.

Hoecker, James J. *Joseph Priestley and the Idea of Progress*. New York: Garland, 1987.

Howell, Wilbur Samuel. *Eighteenth-Century British Logic and Rhetoric*, 632–47. Princeton: Princeton University Press, 1971.

Kramnick, Isaac. "Eighteenth-Century Science and Radical Social Theory: The Case of Joseph Priestley's Scientific Liberalism." *Journal of British Studies* 25.1 (1986): 1–30.

Lawson, Chester A. "Joseph Priestley and the Process of Cultural Evolution." *Science Education* 38.4 (1954): 267–76.

Moran, Michael G. "Joseph Priestley, William Duncan, and Analytic Arrangement in 18th-century Scientific Discourse." *Journal of Technical Writing and Communication* 14.3 (1984): 207–15.

Warnick, Barbara. "The Bolevian Sublime in Eighteenth-Century British Rhetorical Theory." *Rhetorica* 8.4 (1990): 349–69.

CHARLES ROLLIN
(1661–1741)

Russell Greer

The son of a master cutler, Charles Rollin was born in 1661 in Paris, France. With the support of a Benedictine monk, who arranged for a scholarship, Rollin was educated at an annex of the Collège du Plessie-Sorbonne, where he showed such promise that he was made professor of rhetoric in 1683 at age twenty-two. Popular as a teacher, he quickly advanced in his profession. He was elected Recteur at the University of Paris in 1693 and was reelected eight more times over a two-year period. His attempts at educational reform met with resistance, however; and when he failed to be reelected for a ninth time, he retired to his home and garden in the Latin Quarter of Paris. In 1699 he became principal of the Collège de Beauvais and successfully served there for thirteen years. In 1712 he again retired—this time under pressure by the Roman Catholic Church because of his support for the heretical Jansenist movement, a religious affiliation that influenced his educational views. The Christian reformers known as Jansenists pessimistically considered "man a fallen being, whose heart was perverted and whose passions were dangerous" (Gaudin 3). Consequently, education for Rollin was extremely important: He believed it had a profound social and moral consequence. In retirement, Rollin prepared an abridged edition of Quintilian's *Institutes of Oratory* in two volumes and emerged briefly from retirement in 1719 to deliver a speech thanking King Louis XV for his financial support of higher education. On this occasion, Rollin's educational views so impressed his colleagues that they urged him to expand his views into a book. Rollin accepted the suggestion, and from 1726 to 1728 he published the four volumes of *The Method of Teaching and Studying the Belles-Lettres* (*Traité*, in French). In his book, Rollin addressed educational reform in the study of languages, poetry, philosophy, history, eloquence, educational administration, and rhetoric. His work was immediately popular, appearing "in twenty-seven French editions prior to 1882, plus six abridged editions and seven editions of Rollin's collected works" (Warnick 49). *Traité* was first translated into English in 1734, just six years after its first French publication. In its English preface, the anonymous English translator described the work as already well known throughout Europe. Translated versions of the work appeared in Russian, German, Italian, and English, although *Traité* "was most popular with the English-speaking public" (Warnick 49). A second English edition appeared just three years after the first, and *Traité* went into eleven English editions, the last one appearing in 1810 (Howells 532).

Educators and writers praised the volumes for their good judgment, good taste, honesty, wit, reason, and excellent examples of good literature (Gaudin x–xi). Voltaire called the work "a book forever useful" that "breathes good sense and sound literature throughout" (Gaudin x). With the English translation of *Traité*, Rollin joined two other French writers—Réné Rapin and Dominique Bouhours—in popularizing in English the term and concept of belles lettres. Although the term had been used as a foreign concept prior to the English translation of Rollin's work, including a very early 1710 appearance in the *Tatler* by Jonathan Swift (Howell 533), the English publication of Rollin's *Traité* was timely. The English language did not have a word for "the kinds of literature and for the disciplines that create literature" (Howell 533). Two years after *Traité* appeared in English, Nathan Bailey's important and influential *Dictionarium Britannicum* listed *belles lettres* for the first time as an English term (Howell 532).

Except for a brief reelection as Recteur at the University of Paris in 1720, Rollin spent the remainder of his life writing books on ancient history. He died in September 1741 at the age of eighty.

ROLLIN'S RHETORICAL THEORY

As a rhetorical theorist, Rollin was a transitional figure. His use of classical writers as rhetorical models—authors such as Quintilian, Cicero, and Longinus—makes him part of the school of traditional rhetoric of the seventeenth century. He broke with earlier rhetorical theory, however, by refusing to accept blindly classical precepts for good rhetoric. Instead, he emphasized audience response as the most important yardstick for measuring the value of a discourse. In one of the few recent studies of Rollin, Barbara Warnick has shown the important influence that Rollin had on English rhetorical theorists. The four volumes of Rollin's *Traité*, including the important second volume on rhetoric (translated into English in 1734), had a wide influence on the fledgling belles lettres tradition in Great Britain. Such British rhetoricians as Adam Smith, George Campbell, and Hugh Blair read Rollin's work.

Rollin's commitment to education played a crucial role in defining his rhetorical theory. Chiefly a handbook for students and teachers, Rollin's

Traité provided hundreds of examples of rhetorical models that Rollin considered worthy of imitation. Studying great classical writers, Rollin believed, formed literary taste, creating an *honnête homme*, or cultured man (Gaudin 9). A student could use the examples "as guides to supply him with certain rules for distinguishing good from bad" (Rollin 1). These examples helped form judgment and good taste, crucial qualities in rhetoric and in life. Rollin wrote that "a corruption of manners will correspond to a corruption of style" (Gaudin 16).

Most of these examples came from classical literature, with Rollin citing Cicero and Quintilian more than any other classical authors (Warnick 50). Rollin felt that classical writers such as Aristotle, Dionsius Halicarnaesseus, Longinus, Cicero, and Quintilian represented the "fountain head" of rhetorical knowledge (Rollin 3). This reliance on classical models has led such scholars as Wilbur Samuel Howell to label Rollin "essentially an eighteenth-century Ciceronian, even if he especially admired Cicero's disciple, Quintilian" (Howell, 547).

Rollin differed from other Ciceronians, however, by also citing contemporary authors as examples of good rhetoric. His favorites among the moderns were Esprit Fléchier (14 citations) and Jacques-Bénigne Bossuet (9 citations); he also cited Jules Mascaron, Paul Pellisson, and François de Malherbe (Warnick 50). By providing students with examples of good rhetoric in their native language, Rollin infused a vitality to rhetorical instruction, emphasizing practical communication at the expense of the florid style typical of the period (Warnick 47).

Rollin demanded that students cultivate a clear but expressive style, free from senselessly ornate language. Yet, while he valued clarity, Rollin felt that the best communication combined clarity with vivid language that could capture and hold an audience's attention.

Students could achieve this rhetorical skill by carefully studying long passages in French and Latin from great authors—a strategy that departed from the traditional instructional method. Typically, students of the time memorized rules for good rhetoric and then applied them by composing Latin passages or by translating passages from Latin to French or French to Latin (Warnick 51). Rollin's emphasis on models over precepts generated some criticism. At least one contemporary French rhetorician, Professor Balthazar Gilbert from the Collège Mazarin, attacked Rollin for his departure from traditional instructional methods. In *Traité*, Rollin justified his method by explaining that when students are exposed to examples of great rhetoric, "a great number of terms and phrases of that tongue in which they propose to write [are created]; so that when an occasion offers for expressing any thought in just and proper language, they have recourse to their memory" (Rollin 71).

Under Rollin's plan, students wrote about topics that they already understood in assignments that grew progressively more difficult and required critical thinking instead of simply applying classical precepts (Warnick 52). Rollin also advocated that colleges should require two years of rhetorical study instead of only one.

Although Rollin believed that rhetoric touched every branch of learning that used discourse, he gave special attention to law and religion. Both, he believed, presented opportunities to evoke a passionate response from an audience. Effective rhetoric, especially in religious matters, could be measured by its ability to "force a tear from the hearers" by "blending the sublime and pathetic with . . . softeness and tenderness" (Rollin 291). Rollin owed his understanding of the sublime to Longinus (Howell 531) and believed that passionate response could be achieved by using whatever appeals to the human heart—specifically, metaphor, simile, repetition, apostrophe, and prosopopoeia (giving life, sentiment or speech to animals or inanimate things). Rollin believed that the sublime "transports the auditor . . . and leaves him . . . struck down and dazzled with its thunder and lightening" (58). The true test of the sublime is its ability to make "an impression which is difficult to resist and, once effected, to forget" (Warnick 55).

This ability to communicate with "force and vehemence" (58) brings with it a responsibility on the part of the educator to infuse good judgment and good taste in the student along with knowledge of rhetoric. Because all disciplines require discourse, rhetoric would apply to every field of study— and, therefore, the educator's task is tremendous. Languages, poetry, history, philosophy, science, religion—they all belong to belles lettres (Howell 530).

Although Rollin himself introduced few completely original ideas, his "comprehensive bringing together of the major tenets of communication under the rubric of a single discipline" (Golden 140) helped to establish a belles lettres tradition in English, which was later further developed in Great Britain by Adam Smith and Hugh Blair. The sweeping scope of Rollin's four-volume study contributed to the broad definition of literary study. His book emphasized the study of literature in the vernacular and helped to establish the link between *rhetoric* and the *belles lettres*, giving "both of these terms a reference to all the forms of discourse" (Howell 535).

BIBLIOGRAPHY

Primary Sources

Rollin, Charles. *The Method of Teaching and Studying the Belles-Lettres.* Vol. 2. London, 1758.

Biography

Gaudin, Albert C. *The Educational Views of Charles Rollin*, 1–8. New York: Thesis Publishing Co., 1939.

Criticism

Golden, James L., Goodwin F. Berquist, and William E. Coleman. *The Rhetoric of*

Western Thought, 136–59. 4th ed. Dubuque, IA: Kendall/Hunt Publishing Company, 1989.

Horner, Winifred Bryan. "The Eighteenth Century." In *The Present State of Scholarship in Historical and Contemporary Rhetoric,* edited by Winifred Bryan Horner, 101–33. Columbia: University Press of Missouri, 1983.

Howell, Wilbur Samuel. *Eighteenth-Century English Logic and Rhetoric,* 529–35. Princeton: Princeton University Press, 1979.

Warnick, Barbara. "Charles Rollin's *Traité* and the Rhetorical Theories of Smith, Campbell, and Blair." *Rhetorica* 3.1 (1985): 45–65.

ANTHONY ASHLEY COOPER, THIRD EARL OF SHAFTESBURY
(1671–1713)

Susan Griffin

Anthony Ashley Cooper was born in 1671 (New Style) at his grandfather's home in London. He was more influenced by his grandfather, the first earl, than by his own father, who was relatively uninvolved in his upbringing. Most notably, his grandfather's friend and secretary was John Locke, who supervised the education of the grandchildren. As a result, the third earl was taught Greek and Latin at a young age and was fluent in these languages for the rest of his life. He briefly attended the Winchester public school and then travelled on the Continent from 1686 to 1689. Despite his reputation as a reclusive scholar later in life, the young Shaftesbury had political ambitions and entered Parliament in 1695. He was forced to retire in 1698 because of chronic asthma, a condition that persisted throughout his life. After his father's death in 1699, Shaftesbury entered public life again, serving in the House of Lords from 1700 to 1701. But a combination of political changes at Anne's accession to the throne and his own fragile health led to his second withdrawal into private life. He turned increasingly to study, writing, and domestic life, marrying Miss Jane Ewer in 1709, with whom he had an only child. In these years, Shaftesbury published several essays on a variety of themes: *Letter concerning Enthusiasm* (1708), on religious zealotry; *Sensus Communis, an Essay on the Freedom of Wit and Humor* (1709), on religious tolerance; *The Moralists: a Philosophical Rhapsody* (1709), a dialogue on moral philosophy; and *Soliloquy; or, Advice to an Author* (1710), a wide-ranging consideration of rhetoric. Along with *An Inquiry concerning Virtue*, an early philosophical work that had been published without the author's permission in 1699, these essays were published together in 1711 as *Characteristics of Men, Manners, Opinions, Times, etc.* In July 1711, Shaftesbury moved to Italy in an attempt to regain his health, which was unsuccessful; he died there in 1713. In these last two years, he worked on several essays on aesthetic theory.

The *Characteristics* was wildly popular throughout the eighteenth century, both in England and on the Continent. There were eleven English editions by 1790, and many translations. Shaftesbury's reputation seemed secure. He had a professed disciple in Francis Hutcheson, the Scottish moral philosopher; Diderot had translated the *Inquiry*; and Alexander Pope, through Bolinbroke, had picked up elements of his philosophy. However, *Characteristics* went unpublished from 1790 until 1901, when John Robertson brought out a new edition. Robertson attributed the decline of *Characteristics* to religious opposition to freethinking. To some extent, Shaftesbury's reputation also suffered from the shift in rhetorical theory, especially as it was represented by the "new" rhetoricians of late eighteenth-century Scotland—that is, Adam Smith, George Campbell, and Hugh Blair, who expressed some disapproval of Shaftesbury, both as a stylist and as a thinker, and discouraged their students from taking him as a model.

Their objections to Shaftesbury's style are predictable, since one of the significant characteristics of the rhetoric that developed in Scottish universities at that time was its endorsement of "plain style"—the unadorned and clear language presumably accessible to any reader. Figurative, recursive, indirect, and ironic—Shaftesbury's style is the antithesis of "plain." Yet it was admired, even in late eighteenth-century Scotland, particularly among younger readers. Educators, then, had to dislodge this perverse taste for linguistic elegance before they could effectively promote a proper taste for simplicity. There was also a strong religious motive—youths who admired Shaftesburian elegance might be led to adopt Shaftesburian anticlericalism and freethinking. Both Campbell and Blair were themselves clerics, as were several other rhetoricians of the late eighteenth century. It is therefore not surprising that Shaftesbury was dismissed, both as a stylistic model and an intellectual guide.

The Scottish rhetoricians, however, regarded Shaftesbury as he is still regarded today—as a moral philosopher, not a rhetorical theorist. Yet one of the essays of *Characteristics*, specifically addressed to aspiring writers, titled *Soliloquy; or, Advice to an Author*, does offer a discernible rhetorical theory—one that differs considerably from the theory espoused by the Scots. That Shaftesbury's *Soliloquy* has not been seen as rhetorical theory is due not only to Shaftesbury's general identification with "moral sense" philosophy but also to the essay's typically Shaftesburian form. Here, theory is not presented systematically, but informally. The essay includes: a charming story about a prince in love; a brief history of Greek literature; comments on what influence patrons, critics, and audiences should have on authors; condemnations of purely speculative epistemological philosophy; and sly attacks on Christianity. This baffling miscellaneousness and a bantering tone seem to have discouraged serious considerations of Shaftesbury's *Soliloquy* as rhetorical theory.

SHAFTESBURY'S RHETORICAL THEORY

The two distinctive characteristics of Shaftesbury's theory are its use of a Platonic epistemology, which contradicts the empirical epistemology of the later Scottish rhetoricians, and a classical notion of *ethos*—that is, that effective rhetoric is linked to good character. What the exercise of soliloquy is supposed to develop, in fact, is the good character that gives authors their persuasive power. According to Shaftesbury, most techniques of self-examination are mere moral inventory, mental surveys of one's own virtues and vices. But the soliloquy is a more complex procedure; it produces the proper public *ethos* by establishing the dominance of a particular internal *ethos*—what Shaftesbury alternately called "reason," "good sense," and "right taste"—in effect, a superior moral wisdom that is at least latent in every human mind.

Shaftesbury began his *Soliloquy* by defining the author's role as essentially normative. According to Shaftesbury, authors are "professed masters of understanding to the age" (104); whether authors consciously accept that role or not, the mere fact of publication gives them a sort of public authority. They thus have a need for wisdom; they must be sure of the value of their own ideas before broadcasting them to the public. The best way to ensure the validity of one's own ideas, Shaftesbury suggested, is to examine them in a soliloquy, a dialectical conversation with oneself. In fact, this exercise is essential, rather than optional: " 'Tis the hardest thing in the world to be a good thinker without being a strong self-examiner and thorough-paced dialogist in this solitary way" (112), he claimed.

These internal dialogues will invariably result in an internal split, "a certain duplicity of soul" (112) that allows internal dialogue. Shaftesbury offered various metaphors to describe the actual exchange of the two "persons." The longest, and most explicitly verbal, is a representation of a sort of internal parliamentary debate. The mind uses a "certain powerful figure of inward rhetoric" (123) to give voice to its own ideas, which then split into two "parties," one on the side of *Appetite*—Shaftesbury's inclusive term for all the less noble human desires—and the other representing *Reason*. At the beginning of the debate, the soliloquizer does not know which party is which. The debate itself reveals the identities of its participants. The odd quality of this debate is that the soliloquizer recognizes the better self, the "party of reason and good sense" (124), by its style, tone, and character, rather than by the substance of its arguments. The voice of reason triumphs not by virtue of the ideas it proposes—the whole purpose of the soliloquy is to judge those ideas—but through its straightforward rhetoric, the "plainer language and expression" (124). Appetite also announces itself rhetorically, with the worst kind of sophistry—"subtle," "insinuating," "specious" (123–24)—remarkable more for what it omits than what it says. In effect, Shaftesbury asked us to accept effective oratory as a sign of virtuous character.

Only when the author has identified his own better ideas can he address the public with authority. And his authority will be effective, because his audience has that same double nature of better and worse, Reason and Appetite. It is evident, Shaftesbury claimed, "that in the very nature of things there must of necessity be the foundation of a right and wrong taste, as well as in respect of inward characters and features as of outward person, behaviour, and action" (216–17). "Right taste" is not immediately apparent; it is, instead, what the process of soliloquy will make clear. Despite his insistence on this universal human capacity for moral knowledge, Shaftesbury was far from implying that it is easily obtained. But his assumption of a common sense of right and wrong allowed him to assume that those arguments that the self approves will be rhetorically effective for the public.

Of course, audiences can also choose to listen to Appetite rather than Reason—and Shaftesbury sadly concluded that the audiences of his day may be ruled by this baser part. He was particularly appalled by his contemporaries' taste for travel literature—those outlandish stories of savage customs and improbable adventure that were the eighteenth-century equivalent of American grocery-store tabloids. Although he lamented this taste for "monsters and monster-lands" (225), he also asserted that "nature will not be mocked. . . . She has a strong party abroad, and as strong a one within ourselves" (228). Readers, it appears, must also use the soliloquy to correct their responses to literature; if they examine bad writing in this way, its defects will become apparent, and their better, or more "natural," taste will again rule. Given a choice between real merit and mediocrity, the audience will choose rightly.

The greater responsibility is still the author's. If the reading public has developed a corrupt taste, the author must correct it, never cater to it. "One would expect it of our writers that if they had real ability they should draw the world to them, and not meanly suit themselves to the world in its weak state," Shaftesbury commented (171).

Shaftesbury could also account for the failure of some thinkers to distinguish right from wrong in their own minds: the distinction is made difficult by the amazing human predilection for self-deceit. Shaftesbury began with the commonplace that no one wants to know their own faults; he even insisted that public denunciation is less threatening than private acknowledgment, "for so true a reverence has everyone for himself when he comes clearly to appear before his close companion, that he had rather profess the vilest things of himself in open company than hear his character privately from his own mouth" (115). Even when this vanity is repressed, self-knowledge is still difficult, because of the inchoate, barely conscious nature of unarticulated thought. We think we know our own minds, Shaftesbury cautioned, "but our thoughts have generally such an obscure implicit language, that 'tis the hardest thing in the world to make them speak out distinctly" (113).

Right and wrong ideas are important not only for persuasion but for conduct. Shaftesbury's ostensible aim in this essay was to give advice to authors: they stand in need of soliloquy, because to publish the right messages, they must know them. But in preparing authors for this public role, the soliloquy also reforms private character. Although Shaftesbury first urged self-knowledge as a method of acquiring knowledge of human nature—a necessity for authors, whether historians, politicians, or poets (1:124)—he also insisted that the process of acquiring self-knowledge is inevitably reforming: for those who practice soliloquy, " 'tis impossible they should fail of being themselves improved and amended in their better part" (135).

The final section of *Soliloquy* is concerned with the development of taste— a process closely linked to the development of *ethos*, but including such external factors as reading the right books and cultivating the right companions. Shaftesbury refrained from extending his discussion to religious matters, however, on the ground "that there can be no rules given by human wit to that which was never humanly conceived, but divinely dictated and inspired" (229). This respectful attitude, however, is quickly undermined by Shaftesbury's comparison between religious dogma and heraldic devices. "Mermaids and griffins were the wonder of our forefathers" (233), Shaftesbury drily observed, and thus should not be changed or criticized. The implication that religious dogma should be equally immune but is equally trivial accurately represents Shaftesbury's resistance to religious authority and explains the rather abrupt conclusion of his essay: that only authors can give truly meaningful advice. And only soliloquy can create the proper authorial *ethos*, "that modesty, condescension, and just humanity which is essential to the success of all friendly counsel and admonition" (234).

This resistance to religious authority is inevitable in an essay proposing such a classical rhetorical theory. After all, Shaftesbury's hypothetical author gives advice that is guaranteed only by his own moral expertise, developed by a private dialectical exercise. His idea of the good is thus independent of any orthodox religious notion of virtue, as given in Scripture or publicly interpreted by the ministers of the Church. As an agent of public reformation, the author is potentially the minister's rival.

This rivalry may account, in part, for the distaste that the Scottish rhetoricians expressed for Shaftesbury's work—two of the more important ones, George Campbell and Hugh Blair, were also ministers. But there is also a tension between the pessimistic Christian view of the self as naturally corrupt and in need of grace, on the one hand, and this brighter vision, on the other. At any rate, Shaftesbury's idiosyncratic interpretation of these classical ideas was eclipsed by what Howell has called the "new" rhetoric of Smith, Campbell, and Blair.

As a moral philosopher, Shaftesbury's reputation withstood the century of silence; he is still regarded as a major influence on Hutcheson and on other moral philosophers, such as David Hume, Adam Smith, and Jeremy Bentham. Very little attention has been paid to his rhetorical theory, however. The bibliography of works about Shaftesbury's philosophy and aesthetics is extensive; I include here only those works that consider some aspect of his rhetoric.

BIBLIOGRAPHY

Primary Source

Cooper, Anthony Ashley, third earl of Shaftesbury. *Soliloquy; or, Advice to an Author. Characteristics of Men, Manners, Opinions, Times, etc.* Edited by John M. Robertson. Vol. 1. Gloucester, MA: Peter Smith, 1963.

Biography

Brett, R. L. *The Third Earl of Shaftesbury: A Study in Eighteenth-Century Literary Theory.* London: Hutchinson's University Library, 1951.
Fowler, Thomas. *Shaftesbury and Hutcheson.* London, 1882.
Voitle, Robert. *The Third Earl of Shaftesbury, 1671–1713.* Baton Rouge: Louisiana State University Press, 1984.

Criticism

Davidson, James W. "Criticism and Self-Knowledge in Shaftesbury's *Soliloquy.*" *Enlightenment Essays* 5.2 (1974): 50–61.
Griffin, Susan. "Shaftesbury's *Soliloquy:* The Development of Rhetorical Authority." *Rhetoric Review* 9.1 (1990): 94–106.
Selby, Scott Finn. "Soliloquy, Colloquy, and Dialectic: The Rhetorical Strategies of Shaftesbury's *Characteristics.*" *DAI* 44.1 (July 1983): 177A–78A.

THOMAS SHERIDAN
(1719–1788)

William Benzie

Thomas Sheridan was born in Dublin, Ireland, in 1719. His father, Dr. Thomas Sheridan, was a prominent Irish clergyman and a close friend of Jonathan Swift; in addition to preaching religion, Dr. Sheridan taught boys Greek and Latin in the family home at Capel Street, Dublin. His son also planned to make teaching his profession. But in 1735 a remark made to him by Swift, his godfather, changed everything. In his *Oration*, Sheridan wrote that soon after his entrance into college, Swift asked him what they taught there: "When I told him the Course of Reading I was put into, he asked me, Do they teach you English? No. Do they teach you how to speak? No. Then, said he, they teach you *nothing*" (19).

Sheridan decided that the English language could never be standardized until the study of oratory was revived; so the revival of oratory became his first step toward remedying the defects in the education system. And realizing that to master the difficult art of speaking required practical experience, he went on the professional stage: starting in 1743 he appeared in various roles at Smock Alley in Dublin and at Covent Garden and Drury Lane in London.

In 1756, Sheridan reverted to his original plan and published his first and most important book *British Education*, in which he presented his thesis that "the Immorality, Ignorance and false Taste" so prevalent in the country were the result of a defective system of education that a "Revival of the Art of Speaking and the Study of our Language" would help to correct. Accordingly, he suggested that British youth be required to study English rhetoric and be encouraged to learn the art of public speaking and the art of reading; in addition, he planned to set up a "vocational college"—that is, after a normal period of training in school, students were to pursue a course of studies designed to benefit them in their future occupations. His "vocational" plan was primarily aimed at the senate, the bar, and the pulpit.

For instance, in his *British Education*, Sheridan reasoned that without skill in speaking, members of the ecclesiastical and legal professions could not perform their duties properly; therefore, according to Sheridan, the study of oratory was essential to the well-being of the British Constitution (172).

Sheridan's contention that oratory would reform pulpit, senate, and bar provoked much deserved ridicule, but *British Education* does reflect the widespread concern at the time about the lack of energy and propriety in the delivery of contemporary speakers; and Sheridan's plan, with its emphasis on the study of English (instead of Latin and Greek), on vocational training, and its concern for the future needs of students is remarkably modern in spirit.

Not one to be silenced by criticism, in 1757 Sheridan began to give public lectures on elocution in Dublin, London, Oxford and Cambridge, Bath, Bristol, and Edinburgh. Generally speaking, these were very successful, notwithstanding their somewhat lukewarm reception in some quarters. For example, despite Dr. Samuel Johnson's prognostication that "Ridicule" had "gone down before him" (Boswell 1:394), Sheridan lectured with great success at Bath and Bristol during 1763 and 1764; and his London lectures were referred to by one of Sheridan's critics in the following terms: "Such was . . . the general desire to become skilled in declamation without much study, that the lecturer proceeded with an increase of hearers and popularity" (Watkins 1:102). The fact that he drew large audiences, sometimes of extremely influential people, indicates that a lively interest in elocution and propriety of speech did exist.

SHERIDAN'S RHETORICAL THEORY

However, Sheridan's claim to be regarded as one of the leaders of the elocution movement rests not so much on the popularity of the lectures as on the influence of his *Course of Lectures on Elocution* (1762), a book that became popular both in Britain and America. Throughout his major works he presented the general theories that he expounded in these lectures: his main concern was with the general aspects of oral delivery and with the factors that contribute to its effectiveness. For instance, he described elocution as the "just and graceful management of the voice, countenance, and gesture in speaking," and in Lectures 2 to 6 he dealt with articulation, pronunciation, emphasis, accent, tones (of the speaking voice), pauses, pitch and management of the voice; in the final lecture, he discussed gesture. Sheridan saw oral delivery as applying to both public speaking and reading; he made distinction of basic techniques between the two forms.

In his *Lectures on Elocution*, Sheridan avoided any mechanical rules or instructions for the expression of various thoughts and emotions. Rather than propose rules for gesture, movement of the body, and changes of countenance, he told the speaker to follow nature: "Let him speak entirely from his feelings; and they will find much truer signs to manifest themselves by, than he could find for them . . . in order to persuade, it is above all things necessary that the speaker should at least appear himself to believe what he utters; but this can never be the case, where there are any evident marks of affection or art" (121). By adopting this approach, Sheridan dissociated himself from the so-called Mechanical School of elocution, whose members, such as John Burgh and Gilbert Austin, analyzed gesture and issued detailed instructions on how to express various emotions; this kind of instruction showed the influence of Johann Kaspar Lavater's *Essays on Physiognomy*, which was popular at the time.

Sheridan's alliance with the more modern "natural" school of elocution has been questioned by some writers, but his repeated insistence that imitation was of negative value and led to artificiality and affectation made his position quite clear: "Avoid all imitation of others; let him [the orator] give up all pretensions to art, for it is better to have none, than not enough; and no man has enough, who has not arrived at such a perfection of art, as to wholly conceal his art" (120). He also insisted that in reading sermons, speeches, and so forth, the reader should try to come as close as possible to relaxed, extemporaneous speaking by using the mode of expression peculiar to conversation for both reading and speaking. Thus, he was opposed to conventional punctuation because it tended to lead the reader into an artificial manner of reciting: "Nothing has contributed so much, and so universally, to the corruption of delivery, as the bad use which has been made of the modern art of punctuation, by introducing artificial tones into all sentences, to the exclusion of the natural," he stated in his *Lectures on the Art of Reading* (1:159–60).

A strong negative response to the prescriptive methods of the "mechanical" school set in near the end of the eighteenth century, and supporters of Sheridan and the "natural" school attacked the methods of the former on the grounds that it produced unnatural and insincere delivery. In America the controversy was kept alive by works on elocution; and although the mechanical method remained popular there through the nineteenth century, many of the early American colleges used Sheridan's *Lectures on Elocution*.

John Walker became the leader of the "Mechanical" school with the publication of his *Elements of Elocution* in 1781; and in the main, writers on elocution both in Britain and America during the eighteenth and early nineteenth centuries followed closely the texts of either Sheridan and Walker, or both. A study of the systems of speech education that have been in use for many years in British and American schools and colleges shows that these systems owe much to the pioneering work of these early elocutionists in particular. Previously, the graces of delivery had been regarded as innate— and, therefore, unteachable. Thus, for the first time an attempt had been made to place elocution upon a scientific basis. Charles Fritz has written: "The ancients . . . gave only general advice on delivery. . . . Aristotle spoke of volume, rhythm and pitch, but did not analyze them. Quintilian spoke of the raising and lowering of the voice as tending to move the feelings of the hearers, but gave no suggestion as to method" (75).

In the end, Walker's influence proved to be far greater than Sheridan's, for the mechanical aspects of the elocutionists' teaching continued to flourish in the nineteenth and twentieth centuries; even by the end of the eighteenth century, Walker's works had virtually become the accepted guides to the art of delivery. Nevertheless, Sheridan's contribution to the elocution movement was considerable, and the following statement by James Murdoch in *A Plea for Spoken Language*, published in 1883, is not an exaggeration: "The combined influence, however, of Walker and Sheridan tended to awaken a new interest in reading, which, up to their time, had been taught in a hard, dry, mechanical manner, entirely devoid of expressive meaning. Save a strict injunction to drop the voice at the end of a sentence, no attempt had been made to give variety to its sounds, but the pupil was allowed to drone on like the buzz of a bee-hive" (26). Furthermore, James Rush in his *Philosophy of the Human Voice* (1827)—which was to become as influential in the American elocution movement as the texts of Sheridan, Walker, and Austin—paid tribute to Sheridan in the following way: "The works of Steele, Sheridan and Walker have made large contributions to the long neglected and still craving condition of our tongue. . . . Mr. Sheridan is well known by his accurate and systematic investigation of the art of reading: and though he improved both the detail and method of his subject, in the department of pronunciation, and emphasis, and pause, he made no analysis of intonation. A regretted omission! The more so, from the certainty, that if the topic has seriously invited his attention, his genius and industry would have shed much light of explanation upon it" (xvii–xviii).

Sheridan's influence on the areas of public speaking that he attacked in *British Education* (the senate, the bar, and the pulpit) is more difficult to determine. The only significant example of his influencing eighteenth-century parliamentary oratory is in the political career of his son, Richard Brinsley Sheridan, who inevitably received a thorough training in elocution from his father: "The father carried out a sort of patriarchal system of education, reading prayers every morning and expounding a portion of Scripture, after which a selection from some sterling author was read aloud with just and due elocution, which he seemed to think the only safeguard for society. The son must have profited—even malgré himself—by these wholesome exercises" (Fitzgerald 1:70).

It is also possible that Sheridan's teaching had some effect on Scottish forensic oratory because of his association with the Select Society of Edinburgh. And it is probably not too much to say that the impetus that Sheridan's lectures in Edinburgh gave to the movement in Scotland to improve public speaking by forming debating societies in the Scottish universities contributed in some measure to the preeminence of the Scottish bar in the latter eighteenth century: "In the summer of 1761, Mr. Sheridan . . . made a visit to Edinburgh, and delivered a course of lectures on elocution. . . . He was patronized by the professors in the College, by several of the clergy, by the most eminent among the gentlemen at the bar, by the judges of the Court of Session and by all who at that time were the leaders of public taste. . . . A rage for the Study of elocution became universal, as if it were the master—excellence in every profession" (Somerville 56–57).

A stronger case can be made for Sheridan's influence on pulpit oratory. A general revival of interest in the more practical affairs of the pulpit seems to have occurred in the late eighteenth and early nineteenth centuries. For instance, there was a marked interest in the publication of books about pulpit action and delivery, and some of the authors of these books either quote Sheridan or follow his methods. In his *Chironomia* (1806), Gilbert Austin, who was particularly concerned about pulpit excellence, quoted freely from Cicero, Quintilian, Walker, and Sheridan. And as late as 1858, the Reverend John Halcombe, Rector of St. Andrew's, Worcester, wrote in the preface to his *Church Reading*: "The manner of reading the Services of the Church of England having lately excited much attention, I have put forward the following pages. . . . The work from which I have mainly quoted was published in 1775, by Thomas Sheridan, Esq., M.A." (v–vii). This is a reference to Sheridan's *Lectures on the Art of Reading*, and it is clear that Sheridan's work relating to preaching was made use of by those who contributed directly to the general revival of interest in pulpit delivery that started at the end of the eighteenth century and continued in the nineteenth century.

In *Art of Reading*, Sheridan dealt with the oral reading of literature (Part One, with prose; Part Two, with verse), and the work was addressed to the clergy and "To all Masters and Mistresses of Academies and Boarding Schools." In Part One he discussed the sounds of the English language and the relation of sound to sense; and in his discussion of emphasis and accent, he was following the *Lectures on Elocution*, except that in *Art of Reading* he emphasized "accentual language" (words uttered in various notes or inflections without regard to meaning) and "emphatical language" (changes of voice regulated by meaning and sentiment); the latter was the natural mode of delivery and the one that should be cultivated.

Having laid down "all the fundamental principles of the art of reading," Sheridan then presented practical observations and examples to confirm his theories. For example, he used marks for emphasis and pause to point out the proper method of reading those parts of the liturgy that were in general use. This preoccupation with grammar and meaning as the directive element in vocal expression is typical of the "natural" school of elocution, despite Sheridan's use of mechanical marks for teaching emphases and his technique of pausing; these instructions were obviously used not only to increase understanding of content but also to steer the reader in the direction of an imitation of natural and meaningful conversation.

In his texts Sheridan tended to theorize and elaborate on the virtues of oratory rather than offer practical methods of teaching the subject. This is less true of the *Art of Reading*, the first part of which, for example, sets out basic directions for the production of vowel and consonant sounds. In the second part of the book, Sheridan turned prosodist and focused his attention on English versification.

To what extent clergymen and schoolmasters responded to Sheridan's strictures in the *Art of Reading*, is impossible to say. But there is no doubt that over the years many parts of his *Lectures* received their widest circulation through their incorporation by Lindley Murray in his celebrated *English Grammar*, a text that went through countless editions after its publication in 1795.

If Sheridan's influence in these areas of public speaking was somewhat peripheral, the effects of his efforts to promote elocution on the English stage were quite central. Indeed, as a leading member of the "natural" school of elocution, his influence on stage presentation seems to have been considerable. The period from 1690 to 1714 was one of classicism, "marked on the stage by formalism and convention and the acceptance of tradition" (Campbell 199); and the main features of stage delivery in tragedy were pompous utterance, a high-flown style of declamation, and a formalism normally associated with grand opera. This artificial style of declamation has a great deal in common with the mechanical school of elocution in its inflexibility and its insistence upon formal and "fixed" gesture. In 1725, Charles Macklin tried but failed to bring the "natural style of acting" to the English stage and later wrote of his lack of success: "I spoke so *familiar*, Sir, and so little in the *hoity-toity* tone of the Tragedy of that day, that the manager told me, I had better go to grass for another year or two" (Cooke 12–13). And although David Garrick's performance of Richard III in 1741 "in the Natural Manner" marked a new age in stage presentation, the Garrick school of acting was in decline after 1776; ironically one reason for this was the growing importance of declamation (an art Garrick did not excel in), a direct result of Sheridan's teaching. Lily Campbell wrote that "to understand the new forces at work in the stage affairs of 1776, it is necessary to go back to trace a new interest that was just coming into an influential place after years of struggle on the part of one man, Thomas Sheridan. It was a two-fold interest . . . an interest in the propriety of speech and an interest in declamation in and for itself" (191).

Sheridan's own success as an actor, and later as a stage manager, accounts for his close association with the stage; on at least one occasion he used his position to deliver his lectures on elocution from the stage at Drury Lane. But it was really his friendship with the great Mrs. Siddons that enabled him to influence English stage presentation. Sheridan taught her a great deal about acting, especially the art of declamation. In his *Memoirs of Mrs. Siddons*, James Boaden described her method of studying a part: "She was fond of having the experience of old Mr. Sheridan to confirm her own judgment; [except] when he went to the theatre with her, 'where *alone*,' she said, 'she could show him exactly what she could do at night' " (1:366–67). When she and her brother John Philip Kemble ruled the London stage from 1782 to 1814, it is not surprising that propriety of speech and elegance of declamation were emphasized. "That this interest [in declamation] was strengthened in the stage world by his [Sheridan's] rule and by his influence exercised through Mrs. Siddons and the younger actors must be immediately evident," Lily Campbell concluded (195).

In 1769, Sheridan embarked upon a new venture, which was really a development of his lectures on elocution: readings and recitations from the works of the best English authors. Boaden recalled these readings: "He [Sheridan] made considerable effect in the speeches of *our* Demosthenes, Lord Chatham, and of his Grecian prototype. Much of the church service, too, he stripped of the usual nasal monotony, and settled the emphasis by a sound logic. In poetry, I consider him to have made more of the *Alexander's Feast*, and the famous *Elegy* by Gray, than even *very* attentive readers could have discovered" (1:367–68). It is significant to the development of an interest in elocution and recitation that during their heyday both Kemble and Mrs. Siddons held "Attic evenings" (as they were called) of their own and also attended Sheridan's readings. That these "Attic evenings," so popular in their day, were not quickly forgotten is seen in the following account written as late as 1793 in *Gentleman's Magazine*: "The names of Sheridan and Henderson, now, alas! no longer to be heard of, some few years back drew crowds to attend their readings; an entertainment which would have honoured the elegant and the refined age of Athenian learning" (1084). The value of the readings in developing an appreciation of English literature is obvious, and it is unlikely they had no influence on the growing interest in propriety of speech and the art of declamation already developed by Sheridan and Walker.

One important by-product of the "Attic evenings" was the appearance during the second half of the eighteenth century of a large number of "elegant extracts"—that is, pieces for reading and recitation selected from the poetry and prose of the best authors. Most of these anthologies (of which Vicessimus Knox's *Elegant Extracts* was the most popular) provided instructions to the student regarding gesture, delivery, pronunciation, and so forth; and many of the publications contained passages made famous by Sheridan and Henderson.

Since progress toward the study of English language and literature was largely determined by the frequency with which English authors were recommended as models for students, the importance of the "elegant extracts" is clear. In the eighteenth century, the Dissenting academies were the most potent force in the development of the study of English and elocution; while the universities continued to provide a classical education, the academies were offering the kind of liberal education that Sheridan advocated in *British Education*. Indeed, had the academies never existed, it is hard to say when the study of elocution and English would have begun. Teachers like Philip Doddridge (Northampton Academy), Joseph Priestley (Warrington Academy), and William Enfield (also of Warrington), as well as the texts that they published on elocution and English, had an enormous effect on subsequent educational practice. For example, Enfield's *The Speaker* (1774) became a well-known textbook in schools, and by 1800 at least eleven editions had appeared. The 1790 London edition of Enfield's work contained two essays, one on elocution and one on taste, and in 1795 the first American edition was published in Boston. Between 1814 and 1858, ten more editions were published in Britain and America.

The Speaker is based on Sheridan throughout. In his "Essay on Elocution," Enfield made it clear that he was a member of the "natural" school of elocution: "FOLLOW NATURE, is certainly the fundamental law of oratory, without a regard to which, all other rules will only produce affected declamation, not just elocution" (vi). Enfield followed Sheridan on the subjects of emphasis, gesture, tones, and so forth; and "Sheridan on Elocution" is listed in the "Select Catalogue of Books in the Library belonging to the Warrington Academy" for the year 1775. *The Speaker* also provides another example of a very popular kind of school text that had its origin in the "Attic evenings" given first by Sheridan. In 1796, appeared *Sheridan's and Henderson's Method of Reading and Reciting English Poetry*. The text gave detailed instructions as to how passages should be read:

For them no more the blazing hearth shall burn
Or busy *housewife* ply her evening care.

The word *housewife* sounds rather clumsy on the ear, and Mr. Sheridan used in consequence to pronounce it as if spelt hussif, which has a much better effect than the other, and we shall therefore recommend the use of it to the scholar.

A taste for polite literature was clearly becoming recognized as a necessary social accomplishment, and the academies regarded belles lettres as part of the educational program for all students, no matter what their future occupation was to be. Elocution had become a recognized subject, and English literature was being used as a storehouse for specimens of good style in the teaching of composition. In short, the displacement of Latin by English had begun, and the groundwork had been done for the educational expansion of the nineteenth century.

Sheridan's exaggerated claims for the powers of oratory and the zeal with which he doggedly promoted the study of elocution naturally made him appear a somewhat ridiculous figure in the eyes of many contemporaries and biographers. Writing about Richard Brinsley Sheridan's fortunes in 1770, Walter Sichel commented: "He was bound for a concert-room where his father, the pompous and indefatigable gentleman-actor and author, the teacher and exemplar of elocution, had advertised recitations and a discourse on the powers of rhetoric 'with a view to the improvement of human nature' " (1:184). This statement and others like it no doubt help to explain why the influence of Sheridan's lifetime work was never properly assessed. Yet, his efforts produced very substantial results in many different ways. For instance, as a leader of the elocution movement he contributed in a very significant way to the development of modern theories of public address in Britain and America. And through his lectures, as well as his "Attic evenings" (and the "elegant extracts" that grew out of them), he did much to promote the study of English language and literature in schools and universities and, at the same time, exerted a strong influence on eighteenth-century social and literary culture.

BIBLIOGRAPHY

Primary Sources

Sheridan, Thomas. *British Elocution*. London, 1756.
———. *An Oration Pronounced before a Numerous Body of the Nobility and Gentry, Assembled at the Musick-hall in Fishamble Street*. Dublin, 1757.
———. *A Course of Lectures on Elocution*. London, 1762.
———. *Lectures on the Art of Reading*. London, 1775.

Biography

Bacon, Wallace A. "The Elocutionary Career of Thomas Sheridan (1719–1788)." *Speech Monographs* 31.1 (1964): 1–53.
Rae, Fraser. "Thomas Sheridan." *DNB* (1963–1964).
Sichel, Walter. *Sheridan*. London, 1909.

Criticism

Benzie, William. *The Dublin Orator: Thomas Sheridan's Influence on Eighteenth-Century Rhetoric and Belles Lettres*. Leeds Texts and Monographs, edited by A. C. Cawley and R. C. Alston, n.s., no. 4. The University of Leeds School of English, 1972.
Boaden, James. *Memoirs of Mrs. Siddons*. 2 vols. London, 1827.
Boswell, James. *Life of Johnson*. 2 vols. Oxford, 1934.
Campbell, Lily B. "The Rise of a Theory of Stage Presentation in England during the Eighteenth Century." *Publication of the Modern Language Association* 32.2 (1917): 163–200.
Cooke, William. *Memoirs of Charles Macklin*. London, 1804.
Croghan, Martin J. "Swift, Thomas Sheridan, Maria Edgeworth and the Evolution of Hiberno-English." *Irish University Review* 20.1 (1990): 19–34.
Enfield, William. *The Speaker; or, Miscellaneous Pieces Selected from the Best English Writers*. London, 1782.
———. *Sheridan's and Henderson's Method of Reading*. London, 1796.
Fitzgerald, Percy. *The Lives of the Sheridans*. 2 vols. London, 1886.

Fritz, Charles. "From Sheridan to Rush: The Beginnings of English Elocution."
    Quarterly Journal of Speech 16.1 (1930): 75–88.

Gentleman's Magazine 63 (1793): 1084.

Halcombe, John. *Church Reading.* London, 1858.

Murdoch, James. *A Plea for Spoken Language.* Cincinnati, 1883.

Rush, James. *The Philosophy of the Human Voice.* Philadelphia, 1827.

Somerville, Thomas. *My Own Life and Times, 1741–1814.* Edinburgh, 1861.

Stephan, Eric. "Sheridan's and Walker's Use of the Pause." *Southern Speech Journal*
    33.2 (1967): 119–23.

Vandraegen, Daniel E. "Thomas Sheridan and the Natural School." *Speech Mono-
    graphs* 20.1 (1953): 58–64.

Watkins, John. *Memoirs of the Public and Private Life of the Right Hon. R. B. Sher-
    idan.* 2 vols. London, 1818.

ADAM SMITH
(1723–1790)

H. Lewis Ulman

Most widely known for *The Wealth of Nations* (1776), his seminal work on economics, Adam Smith was also among the first to articulate the new rhetoric that emerged in Britain during the second half of the eighteenth century. He lectured on rhetoric from 1748 to 1763, first to public audiences in Edinburgh and later at Glasgow University, but he never published his lectures; and for over one and one-half centuries after his death, his rhetorical theory remained somewhat of an enigma, known to historians only through contemporary reports that summarized and attested to the quality and influence of his lectures. However, in 1958 two volumes of carefully recorded student notes from the Glasgow lectures were discovered and in 1963 were published as *Lectures on Rhetoric and Belles Lettres*, allowing scholars at long last to assess Smith's rhetorical theory in detail, if not at first hand. One of the most authoritative of those assessments is that "Adam Smith's lectures gave [the] new rhetoric its earliest and most independent expression" (Howell 541).

STUDENT, LECTURER, AND PROFESSOR

Adam Smith was born on June 5, 1723, in Kirkcaldy, Scotland, a small fishing village near Edinburgh. He was the son of Adam Smith, a customs official, and Margaret Douglas, who raised him by herself after her husband died early in 1723. Smith attended the burgh school of Kirkcaldy, then studied at Glasgow University from 1737 to 1740, where he was taught by Francis Hutcheson and received his M.A., graduating with distinction. He then won a scholarship (the Snell Exhibition) to Balliol College, Oxford, where he studied from 1740 to 1746, focusing on history, philosophy, and Greek and Latin literature. As a condition of his scholarship, Smith was expected to take orders in the Church of England, but he was reluctant to do so. He returned to Kirkcaldy, where he lived from 1746 to 1748, the year in which he first gave the course of lectures on rhetoric and belles lettres that constitute his major contribution to rhetorical theory (Mossner and Ross xix; Lothian xiv; Stephen).

Reportedly at the invitation of Lord Kames and other Edinburgh literati, Smith delivered his lectures before public audiences, perhaps under the auspices of the Philosophical Society of Edinburgh (Bevilacqua 559). The potential influence of these lectures is suggested by the roster of notable men of letters who are known to have attended: Lord Kames; Alexander Wedderburn, who edited the *Edinburgh Review* from 1755 to 1756; William Robertson, a historian who later became Principal of Edinburgh University; and Hugh Blair, who acknowledged his debt to Smith's lectures in his own *Lectures on Rhetoric and Belles Lettres* (Lothian xxi; Bryce 8). Another indication of the success of the lectures was the subsequent history of rhetoric at Edinburgh. After Smith's departure for Glasgow University in 1751, Robert Watson offered a similar course, followed in 1759 by Hugh Blair, who in 1762 became the first Regius Professor of Rhetoric and Belles Lettres at Edinburgh—the first professorship of its kind in Britain.

Smith was appointed Professor of Logic at Glasgow University in 1751, a post that traditionally included the teaching of rhetoric (Bryce 9). The following year, however, he was translated to the Chair of Moral Philosophy, a position he occupied from 1752 until 1763, after which he left the university, serving for three years as tutor to Henry Scott, Third Duke of Buccleuch, and living thereafter on a pension from the Buccleuch estates and income from a government post. As Professor of Moral Philosophy at Glasgow, it was no longer Smith's official duty to lecture on rhetoric, but he chose that subject for his "private" class. The students in that class would have previously attended lectures on rhetoric from the Professor of Logic and would be attending—or would have attended—Smith's "public" course of lectures on ethics, politics, jurisprudence, and natural theology (Bryce 9).

Unfortunately, Smith's manuscripts were burned at his request shortly before his death in 1790, and aside from published reports by those who heard Smith's public and university lectures on rhetoric, the only record that we have of the lectures is a set of student notes from Smith's 1762–1763 "private" class on rhetoric at Glasgow. Discovered in 1958 at an Aberdeen auction, these manuscripts appear to have been transcribed primarily by two hands, presumably from notes taken during the lectures (Bryce 3). Although evidence suggests that Smith's lectures on rhetoric and belles lettres from 1762 to 1763 follow his Edinburgh lectures closely and that the students' notes are quite faithful representations of the lectures, readers should keep in mind the nature of the text that has come down to us (see Howell 544–45). Nevertheless, the discovery of a nearly complete set of notes from Smith's lectures (notes from the first lecture are missing) provided the first substantial evidence on which to base assessments of Smith's contribution to eighteenth-century rhetorical theory.

SMITH'S RHETORICAL THEORY

The general plan of Smith's lectures embodies the nature of his contribution to rhetorical theory and secures his place as one of the earliest proponents of the new rhetoric; unfortunately, the state of the text renders some details of Smith's plan difficult to reconstruct. Wilbur Samuel Howell has proposed two main divisions, arguing that Lectures 2 through 11 deal with communication and that lectures 12 through 30 analyze various forms of discourse. Howell saw the first division as breaking from the old rhetoric's focus on persuasion by establishing *communication* as a new, broader aim for rhetoric. Further, he has noted that the second division extends the realm of rhetoric beyond the civic forums analyzed by ancient rhetoricians; Smith's plan encompasses a much broader range of discourse, including poetry, history, and scientific writing (548). More specifically, the matter of the second section of the lectures is *composition*, a term that highlights the practical bent of Smith's rhetoric and is, in fact, the term most often used in the lectures to refer to kinds of writing or, to use Smith's phrase "Species of Composition" (62).[1]

Communication

Like other eighteenth-century rhetoricians who viewed rhetoric as a general art of communication, Smith grounded rhetoric, in part, on the study of language. His first ten lectures (2–11) focus, in turn, on the bases of perspicuity in language, the "origin and design of language," the general rules of prose style, and the relations between prose style and character. In the initial extant lecture, on perspicuity, Smith first compared native and foreign words, arguing that "foreigners though they may signify the same thing never convey the idea with such strength as those we are acquainted with and whose origin we can trace" (3). Smith argued that the many foreign terms in English constitute a defect in the language: "Most terms of art and most compounded words are borrowed from other languages, so that the lower sort of People, and those who are not acquainted with those languages from whence [*sic*] they are taken can hardly understand many of the words of their own tongue"—and, consequently, misuse them (4). Turning next to the dependence of perspicuity on propriety and purity of style, Smith argued that words must be "agreeable to the custom of the country" but that the language of "men of rank and breeding" is the most agreeable to us (4); thus, he developed strong links among national identity, social rank, sympathy, and linguistic influence. Caught in the bind of basing linguistic standards on custom but dismissing the custom of the majority, he appealed to a *standard* as opposed to that which is "mean and Low," however widely used (4). In short, "It is the custom of the people that forms what we call propriety, and the custom of the better sort from whence the rules of purity of stile [i.e., *style*] are to be drawn" (5). In the rest of the lecture, Smith considered in turn the order of words, sentence length, figurative language, and the use of pronouns, illustrating his analysis with examples from classical and contemporary authors. In the lecture on perspicuity, then, we find several approaches to language characteristic of the new rhetoric: (1) comparing languages and identifying their relative strengths and defects; (2) emphasizing the vernacular while supporting and illustrating arguments through examples drawn from both classical and contemporary writers; (3) linking phonological, grammatical, and stylistic standards to national custom and social hierarchy.

Turning next to the origin and progress of language,[2] Smith first presented a speculative account of two savages trying to name specific things, assuming that names for substantives occurred first in the evolution of language. The problem that he posed concerns the development of general names, adjectives, and prepositions, all of which seem to require greater powers of abstraction than he was willing to assign to early man (9–11). Smith sided with those who would resolve this problem by arguing, for instance, that "all the primitive and simple languages . . . express by various modification of the same word what would otherwise require a preposition" (11); or, more generally, "the simpler the language the more complex" its grammar (13). Again, he cited the mixing of nations as a source of linguistic transformation. Foreigners looking for simple ways to say something, he argued, will drop inflections: for instance, "prepositions would be put . . . in the place of the declensions of nouns" (13). Interestingly, Smith compared this evolution to that of machines, which, he claimed, become simpler as they are refined. But while simpler machines that accomplish the same task are always to be preferred, simple languages will often have less "variety and harmony of sound," will be less capable of "various arrangement," and will be more "prolix" (13). Two aspects of Smith's historical argument are particularly representative of eighteenth-century rhetoricians' investigations of the origins of language: (1) his comparative analysis of languages again emphasizes relative strengths and defects, and (2) his speculations about differences between savage and cultured nations and primitive and refined languages are grounded in an ideology of progress and parallel his analysis of the relations between language and social and intellectual differences in contemporary society.

Having established some basic assumptions about language, Smith turned next to explicit rules of style relating to the arrangement of words and the use of tropes and figures. After first outlining the constituent parts of sentences ("periods," phrases, etc.), he established a general principle of order: contrasting the "animated and Eloquent" to the strictly "grammaticall," he argued that "whatever is most interesting in the sentence, on which the rest depends, should be placed first; and so on thro' the whole," thus linking the rules of style to the passions, imagination, and understanding in concert (18, 19). To this general rule of arrangement he added only a subordinate injunction to arrange prose so that "your Sentence or Phrase never drag [*sic*] a Tail"—that is, to place qualifications before affirmations in order to give the impression of "accurate and extensive views" (24). In the course of this argument, he again linked style to the passions, comparing the regularity and irregularity of various passions to the prose cadences that best express them. Two simple rules, then, constitute Smith's doctrine of arrangement, and he made no bones about his impatience with more elaborate rhetorical systems: "Many other rules for arrangement have been given but they do not deserve attention" (24).

Similarly, Smith refused to offer a detailed taxonomy of tropes and figures, calling ancient and modern rhetorical treatises based on such taxonomies "a very silly set of Books" (26). He took issue with the assumption that figurative language gives "the chief beauty and elegance to language," arguing instead that "when the sentiment of the speaker is expressed in a neat, clear, plain and clever manner, and the passion or affection he is possessed of and intends, *by sympathy*, to communicate to his hearer, is plainly and cleverly hit off, then and then only the expression has all the force and beauty that language can give it" (25). This key passage provided the foundation from which Smith argued that it is not figures themselves but their relations to the sentiments, characters, and circumstances of speakers that make such expressions agreeable and effective. Accordingly, he concluded that styles will vary with characters, each having its proper complement (34).

Smith next summarized his discussions of particular aspects of style, noting three general principles governing the "beauties of stile": (1) words should "neatly and properly" express "the thing to be described" and convey "the sentiment the author entertained of it and desired to communicate by sympathy to his hearers"; (2) styles will vary with sentiments; and (3) "when all other circumstances are alike the character of the author must make the stile different" (40). Ever the champion of simplicity in rhetorical principles, Smith admitted that these and "all the Rules of Criticism and morality when traced to their foundation, turn out to be some Principles of Common Sence [*sic*] which every one assents to; all the business of those arts is to apply these Rules to the different subjects and shew what their conclusion is when they are so applyed" (55). Accordingly, he devoted much of lectures 7 through 11 to analyses of the "character of some of the best English Prose writers" in order to illustrate and substantiate his rhetorical principles (55).

For instance, Smith illustrated his argument about the variety of styles by examining the characters and styles of Jonathan Swift and William Temple as representative of "plain" and "simple" men, respectively. Similarly, he examined Swift and Lucian as representative of two forms of ridicule and the characters appropriate to them. Further, he presented Joseph Addison as an exemplar of "gaiety" and "modesty" of character and style, and Shaftesbury as a negative example of someone who has "formed to himself an idea of beauty of Stile abstracted from his own character" (56). All of these case studies illustrated Smith's three requirements of a good writer, who must (1) have "complete knowledge of his Subjects," (2) "arrange all parts of his Subject in their proper order," and (3) "describe the Ideas he has of these severall in the most proper and expressive manner" (42). These requirements and Smith's other principles of style ground an art of communication that intimately links style to knowledge, character, and social contexts rather than treating it as an adornment or embellishment of discourse.

Composition

The second major section of Smith's course (Lectures 12–30) concerns the "different parts and Species of Composition" (62). Arranged according to a taxonomy of kinds of composition, these lectures emphasize practical rules and principles governing the ends, means, arrangement, and expression appropriate to each form of composition. Smith also provided historical sketches of the forms and analyzed the work of writers who had "succeeded most happily in all these branches" (63).

Smith began his taxonomy with a division between discourses whose purpose is "barely to relate some fact" and those that aim additionally "to prove some proposition" (62). The first kind he called narrative, which he eventually divided further into descriptive and historical writing, the former a general method of relating facts, the latter a distinct form of composition. The second kind (discourses that aim to prove propositions) he divided into two subcategories, the didactic and the rhetorical, distinguished by their ends and means. Didactic writing aims primarily at instruction and only secondarily at persuasion; therefore, it "proposes to put before us the arguments on both sides of the question in their true light" (62). Rhetorical writing aims primarily at persuasion and only secondarily at instruction; therefore, it "magnifies all the arguments on the one side and diminishes or conceals" arguments that favor the opposing side (62). Smith further divided rhetorical writing according to the classical categories of demonstrative, deliberative, and judicial eloquence, though he went out of his way to distance himself from the classical tradition on this point: "It is rather reverence for antiquity than any great regard for the Beauty or usefullness of the thing itself which makes me mention the Antient divisions of Rhetorick" (63). Thus, since Smith also considered poetry and drama in Lecture 21, his broad treatment of communication and composition encompassed discursive territory that once belonged to the realms of rhetoric, dialectic, and poetics (Howell 575).

Smith turned first to the description of facts, the basis of narrative writing and of its prototypical form of composition, history. However, it is important to remember that in his taxonomy Smith often blended analytical principles, sometimes emphasizing ends, at other times means. Further, his categories overlap, as he noted at the beginning of Lecture 17, where he applied "to the historicall stile" what he had said about description: "Besides the narration makes a considerable part in every Oration. It requires no small art to narrate properly those facts which are necessary for the Groundwork of the Oration. So that I would be necessitated to lay down rules for narration in generall, that is for the historicall Stile, before I could thoroughly explain The Rhetoricall composition" (89). Indeed, Smith's categorical divisions among the forms of composition are most interesting not for the categories themselves but for what they reveal about his manner of analyzing the ends, means or matter, arrangement, expression, and history of discourse.

Smith employed two schemes for categorizing compositions according to their aims or ends. In the first he followed classical tradition and focused on the effects of a discourse on its audience—specifically, instruction, persuasion, and amusement. Allowing for primary and secondary aims, Smith claimed that historical and didactic compositions share the primary aim of instruction but differ in that the secondary aim of history is to amuse, while the secondary aim of didactic writing is to persuade. In Smith's scheme the aims of didactic writing are shared by all forms of rhetorical composition, but with reverse emphasis—persuasion is primary, instruction secondary. Smith designated amusement as the chief aim of poetry without explicitly naming any secondary aims (118). Finally, because description is basic to all compositions, we can surmise that it lends itself to all ends of writing. In his second scheme for categorizing the aims of compositions, Smith focused on whether the speaker or writer's personal interests were invested in the matter at issue. From this perspective, Smith associated history and didactic writing ideally with disinterestedness and associated all forms of rhetoric with interestedness. Disinterestedness should not be taken to imply lack of sentiment, however, as Smith's discussions of the means or matter of the various species of composition amply illustrate.

Since the description of facts constitutes the basic matter of all the types of discourse in Smith's scheme, it is no surprise that he provided a fairly elaborate taxonomy of facts. First, he divided facts into two general categories: *external* facts ("transactions that pass without us") and *internal* facts ("the thoughts sentiments or designs of men") (63). After further subdividing simple objects, he identified two kinds of complex objects—characters and actions. Smith associated each of these types of facts first with some general rules of description and, throughout his remaining lectures, with rules for describing and developing the matter of each sort of composition.

Smith's rules of description and development build upon his basic distinction between external and internal facts, emphasizing the latter and, thereby, grounding his rhetorical theory in sentiment, sympathy, and character. For instance, he identified two general means of describing simple objects: *directly*, by describing "parts that constitute the quality we want to express," and *indirectly*, by "describing the effects this quality produces on those who behold it" (67). Similarly, he noted two causes of internal facts: *internal causes*, or "dispositions of mind as fit one for that certain passion or affection," and *external causes*, or "such objects as produce these effects on a mind so disposed" (68). Turning to complex objects, Smith advised that descriptions of character may be either *direct*, in which case we "relate the various parts of which it consists" (78), or *indirect*, in which case we "relate the effects it produces on the outward behaviour and Conduct of the person" (80). Generally, he preferred the indirect method of describing character, as he did for describing actions: "When we mean to affect the reader deeply we must have recourse to the indirect method of description, relating the effects the transaction produced both on the actors and Spectators" (86–87).

According to Smith, each of the forms of composition builds upon these basic principles for the description of facts. In history, Smith advised, the central facts should be the actions of men, for "Design and Contrivance" interest us more than "chance, and undesigning instinct," and descriptions of actions arouse in us "Sympatheticall affections" (90). Further, because the chief aim of history is instruction, it ideally describes the internal and external causes of "the more interesting and important events of human life . . . and by this means points out to us by what manner and method we may produce similar good effects or avoid Similar bad ones" (90). Similarly, in demonstrative oratory, we describe actions and characters, focusing on actions if they show success, on character if it shows admirable qualities in the face of adversity or defeat—always with the aim of establishing a hierarchy of virtues. Stressing character as well in his discussion of poetry and drama, Smith considered the traditional rules concerning the unities of interest, time, and place, noting how each rule might be violated without ill effect but insisting that the one rule that "must be always observed" is propriety of character (123–24).

In his discussions of didactic, demonstrative, deliberative, and judicial compositions—all forms that depend on proving propositions as well as relating facts—Smith considered means of development uniquely suited to each form. He identified two methods in didactic writing—proceeding from principles to phenomena or vice versa—related to the methods of natural philosophy, which he styled Newtonian and Aristotelian, respectively (though, as Howell has noted, the latter method can be traced at least to Ramus, if not to Plato's time [563–64]). Similarly, Smith argued that deliberative oratory employs two analogous methods of development, the Aristotelian and Socratic, the former stating the point to be proven "boldly at the Beginning," the latter "bringing on the audience by slow and imperceptible degrees to the thing to be proved" (146–47). Finally, in his analysis of judicial orations, Smith identified two subject matters, fact and law, which give rise to three kinds of issues: (1) the "reality of a [disputed] fact"; (2) the "Existence of a certain Point of Law"; and (3) the "Extent of that law" (170). As he acknowledged, these three issues follow classical methods for determining the question at issue in a judicial oration. Smith further noted that questions of fact may be argued from causes or effects, questions of law may be argued from precedents or statutes, and questions regarding the extent of the law may appeal to the letter or spirit of the law. In all these discussions of the means or matter of composition, Smith borrowed from classical tradition when he saw fit but carefully noted circumstances in which a contemporary rhetoric must depart from tradition.

Belying the common notion that the new rhetoric was primarily a rhetoric of management rather than substance, Smith had relatively little to say about the organization of the various forms of composition, and what he did say about arrangement did not simply outline traditional structures but related arrangement to the capacities of hearers and the mechanisms of sympathy. In history, for instance, his general rule was to arrange narration "in the same order as that in which the events themselves happened" because "the mind naturally conceives that the facts happened in the order they are related, and when they are by this means suited to our naturall conceptions the notion we form of them is by that means rendered more distinct" (98). Similarly, in didactic writing Smith advocated organizing materials in divisions and subdivisions because they "assist the memory in tracing the connection of the severall parts" but warned against more than two levels of organization because "subsubdivisions . . . become too intricate for our memory to comprehend" (144). In regard to demonstrative oratory, his students were advised to begin with actions, for character "only appears in perfection when it is called out into action" (132). It is in his discussion of judicial oratory that Smith dealt most explicitly with the classical doctrine of *dispositio* or arrangement. He outlined the five traditional parts of judicial orations—exordium, narration, confirmation, refutation, and peroration—but was careful to point out ways in which this classical structure was no longer suited to modern courts.

Similarly, in his analyses of exemplary writers of the different forms of composition, Smith linked the ends, means, arrangement, and expression of writers' work to their cultural circumstances.[3] In his history of historians, he first traced the development of the form. The poets, he said, were the first historians, though their primary aim was to please. Herodotus, according to Smith, extended "the plan of history" by providing information about "the Customs of the different nations" and other interesting facts, but his design "seems to have been rather to amuse than to instruct" (105). Thucydides, Smith argued, was the first to aim at "a proper design of historicall writing" because he aimed to present the causes of the Peloponnesian War (106). This account of history is tied to the state of knowledge in society. Early writers, Smith argued, focused on the marvelous; but when knowledge displaced their material, writers who wished only to please turned to tragedy and romances. Continuing that line of reasoning, Smith offered a cultural critique of Tacitus's *Annales* and *History*, sketching the state of Rome at the time and arguing, "Sentiment must bee [*sic*] what will chiefly interest such a people" (112). Similarly, he compared Machiavelli and Guicciardini, chiefly to contrast the degree to which their histories were or were not contaminated with the party spirit of their times. And, finally, he faulted the English historians Clarendon and Burnet on this same count, concluding that "it has been the fate of all modern histories to be wrote [*sic*] in a party spirit" because "the Truth and Evidence of Historicall [*sic*] facts is now in much more request and more critically Examined than among the Antients [*sic*] because of all the Numerous Sects among us whether Civil or Religious, there is hardly one the reasonableness of whose Tenets does not depend on some historicall fact" (116, 102). The problem is that such an attitude toward history violates the principle of disinterestedness.

Another striking example of the connections that Smith drew between cultural conditions and forms of composition occurs in his history of deliberative rhetoric. Analyzing Demosthenes's oratory, Smith first considered "the state the Athenian affairs were in at the time these Orations were composed" (149). Explaining that the Athenians needed to be persuaded to go to war to defend themselves against Philip of Macedon, Smith focused on Demosthenes's means of engaging his audience: "His manner is that of one who spoke to a favourable audience; for tho the Athenians were sluggish and Dilatory in undertaking the war they saw well enough that it was for the good of the State" (152). Similarly, in his subsequent analysis of Cicero's orations, Smith began with "some observations on the State of the Roman Commonweal" (154). Here he focused on the differences of rank in Roman culture, contrasting that to the more democratic society of Athens: "In the one country the People at least the Nobles would converse and harangue with Dignity, Pomp and the air of those who speak with authority. The language of the others would be that of freedom, ease and familiarity" (158). Smith concluded that the "differences in the Stile of these orators may probably arise from the different condition of the countries in which they lived," thus linking rhetorical theory and practice to cultural contexts (160).

Smith's Influence and Significance

Though Smith's decision not to publish his lectures certainly meant that his rhetorical theory would be far less influential than George Campbell's or Hugh Blair's, the discovery of student notes from Smith's lectures has given scholars a fuller understanding of the emergence of the new rhetoric at midcentury. Moreover, scholars have found in Smith's lectures the principles of a distinctive historiography (Hogan) and evidence that his conjunction of rhetoric and belles lettres was but the precursor to their later split—that is, the split between the study of literature and the teaching of writing (Carter, Court, Lothian). Clearly, to read Smith's lectures is to examine a pivotal point in the history of rhetoric.

NOTES

1. Passages from Smith's *Lectures on Rhetoric and Belles Lettres* quoted in this essay are from *The Glasgow Edition of the Works and Correspondence of Adam Smith*.

2. Bryce has noted that Lecture 3 is a short version of Smith's "Considerations concerning the First Formation of Languages," first published in *The Philosophical Miscellany* (1751) and subsequently appended to the third and later editions of *The Theory of Moral Sentiments*, published during Smith's lifetime (27–28).

3. Having devoted his early lectures to matters of language and style, Smith presented little in the way of rules or principles regarding expression in the various forms of composition treated in the second half of the course.

BIBLIOGRAPHY

Primary Sources

Smith, Adam. *The Correspondence of Adam Smith*. Edited by Ernest Campbell Mossner and Ian Simpson Ross. New York: Clarendon Press, 1977.

Smith, Adam. *Lectures on Rhetoric and Belles Lettres, Delivered in the University of Glasgow by Adam Smith, Reported by a Student in 1762–63*. Edited and with an introduction by John M. Lothian. Carbondale and Edwardsville, IL: Southern Illinois University Press, 1963.

Smith, Adam. *Lectures on Rhetoric and Belles Lettres*. Edited and with an introduction by J. C. Bryce. Vol. 4 of *The Glasgow Edition of the Works and Correspondence of Adam Smith*. New York: Oxford University Press, 1983.

Bibliography and Biography

Lightwood, Martha Bolar. *A Selected Bibliography of Significant Works about Adam Smith*. Philadelphia: University of Pennsylvania Press, 1984.

Rae, John. *Life of Adam Smith*. London: Macmillan, 1895.

Scott, William Robert. *Adam Smith as Student and Professor, With Unpublished Documents, Including Parts of the "Edinburgh Lectures," a Draft of "The Wealth of Nations," Extracts from the Muniments of the University of Glasgow, and Correspondence*. Glasgow: Jackson, Son and Co., 1937.

Stephen, Leslie. "Smith, Adam." *DNB* (1949–1950).

Criticism

Bevilacqua, Vincent M. "Adam Smith and Some Philosophical Origins of Eighteenth-Century Rhetorical Theory." *Modern Language Review* 63.3 (1968): 559–68.

———. "Adam Smith's *Lectures on Rhetoric and Belles Lettres*." *Studies in Scottish Literature* 3 (1965/66): 41–59.

Carter, Michael. "The Role of Invention in Belletristic Rhetoric: A Study of the Lectures of Adam Smith." *Rhetoric Society Quarterly* 18.1 (1988): 3–13.

Court, Franklin E. "Adam Smith and the Teaching of English Literature." *History of Education Quarterly* 25.3 (1985): 325–40.

Golden, James L. "The Rhetorical Theory of Adam Smith." *Southern Speech Journal* 33.3 (1968): 200–215.

Griswold, Charles L., Jr. "Rhetoric and Ethics: Adam Smith on Theorizing about the Moral Sentiments." *Philosophy and Rhetoric* 24.3 (1991): 213–37.

Hogan, J. Michael. "Historiography and Ethics in Adam Smith's Lectures on Rhetoric, 1762–63." *Rhetorica* 2.1 (1984): 75–91.

Howell, Wilbur S. *Eighteenth-Century British Logic and Rhetoric*, 536–76. Princeton: Princeton University Press, 1971.

Mossner, Ernest Campbell, and Ian Simpson Ross, eds. "Introduction." *The Correspondence of Adam Smith*. New York: Clarendon Press, 1977.

Spencer, Patricia. "Sympathy and Propriety in Adam Smith's Rhetoric." *Quarterly Journal of Speech* 60.1 (1974): 92–99.

JOSHUA STEELE
(1700–1791)

Yvonne Merrill

Musical prosodist Joshua Steele was born in Ireland in 1700, but resided for many years in London. Elected to the Society of Arts in 1756, he established a similar society in Bridgetown, Barbados, in 1781, following his removal there in 1780 to assume personal management of his Barbados estates. A champion of the liberal treatment of slaves, he found considerable opposition from members of the Bridgetown Society of Arts when, in 1789, he raised his estates to manors and made his Negroes copyholders. His opponents, as a result of their opposition, disbanded the society. The success of his manoral system, however, supported Steele's argument for humane management (Carlyle 1016).

Among his other humanitarian efforts were the abolition of arbitrary punishment, the establishment of Negro courts for the treatment of offenses, the promotion of voluntary labor among Negroes through the payment of wages, and the encouragement of native and imported industries for the employment of the poor white population. A pamphlet entitled *An Account of a late Conference on the Occurrences in America, In a Letter to a Friend*, published in London in 1766, has been attributed to Steele; and his letters, entitled *Mitigation of Slavery in Two Parts*, describing the management of his estates written to Thomas Clarkson, were published in 1814 by William Dickson. He died in 1791 (Carlyle 1016).

STEELE'S CONTRIBUTION TO RHETORIC

In 1775 while living in London, Steele had published three essays: two on musical instruments, which he contributed to the *Philosophical Transactions*, and one entitled "An Essay towards establishing the Melody and Measure of Speech to be expressed and perpetuated by certain Symbols." This latter essay was augmented and reissued in 1779 under the title *Pro-*

sodia Rationalis, becoming his major theoretical work. Phonetician Magdelena Sumera has attributed to it the beginning of a 150-year history of
musical (or temporal) prosody, culminating with the work of William
Thomson in the early twentieth century.

Prosody is the study of verse meter and the pronunciation of words, giving
attention to accent, quantity (temporal length), emphasis, pause, and tone
(level of pitch). According to Sumera, the difference between traditional
prosodists and musical prosodists is that the latter have given more consideration to questions of rhythm and its effects on musical scansion. Specifically, musical prosodists have differed from traditional prosodists concerning
the basis of rhythm, the unit of rhythm and its characteristics, the range of
syllable quantities contained in rhythmic units, the method of assigning the
units, the method of scansion, and the goal of analysis (Sumera 100). Steele,
for example, made the following assertion in *Prosodia Rationalis* about the
features that distinguish the pronunciation of English as illustrated by its
best speakers: "This essential quality is chiefly owing to the speaker's dwelling with nearly uniform loudness on the whole length of every syllable, and
confining the extent of the accents, acute and grave, within the compass of
four or five tones; and also to adopting, in general, a deliberate instead of
a rapid measure" (48–49).

As a member of the landed gentry and citizen of a British subject nation,
Steele was probably sensible to the need for "correct" English pronunciation felt by non-English members of the Empire who aspired to success in
the great world (Bizzell and Herzberg 649). Steele, who had a grounding
in musical theory, devised a notational system, drawing heavily from music,
for transcribing the phonetic features of spoken language. By so doing, he
hoped to demonstrate language's rhythmic regularity and musical qualities,
while providing a method for its scientific description and teaching. Such a
tool could be expected to find favor in a century obsessed both with scientific method and with articulating standards of taste, particularly in the
use of language. Sumera has recognized him today as the founder of musical
prosody and early contributor to quantitative phonetics (100). But he contributed significantly to eighteenth-century rhetoric by indirectly founding
the Elocutionary Movement (Howell 249–250; Newman 65ff).

Prosodia Rationalis was not ostensibly intended as a pronunciation manual but as a scientific treatise addressed to the Royal Society in response to
an essay by James Burnett, Lord Monboddo, entitled "The Origin and Progress of Language." In *Prosodia Rationalis*, Steele argued that speech is a
musical genus because it has melody and rhythm but that it differs from the
genus of song because it progresses in scale and time through slides akin to
the sound produced by fingers moving up and down the finger-board of a
bass viol rather than through leaps of pitch, as in the melody of a song (14–
16) (see also Newman 68). Steele's innovation in prosodic theory was that
prosody should examine the actual features of speech and voice (Sumera

100; Newman 70). As a means of representing these features, he posited quarter tones for recording pitch variations and regular rhythmic pulsations as the underlying basis of natural speech, which permitted him the establishment of uniform units of rhythm.

As stated in *Prosodia Rationalis*, Steele found physiological analogies for his belief in regular periodicity in the natural rhythms of breathing, pulse, and walking: "Our animal existence being regulated by our pulse, we seem to have an instinctive sense of *rhythmus*, as connected with, and governing, all sounds and all motions; whence it follows, that we find all people feel the effects of *rhythmus* . . . so that, without searching for the reason, it has generally been passed over as a first principle, or self-evident truth" (67). According to Steele, each of these natural "cadences" has two motions, raising and posing, which in Greek are *arsis* and *thesis*, respectively. Steele found these motions also in the heavy and light stresses ("poizes") of speech. In contrast to the four metrical feet comprising the traditional prosodic measures, all of Steele's units of rhythm, or cadences, begin with a heavy stress and end with a light. In a normal walking step, for example, the *thesis* marks the first beat, or "posing" of the foot, and the *arsis* marks the lifting, or lighter, beat. A pace constitutes two such cadences and produces the equivalent of what in musical terminology is a measure of common time—namely, two heavy beats alternating with two lighter beats, all of equal duration (20–21).

Steele's other primary cadence begins on the heavy stress, ends with a lighter stress, and adds a still lighter stress in the middle. For his illustration, he used the gait of a lame person, whose walk results in a three-beat measure because one foot remains on the ground twice as long as the other, thereby producing a pace divisible by six, instead of by four. Between the fall of the stronger foot and that of the lighter foot, the lightest beat marks the additional time during which the stronger foot remains posed. From such analogies, Steele maintained that all cadences for which we have a natural affinity, or "affection," are divisible either by two, double time, or by three, triple time (21).

Steele placed the symbols for these three beats below the traditional five lines of the musical staff, on which he recorded the "melody" or intonation and the relative time lengths for each sound unit (6–9), which do not always bear an exact relation to individual syllables, syllabication being subordinate to the measure in which it occurs. Rhythmic measures can be either short or long, resulting in heavy or light cadences (21–29) (see also Sumera 101–2).

The most significant aspects of Steele's system of notation are his scheme for indicating how long the voice remains on a particular sound, relative to the preceding and following sounds, and his use of a quarter–tone system to record the range of pitch actually traversed in natural speech. To indicate duration, or "quantity," Steele employed modified musical notes and their dotted equivalents, which, together with rests, yield nine possible quantities.

He employed rising and falling lines attached to the note stems to indicate "acute" and "grave" accents, or the number of quarter tones through which the voice "slides" during a particular syllable (7–9, 24). By "circumflex," he intended the phenomenon by which both acute and grave accents occur on the same syllable (85).

Through analyzing spoken and written verse using his system, Steele discovered that volume, pitch, and duration could vary within the sounding of a single syllable. He also made the startling observation that English heroic meter, if accurately marked, actually has six or possibly even eight cadences, rather than five, when natural accents and pauses are accurately recorded (26, 77). In response to actor David Garrick's question whether his notational system would make it possible for any person to pronounce words in the same tone and manner as the original speaker, Steele responded, "Though these rules may enable a master to teach a just application of accent, emphasis, and all the other proper expressions of the voice in speaking, which will go a great way in the improvement of elocution, yet they cannot give a sweet voice where Nature has denied it" (55). Citing the natural delivery style of Garrick for illustration, Steele showed that the sense of English expressions depends on the appropriate recognition of regularly occurring accent and that the sense could be altered with its shift (149, 151).

Throughout his treatise, consisting mostly of Steele's correspondence with Lord Monboddo addressing the latter's queries, Steele made clear his purpose to forward a method whereby the elocutionary features, particularly those of accent, rhythm, pause, and force could be scientifically transcribed, analyzed, and passed on to posterity. The lasting contribution that he hoped to make was the invention of a means by which English could rival ancient Greek and Latin in musical beauty and perfection. In providing a scientific way to analyze the rhythm and melody of speech, he envisioned a perfectible national language that capitalized on the music inherent in it.

This contribution did, in fact, secure a place for Steele in the history of rhetoric through his influence on the elocutionary movement, as well as make him a founding figure in the history of phonetics (Sumera 100, 111). However, John Newman has argued that it was actually John Walker who applied Steele's method to elocution through plagiarizing Steele's scheme after the latter had left England (67–69), a charge countered by Wilbur Samuel Howell (249, 250n) and by Jack Hall Lamb, who has cited Walker's claim not to have understood music well enough to comprehend Steele's method (414–15). Since Steele's work was admittedly unpolished and theoretical (see the preface to his work), it received little notice at the time, though most of the major elocutionists and musical prosodists ultimately gave him credit, both in England and in America, into this century (Newman 69–70; Sumera 100). Gilbert Austin, for example, invited the readers of his famous oral interpretation manual *Chironomia* to compare his own notational system to Steele's (Austin 739). Howell has confirmed Walker's debt to Steele, thereby giving Steele credit for helping found the elocutionary movement (Howell 250n), though it would be a mistake to attribute to Steele the so-called Mechanical School of delivery founded by Walker. Steele's system resulted solely from a scholarly interest in and scientific analysis of language, for the purpose of description and recording.

Steele found precedence for his uniting of musical analysis with prosody in the single figure of the ancient Greek bard, who was both musician and poet. Allying literature with art instead of logic, and appealing to classical models moved him in the direction of belles lettres, which came to full flower in the eighteenth century. Rhetoric in its own right had been increasingly under attack by the rational scientists, who wanted it stripped of ornament and reduced to plain language. But in seventeenth-century France, rhetoric had gained renewed prestige through association with history, art, and literary criticism—the heart of belles lettres (Bizzell and Herzberg 644). Steele avoided direct confrontation with the supporters of plain language by firmly allying speech with poetry and music and by arguing, in *Prosodia Rationalis*, for a standard of taste: "If we wish to improve our language, the grammarian, the poet, and the musician, must again be united in the same person (173).

Also, in his desire to make English pronunciation natural and easily transmittable, Steele joined forces with fellow Irishmen Thomas Sheridan and Gilbert Austin in their effort to see that their countrymen were able to compete in the public arena, specifically in the worlds of theater, university, church, and parliament. Although the *Prosodia Rationalis* had really nothing to do with elocution per se, as Newman has asserted (68), the book was quickly appropriated for use by those ambitious to acquire the prestigious dialect. Actors Sheridan (also usually credited with founding the elocutionary movement) and Garrick, who responded favorably to Steele's scheme, were the leaders in the natural-delivery movement.

Therefore, through providing a scientific method by which the music of natural English pronunciation could be accurately recorded and transmitted, Steele contributed to the eighteenth-century elocutionary and belles lettres movements as well as to the nascent field of phonetics, for which he devised an amazingly precise notational system.

BIBLIOGRAPHY

Primary Source
Steele, Joshua. *Prosodia Rationalis.* New York: Georg Olms Verlag, 1971.

Biography
Carlyle, Edward Irving. *DNB* (1973).

Criticism and References
Austin, Gilbert. *Chironomia.* In *The Rhetorical Tradition,* edited by Patricia Bizzell and Bruce Herzberg, 738–45. Boston: Bedford, 1990.

Bizzell, Patricia, and Bruce Herzberg. "Eighteenth-Century Rhetoric." In *The Rhetorical Tradition*, edited by Patricia Bizzell and Bruce Herzberg, 645–60. Boston: Bedford, 1990.

Howell, Wilbur Samuel. *Eighteenth-Century British Logic and Rhetoric*, 248–50. Princeton: Princeton University Press, 1971.

Lamb, Jack Hall. "John Walker and Joshua Steele." *Speech Monographs* 32.4 (1965): 411–19.

Newman, John B. "The Role of Joshua Steele in the Development of Speech Education in America." *Speech Monographs* 20.1 (March 1953): 65–73.

Sumera, Magdelena. "The Keen Prosodic Ear: A Comparison of the Notations of Rhythm of Joshua Steele, William Thomson and Morris Croll." In *Towards a History of Phonetics*, edited by R. E. Asher and Eugenie J. A. Henderson, 100–112. Edinburgh: Edinburgh University Press, 1981.

JOHN STIRLING

Michael G. Moran

Little is known about John Stirling's life except that he held an M.A., served as chaplain to the Duke of Gordon, and wrote a large number of elementary books "designed to teach Latin and English, most of which are extremely rare" (Alston). These books include English titles such as *A Short View of English Grammar* (1735), *A Course of Theology* (1750), *The Private Tutor to British Youth* (1778), and *Cato's Moral Distichs and Lily's Pedagogical Admonition* (1787); but Stirling's most important publication was *A System of Rhetoric* (1733), an elementary-school text based on the classical rhetorical figures. The book went through about eighteen editions, including American ones in 1788 and 1789, and remained in print through 1833, one hundred years after it was first published. In 1786, Stirling's work was combined with John Holmes's *The Art of Rhetoric Made Easy* (Howell 137). As Wilbur Samuel Howell has noted, however, the combination of the two works was not entirely fortunate because Holmes's *Art* already summarized four of the arts of Ciceronian rhetoric, including style. Stirling's contribution, therefore, was redundant since it addressed itself exclusively to style (137–38).

The confusion about the purpose of Stirling's book is intensified by its title, which suggests that the book will cover all of rhetoric, including the arts of invention, arrangement, memory, and delivery, in addition to style. Such narrowing of traditional rhetoric follows in the seventeenth-century tradition that reduced rhetoric to stylistics. This tradition included Thomas Farnaby's *Troposchematologia* (1648) and Thomas Gibbons's *Rhetoric; or, a View of Its Principal Tropes and Figures* (1767), both of which used the term *rhetoric* in the sense of stylistics.

The importance of Stirling's rhetoric should not be overlooked, however, for his book and its popularity prove that "rhetoric was by no means a neglected subject in eighteenth century education" (Alston) on the elementary level. Since the first part of the book is in English, *The Art of Rhetoric* also represents an important development in the curriculum as it moved from Latin-based to English-based instruction. Stirling's work also demonstrates a representative eighteenth-century pedagogical method for teaching rhetorical figures to young students as a tool for analyzing texts.

STIRLING'S RHETORICAL THEORY

To understand Stirling's work we must first recognize that his goal, as he noted in his preface, was to teach his elementary students "a right Understanding of the Classics." To accomplish this goal, he began his book with his own explanation in English of the various rhetorical figures. The second part of the text discusses the same figures in Latin. Stirling admitted that he took this section "mostly" from Thomas Farnaby's seventeenth-century Latin primer. One of Stirling's main contributions, therefore, was that he defined the classical rhetorical figures in the vernacular.

These definitions were versified into distiches, or rhymed couplets, to help students memorize the figures. In the preface Stirling explained his method. While the Latin section could explain each figure in a single line, his English equivalent had to be longer because the English language is not as "concise" as the Latin. Therefore, he presented each figure in a distich so that he could define it "in an intelligible and easy Turn of Expression, a full and exact Definition of the Figure, its Nature and Use, and what Observation is sometimes equally necessary with the very Definition" (see the preface). He was also concerned about his student's ability to commit the figure and its definition easily to memory, so he made certain that the name of the figure appeared first, with the definition following. This order is more natural, Stirling argued, and fosters ease of memorization. This may be true, but as Howell has accurately noted, much of this verse would not have "advanced the cause of poetry in the eyes of schoolboys of the time" (138). A brief sample from the section headed "Affections of Tropes" will suffice to justify this view:

> A *Catachress* Words too far doth strain:
> Rather from such Abuse of Speech refrain.
> *Hyperbole* soars high, or creeps too low;
> Exceeds the Truth, Things wonderful to shew.
> By *Metalepsis,* in one Word combin'd,
> More Tropes than one you easily may find.
> An *Allegory* Tropes continue still,
> Which with new Graces every Sentence fill. (2)

While this doggerel might well help students remember the names and uses of the tropes, it would not have encouraged a taste for good poetry.

In addition to the couplets, Stirling provided his students with additional learning aids. First, he numbered the name of each figure at the end of the line of poetry in which it was mentioned. This number referred students to a list of examples of the figure used in English. Stirling intentionally separated the example from the rule for two reasons. First, he assumed that students did not have the judgment to distinguish the rule from the example—which would cause confusion. Second, to include the examples in the poetry would lead to infelicities—no small problem already. An example of this problem is made clear by Stirling's treatment of metonymy, which Stirling defined as the trope that "does new Names impose / And Things for Things by near Relation shews" (1), offering the following examples:

The Inventor is taken for the invented: As Mars (War) rages. The Author for his Works: as, read Horace, i.e. his Writings. The Instrument for the Cause; as, his Tongue (Eloquence) defends him. The Matter for the Thing made; as, the Steel (Sword) conquers. The Effect for the Cause; as, cold Death, i.e. Death that makes cold. The Subject containing for the Thing contained; as, I feast on Dishes, i.e. Meats. The Adjunct for the Subject; as, the Mace (Magistrate) comes. (1)

While they do illustrate the various figures, the examples would not have helped the elementary student. They tend to be abstract and difficult to follow, especially since they do not appear in context. The teacher would probably have to explain them to students in some detail, perhaps pointing out their uses in texts the students read. The examples also do not illustrate all kinds of metonymy. Again, the teacher would have to expand on the types for the class.

Stirling's final pedagogical tool in the text is the section labelled "Terms English'd," by which he meant to give students English terms equivalent to the Greek and Latin ones. These English names are tied to the original names via the numbering system. Stirling justified this method in his preface on the grounds of association psychology. He argued that since the names are mostly Greek, they "cannot excite in the Mind the proper ideas affixed to them, without a tolerable Acquaintance with the Original" (see the preface). He therefore offered English equivalents "that the young Student might not only understand the Figure itself, but also the particular meaning of its Name" (see the preface). These translations, however, must have caused considerable confusion in the students' minds because many of the Anglicized names are at best loosely equivalent to the Greek or Latin terms. For instance, metaphor becomes "Translation"; metonymy, "Changing of Names"; synecdoche, "Comprehension"; and irony, "Dissimulation" (1). None of these precisely duplicates the original terms, and, since they were well established in English at the time, it is hard to see the benefits of including English equivalents. While Stirling thought that his elementary students needed an English word to associate with the rhetorical term to root the term in experience, the modern reader cannot help but wonder if this imprecise language did not lead to obfuscation rather than clarification.

Some of the most interesting sections of the preface discuss the four-week syllabus that Stirling developed to teach his "Scholars" all figures, beginning with the English section and moving to the Latin. Since he had ninety-four figures to teach, he required his students to memorize eight of them during the school day and eight more "at home for their Evening Exercise" (see the preface), transcribing all sixteen from the book. Therefore, he noted with some satisfaction, he could finish the English system in six days. During the second week, the students were to repeat the assignments of the first week, after which they would be ready to begin the Latin section. Since they already understood the concepts from the English section, they could speed through the Latin material "because it contains no more than half the Number of Lines" (see the preface). He did not mention how proficient students were in Latin, but they must not have been beginners because by the end of the third week he claimed that they could recite from memory all the Latin verses as well as the English. Stirling concluded his preface with a boast common to many textbook authors about the effectiveness of his method:

In the fourth Week, as they are become very easy and familiar, the Scholar will have no hard Task to go through the whole again both in English and Latin: After which, with a constant *Praxis* in daily reading the Classics, and rehearsing them every Saturday, they must soon be fixed so strongly in their Memory, as scarcely ever to be forgotten, and render even the Poets as easy and more pleasant to Boys than the Prose Authors (Preface).

One can only speculate about how the young scholars viewed the program after being forced to memorize Stirling's doggerel.

It is important to note, however, that Stirling's purpose for developing his rhetoric was not to produce effective speakers or even graceful writers. He taught his scholars the rhetorical figures to make them better readers of the classics. Furthermore, Stirling conceived of his rhetoric as part of a larger system of text analysis that he presented in another volume, *A Short View of English Grammar* (published in 1735), which included three parts: etymology, syntax, and prosody. His rhetoric made up the fourth part of this system (22). Rhetoric as Stirling conceived it therefore fell logically under grammar as part of the methodology that students learned in order to analyze literature, especially the classics. Given the current interest in the rhetoric of reading, Stirling appears somewhat modern in his approach.

Although flawed, Stirling's *Art of Rhetoric* is an important text for several reasons. It indicates that the rhetorical figures were being taught in some elementary schools throughout the eighteenth century. The large number of editions of the book points to its popularity. By discussing its material first in English, then in Latin, the book represents a step in the direction of vernacular instruction. Finally, although the poetry is bad, Stirling developed in the book a new pedagogical approach to teach students to read the classics; and this approach must have helped them with their speaking, reading, and writing of English.

BIBLIOGRAPHY

Primary Source

Stirling, John. *A System of Rhetoric.* 1733. Reprint. Edited by R. C. Alston. Menston, Eng.: Scolar Press, 1968.

Criticism

Alston, R. C., ed. "Note." In *A System of Rhetoric,* by John Stirling. Menston, Eng.: Scolar Press, 1968.
Howell, Wilbur Samuel. *Eighteenth-Century British Logic and Rhetoric,* 137–38. Princeton: Princeton University Press, 1971.

JOHN WALKER
(1732–1807)

Byron K. Brown

John Walker was born in 1732 to a Dissenting family in the Middlesex village of Colney Hatch. When Walker was still a child, his father died; and the boy was taken from grammar school to learn a trade. Walker's inclinations were literary, however; and although he attempted several trades, he succeeded at none. After his mother died when he was seventeen, Walker pursued a career on the stage, performing for a time in provincial theaters before playing supporting roles under David Garrick's management at Drury Lane. In 1758 Walker married a comic actress and moved to Dublin to perform at Spranger Barry's new Crow Street Theatre, which opened in competition with Thomas Sheridan's Theatre Royal. At Crow Street, Walker played various leading roles, and the success of his company might have encouraged Thomas Sheridan to end his theatrical career in 1759. In 1762 Walker and his wife returned to London to perform at Covent Garden, returned briefly to Dublin in 1767, and performed in Bristol in 1768 before retiring from the stage that same year (Cooper; Howell 248–51; see also "Mr. John Walker").

Soon after his marriage, Walker had converted to Roman Catholicism, and in January 1769 he and James Usher formed a school for Catholic youth. Walker taught elocution there until 1771, when he quit the school and began lecturing on elocution, touring both Scotland and Ireland as well as England (see "Mr. John Walker" 78–79, 83). Soon afterward, Walker began publishing a series of dictionaries and elocutionary texts that established him as an authority on the correct pronunciation of both words and sentences. His first major work was *A Dictionary of the English Language, Answering at Once the Purposes of Rhyming, Spelling, and Pronouncing* (1775), later published under the more familiar title of *A Rhyming Dictionary*. In 1781 he published *Elements of Elocution*, which went through numerous English and American editions and profoundly influenced the teaching of elocution, especially in America, during the first half of the nineteenth century (Grover 289; Guthrie 27n; Robb 179–80). In *A Rhetorical Grammar* (1785), Walker simplified and expanded his elocutionary system for younger students.

In 1791 Walker published his immensely influential *Critical Pronouncing Dictionary and Expositor of the English Language*, a work that quickly gained a reputation as "the statute book of English orthoepy" (see "Mr. John Walker" 81). Like Walker's *Elements of Elocution*, this volume was dedicated to Samuel Johnson, and Walker"s "Principles of English Pronunciation" was bound with Johnson's dictionary several times during the nineteenth century. In 1798 Walker followed this book with *A Key to the Classical Pronunciation of Greek and Latin Proper Names . . . To Which is added a Complete Vocabulary of Scripture Proper Names*. Toward the end of his life, Walker turned once again to elocution, publishing several minor school texts before he died in 1807 at age sixty-seven, leaving an estate of £7,000 to testify to his works' popular success (see "Mr. John Walker" 81–84).

WALKER'S RHETORICAL THEORY

John Walker's career paralleled Thomas Sheridan's in remarkable ways: both were actors who, at age thirty-seven, left the theater to become teachers, lecturers, and lexicographers (Haberman 116–17). Both were probably influenced by David Garrick's forceful, natural stage delivery and perhaps saw the commercial possibilities of teaching this new style (Lamb 412). Unlike Sheridan, though, Walker offered a complex system of rules to govern delivery, and for this reason he is described as founder of the "mechanical" school of elocution, as opposed to Sheridan's "natural" school. However, this juxtaposition is oversimplistic since neither Sheridan nor Walker believed that rules and nature were mutually exclusive.

Like most elocutionists, Walker accepted a Ramistic definition of rhetoric that restricted the art to the study of style (which it reduced to figurative expression) and delivery (which it divided into voice and gesture). Walker's most significant contributions were in the area of voice, but the corpus of his work addresses all three areas. Unlike his fellow elocutionists, though, Walker broke with traditional elocutionary practice by also including a discussion of invention, which he extracted from John Ward's *System of Oratory*, in the third edition (1801) of *A Rhetorical Grammar* (Howell 248).

In his discussion of voice in *Elements of Elocution*, Walker focused on the importance of inflection, or the rising and falling tonal shifts that run throughout spoken language. Proper inflection, Walker insisted, is essential to the semantics as well as the aesthetics of language: it "shows the import of the pauses, forms the harmony of a cadence, distinguishes emphasis into its different kinds, and gives each kind its specific and determinate meaning" (1:114). Although Walker claimed to have independently discovered that speech employs upward and downward slides rather than the stable tones of music, his discussion bears an unmistakable debt to Joshua Steele's *Prosodia Rationalis*, which appeared six years before. In fact, although Walker acknowledged reading Steele's work in the first edition of *Elements of Elocution* (1:xi), in later editions he omitted all reference to Steele's work; consequently, accusations of plagiarism were leveled against Walker as early as 1823 and have continued to the present (Lamb 416). However, because Walker extended Steele's ideas and explored the relationship between inflection, pause, emphasis, and harmony, he substantiated his claim that *Elements of Elocution* proceeded "one step farther, in the art of reading, than any author has hitherto ventured to go" (1:114).

The proper use of pauses dominates the first volume of Walker's *Elements of Elocution*. Noting, as Sheridan does, that conventional rules of punctuation reflect grammatical structure rather than rhetorical cadence, Walker devoted over a hundred pages to demonstrating the inadequacy of existing rules and outlining a system of "rhetorical" punctuation. Concluding that "if we would speak well, we must pause upon an average at every fifth or sixth word" (1:111), Walker laid down sixteen rules designed to reflect the type of frequency of pauses actually used by speakers. Rule 7 illustrates the general tenor of his advice: "When two verbs come together, and the latter is in the infinitive mood, if any words come between they must be separated from the latter verb by a pause" (1:82). Walker intensively analyzed each rule and illustrated its application in a variety of prose and verse passages.

Walker next explored the forms of inflection appropriate to the different pauses required by various sentence types. First, he established the basic principles that falling inflections generally accompany the longer pauses marked by semicolons and colons, rising inflections the shorter pauses marked by commas. Next, he laid down twenty additional rules for properly inflecting the pronunciation of two to twenty-three items in a simple series, eleven more for items in a compound series.

In the second volume, Walker devoted over a hundred pages to both emphasis and harmony, two other major attributes of voice. He insisted that proper inflection is crucial to each. Emphasis, he argued, is integral to meaning, signaling either stated or implied contrast. In his words, "Emphasis, so called, always supposes contradistinction or antithesis, either expressed or understood" (2:42). However, he argued that emphasis depends as much upon inflection as it does upon force, and he required that in contrasted pairs the positive word receive a falling inflection and the negative word, a rising one, regardless of word order (2:69). He similarly saw the proper variation of rising and falling inflections as the key to harmony, and he recommended ending sentences with one of two inflectional patterns. In the same connection, he delivered nine rules for reading verse effectively. Voice management is the only part of voice that he did not relate to inflection, but he did give advice frequently repeated throughout the next century:

speakers should discover their natural pitch, strengthen their middle tone, and resist the impulse to confuse pitch and volume.

Like Thomas Sheridan, Walker drew heavily on James Burgh's *Art of Speaking* in his discussion of gesture—a debt that he, unlike Sheridan, readily acknowledged (Murphy 141). In *Elements of Elocution*, Walker devoted over 150 pages to gesture, explaining the importance of gesture and using contemporary psychology to defend the imitation of passions. In *Elements of Gesture* (1788), Walker contributed significantly to the teaching of gesture by being the first to use copperplates to illustrate posture and gesture, anticipating Gilbert Austin's more extensive and well-known method in *Chironomia* (see "Mr. John Walker" 80–81).

Although Walker's discussion of style was peripheral, even accidental, to his elocutionary system, he did draw some interesting connections between style and delivery. In *Elements of Elocution*, he made implicit stylistic recommendations for writers when he advocated the use of certain inflectional patterns at the close of periodic sentences. In *A Rhetorical Grammar* he explicitly addressed the canon of style and offered an elocutionary twist on the traditional division of figures of speech by distinguishing between rhetorical figures and oratorical ones. Walker argued that rhetorical figures—generally equivalent to classical tropes, including metaphor, metonomy, and synecdoche—do not depend upon proper pronunciation for their meaning, but oratorical figures—which include many classical schemes—do; and he devoted over fifty pages to the proper delivery of these oratorical figures.

Although John Walker was primarily a pedagogue who modified and extended the work of others, his contributions to elocutionary practice are noteworthy. He did much to popularize the ideas of Joshua Steele and James Burgh, among others; and as the first to develop a systematic, rule-based approach to teaching delivery, he powerfully influenced the pedagogy of elocution well into the nineteenth century.

BIBLIOGRAPHY

Primary

Walker, John. *A General Idea of a Pronouncing Dictionary of the English Language.* London, 1774.

———. *A Dictionary of the English Language, Answering at Once the Purposes of Rhyming, Spelling, and Pronouncing.* London, 1775.

———. *Exercises for Improvement in Elocution.* London, 1777.

———. *Elements of Elocution.* 2 vols. London, 1781.

———. *Hints for Improvement in the Art of Reading.* London, 1783.

———. *A Rhetorical Grammar.* London, 1785.

———. *The Melody of Speaking Delineated; or, Elocution Taught like Music.* London, 1787.

———. *A Critical Pronouncing Dictionary and Expositor of the English Language.* London, 1791.

————. *A Key to the Classical Pronunciation of Greek and Latin Proper Names . . . To Which is added a Complete Vocabulary of Scripture Proper Names.* London, 1798.

————. *The Academic Speaker.* Dublin, 1789.

————. *The Teacher's Assistant in English Composition.* Carlisle, 1808.

————. *Outlines of English Grammar.* London, 1805.

Biography

Cooper, Thompson. "Walker, John (1732–1807)." *DNB* (1912).

"Mr. John Walker." *The Athenaeum* 3.1 (1808): 77–84.

Criticism

Grover, David. "John Walker: the 'Mechanical Man' Revisited." *Southern Speech Communication Journal* 34.4 (1969): 288–97.

Guthrie, Warren. "The Development of Rhetorical Theory in America 1635–1850. V: The Elocution Movement—England." *Speech Monographs* 18.1 (1951): 17–30.

Haberman, Frederick W. "English Sources of American Elocution." In *A History of Speech Education in America*, edited by Karl R. Wallace, 105–26. New York: Appleton-Century-Crofts, 1954.

Howell, Wilbur Samuel. *Eighteenth-Century British Logic and Rhetoric*, 248–51. Princeton: Princeton University Press, 1971.

Lamb, Jack Hall. "John Walker and Joshua Steele." *Speech Monographs* 32.4 (1965): 411–19.

Murphy, Mary C. "Detection of the Burglarizing of Burgh: A Sequel." *Communication Monographs* 43.2 (1976): 140–41.

Newman, John B. "The Role of Joshua Steele in the Development of Speech Education in America." *Speech Monographs* 20.1 (1953): 65–73.

Robb, Mary Margaret. "The Elocutionary Movement and Its Chief Figures." In *A History of Speech Education in America*, edited by Karl R. Wallace, 178–201. New York: Appleton-Century-Crofts, 1954.

JOHN WARD
(1679?–1758)

Kathleen Massey

John Ward was born in London about 1679. He was the son of a Dissenting Baptist minister of the same name. Out of a family of fourteen children, only two—John and his sister Abigail—survived their father, who died in 1717. Abigail, who at Gresham College, kept house for her brother, a life-long bachelor, died some years before her brother did. John Ward, Sr., was an officer in the English Revolution under Oliver Cromwell. His epitaph, composed by his son, speaks of him as a man "who had suffered much for the sake of integrity and religion, and borne it with a valiant and lofty spirit" (Tongue 7). One of Ward's older brothers, Thomas, came to the American colonies at the restoration of Charles II, in 1666. Shortly after this date, Thomas's name appears on the records as a member of the Seventh-Day Baptist Church of Newport, Rhode Island. He was a prominent member of the legislature of the colony. Thomas Ward died in 1689, survived by his son Richard, born in the same year. Both son and grandson became governors.

Although John Ward referred little throughout his long life to the subject of personal religion—his natural caution and reserve did not suit ecclesiastical controversy—he was a Baptist with strong connections to the Dissenting ministers Drs. Joseph and Samuel Stennett, father and son. Stennett the elder served as Ward's minister and as one of the first five trustees of the Ward educational trust, and the younger Stennett preached Ward's funeral sermon. Ward is buried in Bunhill Fields, the cemetery for Dissenters in London.

Owing to a lack of funds and severe religious restrictions, Ward received no extensive formal education. He studied privately under John Ker (1639–1723) (an Irishman who had studied under Thomas Doolittle, and graduated with an M.A. at Edinburgh in 1664) at Bethnell Green Academy in London and served as a clerk at the Navy Office. In 1710, he undertook the education of a certain number of the children of his friends by starting his own school in Tenter Alley, Moorfields. Ward ran this school from 1710 until 1734. In 1720, at the age of forty-one, Ward was elected Professor of Rhetoric at Gresham College. His close friend Dr. Thomas Birch noted that Ward was chosen as professor for "his knowledge of polite literature, as well as antiquity" (10).

John Ward was a remarkable man. He exhibited a conscious and robust purpose embodied in his continuing concern with and loyalty to a series of larger communities: his dedication to Gresham College and his auditors; his religious beliefs, confirmed in part by his long-term work as founder and tutor of the school in Tenter Alley; his enduring membership in the Royal Society, including his contributions to the *Philosophical Transactions*; his work as a historian, particularly as author of *The Lives of the Professors of Gresham College* (1740); his work as editor of a book that holds an important place in the tradition of education in England, the Lily-Colet *Grammar* (1732); his work as one of the original trustees of the British Museum; and the establishment of the Ward Scholarship, which was still in force as late as 1951. Ward worked steadily to the end of his life, dying at eighty, having, as Birch noted, "gone well to bed" (22).

One of Ward's students, Thomas Hollis, who in his *Memoirs* referred to Ward as his "old excellent master and much-honoured friend" (5), commissioned the only known portrait of Ward, which is now in the National Gallery and reproduced as the frontispiece to the work on Ward by Edwin Tongue.

WARD'S RHETORICAL THEORY

Founded in 1597, Gresham College, where Ward delivered the lectures that became *A System of Oratory*, was, as Christopher Hill has pointed out in *Intellectual Origins of the English Revolution*, a "center of adult education," open to all comers, without charge, and without the necessity of exams or degrees, in sharp contrast to Oxford and Cambridge. In the "Appendix" to his *Lives*, Ward pointed out that the "Rules and Orders for the Readers in Gresham College" outlined in Sir Thomas Gresham's will and later confirmed by the trustees of Gresham—the Mercers Guild and the Mayor and City Council of London—stipulated that the lectures were to be chiefly in English so that "the good, that will ensue, wilbee [*sic*] more publique," for "the founder seemeth to have a speciall [*sic*] respect of the citizens, of whome fiew [*sic*] or none understand the Latine tongue" (13). The lectures were to be practical, aimed at the "common people"; and as in the "rules" for the professor of "lawe," the lectures were to be selected "as best may serve to the good liking and capacitie of the saied auditorie, and ar [*sic*] more usual in common practice" (18).

Thus, Ward's charge at Gresham was to teach the "basics" that would be of most use to the merchant class, tradesmen, and the general population. Ward had to post a £500 bond to the Mercers Company—"for the due performance of the said place, according to the founders Will"—which guaranteed his adherence to the "rules" (see J. Ward, Misc. Papers, BL, Add. MSS 6271/118.f).

In fact, the trustees of Gresham could not have chosen a man better qualified to lecture to these particular students. Ward had been a part-time student himself, having worked in the Navy Office while reading under John Ker's tutelage in his spare time. Ward understood the challenges faced by his Gresham students, who were compelled to study without the formal graces of college. He was intimately familiar with the handicaps typical of his auditors, and he recognized these handicaps in Lecture 4 of his *System of Oratory*: "All are not born with a like happy genius, and have not the same opportunity to cultivate their minds with learning and knowledge" (1: 51). Ward was a careful reader of his audience. "The great thing," he said in a letter written in 1735, just after turning his school in Tenter Alley over to others, "is to make [students] understand what they are about. I am inclined to apply this maxim to the case, *Frustra fit per plurg quod fieri potest per pauciora*" (Brock 3–4).

Furthermore, just as Ward knew how vital Gresham College was for including a certain type of auditor, so he also knew personally how important Gresham was for those excluded by religious belief from Oxford and Cambridge. As a Dissenter, Ward was at a disadvantage in a society shaped by the Toleration Acts of 1689. Those Acts assured that the forum for public discourse was not open to Ward in some important ways; and since Gresham was set up to adhere to the Church of England, the professors were, in the "Rules," expected to operate within the strictures of the Church. Ward was understandably cautious in his responses to the political and social issues of his time, and he voiced his cautionary stance early on in his *System*:

The orator should (as he ought indeed upon all occasions) well consider where, and to whom he speaks. . . . Different opinions prevail, and gain the ascendant, at different times.

A prudent orator therefore will be cautious of opposing any settled and prevailing notions of those, to whom he addresses; unless it be necessary, and then he will do it in the softest and most gentle manner. (1:105–6)

Ward must have felt sharply the same sensations as his own bright pupils in Tenter Alley caused by their exclusion from Oxford and Cambridge. Indeed, the depth of his feeling and commitment is reflected in the Ward Scholarship (activated in 1759 as a condition of his will), which ensured that such young scholars could attend universities in Edinburgh and Aberdeen, where they studied under Thomas Reid, Alexander Gerard, and George Campbell. It is a striking fact that Ward's Scholarship survived well into the twentieth century.

Within these powerful constraints Ward thought of rhetoric as a response of the good citizen. He was "the eminent Gresham professor," as one biographer stated (Edwards 336). Ward considered what his auditors at Gresham might do with the classical art of rhetoric that they were learning from him as they put its precepts to use in their everyday lives. Indeed, Ward intended *A System of Oratory* for the specific audience he was charged to address at Gresham—namely, the citizens, merchants, and artisans of London. Because Ward took the original instructions to Gresham professors very seriously, he designed his series of lectures to teach the practical art of persuasion and, in keeping with the "rules," to give the people "soe [*sic*] much tast [*sic*] of learning, as that they shall not dispise [*sic*] it," as stated in the "Appendix" to his *Lives* (13). Thus, what he devised was a *sturdy* pedagogy derived primarily from classical rhetoric—an approach to education that was systematized and clear, designed for the needs of a nonelitist audience interested in acquiring practical knowledge.

A System of Oratory, in two volumes, was published in 1759, the year after Ward's death. He continually revised his lectures over the thirty-eight years that he delivered them to the auditors at Gresham and had carefully prepared them for publication. In the first of fifty-four lectures, Ward promised to "form the best system of oratory," collecting the finest precepts from Aristotle, Cicero, Quintilian, Longinus, "and other celebrated authors," using examples "taken from the choicest parts of the purest antiquity" (1:15). He added that he would not take up later and recent authors of rhetorics, although he used other examples from such contemporary writers as John Milton, John Locke, Isaac Newton, and Joseph Addison. Indeed, his *System*, unmistakeably classical in its sources, contains noticeable echoes of ideas current in his time. For example, in Lecture 51, "Of Memory," Ward said that "memory, as considered by philosophers, is a faculty of the mind, which receives, retains, and exhibits again, as occasion requires, all sorts of ideas presented to the understanding" (2:378); in Lecture 11 "Of the Passions," Ward noted that "joy is an elation of the mind, arising from a sense of some present good. Such a reflection naturally creates a pleasant and agreable sensation, which ends in a delightful calm and serenity" (1:159); he also referred to "divine testimony" as incontestable, but not, as he quickly pointed out, to be confused with the divine testimony of the "antient Greeks and Romans" who "esteemed the pretend oracles of their deities, the answers of their augers, and the like fallacies" as divine (1:62). "With us," Ward added, "no one can be ignorant of their true notion" (1:62).

In Lecture 3 of his "Division of Oratory," Ward separated logic from rhetoric, recognizing logic as distinct, aiming not at action, but at truth, and he alluded to Peter Ramus with these words: "Indeed some have excluded both *invention* and *disposition* from the art of oratory, supposing they more properly belong to logic; but, I think, without any just reason" (1:31).

Of note, too, are Ward's lectures on imitation and on history. Lectures 53 and 54 presented a view of imitation that seems not only to address Sir Francis Bacon's attack on *imitatio* in book 1 of the *Advancement of Learning*, but also anticipated the objections of Ward's twentieth-century critics who see him as slavishly copying the ancients. He presented several major objections to imitation and answered each: "Imitation," he noted, "does not tie us down to [a] slavish attendance, of following another's steps; but permits us, where we find it proper, to leave the tract, come up with him, and if we can, to get before him" (2:415). The lectures on history, 42 through 45, focus on civil history, "a narrative of such facts, as are fit to be transmitted to posterity, for the use of mankind, and the better conduct of human life" (2:231). Just as the "professor of lawe" was exhorted, in the "rules" of Gresham College, to lecture on those branches of law deemed most useful to the intended auditors, "marchants [*sic*] and other citizens," in the "Appendix" to the *Lives* (18), so too does our orator Ward, following Cicero, lecture on civil history. This "modern" infusion of history may reflect Ward's training with Ker, who was known as a liberal in pedagogy and was a product of the Scottish universities, which strove to reach all classes of society and not merely the privileged.

Looking closely at the examples that Ward used from Cicero and Quintilian in the *System*, one sees that he was teaching a kind of action that the common man might take on his own behalf. In fact, in *Lives of the Professors of Gresham College*, Ward, in his preface, lauded Sir Thomas Gresham, "whose regard for the honour of this renowned city [London] was so great, that he chose to have all those liberal arts professed . . . which might be of the greatest service, either for the ornament of [his fellow citizens'] minds, or conduct of their lives" (ii). Ward's lectures were "careful reinterpretations" of Cicero for those for whom the "basics" were of most *use*—namely, his auditors, those who represented the flourishing city of London most readily to the rest of the world and who would benefit from an education that would make them stellar representatives of such an important city. This is the framework that Ward, well within reason, expected his auditors to bring to his lectures.

In looking at another aspect of the *System* and its place in the education of the citizens of London, it is important to note that Ward read the moderns apparently as much as he read the ancients. Samuel Pufendorf, Hugo Grotius, Jean Le Clerc, and John Locke all were part of his education under Ker and part of his reading outside school. It is not, then, out of line to look at the *System* as, say, a response to Locke's criticisms of rhetoric in his *Thoughts concerning Education*, where Locke advised, "If you would have [the student] speak well, let him be conversant in *Tully*, to give him the true *Idea of Eloquence*; and let him read those things that are well writ in

English, to perfect his Style in the purity of our Language" (324–25). Locke recommended Tully also when teaching history, ethics, and civil law. A close examination of the *System* reveals that history, ethics, and civil law were an integral part of Ward's lectures on rhetoric; in fact, by the time one has read both volumes, the passages from Cicero alone add up to a clear lesson on good citizenship.

John Ward's *System of Oratory* exemplifies and contributes to what constitutes a "strong strain of 'nonphilosophical' rhetorics" in the eighteenth century, rhetorics that address the practical demands of society and that consider the roles that rhetoric was meant to play in that society (Conley 193). Strongly Ciceronian rhetorics, such as Ward's, seem "self-consciously opposed to the New Philosophy" (Conley 199). A good example of this pragmatic, nonphilosophical rhetoric is evident in Ward's treatment of invention.

In Lecture 4, "Of Invention in general, and particularly of Common Places," Ward conceded that "a lively imagination and readiness of thought are undoubtedly a very great help to invention" (48–49). He recognized that although "some persons are naturally endued with that quickness of fancy, and penetration of mind," in that "they are seldom at a loss for arguments either to defend their own opinions, or to attack their adversaries," those with these "gifts of nature" do not need the help of the art of invention. Instead, with his auditors clearly in mind, Ward acknowledged that "because all are not born with an like happy genius, and have not the same opportunity to cultivate their minds with learning and knowledge" (1: 51), art provides method through the use of the Greek *topics*.

It is important to understand why it continued to make sense to John Ward to teach a system of invention that others believed was being superseded. Since Ward was a member of long and good standing in the Royal Society and conversant with the ideas of his time, he was well aware of John Locke's idea of *accuracy* as the test of truth. But it is obvious that Ward, to use Lloyd Bitzer's crucial distinction, created a rhetoric that was intended to operate in the "scene of action," with people, rather than in the "scene of truth," for philosophy (1). Ward, one might suggest, made his own philosophic and ethical choice to craft a rhetoric that was predominantly pedagogic in its aim.

Although *A System of Oratory* did not go into multiple editions, Ward's book influenced the rhetorics of others, most notably, as Lloyd Bitzer has suggested (personal communication, July 1990), John Quincy Adams in his *Lectures on Rhetoric and Oratory* (1810). Adams used Ward's *System* as a model for his own series of lectures at Harvard; and although Adams expressed his hesitation at presenting invention—and, thus, the topics—he chose to do so because he believed that "they are not so entirely useless, as in modern times they have generally been considered" (208). Interestingly enough, and in spite of his hesitation, Ward treated invention in eight lectures (a total of 131 pages), whereas Adams treated it in ten (for a total of 182 pages).

At the same time, we can see that other rhetoricians were dismissing the topics. So, for example, in contrast with the treatment of invention in Ward and Adams is that in the rhetoric of John Witherspoon also published in 1810. In his *Lectures on Moral Philosophy and Eloquence*, delivered at Princeton, Witherspoon asserted that "there is no necessity of teaching it, and where it is necessary, I believe it exceeds the power of man to teach it with effect. . . . [I]nvention need not be taught unless it be to one that never yet composed a sentence" (233, 235). Indeed, Witherspoon devotes two pages overall to this by-then-disputed head of rhetoric.

The crucial point here is that Ward recognized the topics as a way to "help everyone to a supply of arguments upon any subject," because, as he pointed out, "art has prescribed a method to lessen in some measure these difficulties" (1:51). It is this *art*, then, that Ward offered those auditors who heard the lectures at Gresham College.

Ward's discussion of arrangement, too, recognized the practical needs of his audience, the practical aims of his lectures. After a detailed discussion of syllogism and "enthymem" in Lecture 15 (1:223–37), Ward put these "several forms and methods of reasoning made use of by orators" (224) into a wisely considered social perspective:

This method is what persons for the most part naturally fall into, who know nothing of the terms *Syllogism* or *Enthymem*. They advance something, and think of a reason to prove it, and another perhaps to support that, and so far as their invention will assist them, or they are masters of language, they endeavour to set what they say in the plainest light, give it the best dress, embellish it with proper figures, and different turns of expression, and, as they think convenient, illustrate it with similitudes, comparisons, and the like ornaments, to render it most agreeable, till they think what they have advanced sufficiently proved. As this method of arguing therefore is the most plain, easy and natural; so it is what is most commonly used in oratory. (1:236)

Ward's treatment of style, likewise, was not one of elaborate schemes of tropes and figures. Wilbur Samuel Howell has noted that Ward "was more selective than many of his predecessors and contemporaries were" when it came to the treatment of figures and tropes; therefore, his discussion of these covered only the "more basic and distinctive of them" (112). In fact, throughout his discussion of style, Ward seems to have followed the Baconian idea that language arises from nature through the senses, not from the imagination.

Ward's interest in and understanding of style was also no doubt shaped by his membership in the Royal Society and his reading of *The Charters and Statutes of the Royal Society of London*. Ward had become a member of the Society in 1723 (all Gresham professors held that distinction), and he later held office in the Society. Hollis's *Memoirs* reveal that in 1759 Hollis had purchased, at the auction of Ward's books, "a sett [*sic*] of the Philosophical Transactions, with Hooke's Collections and Lectures, and the Cronian Lectures; being the completest and best collection ever sold; and so completed by Dr. Ward himself" (494). On the other hand, Ward's Memoranda (June 2, 1752, Add. MSS 6268) show that he was aware of a satire, *The Transactioneer With some of his Philosophical Fancies* (1700), by William King, which lampooned the scientific writing of the age and the moral implications of modern style as exemplified by the Royal Society.

What the *Transactioneer* lampooned, and what Ward showed in his lectures, was an awareness of the potential complexity in the idea of plain language as posed by the Royal Society. The mandate of *The Charters and Statutes* that "in all Reports of Experiments . . . the Matter of Fact shall be barely stated, without any Prefaces, Apologies, or Rhetorical Flourishes" (48) and the call in Thomas Sprat's *History of the Royal Society* for a return to "the primitive purity" of the language "when men deliver'd so many things, almost in an equal number of words" (113) were heeded in Ward's lectures on style. Ward saw the distinguishing mark of the "low or plain stile" as "pure nature, without any colouring, or appearance of art. . . . The design of it is to make things plain and intelligible" (2:144). Any discourse "that ought to be treated in a plain and familiar manner, without much ornament, or address to the passions," such as epistles, dialogues, and "philosophical dissertations," are the proper subjects of this style, which has its "own native beauty and simplicity" (2:145–46).

Even the "true sublime" Ward saw as consistent with "the greatest plainness and simplicity of expression" (2:173). Generally speaking, he said, "the more plain and natural the images appear, the more they surprize [*sic*] us. How succinct, and yet how majestic, is that expression of Caesar, upon his victory over Pharnaces? 'I came, I saw, I conquered' " (2:173). Whether with subjects divine or those held in the highest esteem, one must, Ward continued, use "ornaments and the assistance of eloquence" with "discretion." For when the mind is in the pursuit of noble ideas, "sublimity must appear rather from the elevation of the thought, attended with a simplicity of expression, than from the ornaments and dreams of the language" (2: 193).

At first sight, this may sound like Sprat's claim that the Royal Society valued the "native easiness" in the language of "Artizans, Countrymen, and Merchants" (113). However, the dialogue in King's *Transactioneer* continually insists on the irony of the Latinisms, twisted syntax, grammatic vagaries, and reliance on metaphor in the "Modern Stile [i.e., *style*]" (7) of the *Philosophical Transactions;* therefore, one of King's frustrated speakers plaintively desires that this prose be translated into "plain English" since, the speaker says, "the Sublimity of this way of Expression is above my mean Capacity" (5) and "the Style is so lofty I am not able to discern it" (11).

One can imagine Ward's recognition of, perhaps even his delight in, this irony reappearing in drier form in his reminder to his students that, although the plain style represents "pure nature, without any colouring, or appearance of art," much art is involved, "for it requires no small skill, to treat a common subject in such a manner," since "the fewer ornaments it admits of, the greater art is necessary to attain this end" (2:144–45). As an exponent of classical rhetoric, Ward was clearly noting the distinction between innocent and sophisticated simplicity.

Among the manuscripts on file at the British Library are letters between Ward's heirs, the Goodwins, and the widow of the printer of the *System*, also named John Ward. These letters, which are mediated by a lawyer, John Loveday, are dated 1760 and 1761 and indicate that a dispute of some sort took place between Ward's heirs and the printer's widow. This may explain why there were no subsequent editions of the *System*. In any case, Ward's lectures apparently enjoyed limited influence on other authors during the eighteenth century. Ward is quoted extensively in the third edition of John Walker's *Rhetorical Grammar; or, Course of Lessons in Elocution* (1801), which contains an account of invention borrowed from Ward's Ciceronian approach in *A System of Oratory*.

It is important to recognize the ways in which classical rhetoric survived the sophisticated and highly influential new philosophic rhetoric of the eighteenth century and to acknowledge that the "ancient topical machinery of invention," as Wilbur Samuel Howell has put it, is alive and doing well in the twentieth century. In this light, Ward should be viewed as an important figure in education in eighteenth-century rhetoric—and as a potentially interesting figure to return to for twentieth-century rhetoricians. His *System* is an example of education in action and, thus, is out of the norm most commonly studied by historians of rhetoric—namely, the high road of prestigious colleges and academies. His contribution goes beyond his lectures in rhetoric and resonates with our own debates about education in a pluralistic democracy.

BIBLIOGRAPHY

Primary Sources

Adams, John Quincy. *Lectures on Rhetoric and Oratory.* Cambridge, MA, 1810.
The Charters and Statutes of the Royal Society of London for improving Natural Knowledge. London, 1728.
King, William. *The Transactioneer With some of his Philosophical Fancies: In Two Dialogues.* 1700. Reprint. The Augustan Reprint Society, 1988.
Sprat, Thomas. *The History of the Royal Society of London.* 1667. Reprint. Edited by J. I. Cope and H. W. Jones. St. Louis: Washington University Studies, 1958.
Ward, John. *The Lives of the Professors of Gresham College.* 2 vols. London, 1740.
———. *A System of Oratory, Delivered in a Course of Lectures Publicly read at*

Gresham College, London. 2 vols. 1759. Reprint. Hildesheim: Georg Olms Verlag, 1969.

Witherspoon, John. *Lectures on Moral Philosophy and Eloquence.* Philadelphia, 1810.

Biography

Birch, Thomas. *An Account of the Life of John Ward, LL.D., Professor of Rhetoric in Gresham College; F.R.S. and F.S.A.* London, 1766.

Brock, William. "John Ward, LL.D., F.R.S., F.S.A." *Transactions of the Baptist Historical Society* 4 (1914–1915): 1–32, 63, 219, 225.

Edwards, Edward. *Lives of the Founders of the British Museum; with Notices of its Chief Augmentors and Other Benefactors, 1570–1870.* London, 1870.

Hollis, Thomas. *Memoirs of Thomas Hollis, Esq., F.R. and A.S.S.* London, 1780.

Tongue, Edwin John. *Dr. John Ward's Trust.* London: The Carey Kingsgate Press Ltd., 1951.

Criticism

Bitzer, Lloyd F. "Some Marks/Characteristics of 18th-Century Rhetorics." Paper read at conference, The Scope of Eloquence: Texts and Contexts of Rhetoric after the Renaissance, UCLA, December 8, 1990.

Conley, Thomas M. *Rhetoric in the European Tradition.* New York: Longman, 1990.

Ehninger, Douglas. "John Ward and His Rhetoric." *Speech Monographs* 18.1 (1951): 1–16.

Howell, Wilbur Samuel. "John Ward's Lectures at Gresham College." *Eighteenth-Century British Logic and Rhetoric,* 83–124. Princeton: Princeton University Press, 1971.

Vicker, Brian, and Nancy S. Struever. *Rhetoric and the Pursuit of Truth: Language Change in the Seventeenth and Eighteenth Centuries.* Los Angeles: University of California, 1985.

ROBERT WATSON
(1730–1781)

Paul G. Bator

Robert Watson is associated primarily with the University of St. Andrews, where he served first as Professor of Logic, Rhetoric, and Metaphysics from 1756 to 1778 and then as Principal of the United College from 1778 to 1781. Robert Watson also achieved reputation as a historian by writing the *History of the Reign of Philip II of Spain*, first published in 1777. Watson, one of the Moderate Ministers of the Church of Scotland, is believed to be a relation of Hugh Blair and may be placed among the noteworthy group of Scottish literati who achieved reputations as historians, philosophers, clergymen, and academics including such well-known Scotsmen as David Hume, Adam Smith, Henry Home (Lord) Kames, and Hugh Blair, as well as lesser-known Scotsmen, among them William Robertson and Adam Ferguson. Prior to assuming his posts as professor and then principal at St. Andrews University, Robert Watson had delivered a series of lectures on rhetoric and belles lettres in Edinburgh. The juncture at which Watson delivered his lectures is important in the history of rhetoric, for Watson was the person who inherited the series of lectures on rhetoric that Adam Smith had launched in Edinburgh.

Watson was born in St. Andrews about the year 1730 to a father—an apothecary and brewer—who had the same name as his son. He studied at St. Andrews University from 1744–1748, and the Graduation Roll shows him to be among three students receiving an M.A. degree on May 6, 1748. In order to "improve himself," Watson moved from his native town and spent time first in Glasgow and then Edinburgh and is assumed to have attended some classes at both universities. After he qualified before the St. Andrews Presbytery (1756) and was licensed for the ministry, Watson applied for a vacancy in one of the local St. Andrews parishes but was not granted the position. Shortly thereafter, however, the Professor of Logic, Rhetoric, and Metaphysics at St. Andrews, Henry Rymer, retired; and under usual agreements, Watson arranged to obtain Rymer's chair for a small sum of money with the proviso that Rymer would continue to receive his salary. Watson was appointed Professor of Logic, Rhetoric, and Metaphysics at St. Andrews on June 18, 1756. During his term as Professor, Watson was among those responsible—perhaps the chief person responsible in one or both cases—for conferring honorary degrees upon Hugh Blair and Benjamin Franklin. Blair was awarded a doctor of divinity degree on June 13, 1757, just two years before he took up Watson's lectures on rhetoric at Edinburgh. Franklin, honored for his "Writings on Electricity," was awarded the doctor of laws degree at St. Andrews on February 12, 1759. Upon assuming his professorial duties, Watson married Margaret Shaw, the daughter of the professor of divinity in St. Mary's College at St. Andrews; his wife gave birth to their five daughters. In order to house his growing family, in 1772 Watson actually made purchase (£200 and a yearly *feu*-duty of £10) of the main St. Leonard college buildings and gardens in the Priory Precinct, what the English might refer to as "the college living," and he and his family resided there for a time. Andrew Cant, the St. Andrews historian, observed: "Professor Watson may well have thought it a bargain. It is not often that one can buy a complete college for so little" (94).

Influenced by the success of David Hume's *History of England* (1759) and William Robertson's *History of Scotland* (1759), Watson decided upon the reign of Philip II of Spain as a proper subject for writing his own historical account. Watson worked on his history of the reign of Philip II for several years, and it gained the light of publication at London in 1777, in two volumes quarto. Six subsequent editions were published between the years 1778 and 1812. Interestingly, just before its initial publication, Samuel Johnson had written to Watson's publisher, William Strahan, offering his editorial assistance: "I am told that you are printing a Book for Mr. Professor Watson of Saint Andrews, if upon any occasion, I can give any help, or be of any use, as formerly in Dr Robertson's publication, I hope you will make no scruple to call upon me, for I should be glad of an opportunity to show that my reception at Saint Andrews has not been forgotten" (October 14, 1776). Indeed, after it was published—whether it was owing to his assistance is uncertain—Johnson found Watson's *History* to be "much esteemed." Watson's *History* went through six successive editions, met with much success, and gained for Watson notoriety at the time as an historian near the rank of William Robertson. At the time of his death, on April 1, 1781, Watson also had completed the first four books of his history of the reign of Philip III, a continuation of his earlier study. The work was completed by the addition of two more books by Dr. William Thompson and published as the *History of the Reign of Philip the Third, King of Spain* in 1783.

On January 9, 1778, Watson was named principal (and in that same year rector) of the United College of Saint Salvator and Saint Leonard in the University of Saint Andrews, succeeding the College's first principal, Thomas Tullideph, who held the position from 12 June 1747 until his death 14 November 1777. The United College minutes show Watson, as professor and principal, to have been involved in a wide range of internal and external affairs on behalf of his university. He was sent to London in 1776, for example, to buy maps and pamphlets "on both sides" of the American question and represented the university before the town council. During Watson's brief tenure as principal of United College from 1778 until his death in 1781, the notable figures at St. Andrews were few but did include the moderate theologian and professor of Greek, George Hill, and the young professor of the humanities, John Hunter.

More significant than Watson's role as historian or principal of St. Andrews, in terms of rhetorical historiography, is the fact that Watson early in his career had been solicited by Lord Kames and others to continue the Edinburgh rhetorical lectures that Adam Smith had initiated and Hugh Blair later popularized. It is probable also that Watson met Adam Smith in Edinburgh and attended Smith's lectures on rhetoric delivered in Edinburgh in the fall and winter of 1748–1749. While in Edinburgh, Watson "secured the friendship of Lord Kames, Mr. Hume, and other eminent men of that day" (Anderson 611–12). Ian Simpson Ross, in his biography of Lord Kames, has stated that it was Kames who did not "let drop" his plan for promoting lectures on rhetoric and belles lettres in Edinburgh after Smith left to take up the Chair of Logic at Glasgow in 1751 and that it was Home who "recruited" Robert Watson to "give courses similar to Smith's" (94). J. C. Bryce has stated that after Smith left Edinburgh for Glasgow, "a rhetoric course continued to be given by Robert Watson til his departure for the Chair of Logic [Rhetoric and Metaphysics] at St. Andrews in 1756" (8). Wilbur Samuel Howell has surmised that it was Smith's lectures on rhetoric that "led to Robert Watson's being named to continue the public lectures on rhetoric after Smith departed for Glasgow" (544), which adds a degree of probability to the suggestion that Watson was among the audience attending Smith's lectures. Henry W. Meikle, furthermore, has characterized Watson as having, with the encouragement of Lord Kames, "continued the course which Smith had initiated" (91). Anderson, in *The Scottish Nation*, reported that it was John Home, the minister and playwright (who later became personal secretary to John Stuart, the Earl of Bute), who had asked Robert Watson to continue the lectures on rhetoric at Edinburgh in Smith's place" (611–12). Exactly when Watson began lecturing at Edinburgh cannot be ascertained; but his lectures must have been presented between 1751, the time that Smith's lectures ended, and 1756, the date that Watson took up his post at St. Andrews.

WATSON'S RHETORICAL THEORY

There are several versions of Robert Watson's lectures on rhetoric in manuscript form; however, none of the manuscripts appears to be a record of

the actual lectures that Watson delivered in Edinburgh between 1751 and
1756. The manuscripts that do exist provide a record of the lectures that
Watson delivered while Professor of Logic, Rhetoric, and Metaphysics at St.
Andrews from 1756–1778. The 1758 St. Andrews manuscript set of Watson's lectures is entitled "A treatise on Rhetorick" and contains thirty-seven
brief chapters in Part One, twelve chapters in Part Two, and an appended
section (pp. 1–5) of observations of the origins of language. A St. Andrews
University librarian has marked on an inserted inside fly-leaf, "Two have
been written in separate note-books and afterwards bound together. They
have been somewhat cropped in the binding." This bound manuscript volume appears to contain two separate sets of notes prepared by two different
note takers; neither student note taker is identified. At the end of the bound
notebook, the student note taker has written: "This Book contains all the
Second Part of Rhetorick, which Mr. Robert Watson taught in the Year
1758. Finis, the End."

The lectures in Part One of "A treatise on Rhetorick" are essentially lectures on language and style. For example, the titles of various lectures, including "Of the general Qualities of Stile [i.e., style]," "Of the Length of
Periods," "Of Tropes & Figures," "Of Perspicuity," "Of Elegance &
Beauty," "Of the natural," "Of Wit," and "Of Description and Narration,"
indicate Watson's rhetorical trajectory: it is toward an analysis of the traditional stylistic elements of polite discourse. The opening of the third chapter,
"Of the general Qualities of Stile," sets forth an outline for the entire first
part of the lectures: "The principal Qualities of Stile are Perspicuity, Elegance or Beauty, Simplicity together with its contrary, and that to which we
give the Name of Natural." Watson proceeded to take up these themes and
elaborate upon their relationships in Part One of his lectures. In Part One,
Watson set forth for his students standard neoclassical refrains of the eighteenth-century Scottish rhetoricians: a concern for "perspicuity of style";
"elegance or beauty" of natural language; attention to the "smoothness"
of words and the length of sentences or "periods"; the appropriate use of
similes and "metaphors"; and a treatment of several figures, including "in-
terrogation," "transposition," and "personification." In Part Two, Watson
presented an extended treatment of poetry, including lectures on the dramatic forms, tragedy and comedy. The student note taker made it clear in
the appendix that "what follows does not belong to Rhetorick [b]ut are
some observations concerning Language."

The Edinburgh manuscript (1764) of Robert Watson's lectures on rhetoric is cataloged "Heads of lectures on rhetoric and belles lettres," with the
manuscript title page reading: "Of Rhetorick by Robert Watson." The manuscript contains what clearly appears to be a set of student notes from Watson's lectures, probably delivered at St. Andrews (since Watson was
Professor of Logic, Rhetoric, and Metaphysics there in 1764). The student
note taker(s) is not identified, and it is possible that more than one set of

student notes was used to compose the final manuscript. The manuscript is divided into three sections: "Part One" contains thirty-one brief chapters on topics related to language and style; "Part 2d" contains twelve chapters on poetry; and an "Appendix" contains three chapters titled "Of Propriety," "Of Simplicity," and "Of History." It appears essentially that Watson had "fixed" his lectures by 1758. The 1764 Edinburgh manuscript "Heads of lectures on rhetoric and belles lettres" includes all of the lectures contained in Part One of the 1758 St. Andrews manuscript "A treatise on Rhetorick," except for the lecture on parentheses, three lectures on words, and the lectures entitled "Of the Use of Precepts," "Of the Proper Emphasis," and "Of Tropes & Figures." The lectures in Part Two of each manuscript version on poetry are essentially repeated. The one important difference between the two manuscripts is that the Edinburgh (1764) manuscript includes the three appendix chapters on "Propriety," "Simplicity," and "History." It should be noted that lectures on "Propriety," "Simplicity," and "History" are also contained as regular chapters in the 1778 St. Andrews manuscript "Notes of Lectures on Logic and Rhetoric by Principal Watson, St. Andrews, 1778," which also contains a new chapter on the "Passions."

In addition to the manuscripts described above recording Watson's lectures on rhetoric and belles lettres, there are additional manuscripts extant that contain a record of Watson's lectures on logic (listed in my bibliography under "Primary Sources"), which he delivered as Professor of Logic, Rhetoric, and Metaphysics. There do not appear to be any separate manuscripts containing lectures on metaphysics. However, in "A System of Logic," Watson did provide a chapter, "Of Pneumatics," in which he discussed the powers of the mind, and elsewhere he took up "practical means of improvement" for his students. Overall, Watson's lectures on logic are decidedly modern, cast in the tradition of Descartes, Bacon, and Locke. As do many of the published logics of the eighteenth century that largely rejected the formal logic of scholasticism, Watson nevertheless retained elements of traditional logic insofar as he prelected on terms, propositions, and syllogisms. Yet Watson's presentation of these traditional elements of logic is contained within his more central framework of an investigation of the nature and operation of human understanding as it searches for truth through reason and judgment. After presenting brief analyses of his terms and their related classes of objects, Watson proceeded to explain the different "terms, Propositions, and Syllogisms," as "signs of the several powers" by which the understanding generally establishes and expresses itself. Watson was attempting to convey to his students at St. Andrews the "modern" logic of Locke, which swept into the logic curricula at each of the other major Scottish universities during the eighteenth century and was evident in Thomas Reid's lectures at Aberdeen, John Stevenson's at Edinburgh, and James Clow's at Glasgow.

Before considering more carefully Watson's lectures on rhetoric, it should be kept in mind that Watson prepared and fixed his lectures prior to 1756, perhaps as early as 1751, when he may have taken over from Smith at Edinburgh. Blair did not begin his series of lectures on rhetoric at Edinburgh until 1759, Campbell presented his lectures to the Aberdeen Philosophical Society between 1758 and 1771, and Kames did not publish his *Elements of Criticism* until 1762. The analysis that follows is based primarily on Watson's Edinburgh (1764) manuscript, "Heads of lectures on rhetoric and belles lettres."

Unlike the extant version of Adam Smith's rhetoric lectures, which do not include an opening or introductory lecture, we do have an introductory lecture from Watson. In his first lecture as recorded in the Edinburgh (1764) manuscript, "Heads of lectures on rhetoric and belles lettres," Watson set forth a qualified definition for rhetoric: "Rhetorick may be defined to be the art which delivers rules for the excellence and beauty of discourse"—which he then proceeded to question and extend. Also referring to rhetoric as a science, Watson deemed it wise to begin his lectures—as recorded in a slightly extended version of the opening lecture in the St. Andrews (1758) manuscript, "A treatise on Rhetoric"—by fixing the "Notion of the Science itself." Watson found fault with those writers on rhetoric who limited themselves to one sort of discourse—for example, public orations. His stated plan was to treat the "many rules of this Art" since an acquaintance with history and poetry, for example, was "at least of equal consequence to the improvement of taste" as an acquaintance with public orations. While obviously restricting oratorical discourse from his primary rhetorical purview, Watson was nevertheless careful not to dismiss eloquence or persuasive discourse from rhetoric's scope but to expand narrower claims for rhetoric by emphasizing nondisputational forms, such as history and poetry. His rhetoric, then, becomes a familiar eighteenth-century French or Scottish rhetorician's expansion of rhetoric's domain by its inclusion of nonoratorical, nonpersuasive discourse. Similarly, there can also be seen in Watson's introductory lecture a shift away from oral eloquence toward increasing concern with written forms of discourse and composition.

By linking the study of nonpersuasive forms of discourse with an "improvement of taste," Watson thereby signaled what he saw as one of the chief advantages of the "rules" of rhetoric. He became even blunter in his second lecture ("Of the Use of Precepts") in the Edinburgh (1764) manuscript "Heads of lectures on rhetoric and belles lettres," when he said, "The first advantage to be drawn from the Rules of Rhetorick, is that they improve our Taste." Subtly, yet deliberately, Watson framed the stated plan for his lectures upon common-sense moral grounds. His practical concern with "improvement" in matters of language and composition was linked to an aesthetic refinement of critical taste. Closely upon such improvement in matters of discourse and taste Watson posited a second "advantage," literally "that the Improvement of Taste is nearly connected with Improvement in Virtue." Watson may be seen as attempting to preserve Cicero's dictum for rhetoric as "the good man speaking well," transformed into "the good man criticising with taste and discernment." Concomitantly, Watson importantly preserved one of rhetoric's chief classical aims—namely, an inculcation of virtue in the rhetor and audience. A further use or advantage for the precepts of rhetoric, Watson believed to be a distinctly practical one: "They enable us to discern the Faults of our own Composition, and to correct them." Lecturing as he was to an audience of young students, Watson was ever mindful of casting his rhetorical advice in workable terms, as his students wrote, criticized, and corrected their compositions. In this respect, Watson's is a practical rhetoric; it does not offer guidelines on elocution or pronunciation but supplies practical guidelines for composing and sufficient examples of the beauties and faults of literature in its several forms. Thus, it is difficult initially to characterize Watson's rhetoric as uniformly "belletristic," insofar as such a characterization implies an exclusive concern with matters of style. For Watson's emphasis upon improving the critical faculties, his offering his students practical advice about writing and correcting their compositions, and his linking of rhetoric with promotion of virtue stamp his rhetorical scope as broader than other rhetorics. Furthermore, Watson's emphases on the representational function of language through narration and description, on the imitative capacity of poetry, and on the instructive measure of history mark his lectures as more than simply stylistic or elocutionary.

Watson planned to explain his subject by a neoscholastic method, which broke away from the plan of those who delivered their rhetorical treatises primarily through "rhetorical rules." An excerpt from his opening lecture in "Heads of lectures on rhetoric and belles lettres" demonstrates Watson's plan: "By the Rules of Rhetorick or fine writing else is meant but observations concerning the particulars which render discourse excellent and useful; it is not proposed to deliver them in the form of rules, but in the form of general Criticisms: illustrated by passages from authors. To what follows therefore may be given either the name of Rhetorick or of Criticism; for if it deserve the name of the one it will deserve the other also." Watson thus established a pedagogical pattern similar to Adam Smith's and Hugh Blair's lectures, wherein Smith and Blair prelected on their subject by providing relevant comparative examples, passages, and illustrations of the topic for their students—not by setting forth the dry rules of the scholastic rhetorician.

In his third chapter ("Of the general Qualities of Stile") of "Heads of lectures on rhetoric and belles lettres," Watson set forth an outline for the lectures that followed, characterizing for his students essential qualities of style and the particulars that contribute toward achieving a proper and elegant style. Watson saw the principal qualities of style as "Perspicuity, Elegance or Beauty, Simplicity, Propriety, and the Natural." For demonstration of the particulars that he intended to discuss as contributing to or detracting from the essential qualities of style, Watson gave the examples of smooth and harmonious periods, metaphors, and personification. These "qualities" are unoriginal—derivative, in the first place, from Cicero, Quintilian, Horace, Demetrius, and Longinus and, in the second place, through Adam Smith, Lord Kames, Alexander Gerard, Joseph Addison, and others. Watson did not slavishly follow any one of the moderns or the ancients in presenting his critical advice; instead, he selected from those authors, ancient and modern, who suited his purpose—a philosophical and pedagogical method common to Smith and subsequent eighteenth-century Scottish rhetoricians. Nevertheless, Watson's singling out "perspicuity" and "propriety" particularly demonstrates his eighteenth-century orientation. Kames, for example, speaking of communication of thought as the chief end of language, made it a rule that "perspicuity ought not to be sacrificed to any other beauty whatever" (255). Similarly, in his opening lecture, Watson pronounced that "language is never found beautiful without being proper and perspicuous." These two aesthetic terms provided a natural, or common-sense, basis for criticism that was tied to the preservation of moral and social standards by the prominent eighteenth-century rhetoricians.

Watson's emphasis on "perspicuity" is worth highlighting for two reasons: it establishes one of Watson's central rhetorical themes; it also allows close comparison with the subject of Adam Smith's first recorded lecture. Perspicuity, as a fundamental quality of style, has ancient grounding in Quintilian and modern emphasis in John Locke. As Wilbur Samuel Howell—placing aside Locke's mistrust of rhetoric—has discussed, Locke declared the art of speaking well to consist chiefly in "perspicuity" and "right reasoning." According to Howell, Locke supplied his own communicative definition: "Perspicuity consists in the using of proper terms for the ideas or thoughts, which he would have pass from his own mind into that of another man's" (499–500). Watson introduced the concept of "perspicuity" in his third lecture, referred to this quality of prose and verse several times during the course of his lectures, and included a separate lecture devoted to the topic. Watson's treatment is similar to Smith's discussion of perspicuity in his "opening" lecture, which is labeled the second chapter. Smith, in his discussion of "perspicuity," advised: "Our words must also be put in such order that the meaning of the sentence shall be quite plain" (5). For Watson, "Perspicuity denotes that Quality of Stile by which an Authors [sic] meaning is easily understood." He cautioned that perspicuity may be hurt and ambiguity arise from "not keeping those words distinct & separate of which the Ideas are distinct & separate." Watson, like Smith, admired Jonathan Swift in this regard: "Dr. Swift's Stile is more remarkable for Perspicuity than Lord Bolinbroke's or [Shaftesbury's] Characteristicks." Judging from the manuscript copy of the student notes, Watson's treatment of perspicuity is briefer and less comprehensive than Smith's. Watson moved through his topic quickly, slowing only to present examples from Swift, Lord Bolingbroke, and the *Spectator*. He made some brief remarks about borrowing words from the Greek and Latin languages, for example, but did not unravel his thoughts upon the subject in as detailed a manner as did Smith. Hugh Blair also included a chapter on "Style—Perspicuity and Precision," providing both discussion and ample illustration of his topic. Blair's treatment of perspicuity, while fuller than either Watson's or Smith's, established identical rhetorical concerns. Tracing perspicuity as a fundamental quality of style to Quintilian, Blair considered perspicuity in writing to thereby exhibit "a degree of positive beauty" (1:235).

Watson provided his definition of propriety in his third lecture, "Of the General Qualities of Stile," an important juncture in his "Heads of lectures on rhetoric and belles lettres" since he provided a framework for the several lectures on language and style that followed. Here Watson came near to resembling Smith's communicative design for rhetoric: "Propriety of Stile consists in its being expressive of the Meaning intended to be conveyed by it." Smith, similarly, in his eighth lecture, stated: "That when the words neatly and properly expressed the thing to be described, and conveyed the sentiment the author entertained of it and desired to communicate by sympathy to his hearers; then the expression had all the beauty language was capable of bestowing on it" (96). Locke had earlier spoken similar sentiments and recommended a pedagogical method: "The way to obtain this [communication], is to read such Books as are allow'd to be writ with the greatest clearness and propriety. . . . I have chose [*sic*] rather to propose this pattern, for the attainment of the Art of Speaking clearly, than those who give rules about it; since we are more apt to learn by example, than by direction" (231, 245). Watson went on, in his separate lecture "Of Propriety," to supply numerous comparative examples of propriety and impropriety, all drawn interestingly enough, from modern authors, such as Joseph Addison, David Hume, Lord Bolingbroke, and William Robertson.

Given Sprat's dictates to the Royal Society for science to adopt a "plain stile," the Scottish rhetoricians were also highly sensitive to the use of tropes (by which they meant primarily metaphors) and figures of speech. In "Heads of lectures on rhetoric and belles lettres," Watson included one lecture entitled "Of Similes" and a following lecture entitled "Of Metaphors." Watson first outlined the positive effects of similes and metaphors for his students within a narrative context of illustration and explanation. He also found that these figures can be advantageously used to render the impression of subjects more "lively and affecting," and, of lesser importance, to "please the imagination" and "relieve the attention." In his lectures, however, he offered examples illustrating both the positive and negative effects that the use of such figures can have. Watson offered relatively strict guidelines for his students by way of presenting "proper" examples, stressing all the while the need for similes and metaphors to bear particular and exact resemblance to their subjects. Properly introduced, the tropes can enhance perspicuity; improperly selected, they risk giving discourses "the appearence of pains and labour." Watson's student note taker recorded several examples of the faulty use of metaphors, including two illustrations from Smith's favorite author, Dr. Swift, one of which is the following: "Another fault in Metaphors is when they are course & indelicate as where Dr. Swift says 'If the Peace of State could be bought by only flinging men a few Ceremonies to devour, it is a purchase which no wise man would refuse.' " Watson appears generally in accord with Blair on the matter of tropes and figures of speech. Although Blair often preferred to use the word *sentiment* when referring to the intent of the speaker, both Watson and Blair acknowledged the role of the passions in giving rise to the natural use of metaphor in language. In comparison to Watson and Blair, Smith took a somewhat stricter approach to figures of speech. Smith's attitude is captured in this well-known passage from Lecture Six: "When the sentiment of the speaker is expressed in a neat, clear, plain and clever manner, and the passion or affection he is possessed of and intends, *by sympathy*, to communicate to his hearer, is plainly and cleverly hit off, then and then only the expression has all the force and beauty that language can give it. . . . It matters not the least whether the figures of speech are introduced or not" (25–26). Yet Smith's stance, represented by this quotation, is not entirely representative of his eclectic rhetorical advice. While stating that the figures have "no intrinsick worth of their own," Smith did allow for their "just and naturall" use as a way of contributing toward the beauty or elegance of language.

Watson ("Of History"), Smith (Lectures 17–20), and Blair (Lectures 35–36) delivered separate lectures on history or historical composition, as one species of prose composition. There is basic agreement among them that the aim of the historian is to relate the truth of past events through a proper narration of facts in order to instruct and enable men to guide their own actions upon past lessons. Smith, however, placed less emphasis upon the historian's moral role than did Watson and Blair. Smith, in language relatively shorn of didactic moral overtones, would allow that historical writing offered more than mere entertainment, for "it has in view the instruction of the reader" (90). Blair and Watson employed more overtly moral voices: In Lecture 36, Blair advised that the historian should "always show himself to be on the side of virtue" (47); in his lecture "Of History," Watson observed that history "has a tendency to give us a lively sense of the vicissitudes to which human affairs are subjected and of the emptiness of every thing but virtue."

Turning to Watson's lectures on poetry can help to draw out his larger rhetorical purview. Watson devoted a significant portion (about twelve chapters) of his "Heads of lectures on rhetoric and belles lettres" to verse or poetry, treating poetry as the equally important "second division" of rhetoric. Watson devoted Part Two of his lectures on rhetoric to a discussion of poetry in its several classical genres, including tragedy, the epic, and comedy. As did Blair, Watson considered poetry within the central domain of rhetoric's compass and deemed it theoretically necessary and pedagogically useful to prelect upon the subject for his audience. Smith gave much less attention to poetry in his lectures, and poetry appears to be a relatively minor matter in Smith's larger rhetorical system.

Watson's neoclassical treatment of poetry is straightforwardly Aristotelian, with Watson referring his students several times to Aristotle's advice in *Poetics*. Watson did not, unfortunately, take up the knottier problems of the "cathartic" effects of tragedy or respond directly to Plato's charges against poetry in *Republic*. Instead, he payed homage to the classical doctrine of the unities of time, place, and action; presented a discussion of the proper subjects for poetry as it should resemble real life; included one lecture on rhyme; and offered separate lectures on tragedy, the epic, and comedy. Watson diverged from a strictly conventional neoclassical critique of poetry in his emphasis on sense experienced through particularity. In his lecture on the "Subjects of Imitation," Watson closely examined individual characters, virtuous and vicious, supplying numerous illustrative examples (Nero, Desdemona, Richard III, Iago) as well as more "contemporary" characters from Congreve's *Mourning Bride*. Watson's attention to individual characters remains largely superficial, however, as he considers characters as representative or not of stock moral virtues and vices. Nevertheless, in his attempt to particularize his critical observations, Watson belongs to a trend toward individual character analysis developing in the criticism of Blair, Kames, Campbell, and others.

In his discussion of the fit subjects for poetry, Watson did not maintain an aesthetic theory of Platonic ideals, as Shaftesbury preferred; rather, Watson agreed with Aristotle and Cicero that the objects of imitation reside in the general nature of man, in real life, whether such representation be of good or evil. Defending his empirical particularity—or "speciality," using Campbell's term—Watson, in "Subjects of Imitation," paraphrased Aristotle: "The purification of the passions is received for the most part in proportion as the imitation is exact." A noteworthy aspect of Watson's treatment of verse or poetry resides in his attempt to frame a foundation for his classical subject in an eighteenth-century metaphysical context. Watson saw poetry as embodying the language of the imagination and the passions, depending more upon nature than upon the faculties of reason or judgment. Watson viewed poetry as emanating from the nature of the human constitution: the poet, through his love of similitude, invents characters, actions, and events similar to those of real life. According to Watson, the intention and design of the poet is based upon a general and natural "principle" of imitation that can be seen in some measure as providing the foundation of the fine arts—indeed, the "Foundation of Society itself."

Equally telling is Watson's statement of the goals or ends of poetic imitation. Fundamentally, Watson ascribed a moral function to poetry, saying that it affords a "profitable exercise to the virtuous passions and affections." In his lectures on rhetoric and belles lettres, Hugh Blair also devoted ample treatment to poetry. Blair stressed the classical motive of imitation less than Watson did; and he found imitation too "loose" a way of supplying a definition of poetry, since several other arts—painting and music, for example—also rely upon imitation. Blair, in concert with Watson, emphasized poetry's primary address to the imagination, not to reason and understanding. Blair also framed his treatment of poetry within the language of the passions, discussing the several methods by which the poet may raise or excite man's sentiments and passions. Blair, however, did not represent the poet's chief function as that of improving virtue; instead, in Aristotelian fashion, Blair, as stated in Lecture 38, believed that the primary aim of the poet is "to please, and to move" (85). Nonetheless, in Lecture 38, Blair quickly added that the poet may and "ought to have it in his view, to instruct, and to reform" (85).

Adam Smith's treatment of poetry, in his lectures on rhetoric, provides marked contrast to Watson's. In the single lecture (21) that he allotted to poetry, Smith declared the chief end of poetry to be "pleasure" or "entertainment." Smith, either deliberately, or through lack of diligence on the part of the single student note taker, ignored the classical treatment of mimesis or imitation, and neglected to provide an alternative basis for the roots and function of poetic composition other than to say that "amusement and intertaiment [sic] was the chief design of the poet" (118). Smith devoted the bulk of his lecture to Aristotle's unities of time and place through his discussion of "unity of interest" (120). Unlike Watson and Blair, Smith did not believe that poetry espoused the causes of virtue but tended to belittle any "truth" value that may be inherent in poetry, comparing the poet at one point to the teller of ridiculous stories: "The Poet is exactly in the same condition; his design is to intertain and he does not pretend that what he tells us is true" (119). Since it is entertainment that we look for from the poet, Smith observed, we allow him the concessions of some "cobling" and are not offended by any embellishments to his story.

Robert Watson neither repeated Adam Smith's Edinburgh lectures on rhetoric nor routinely relinquished his notes for Hugh Blair to use for his Edinburgh lectures after Watson departed for St. Andrews. Nonetheless, it must also be concluded that while individually preparing and delivering his own set of lectures, Watson was articulating a philosophy squarely representative and supportive of the developing rhetoric of the Scottish Enlightenment. Watson's lectures at St. Andrews reflect the emergent rhetoric of the Scottish Enlightenment and add corroborating evidence for the shift from scholasticism toward a neoclassical, "belletristic" rhetoric. Having read and examined Watson's lectures, I find that they provide added evidence for Bevilacqua's claim that the "Scottish view was the close psychological connection of logic and rhetoric" (207). I would add Robert Watson's name to Bevilacqua's list of those—Smith, Kames, George Campbell, Joseph Priestley, and Blair—who "reoriented mid–eighteenth-century rhetorical theory in terms of human nature, thereby connecting rhetoric to such related studies as ethics, aesthetics, and criticism" (207). What distinguishes Watson's rhetoric lectures, then, is not an innovative contribution to rhetorical theory of the rank of Smith, Kames, Gerard, or Campbell, but their contribution to our understanding of the nature, method, and role of rhetoric in the general Scottish university curriculum in the eighteenth century.

Watson, in accord with Smith, Blair, and Cambpell, subscribed to an attenuated theory of rhetorical invention. Watson, particularly, having ignored the disputational or persuasive function of classical rhetoric, gave classical *inventio* no prominence in his lectures on rhetoric. For Watson, like most of the eighteenth-century rhetoricians who were influenced by emerging scientific methods of inductive inquiry, the discovery of materials was a matter for natural, or empirical, logic to discern through an investigation or analysis of particular examples. Watson's logic of inquiry—insofar as it represented an inventional scheme that accompanied his rhetoric—suggests a practical science of induction based upon assembling or associating facts, examples, and instances, not upon discovering them. Watson, importantly, joins Smith, Blair, and Campbell in emphasizing the "communicative" capacity and role of rhetoric. The rhetoric of the eighteenth-century resulted in an emphasis upon style: the order and arrangement of materials already discovered through other (scientific) means. In his lectures on rhetoric, Watson also demonstrated that the foundation for grammar, logic, and rhetoric is essentially the same: human nature, as articulated through the Scottish "common sense" school of philosophy (advocated notably by Thomas Reid) and through associational or "faculty" psychology (as articulated initially by David Hartley). Thus, there was for Watson—as for Smith, Kames, Blair, and Campbell—a common epistemological basis for rhetoric, resting upon the metaphysical powers of the understanding, reason, judgment, and imagination and evidenced in the production of belles lettres, encompassing science, history, letters, poetry, and vernacular literature. Watson, particularly, since he taught logic and rhetoric (as did his successor at St. Andrews, William Barron), exemplified the cautionary influence of Francis Bacon and Locke on the epistemological design of both subjects. For Watson, while reason and understanding were the natural powers of the human mind most closely associated with logic, they—along with such faculties as imagination, taste, genius, and judgment—provided the common epistemological foundation for rhetoric.

While Robert Watson was but a shadow compared to the popular and influential figure of Hugh Blair, Watson may be seen, nevertheless, as enjoining Blair's effort to blend elements of stoicism, Ciceronian virtue, and a lingering sense of civic humanism with orthodox Presbyterian values and recommending such attitudes and resultant habits to his students. Richard Sher has characterized the primary goal of Moderate moral teaching and preaching as making men "virtuous and happy, which is to say, benevolent in thought and deed and appreciative . . . of the established social, political, and religious order" (211). Watson was one of those whose lectures on rhetoric reflected his desire to inculcate virtue in the hearts and minds of his students. Watson's was a practical moral rhetoric, for he gave his students not only useful lessons in literary criticism but also supplied them with lessons about everyday life through understanding and interpretation of the character, habits, and passions of literary subjects. While promoting an innovative movement away from traditional rhetoric and toward the enlightened rhetoric of the eighteenth century, Watson must also be seen as a promotion of traditional political order and social virtue. Watson's lectures thus reinforced what John Dwyer has remarked upon as "the significance which the literati attached to the smooth functioning of the traditional moral community in Scotland" (5). It is this designed classical emphasis upon virtue, notably, that joins Robert Watson's lectures on rhetoric to Hugh Blair's and distinguishes them from Adam Smith's.

BIBLIOGRAPHY

Primary Sources

Watson, Robert. "Compend of Logic." MS. 3125, Fol. 30. National Library of Scotland, Edinburgh.

———. "A compend of logic and universal grammar. 1776." MS. BC6.W1. St. Andrews University Library, Fifeshire, Scotland.

———. "A compend of Logic, as taught by Dr. Robert Watson. 1770." MS. Murray 3. Glasgow University Library.

———. "Dictates of Rhetoric by Robert Watson. Professor of Logic, St. Andrews, 1762. Taken down by Robert Rintoul." MS. PN 173.W2. St. Andrews University Library, Fifeshire, Scotland.

———. "Heads of lectures on rhetoric and belles lettres." MS. Dc. 6.50/2. Edinburgh University Library.

———. The History of the Reign of Philip the Second, King of Spain, 2 vols. London, 1777.

———. "Notes of Lectures on Logic and Rhetoric by Principal Watson, St. Andrews, 1778." MS. BC6.W2. St. Andrews University Library, Fifeshire, Scotland.

———. "A System of Logic. St. Andrews. 1764–65." MS. Dk. 3.2. Edinburgh University.

———. "A treatise on Rhetorick." MS. PN 173.W1. St. Andrews University Library, Fifeshire, Scotland.

———. "Universal grammar and compend of logic." MS. 36978. St. Andrews University Library, Fifeshire, Scotland.

Biography

Anderson, William. The Scottish Nation and Biographical History. Edinburgh, 1863.

Boswell, James. Life of Johnson, edited by George Birbeck Hill. Vol. 5, The Tour To

The Hebrides and The Journey Into North Wales. Oxford: Oxford University Press, 1964.

Bryce, J. C., ed. *Lectures on Rhetoric and Belles Lettres,* by Adam Smith. Oxford: Oxford University Press, 1983.

Cant, R. G. *The University of St. Andrews.* Edinburgh: Scottish Academic Press, 1970.

Johnson, Samuel. *The Letters of Samuel Johnson.* Edited by R. W. Chapman. Vol. 2, 1775–1782. Oxford: Clarendon Press, 1952.

Ross, Ian Simpson. *Lord Kames and the Scotland of His Day.* Oxford: Clarendon Press, 1972.

St. Andrews University Minutes. Vol. 7, March 1753–May 1766. St. Andrews University, Fifeshire, Scotland.

Schmitz, Robert Morell. *Hugh Blair.* New York: King's Crown Press, 1948.

Criticism

Bator, Paul G. "The Formation of The Regius Chair of Rhetoric and Belles Lettres at The University of Edinburgh." *Quarterly Journal of Speech* 75.1 (1989): 40–64.

Bevilacqua, Vincent M. "Philosophical Influences in the Development of English Rhetorical Theory: 1748 to 1783." *Proceedings of the Leeds Philosophical and Literary Society* 12, pt. 6 (1968): 191–215.

Blair, Hugh. *Lectures on Rhetoric and Belles Lettres.* 3 vols. New York: Garland Publishing, Inc., 1970.

Court, Franklin E. *Institutionalizing English Literature.* Palo Alto: Stanford University Press, 1992.

Dwyer, John. *Virtuous Discourse: Sensibility and Community in Late Eighteenth Century Scotland.* Edinburgh: John Donald, 1987.

Horner, Winifred Bryan. *Nineteenth-Century Scottish Rhetoric.* Carbondale: Southern Illinois University Press, 1993.

Howell, Wilbur Samuel. *Eighteenth-Century British Logic and Rhetoric.* Princeton: Princeton University Press, 1971.

Irvine, James R., and G. Jack Gravlee. "Rhetorical Studies at Edinburgh: A Select Inventory of Manuscripts in Scottish Archives." *Communication Monographs,* 43.4 (1976): 295–99.

Kames, Henry Home, Lord. *The Elements of Criticism.* New York, 1852.

Locke, John. *A Collection of Several Pieces of Mr. John Locke.* London, 1720.

Meikle, Henry W. "The Chair of Rhetoric and Belles Lettres in the University of Edinburgh." *University of Edinburgh Journal* 13 (1944): 89–103.

Miller, Thomas P. "Where Did College English Studies Come From?" *Rhetoric Review* 9.1 (1990): 50–69.

Murphy, James J., ed. *A Short History of Writing Instruction: From Ancient Greece to Twentieth-Century America.* Davis, CA: Hermagoras Press, 1990.

Sher, Richard B. *Church and University in the Scottish Enlightenment: The Moderate Literati of Edinburgh.* Edinburgh: Edinburgh University Press; Princeton: Princeton University Press, 1985.

Smith, Adam. *Lectures on Rhetoric and Belles Lettres.* Edited by J. C. Bryce. Oxford: Oxford University Press, 1983.

NOAH WEBSTER
(1758–1843)

David Payne

Noah Webster was born on October 16, 1758, in West Hartford, Connecticut, and if we measure him by the standards of his countrymen, he was born into relative comfort. He descended from John Webster (one of the earliest Boston settlers) on his father's side, and from William Bradford of Plymouth Colony on his mother's side. The family farm, though small, stood the mortgage for Noah's education at Yale (he graduated in September 1778). Nonetheless, Webster's adult recollection of his college period reflects a sense of disinheritance, when his "country was impoverished by war and when few encouragements offered to induce young men to enter into professional employments," so that Webster saw himself as "being set afloat in the world at the inexperienced age of twenty" by both father and alma mater (Webster to Thomas Dawes Dec. 20, 1808). At that time, "his father put into his hands an eight dollar bill of continental currency, then worth three or four dollars; saying to him 'take this; you must now seek your living; I can do no more for you' " (Rollins 133). Likewise, his memory of Yale centered upon the gaps in his education. Since the Revolution "occasioned various interruptions of the collegiate studies," as various classes were dismissed or "stationed in different towns," Webster noted that "the advantages then enjoyed by the students, during the four years of college life were much inferior to those enjoyed before and since the Revolution, in the same institution" (Rollins 132). Webster recalled, "I was within sound of the church bell in New Haven, a freshman in college, when the news arrived of the shedding of blood in Lexington" (Webster to Lewis Gaylord Clark Nov. 15, 1838).

Webster turned to teaching in the Hartford area (1779–1780), read the law in Litchfield (1780–1781), and was admitted to the bar in April 1781. Teaching occupied him again in Sharon, Connecticut (the summer and fall of 1781) and in Goshen, New York (1782–1783). By the time that he began the practice of law in Hartford in the spring of 1783, he had developed ideas of simplified spelling, which had undoubtedly occurred to him during his teaching stints, and had written Part 1 of the *Grammatical Institute*, a speller which was published in October 1783 but did not reach its best-known "blue-backed" form until its 1827 revision as *An Elementary Spelling Book*. The 1783 speller was followed by Part 2 of the *Grammatical Institute*, in 1784.

Webster's only public pronouncements on rhetoric appear in Part 3 of the *Grammatical Institute* (later known as *An American Selection of Lessons in Reading and Speaking*), published in his 1785 reader. Following that publication, he went on a lecture tour in support of his ideas of a national language (1785–1786). He moved to Philadelphia late in 1786, almost concurrent with the Constitutional Convention (1787), where he edited the *American Magazine* (1787), married, collected his philological thoughts in *Dissertations on the English Language* (1789), and attended to his growing family. His work on the famous dictionary began in 1800, and he produced the *Compendious Dictionary* in 1806, a small version of what would follow. In 1808 he experienced an emotional conversion from "a *rational religion*" and fear "of being misled by the passions" (Webster to Thomas Dawes Dec. 20, 1808) to a complete acceptance of evangelical Protestantism, even at the danger of being accused of enthusiasm. Webster's mild interest in word radicals, remnants of an original Adamic language, grew to obsessive proportions as he found a religious end for his etymological work.

Having moved a number of times in three decades as editing jobs and other circumstances led him, in 1822 he settled in New Haven. Largely in an effort to bolster the etymological accuracy of his dictionary, he spent 1824 and 1825 in England and France, completing his full dictionary in Cambridge. Although the 1827 revision of his speller (*An Elementary Spelling Book*) would bring him the most contemporary fame, Webster's interest lay in the dictionary, for which he finally found a publisher in 1828. His interest in recovering Adamic language also led him to produce a new edition of the Bible, amended and bowdlerized from the King James edition: "Whenever words are understood in a sense different from that which they had when introduced, and different from that of the original languages, they do not present to the reader the *Word of God* . . . the *first ideas* suggested to the reader should be the true meaning of such words, according to the original languages" (qtd. in Rollins 109). A second edition of Webster's dictionary was issued in 1841, as a second salvo in the "war of the dictionaries" in competition with Joseph Worcester's *Comprehensive, Pronouncing and Expository Dictionary of the English Language* (1830). The debate grew far beyond both authors as each lost control of his masterwork to respective publishers. In the midst of this commercial conflict, Webster died in 1843.

WEBSTER'S RHETORICAL THEORY

Webster's overt statements about rhetoric may be termed predictable or even derivative. But his views of the nature and origin of language affect his legacy to American rhetoric in powerful though indirect ways.

Webster, "perhaps the single most influential educator of the early national period" (Davidson 63), offered pedestrian views of declamation, which were, nonetheless, molded to his goals: Webster "reacted to disorder with strenuous attempts to restore order" (Lawson-Peeples 79) by political uses of language and should be considered, however the title may be valued, "America's first language strategist" (Weinstein 92). Some critics have even suggested that Webster "intentionally manipulated the meanings of individual words throughout his career so as to instruct Americans in what he considered to be their duties and responsibilites as a nation" (Jordan 3). For school children, Webster envisioned a common selection of readings and lessons that would "instill the ideals of republican duty, patriotism, moderation, piety, and good sense and would thereby solve a range of social ills from private personal laziness to public political dissension" (Davidson 64). One can only explain these actions by observing that Webster believed that he had a special access to the truth.

Webster, in fact, had looked with Johann Michaelis and other language theorists to "national, colloquial language for a means of access to absolute, universal truth" (Bynack 107). His *Compendious Dictionary* (1806) reveals that, even before his conversion, Webster believed that Saxon-based English had a sacred background that English philologists overlooked: for example, according to Webster, Samuel Johnson mistraced words "which he should have traced back to the Hebrew, as *earth*, which is certainly of Hebrew origin" (xviii). But after his conversion, Webster was even more certain that there was a "sense to which all words were reducible, a level of signification that could be seen, in its turn, as determinative of cultural difference" (Bynack 111). This special reading of the primary thirty-four verbs of Adam-given language (see Webster, *Dictionary* [1828] 21), possible only for an etymologist such as Noah Webster, "could serve as the principle of order Americans needed as the basis of national character" (Bynack 112).

Virtually everything Noah Webster had to say about rhetoric he recorded in the beginning of *A Grammatical Institute of the English Language: Part 3*, later titled *An American Selection of Lessons in Reading and Speaking*. The "Rules for Reading and Speaking" (pp. 5–10) of this 1785 work cite *The Art of Speaking* as source, without naming the author; but undoubtedly Webster referred to James Burgh's *The Art of Speaking*, which appeared in 1762 in England and 1775 in America, where it "had a great vogue" (Howell 245 n.267). Burgh, a member of the "mechanical" school of elocution, furnished much of Webster's discussion of oratory. Burgh offered, for example, this description: "Fear . . . opens very wide the eyes and mouth;

shortens the nose; draws down the eyebrows; gives the countenance an air of wildness; . . . One foot is drawn back behind the other. . . . The heart beats violently (21). In *Lessons in Reading and Speaking*, "General Directions for expressing certain passions or sentiments," Webster merely edited Burgh: "*Fear* opens the eyes and mouth, shortens the nose, draws down the eyebrows, gives the countenance an air of wildness; . . . one foot is drawn back, the heart beats violently" (8). Webster mapped the expressions upon the face and body of the prospective orator in like fashion and echoed the other emotions which Burgh had described in similar form in pages 16–35 of his book: "*Hope* brightens the countenance, arches the eyebrows, gives the eye an eager wishful look, opens the mouth to half a smile, bends the body a little forward" (9); "*Malice* sets the jaws, or gnashes with the teeth, sends flashes from the eyes, draws the mouth down towards the ears, clenches the fist, and bends the elbows. *Envy* is expressed in the same manner, but more moderately" (10).

Those elements of Burgh's work which are *not* echoed in Webster are also revealing. Burgh warned that "an artful and eloquent statesman . . . has it greatly in his power to mislead the judgement" (4). And Burgh at least paid lip service to the necessity of analyzing a work to be read: "And no person reads well, till he comes to speak what he sees in the book before him in the same natural manner as he speaks his thoughts, which arise in his *own* mind. And, hence it is, that no one can *read* properly what he does not *understand*" (11). Although Webster took generous helpings of Burgh on every other topic, he left all discussion of analysis on the table.

Webster's lack of interest in the analysis of rhetorical efforts may simply reflect a commonplace in the early national period: an "unswerving faith in the truth-telling power of language" (Gabler-Hover 36). Eventually, however, "Webster's fears of a republican Babel led him . . . into a long and committed study of language, in his case to devise a unitary system which he could impose on his country" (Lawson-Peeples 80). Nonetheless, Webster offered no guide to analysis of the material to be read. Instead, he identified the prerational appeal of his selections with a headnote from the Washington-deifying Comte de Honoré Mirabeau: "Begin with the Infant in his Cradle: Let the first Word he lisps be Washington" (*Lessons*, 1).

In his rules for reading, in fact, Webster spent no time on the analysis of the words to be read but depended on the power of those words to move and persuade:

Rule 1: Let your articulation be clear and distinct. (5)

Rule 2: Observe the Stops, and mark the proper Pauses, but make no pause where the sense requires none. (5)

Rule 3: Pay the strictest attention to Accent, Emphasis, & Cadence. (6)

Rule 4: Let the sentiments you express be accompanied with proper Tones, Looks, and Gestures. (7).

All of Webster's suggestions support the expressive power of the words, with the understanding that the words will be immediately efficacious. Webster's elocutionary rules may be summarized concisely: "*Let a reader or speaker express every word as if the sentiments were his own* [Webster's italics]" (*Lessons*, 8).

An inordinate portion of Webster's discussions in his speller, reader, and *Dissertations* detail uniform pronunciation, but even this detailing reveals the political goals behind his rhetorical efforts as stated in *Dissertations*: "Nothing but the establishment of schools and some uniformity in the use of books, can annihilate differences in speaking and preserve the purity of the American tongue. A Sameness of pronunciation is of considerable consequence in a political view" (19). In his 1806 dictionary, he pointed out the region that should furnish such a standard: "The common unadulterated pronunciation of the New England gentlemen, is almost uniformly the pronunciation that prevailed in England, anterior to Sheridan's time" (xvi). And since Webster found a number of Adamic remnants in the more archaic forms of English, he made the New England standard of language and culture a holy thing, of which he was the prophet.

In the preface to Part 3 of the *Grammatical Institute*, Webster included a trio of goals intended to justify all three numbers of the *Grammatical Institutes*: "To refine and establish our language, to facilitate the acquisition of grammatical knowledge, and diffuse the principles of virtue and patriotism, is the task I have labored to perform" (4). Likewise, Webster's rhetorical stance reveals itself even more clearly in the full title: *An American Selection of Lessons in Reading and Speaking; Calculated to Improve the Minds and Refine the Taste of Youth. And also to Instruct them in the Geography, History, and Politics of the United States, to which are prefixed, Rules in Elocution, and Directions for Expressing the Principal Passions of the Mind.*

Webster's selections in this reader aimed at a unified, national culture stamped firmly by his hand. For example, we find a special revision of Columbus as an agent of American destiny, "whose extraordinary genius led him to the discovery of the continent, and whose singular sufferings ought to excite the indignation of the world" (77). Webster implied that Columbus somehow sensed that another great continent might actually lie in his path to India: "Columbus drew this conclusion, that the Atlantic Ocean must be bounded by the west, either by India itself or by some *great* [italics added] continent not far distant from it" (78). According to Webster, Columbus was "prompted by . . . the advantages that would result to mankind from such discoveries" (80). In like manner, many of Webster's other selections clearly show his intention of giving America not just one language, but one culture.

Noah Webster's motives, then, for his linguistic efforts were almost entirely political, though, as his later biographers have noted, his national politics changed during his lifetime from a rather unfocused egalitarianism to a rigid republicanism. His selections and his rhetoric glossed over any danger of misreading in his certainty that the virtues inculcated from reading and declaiming the selections would be identical to his own. Given an appropriate selection of readings (as Webster would assume he had collected), the effect of the materials would be unequivocal. In fact, Webster's trust in the power of his selection of words may follow from his belief in the remnants of Adamic language. As he noted in the preface to his 1828 dictionary: "All nations, as far as my researches extend, agree in expressing the sense of *justice* and *right*, by *straightness* and *sin, iniquity, wrong*, by a deviation from a straight line or course. Equally remarkable is the simplicity of the analogies of language, and the small number of radical significations; so small indeed, that I am persuaded that the primary sense of all the verbs in any language, may be expressed by thirty or forty words" (21). Since "we are not however to suppose the language of our first parents in paradise to have been copious," and since "many of the primitive radical words may and probably do exist in various languages," then we can assume that Webster believed he had some idea which thirty or forty words were Adamic and primordially effective. His fascination with Adamic radicals led him to assert in the 1828 dictionary that Chaldean, not Hebrew, "must then have been the oldest or the primitive language of man" (3). Indeed, Webster found that "the Chaldee dialect, in the use of dental letters instead of sibilants, is much the most general in the Celtic and Teutonic languages of Europe" (4). In arguing his tortuous Hebrew-to-Celtic-to-Saxon-to-America thread, Webster in his *Dissertations*, stated that "the Irish seems to be a compound of *Celtic* and *Punic*. . . . The Hebrew was the root of the Phenician and the Punic. The Maltese is evidently a branch of the Punic; for it approaches near to the Hebrew and Chaldaic, than to the Arabic" (354), and that "in several particulars the Irish bears a close affinity to the Hebrew and Greek" (355). Webster also cited common points of worship (facing east, for example), much as other theorists, before and after, have compared Indians and Hebrews to bolster their argument that one or more of the Lost Tribes of Israel had engendered America's native population. From this point, Webster needed only to make a short leap of inference to make the etymological study of English words a holy undertaking. The learned men of Europe were misled by classical languages, and "neglected to resort for the radical words to some of the best sources for correct knowledge, the Celtic and Teutonic dialects, which, next to the Hebrew, are the purest remains of the primitive language" (Webster to the Friends of Literature Feb. 25, 1807).

Even though Webster's interest in Adamic language spawned an American Renaissance motif for truth hidden in a "lost language . . . which mortals are no longer capable of understanding" (Scherting 15), Noah Webster remained certain that he had found inarguable certainty. His beliefs, which he intended to be expressed through the elocutionary techniques of the "mechanical" school, did not produce the immediate converts to his social, political, and religious views that he had expected. Since Webster's rhetoric neither contained nor taught any methods of analysis or argumentation, Webster could only rail at his political opponents through Biblical analogy, as when, in his *Address to the Citizens*, he recalled "Absalom, the revolter, the great democrat of Israel" (22), or, in his letter to Emily Webster Ellsworth, he grieved over American political rhetoric (referring to William Henry Harrison): "But the Log Cabin—oh how our country is degraded, when even men of respectability resort to such means to secure election! I struggled, in the days of Washington, to sustain good principles—but since Jefferson's principles have prostrated the popular respects for sound principles, further efforts would be useless. And I quit the contest forever" (qtd. in Rollins 115).

BIBLIOGRAPHY

Primary Sources

Webster, Noah. *An Address to the Citizens of Connecticut.* New Haven, 1803.
———. *An American Dictionary of the English Language.* 2 vols. New Haven, 1828.
———. *An American Dictionary of the English Language.* 2 vols. New Haven, 1841.
———. *An American Selection of Lessons in Reading and Speaking; Calculated to Improve the Minds and Refine the Taste of Youth. And also to Instruct them in the Geography, History, and Politics of the United States. To which are prefixed, Rules in Elocution, and Directions for Expressing the Principal Passions of the Mind. Being the Third Part of A Grammatical Institute of the English Language. To which is added, an Appendix, Containing several new Dialogues.* Newburyport, 1811.
———. *A Collection of Essays and Fugitiv* [sic] *Writings on Moral, Historical, Political and Literary Subjects.* 1790. Reprint. Edited by Robert K. Peters. Delmar, NY: Scholars' Facsimiles and Reprints, 1977.
———. *A Compendious Dictionary of the English Language.* New Haven, 1806.
———. *Dissertations on the English Language: With Notes, Historical and Critical. To which is added, By way of Appendix, An Essay on A Reformed Mode of Spelling, with Dr. Franklin's Arguments on that Subject.* Boston, 1789. Reprinted in *English Linguistics, 1500–1800*, no. 54, edited by R. C. Alston. Menston, Eng.: Scolar Press, 1967.
———. *A Grammatical Institute of the English Language: Part I.* 1783. Reprinted in *English Linguistics, 1500–1800*, no. 89, edited by R. C. Alston. Menston, Eng.: Scolar Press, 1968.
———. *A Grammatical Institute of the English Language: Part 2.* 1784. Reprinted in *English Linguistics, 1500–1800*, no. 90, edited by R. C. Alston. Menston, Eng.: Scolar Press, 1968.
———. *A Grammatical Institute of the English Language: Part 3.* 1785. Reprinted as *An American Selection.*
———. *History of the United States: To Which is Prefixed a Brief Historical Account of Our English Ancestors, from the Dispersion of Babel, to Their Migration to America; and of the Conquest of South America by the Spaniards.* New Haven, 1832.

————, ed. *The Holy Bible, Containing the Old and New Testaments, in the Common Version. With Amendments of the Language.* New Haven, 1833.

Biography

Ford, Emily Ellsworth Fowler. *Notes on the Life of Noah Webster.* 2 vols. New York: Privately printed, 1912.

Rollins, Richard M., ed. *The Autobiographies of NW [Noah Webster]: From the Letters and Essays, Memoir, and Diary.* Columbia: University of South Carolina Press, 1989.

Webster, Noah. *Letters of Noah Webster.* Edited by Harry R. Warfel. New York: Library Press, 1953.

Criticism

Burgh, James. *The Art of Speaking.* 1775. Reprint. Baltimore, 1804.

Bynack, Vincent P. "Noah Webster's Linguistic Thought and the Idea of an American National Culture." *JHI* 45.1 (1984): 99–114.

Davidson, Cathy N. *Revolution and the Word: The Rise of the Novel in America.* New York: Oxford University Press, 1986.

Gabler-Hover, Janet. *Truth in American Fiction: The Legacy of Rhetorical Idealism.* Athens: University of Georgia Press, 1990.

Howell, Wilbur Samuel. *Eighteenth-Century British Logic and Rhetoric.* Princeton: Princeton University Press, 1971.

Jordan, Cynthia S. *Second Stories: The Politics of Language, Form, and Gender in Early American Fictions.* Chapel Hill: University of North Carolina Press, 1989.

Lawson-Peeples, Robert. *Landscape and Written Expression in Revolutionary America: The World Turned Upside Down,* 73–83. Cambridge: Cambridge University Press, 1988.

Scherting, Jack. "The Chaldee Allusion in M-D: Its Antecedents and Its Implicit Skepticism." *MSex* 49 (1982): 14–15.

Weinstein, Brian. "NW [Noah Webster] and the Diffusion of Linguistic Innovations for Political Purposes." *International Journal of the Sociology of Language* 38 (1982): 85–108.

JOHN WITHERSPOON
(1723–1794)

Thomas P. Miller

Like a handful of others in the rhetorical tradition, most notably Cicero, John Witherspoon was first of all a practitioner of the art of rhetoric. Witherspoon was far more influential as a religious and political orator and writer than as a theorist, though his approach to the study of rhetoric does provide an important counterpoint to the dominant trends in eighteenth-century rhetoric. After studying alongside Hugh Blair at Edinburgh University, Witherspoon emigrated in 1768 to become the president of the college that New Light Presbyterians had founded at Princeton, and he soon became a leading figure in the Presbyterian Church in America. At what would become Princeton University, he broadened the curriculum beyond the classics; and he himself taught rhetoric, moral philosophy, and modern history to such students as James Madison, who stayed on after graduation for further studies with Witherspoon (see Walsh; Wills; Smylie). Witherspoon also preached influential sermons on behalf of independence, helped to organize resistance to the British government, and became the only minister to sign the Declaration of Independence. As a theorist of rhetoric, Witherspoon is noteworthy because he is an example of how differing sociopolitical contexts shaped the reformation of rhetoric in the eighteenth century. While he had studied English literature and criticism alongside Hugh Blair and drew on the common-sense philosophy that shaped George Campbell's epistemologically oriented theory of rhetoric, Witherspoon was less concerned with belles lettres or epistemology than with the practical art of speaking to public controversies. Witherspoon's civic perspective on rhetoric and moral philosophy is a notable, though less influential, alternative to the belletristic and epistemological approaches that shaped how classical rhetoric was translated into the study of English (see my essay "John Witherspoon").

Witherspoon entered Edinburgh University in 1736 at the age of thirteen.

He studied with Hugh Blair under John Stevenson, who was perhaps the first university professor to lecture in English on English. As professor of Logic and Metaphysics from 1730 to 1777, Stevenson drew on the theories of Locke and Bacon as well as Cicero and Quintilian to develop an eclectic course of lectures on logic, rhetoric, composition, and criticism. Reports of students, archival materials, and published accounts show that Stevenson took a belletristic approach that moved from Longinus and Aristotle's *Poetics* to contemporary French and English critics to cover the principles of English composition and literary criticism. Although his interdisciplinary approach challenges modern assumptions about the boundaries of literary studies, understanding Stevenson's belletristic synthesis of classical and contemporary sources is important because he was a formative influence on both Blair and Witherspoon according to their biographers (see my introduction to Witherspoon's *Selected Writings*, 3–7). The student essays from Stevenson's class suggest that he taught the virtues of polite taste in the manner that Blair's belletristic approach popularized, and the thesis that Witherspoon wrote for his M.A. (which is reprinted in Rich) shows that even as a student he had begun to turn to common-sense doctrines as a hedge against skepticism in moral philosophy.

While he was introduced to the study of Locke's inductive logic in Stevenson's course, Witherspoon was also broadly influenced by his studies in moral philosophy, which was becoming the culminating study of the reformed curriculum in Scotland. John Pringle—as well as Francis Bacon and such Continental natural rights advocates as Pufendorf—was lecturing at Edinburgh on the moral philosophy of Cicero. While the English universities would confine themselves to dead languages and a moribund classicism through most of the next century, the moral philosophers of Pringle's generation broadened the curriculum to include the study of modern social and cultural affairs, with none more influential in defining those studies than Francis Hutcheson. Like Pringle at Edinburgh, Francis Hutcheson and George Turnbull were among the first to lecture in English at Glasgow and Aberdeen; and they had a major influence on their students, who included Adam Smith, Thomas Reid, and the other moral philosophers who shaped the institutionalization of English studies in Scotland. The generation of Hutcheson and Pringle translated the classical tradition into the contemporary idiom, but their successors were also influenced by Ciceronian humanism. Even more fully than Adam Smith—who also lectured on both rhetoric and moral philosophy—Witherspoon maintained the integral relationship among rhetoric, ethics, and politics that is central to the civic humanist tradition. While Smith and Blair's emphasis on stylistic criticism had continuities with Ciceronianism, Witherspoon's emphasis on public discourse and civic virtue is more broadly consistent with the rhetoric of Ciceronian humanism, as will be discussed when I turn to Witherspoon's lectures on rhetoric and moral philosophy.

After graduating from Edinburgh, Witherspoon came into conflict with his former classmate when Blair and William Robertson established the Moderate party as the dominant force in the Scottish Church in the early 1750s. As cultural liberals, the Moderates defended David Hume against censure; and as political conservatives, they spoke for the authority of upper-class patrons to select clergymen, who had traditionally been chosen in consultation with local congregations. In Witherspoon's *Selected Writings*, we learn that as a leader of the Orthodox or Popular opposition in the church, Witherspoon attacked the Moderates in *Ecclesiastical Characteristics; or, the Arcana of Church Policy, being an Humble Attempt to open up the Mystery of Moderation* (1753) (57–102). Witherspoon ridiculed the Moderates for defending a skeptic's freedom of opinion while censuring those who resisted their authority in the church. Drawing on traditional Calvinist assumptions about individual conscience, Witherspoon supported the democratic selection of clergy and the rights of individuals to dissent from established authorities. *Ecclesiastical Characteristics* foreshadows Witherspoon's writings in revolutionary America, but the work is also important because it documents his aversion both to polite sermonizing on moral properties and to the Addisonian tendency to treat ethical issues as matters of polite sentiment. While he drew on Hutcheson's doctrines of civic virtues and natural rights, Witherspoon was too much of a traditional Calvinist to be responsive to Hutcheson's tendency to conflate moral responsiveness and aesthetic sensitivity in terms of the polite sensibility. Blair's rhetorical practice and theory stands in direct opposition to Witherspoon on these points.

With the urging of the New Lights in the American Presbyterian Church, Benjamin Rush persuaded Witherspoon to come to Princeton to take control of the college that had been founded during the Great Awakening of antiestablishment evangelism in the 1740s (see Butterfield; Sloan). Witherspoon's evangelical predecessors—most notably Gilbert Tennent, Samuel Finley, and Samuel Davis—had close ties with the Scottish universities and English Dissenting academies and, thus, were responsive to the intellectual and institutional trends that were broadening the curriculum to include modern scientific and cultural studies (see Guder; Maclean). Witherspoon's predecessors also prepared the way for the political philosophies that were used to justify the American revolution. In sermons like Tennent's *Danger of an Unconverted Ministry* (1740), New Light clergy reasoned from the equality of all before God to argue for individuals' rights to dissent from institutionalized authorities in matters of personal conscience. Such debates helped to popularize doctrines of natural rights; and in America, as in Britain, shared traditions of religious dissent laid the foundations for public challenges to established political authorities.

Scottish ideas and immigrants influenced the development of colleges—like those at Princeton and Philadelphia—that were founded as alternatives to the established universities (see Sloan). The Scots provided an alternative to the elitist classicism of the English universities; and Benjamin Franklin and others interested in educational reform were quite interested in the reforms that had followed from the philosophies of Hutcheson, Turnbull, and their colleagues. The effect of such trends of thought was not confined to the classroom. As Garry Wills has discussed in *Explaining America*, "The education of our revolutionary generation can be symbolized by this fact: At age sixteen Jefferson *and* Madison *and* Hamilton were all being schooled by Scots who had come to America as adults" (63). In each case, what was studied was Scottish moral philosophy and rhetoric. According to Wills, Scottish views of natural rights, the social contract, and the division of powers within government had a far greater impact than has been recognized by those who have made Locke the definitive source for understanding American revolutionary thought. As we broaden our understanding of the Scots' influence on the education of Jefferson, Madison, and their generation, we may also deepen our understanding of the political theories and rhetorical practices that shaped the formation of America. Few figures will be more central to such an understanding than Witherspoon (see McAllister).

Even before Witherspoon arrived at Princeton, the college was giving more attention to the contemporary idiom than more classically oriented colleges like Harvard and Yale. Witherspoon instituted reforms that made the study of rhetoric and moral philosophy the culminating studies of the curriculum—a curriculum that gave more emphasis to the study of oratory than any other college of the period according to some authorities (see Witherspoon 103–115; Bohman 68; see also Halloran, "Rhetoric in the American College Curriculum"). To further enhance the emphasis given to public speaking, Witherspoon instituted awards for the best compositions and revived the student debating societies that had been suppressed out of fear of their independence from supervision. As indicated in his *Selected Writings*, Witherspoon, like other Scottish educators, assumed that moral philosophy covered "the whole business of active life," to which the studies of rhetoric, composition, and criticism should be subordinate (229) (see also Fiering and Fechner). Witherspoon's lectures on rhetoric and moral philosophy took up most of the last two years of the curriculum at Princeton, with compositions serving as exercises for the lessons on ethics and politics that had been taught in moral philosophy (see Guder and Broderick). The graduation orations that students delivered in the years leading up to independence show how they were being taught to draw on changing political philosophies to speak to public controversies (see my introduction to Witherspoon's *Selected Writings*, 22–24). Faced with the conflicts of the time, students came to view rhetoric as a political art of considerable significance— which is a quite different perspective from that which Blair was teaching his students at Edinburgh. To understand how the contexts of preindependence America and post-Union Scotland shaped the translation of classical rhetoric into English, one need only compare Witherspoon's career as a religious and political leader with Blair's popularity as a preacher of the virtues of the polite sensibility (see my essay "Blair and Witherspoon").

Soon after arriving in America, Witherspoon began taking an active part in public affairs, first in the Church and then in politics. The Presbyterian Church was the second largest in America, and Witherspoon played a leadership role from 1769, when he first attended the synod that had reunified the New Lights and established clergy. Witherspoon was instrumental in aligning the Presbyterian Church behind the cause of independence. He coauthored a pastoral letter that encouraged congregants to view the conflict with Britain as a choice between defending constitutional rights and accepting slavery—a choice that left them with no alternative but to support the Continental Congress as the legitimate defenders of their rights. Witherspoon's most influential statement of support for independence was probably "The Dominion of Providence over the Passions of Men," a sermon preached on May 17, 1776 (see his *Selected Writings*, 126–47). Witherspoon argued that times of disorder testified to divine providence, that history shows that religious and political freedoms are part of the same providential order, and that the American cause was the "cause of justice, of liberty, and of human nature" (140). The sermon was discussed in leading periodicals, went through nine editions in America and Britain, and became perhaps the most important sermon delivered on behalf of the American cause in the Revolutionary period. According to the "Elucidating remarks" of the two Glasgow editions published in 1777, the unrest in America was due to "clerical influence: and none . . . had a greater share . . . than Dr Witherspoon" (see my introduction to Witherspoon's *Selected Writings*, 30).

With the delivery of "The Dominion of Providence," Witherspoon became active in the political developments that led to independence. In the same month that he delivered the sermon, he joined the New Jersey provincial assembly as a leader of the most radical delegation. He was influential in removing the Royalist governor (Benjamin Franklin's son William) and setting up an independent assembly. Witherspoon went on from the New Jersey Assembly as a representative to the Continental Congress and became a signatory of the Declaration of Independence. The delegation from New Jersey arrived at a pivotal point in the debate, and Witherspoon played a disputed but apparently decisive role in speaking for independence (Collins 2:218–21). Although set apart by a heavy Scottish accent and the somber character of a staunch Calvinist clergyman, Witherspoon was active in the debates and maneuverings that shaped the formation of the American government. Witherspoon's rhetorical practice was characterized by a simple style, a clear and direct line of argument, and a concern for the practical implications of disputed issues. His delivery was reportedly uninspired, but he apparently recognized the importance of the rhetorical situation. He was known for waiting for the right moment to enter the debate and then speaking to the immediate situation in terms that were relevant to what had already been said (Maclean 396; see also Paul). In any case, the continuities between Witherspoon's rhetorical practice and theory are far deeper than mere matters of technique. Those continuities become clear when his theories of rhetoric are read along with his moral philosophy against the political debates of the time.

WITHERSPOON'S RHETORICAL THEORY

Witherspoon's *Lectures on Moral Philosophy*, like his *Lectures on Eloquence*, are lecture notes that were edited and published after his death. As Witherspoon himself noted in his *Selected Writings*, the notes thus lack "that high and complete polish that might be expected in what is prepared for publication" (232–33). The lectures were published in his collected works (1800–1801) and then in a separate edition in 1810. This edition, which has been called "the first complete American rhetoric," included the lectures on both rhetoric and moral philosophy (Guthrie 56). Witherspoon was far from being the only figure to link the two subjects. The historical ties between rhetoric and moral philosophy are most obvious in the classical period, but the same two classical authorities—Aristotle and Cicero—shaped both rhetoric and moral philosophy into the eighteenth century. Even then, Adam Smith delivered his lectures on rhetoric as a professor of moral philosophy, as did James Beattie; and the two areas of study retained a vital, though limited, relationship in the case of common-sense moral philosophy and the rhetoric of George Campbell. With the common-sense philosophers, moral philosophy was reoriented from the civic to the psychological sphere, and the purposes of rhetoric were reconceptualized to reflect the workings of the human mind. A brief review of Witherspoon's civic philosophy is thus important, not just for a full understanding of his rhetorical theory, but also for a fuller understanding of how the eighteenth-century emphasis on belles lettres and epistemology redefined the traditional ties between rhetoric and the political and ethical concerns of moral philosophy.

Witherspoon has generally been viewed as having introduced Scottish common-sense moral philosophy into American higher education, where it remained predominant into the latter half of the nineteenth century. Historians such as Henry F. May and Terrence Martin have argued that Thomas Reid, Dugald Stewart, and other common-sense philosophers like Witherspoon responded to Humean skepticism by propagating a close-minded conservatism that treated accepted beliefs as the unassailable truths of an innate common sense. James Berlin has drawn on these accounts to argue that common-sense philosophers instituted a perspective that was tacitly accepted into the twentieth century as "current traditional rhetoric." While Berlin's argument has had an important influence on the politics of contemporary composition studies, sweeping condemnations of common-sense philosophy have tended to foreclose more nuanced analyses of why "common sense" became such an issue in the eighteenth century. Discussions of common sense addressed broader questions about the nature and authority of shared knowledge, the sort of public knowledge that has been a historical concern of moral philosophy because of its traditional engagment with practical action from shared values toward common goals. Modern theories of the social construction of shared knowledge follow from Hume, not the common-sense philosophers; but rather than choose sides in the debate over common sense, we should first recognize that the debate itself marks a major shift in the focus of analysis, an introspective turn toward epistemology that shaped the formation of the modern rhetorical tradition (see Crowley).

In *Lectures on Moral Philosophy*, Witherspoon began with lectures on the Lockean epistemology that provided the starting point for common-sense philosophy. Following Locke, Witherspoon divided the mind into the understanding, will, and affections and treated knowledge as a product of reflection from the senses, which provided reliable information about the world according to Witherspoon and the common-sense philosophers. From Hutcheson, Witherspoon adopted the notion of a moral sense that balances benevolent and selfish feelings. After summarizing some of the major theories of epistemology and ethics, Witherspoon turned in Lecture 5 to the topics that take up the majority of his moral-philosophy course: civic duties, natural rights, and their practical implications for political relations and jurisprudence. Following in a tradition that reached from Cicero through Hutcheson, Witherspoon assumed the perspective of a practical moralist who is less concerned with constructing an academic system of thought than with surveying existing theories to prepare students to act and speak to public affairs (see Scott). Practical moralists like Hutcheson and Witherspoon (and Cicero, for that matter) were little bothered that civic duties and natural rights seem to rely on inconsistent conceptions of the relationship between the individual and the state. In line with the civic humanist tradition, Witherspoon defines the individual as a citizen who has the duty to speak for the common good in public life and concluded that engaging in the duties of an active political life fulfills the highest potentials of human nature. Witherspoon also argued that the social contract bestows rights to life, liberty, the products of one's labors, a presumption of innocence before the law, and freedom of opinion and association. Most importantly for the colonies, individuals also have the right to resist governments that fail to serve the common good. All these positions can be found in Hutcheson as part of a democratic political philosophy concerned with dividing the powers of government and enlisting the participation of citizens in the practical duties of self-government (see Robbins; Norton).

Like his *Lectures on Moral Philosophy*, Witherspoon's *Lectures on Eloquence* provide a survey of practical issues oriented toward preparing students for public life. After three introductory lectures on the general principles and history of rhetoric, Witherspoon summarized the aims of the rest of his lectures in this way:

1. To treat of language in general—its qualities and powers, eloquent speech, and its history and practice as an art. [Lectures 4–5]

2. To consider oratory as divided into its three great kinds—the sublime, simple, and mixed; their characters, their distinctions, their beauties, and their uses. [Lectures 6–10]

3. To consider it as divided into its constituent parts—invention, disposition, style, pronunciation, and gesture. [Lectures 11 and 12[

4. To consider it as its object is different—information, demonstration, persuasion, entertainment. [Lecture 13]

5. As its subject is different—the pulpit, the bar, and the senate, or any deliberative assembly. [Lectures 14 and 15]

6. To consider the structure and parts of a particular discourse—their order, connection, proportion, and ends. [Lecture 15]

7. Recapitulation, and an inquiry into the principles of taste, or of beauty and gracefulness, as applicable not only to oratory, but to all the other (commonly called) fine arts. (*Selected Writings* 247–48)

Throughout his discussion of these topics, Witherspoon cited major sources and briefly summarized the differences among them to provide a comprehensive introduction to "eloquence, or as perhaps it ought to be called from the manner in which you will find it treated, composition, taste, and criticism" (*Selected Writings* 231) (see also Halloran, "John Witherspoon on Eloquence").

Unlike Blair, Witherspoon actually devoted less attention to criticism and taste than to composition. In his discussions of the arts of rhetoric (invention, arrangement, style, delivery, and memory), he covered such practical concerns as theses statements, outlining, topic sentences, and paragraphing as well as speaking in the pulpit, bar, and political assembly. However, as indicated in his *Selected Writings*, Witherspoon, like other "new" rhetoricians, felt that classical aids to invention had little practical value, and he rejected the elaborate form and techniques that had been propagated by scholarly explicators of the classical tradition (279–80) (see also Howell 680–81). From his *Selected Writings*, we learn that Witherspoon distilled classical precepts down to useful advice on how to speak and write for public audiences, stressing throughout that rhetoric was the art of speaking in political forums, "there it reigned of old, and reigns still by its visible effect (258). He categorized the aims of discourse, not in terms of a systematic model of the faculties of the human mind, as Campbell would do, but by the practical ends proposed: to inform, to demonstrate, to persuade, and to entertain. In his final lectures, Witherspoon also discussed some of the literary issues that Blair addressed, including the nature of the sublime and the primitive genius exemplified by the Ossianic poems that James Macpherson had fabricated from the Gaelic traditions being suppressed in the Highlands. The crucial difference between Blair and Witherspoon is that Witherspoon maintained that the ancient art of rhetoric was still most valuable as the civic art of speaking to political controversies, while Blair, in his *Lectures on Rhetoric and Belles Lettres*, nostalgically valorized ancient eloquence and concluded that the time for heated public debate had passed in an age when "ministerial influence" and polite taste had become more important (2:43).

While it was Blair, the teacher and theorist, and not Witherspoon, who had a formative influence on the introduction of English, composition, literature, and rhetoric into higher education, Witherspoon, an influential practitioner of the art of rhetoric, needs to be included within the history of college English studies precisely because he challenged us as rhetoricians to question what was lost when English studies became synonymous with literary studies. Wilbur Samuel Howell concluded his history of the "new" rhetoric with Witherspoon precisely to raise such questions (689–91). In his *Selected Writings*, Witherspoon himself questioned why historians of rhetoric have concentrated on "teachers of that art" rather than on "its progress and effects" as a practical political art (254). Following from trends that are evident in Blair's belletristic perspective, college English studies would subordinate rhetoric to literature, with the composition of political discourse given far less emphasis than the criticism of poetry and fiction in departments of English. Within the history of rhetorical and cultural studies, Witherspoon is significant largely as a historical counterpoint to the more influential approaches of figures such as Blair and Campbell. In contrast to Blair, Witherspoon maintained the classical continuities between rhetoric and moral philosophy; and unlike Campbell, he did not narrow moral philosophy to epistemology. While Witherspoon spoke to American audiences concerned with how rhetoric could be used to address the pressing political conflicts of the time, Blair lectured Scottish students who had limited access to political forums and who were more interested in mastering the taste and usage of England. The belletristic perspective on rhetoric that became institutionalized in Scotland is an influential example of the shift in rhetorical studies from political oratory to literature, a historical transition that George Kennedy has discussed in terms of *letteraturizzazione* (5, 237–38).

It is important to underline the limitations as well as the possibilities of the alternative approach to rhetoric that Witherspoon took. Witherspoon's most obvious limitations were his lack of understanding of the inventive possibilities of writing and reading and his belief that the truths of common sense are authorized by human nature itself. We also need to be aware of the practical political functions of the civic ideal of the good man speaking well for public virtue. Historians who have valorized public discourse have often failed to recognize that the public domain is a politically constituted space from which many groups have historically been excluded, and the ideal of the civic orator obviously served to justify the hegemony of a few good men. In Scotland and America, Witherspoon took comparatively democratic positions on public issues, and as a traditional Calvinist, he took a less elitist view of public discourse than those who assumed that good taste and a polite sensibility were essential qualifications for anyone who would speak to the public. However one situates Witherspoon's rhetorical theory and practice, his historical importance stems from the fact that he taught the discourses of power to students who formed the intellectual and political elite of the new nation. James Madison learned much from Witherspoon's lectures on politics and rhetoric, and few texts are more important for understanding the political ideologies and rhetorical practices that constituted America than Madison's *Federalist* Number 10. Witherspoon is a pivotal figure for assessing how the study of rhetoric contributed to such powerful pieces of public discourse, which were quite different from the belletristic *Spectator* essays that Blair taught his students to imitate as a model of the polite style and sensibility. Such political texts provide important opportunities for research on how changing rhetorical theories affected the political practices that established the American system of government. The rhetorical theories of Witherspoon provide an important point of departure for scholars who are interested in moving beyond the history of ideas about rhetoric to develop research on existing rhetorical practices.

BIBLIOGRAPHY

Primary Sources

Blair, Hugh. *Lectures on Rhetoric and Belles Lettres.* Edited by Harold F. Harding. 2 vols. Carbondale: Southern Illinois University Press, 1965.
Witherspoon, John. *Lectures on Moral Philosophy, and Eloquence.* Philadelphia, 1810.
———. *Lectures on Moral Philosophy.* Edited by Varnum Lansing Collins. Princeton: Princeton University Press, 1912.
———. *Lectures on Moral Philosophy.* Edited by Jack Scott. East Brunswick, NJ: Associated University Presses, 1982.
———. *The Selected Writings of John Witherspoon.* Edited by Thomas P. Miller. Carbondale: Southern Illinois University Press, 1990.
———. *Works.* 4 vols. Philadelphia, 1800–1801.
———. *Works.* 9 vols. Edinburgh: J. Ogle; Glasgow: M. Ogle; London: Duncan and Cochran; Dublin: T. Johnston, 1815.

Biography

Butterfield, Lyman H., ed. *John Witherspoon Comes to America.* Princeton: Princeton University Press, 1953.
Collins, Varnum Lansing. *President Witherspoon.* 2 vols. Princeton: Princeton University Press, 1925.

Rich, George Eugene. "John Witherspoon: His Scottish Intellectual Background." Ph.D. diss., Syracuse University, 1964.

Stohlman, Martha Lou Lemmon. *John Witherspoon: Parson, Politician, Patriot.* Philadelphia: Westminster Press, 1976.

Criticism

Berlin, James A. *Writing Instruction in Nineteenth-Century American Colleges.* Carbondale: Southern Illinois University Press, 1984.

Bohman, George V. "Rhetorical Practice in Colonial America." In *History of Speech Education in America,* edited by Karl R. Wallace, 60–79. New York: Appleton, 1954.

Broderick, Francis L. "Pulpit, Physics, and Politics: The Curriculum of the College of New Jersey, 1746–1794." *William and Mary Quarterly* 6.1 (1949): 50–51.

Crowley, Sharon. *The Methodical Memory: Invention in Current-Traditional Rhetoric.* Carbondale: Southern Illinois University Press, 1990.

Fechner, Roger Jerome. "The Moral Philosophy of John Witherspoon and the Scottish-American Enlightenment." Ph.D. diss., University of Iowa, 1974.

Fiering, Norman. "Moral Philosophy in America, 1650–1750, and Its British Context." Ph.D. diss., Columbia University, 1969.

Guder, Darrel L. "The Story of Belles Lettres at Princeton: An Historical Investigation of the Expansion and Secularization of Curriculum at the College of New Jersey with Special Reference to the Curriculum of English Language and Letters." Ph.D. diss., University of Hamburg, 1964.

Guthrie, Warren. "Rhetorical Theory in Colonial America." In *History of Speech Education in America: Background Studies,* edited by Karl R. Wallace, 48–59. New York: Appleton-Century-Crofts, 1954.

Halloran, Michael S. "Rhetoric in the American College Curriculum: The Decline of Public Discourse." *Pre/Text* 3 (1982): 245–69.

———. "John Witherspoon on Eloquence." *Rhetoric Society Quarterly* 17.2 (1987): 177–92.

Howell, Wilbur Samuel. *Eighteenth-Century British Logic and Rhetoric.* Princeton: Princeton University Press, 1971.

Kennedy, George A. *Classical Rhetoric and Its Christian and Secular Tradition from Ancient to Modern Times.* Chapel Hill: University of North Carolina Press, 1980.

McAllister, James L. "Francis Alison and John Witherspoon: Political Philosophers and Revolutionaries." *Journal of Presbyterian History* 54 (1976): 33–60.

Maclean, John. *History of the College of New Jersey, 1746–1854.* New York: Arno Press, 1969.

Martin, Terence. *The Instructed Vision.* Bloomington: Indiana University Press, 1961.

May, Henry F. *The Enlightenment in America.* Oxford: Oxford University Press, 1976.

Miller, Thomas. P. "John Witherspoon, Scottish Moral Philosophy, and the Origins of College English Studies in America." *Rhetorica* (in press).

———. "Blair, Witherspoon and the Rhetoric of Civic Humanism." *Scotland and America in the Age of Enlightenment.* Edited by Richard Sher and Jeffrey Smitten. Edinburgh: Edinburgh University Press, 1989.

————. Introduction to *The Selected Writings of John Witherspoon*, edited by Thomas P. Miller. Carbondale: Southern Illinois University Press, 1990.

Norton, David Fate. "Francis Hutcheson in America." *Studies in Voltaire and the Eighteenth Century* 154 (1976): 1547–68.

Paul, Wilson P. "John Witherspoon's Theory and Practice of Public Speaking." *Speech Monographs* 16.2 (1949): 272–89.

Robbins, Caroline. *The Eighteenth-Century Commonwealthman: Studies in the Transmission, Development and Circumstances of English Liberal Thought from the Restoration of Charles II until the War with the Thirteen Colonies.* Cambridge, MA: Harvard University Press, 1961.

Scott, William Robert. *Francis Hutcheson: His Life, Teaching and Position in the History of Philosophy.* 1900. Reprint. New York: A. M. Kelley, 1966.

Sloan, Douglas. *The Scottish Enlightenment and the American College Ideal.* New York: Teachers College Press, 1971.

Smylie, James H. "Madison and Witherspoon: Theological Roots of American Political Thought." *Princeton University Library Chronicle* 22.3 (1961): 118–32.

Walsh, James J. *Education of the Founding Fathers of the Republic.* New York: Fordham University Press, 1935.

Wills, Garry. *Explaining America: The Federalist.* Garden City, NY: Doubleday, 1981.

MARY WOLLSTONECRAFT
(1759–1797)

Brenda H. Cox

Although several scholars have written about the rhetoric of Mary Woll-stonecraft, she is not usually thought of as a rhetorical theorist since she did not publish a specific treatise on the subject (Barker-Benfield 1989; Conger 1987; Finke 1987; Jacobus 1986; Tomalin 1974; Wardle 1951; Wang 1991). We can, however, discern her views on rhetoric embedded in her works on education and philosophy. It seems fitting that her ideas on rhetoric be submerged, available to us only through a close scrutiny of her texts on other subjects. Women in the eighteenth century had long been denied access to the public arenas of political, philosophical, and moral discourse. In addition, because women were usually denied a formal education, they were further prevented access to these firmly established arenas of male privilege. Nevertheless, Wollstonecraft ventured to write in both traditionally feminine and masculine genres. In *Thoughts on the Education of Daughters* (1787), *The Female Reader* (1789), *A Vindication of the Rights of Men* (1790), and *A Vindication of the Rights of Woman* (1792), Wollstonecraft conveyed her views on the value of emotion and reason in rhetoric both in the development of the intellect and as a vehicle for philosophical and moral ideas. Her views on the power of effective rhetoric carried special significance for the education of women whose subordinate position in society was directly associated with—and perhaps the direct result of—their lack of opportunities to learn and practice reasoned, intellectual discourse.

Mary Wollstonecraft, the eighteenth-century feminist, philosopher, literary critic, and writer, was born the second of seven children on April 27, 1759, to Elizabeth Dickson and Edward John Wollstonecraft. The father moved the family from London to the English countryside and back again numerous times in his vain attempt to establish himself as a gentleman farmer. Eventually, he became an uncontrollable alcoholic, thrusting Mary into the role of her mother's protector. The family's financial losses as well as the father's alcoholism, though painful, thus provided Mary with poignant insight into the sad fate of middle- and upper-class eighteenth-century women. Because they lacked a practical education, these women were socially and financially dependent on marriage, too often to an indifferent or abusive husband. If single, they were usually dependent on relatives or left desperate to fend for themselves when, to use Mary's description in *Thoughts*, "Fashionably Educated, and Left Without a Fortune" (25). The devastating effects of dependence created by an inferior system of education for women became a driving force in Wollstonecraft's personal and publishing career.

Mary Wollstonecraft left home at nineteen and experienced first-hand the limited vocational opportunities open to respectable eighteenth-century middle-class women: lady's companion, governess, and school mistress. However, working in these positions also provided opportunities to expand her education in the social and political thought of the Enlightenment. While employed in several upper-class homes and during her tenure as mistress of the school that she and Fanny Blood established at Newington Green, she met the leader of the Nonconformist Enlightenment, Richard Price; writers Henry Gabell and George Ogle; the painter and writer Henry Fuseli; and the publisher Joseph Johnson, who encouraged her to pursue her unconventional quest to become a professional woman writer.

However, during the nine years after leaving her father's house, Wollstonecraft also found herself obliged to take care of family and friends in need. She returned home to nurse her fatally ill mother. Later, she became the "shameful incendiary" of a plot to help her sister Eliza, who had suffered a postpartum breakdown, to escape from an abusive husband. Also, she traveled to Portugal to tend Fanny Blood at the birth of her baby, only to see both the consumptive mother and the child die. After a long, tumultuous common-law relationship with American entrepreneur, Gilbert Imlay, which produced a daughter and provoked several suicide attempts, Wollstonecraft married philosopher William Godwin, with whom she had another daughter, Mary Wollstonecraft Shelley. However, Wollstonecraft herself would die from complications of Mary's birth in 1797.

Despite personal and financial hardships as well as obligations to friends and family, Wollstonecraft continued her self-education in the political and social theories of John Locke, Edmund Burke, and Jean-Jacques Rousseau—which, in turn, stimulated further the development of her Dissenter ideals on the need for better education of women. Although she did not reject the conventional role of a woman as wife and mother, throughout her life Wollstonecraft consistently criticized the fashionable but superficial education of daughters that restricted vocational choices and limited their opportunities for intellectual and moral development. The consequences of women's oppression later served as the theme for Wollstonecraft's unfinished novel, *Maria; or, The Wrongs of Woman*, published posthumously in 1799.

Her first attempt at a career as an independent writer came in 1787 with the publication of *Thoughts on the Education of Daughters* in a respectably feminine genre, a collection of essays in the tradition of conduct books for the genteel deportment of young ladies. However, in her *Thoughts* Wollstonecraft subverted the tradition of manners books and social customs by warning young women to resist developing infantile and artificial charms rooted in vanity and affectation. Her book also served as a popular rhetoric for enlightened young women. Through her aphoristic style, she urged women to reject the affected "prattle" of the nursery and to rely on intellect and reason guided by devotion to God—which would thus enable young women to take on the "virtues and graces" of maturity, modesty, sensibility, and sincerity: these traits she saw as necessary "to prepare a woman to fulfill the important duties of a wife and mother" (22). Although not a twentieth-century model feminist, as an eighteenth-century woman advocating that females cultivate the same independent, rational thought traditionally regarded as the prerogative of males, Wollstonecraft established herself as the major British feminist thinker of her day.

Eighteenth-century gentlemen in the Dissenting academies were trained in the art of elocution and practiced their oratory using readers such as William Enfield's *The Speaker* (1774). For women, Wollstonecraft published *The Female Reader* in 1789 under the pseudonym of "Mr. Cresswick, teacher of elocution." Women, however, were restricted from making speeches in public. She admitted in her preface that "females are not educated to become public speakers or players," yet she believed that elocution exercises for women "scholars" would "imprint some useful lessons on the mind and cultivate the taste at the same time" (55). The broad variety of rhetorical exercises in *The Female Reader*, then, were for the purpose of improving the reason and intellect of young women whom Wollstonecraft believed to be equally as capable as their male counterparts, but who usually received training only in shallow sentimentality and feminine, genteel manners. In her usual aphoristic fashion, she claimed: "Exterior accomplishments are not to be obtained by imitation, they must result from the mind, or the deception is soon detected, and admiration gives place to contempt" (59).

Although originally published anonymously in 1790, *A Vindication of the Rights of Men* obtained for Wollstonecraft the access to the public and political arena traditionally denied women. She had previously published a number of critical articles for Joseph Johnson's *Analytical Review*. However, her reply to Edmund Burke's *Reflections on the Revolution in France* in *Rights of Men* established her as a learned and capable Dissenter political critic and later as a learned and capable woman working in the traditionally male genre of political discourse after she published the second edition under her own name. In this work, she opposed Burke's defense of "dignified obedience" to tradition and class privilege and argued, instead, for the right of the moral and intellectual individual over that of the state.

In her attack on Burke, Wollstonecraft expressed her ideas about proper political discourse and argument. Once again, she advocated for discourse the same values that she advocated for the intellect—what she regarded as "manly" qualities of reason, moral virtue, and candor. She thus condemned what she regarded as Burke's deliberate invocation of sophistry. In *Rights of Men*, she wrote: "Words are heaped on words, till understanding is confused by endeavoring to disentangle the sense, and the memory by tracing contradictions . . . you have often sacrificed your sincerity to enforce your favorite arguments, and called in your judgment to adjust the arrangement of words that could not convey its dictates" (127). Assuming language to be a conduit for thoughts and ideas, Wollstonecraft rejected "pampered sensibility" that allowed the "passions" to obscure enlightened argument, yet she valued true sentiment—sincerity and strong personal conviction—in writing.

Having established her political views about the importance of the rights of the individual over those of the state, Wollstonecraft then claimed those same rights for women. *A Vindication of the Rights of Woman* was published in 1792 in response to the French plan for a system of national education that would exclude females. In this work Wollstonecraft provided greater insight into ideas on effective rhetoric and its particular importance in the development of women's intellectual capacities, which were usually "enfeebled by false refinement" (2). In *Rights of Woman*, Wollstonecraft continued to promote the role of motherhood, but she stated that the purpose of women's education should be to develop the intellect since women's "first duty is to themselves as rational creatures" (331).

In her introduction to *Rights of Woman*, Wollstonecraft stated her thoughts about ideal rhetoric: "I shall disdain to cull my phrases or polish my style;—I aim at being useful, and sincerity will render me unaffected; for, wishing rather to persuade by the force of my arguments, than dazzle by the elegance of my language . . . I shall try to avoid that flowery diction which has slided from essays into novels, and from novels into familiar letters and conversation" (7–8). She also praised Catherine Sandbridge Macaulay's style of rhetoric in Macaulay's *Letters on Education*. Wollstonecraft, in *Rights of Woman*, claimed that Macaulay "writes with sober energy and argumentative closeness; yet sympathy and benevolence give an interest to her sentiments, and that vital heat to arguments, which forces the reader to weigh them" (164). By contrast, she criticized Dr. James Fordyce's "affected style," "sentimental rant," and "display of cold artificial feelings" in his *Sermons to Young Women* (206–9). Wollstonecraft, then, valued rhetoric characterized by the same qualities of mind that she urged women to develop: virtue, sincerity, reason, and intellect.

Perhaps the most compelling example of Wollstonecraft's ideas about rhetoric is her own blend of feminine and masculine rhetoric demonstrated in *Rights of Woman*. After her death, Godwin, referring in his *Memoirs* to

Rights of Woman, argued for "the importance of its doctrines" and praised "the eminence of genius it displays" but also called it "a very uneven performance, and eminently deficient in method and arrangement" (56). Modern scholars have also criticized her personal digressions and lack of organization (Wardle 1950; Tomalin 1974). However, these judgments are based on purely traditional standards of masculine philosophical discourse. *Rights of Woman* actually becomes a critique of philosophical discourse itself. Politically disenfranchised as a woman, Wollstonecraft had to construct her argument for women's rights by appropriating a masculine political genre that inadequately served the purpose of reflecting women's experiences. To establish her authority with a primarily male audience trained in the adversarial discourse of philosophy, Wollstonecraft had to demonstrate that she was capable of masculine rhetoric: rational, strenuous, agonistic argument. However, speaking as a woman about the lives of women, as she constructed her argument she also blended a personal point of view, domestic images, issues from women's daily experiences, and personal digressions characteristic of feminine rhetoric. As Laurie Finke has explained, "Wollstonecraft must constantly move between two poles, between a masculine posture of confrontation and a feminine strategy of indirection, between reason and emotion" (167). The tension created by Wollstonecraft's stated preference for masculine rhetoric and her own rhetorical practice that blended both masculine and feminine features thus parallels the tension created when a woman of intellect and reason must speak about the personal experience of women in masculine philosophical discourse (Poovey 1984; Jacobus 1986; Kaplan 1986). But more importantly, *Rights of Woman* represents an example of a new rhetoric that produced in philosophical discourse a dialectic between masculine reason and rationality, on the one hand, and feminine emotion and personal experience, on the other. This is, perhaps, Wollstonecraft's least appreciated but most important contribution to the study of rhetoric.

BIBLIOGRAPHY

Primary Sources

Wollstonecraft, Mary. *The Female Reader*. 1789. Reprint. Edited by Janet Todd and Marilyn Butler. New York: New York University Press, 1989.
———. *Thoughts on the Education of Daughters: With Reflections on Female Conduct, in the More Important Duties of Life*. 1787. Reprint. Edited by Janet Todd and Marilyn Butler. New York: New York University Press, 1989.
———. *A Vindication of the Rights of Men, in a Letter to the Right Honourable Edmund Burke*. 1790. Reprint. Edited by Janet Todd and Marilyn Butler. New York: New York University Press, 1989.
———. *A Vindication of the Rights of Woman: With Strictures on Political and Moral Subjects*. 1792. Reprint. Edited by Janet Todd and Marilyn Butler. New York: New York University Press, 1989.

Biography

Flexner, Eleanor. *Mary Wollstonecraft: A Biography.* New York: Coward, McCann, and Geoghegan, 1972.

Godwin, William. *Memoirs of the Author of a Vindication of the Rights of Woman.* 1798. Reprint. Edited by W. Clark Durant. London: Constable, 1927.

Tomalin, Claire. *The Life and Death of Mary Wollstonecraft.* New York: Harcourt, Brace, Jovanovich, 1974.

Wardle, Ralph. *Mary Wollstonecraft: A Critical Biography.* Lawrence: University of Kansas Press, 1951.

Criticism

Barker-Benfield, G. J. "Mary Wollstonecraft: Eighteenth-Century Commonwealth Woman." *Journal of the History of Ideas* 50.1 (1989): 95–115.

Conger, Syndy McMillen. "The Sentimental Logic of Wollstonecraft's Prose." *Prose Studies* 10.2 (1987): 143–58.

Ferguson, Moira, and Janet Todd. *Mary Wollstonecraft.* Boston: Twayne, 1984.

Finke, Laurie A. "A Philosophic Wanton: Language and Authority in Wollstonecraft's *Vindication of the Rights of Woman.*" In *The Philosopher as Writer: The Eighteenth Century,* edited by Robert Ginsberg, 155–76. London: Associated University Press, 1987.

Jacobus, Mary. "The Difference of View." In *Women Writing and Writing About Women,* edited by Mary Jacobus. New York: Barnes and Noble, 1979.

Kaplan, Cora. "Wild Nights: Pleasure/Sexuality/Feminism." In *Sea Changes: Essays on Culture and Feminism,* 31–57. London: Verso, 1986.

Poovey, Mary. *The Proper Lady and the Woman Writer: Ideology as Style in the Works of Mary Wollstonecraft, Mary Shelley, and Jane Austen.* Chicago: University of Chicago Press, 1984.

Wang, Orrin N. C. "The Other Reasons: Female Alterity and Enlightenment Discourse in Mary Wollstonecraft's *A Vindication of the Rights of Woman.*" *Yale Journal of Criticism* 5.1 (1991): 129–45.

GENERAL BIBLIOGRAPHY

Scholars looking for a wealth of research on eighteenth-century rhetoric and rhetorical theory will find that the area has not yet been fully explored, nor have many of the new critical methodologies—such as semiotics, deconstruction, and cultural studies—been brought fully to bear on the material (although this is now changing). As the bibliographies of the individual entries in this volume suggest, while the major figures of the period—such as Adam Smith, Hugh Blair, and George Campbell—have been discussed in some detail, many of the minor figures have received scant attention, as their short bibliographies confirm. Fortunately, the reader interested in studying the rhetoric of the century in more depth will find important seminal works to consult. I will limit my discussion to these and refer interested readers to the essays in the volume on individual rhetoricians for more focused bibliographical information.

BIBLIOGRAPHIES

There exist several important bibliographies that cite the research on the subject. The most thorough is Winifred Bryan Horner's essay, "The Eighteenth Century," which is Part Four of her edited volume entitled *Historical Rhetoric: An Annotated Bibliography of Selected Sources in English* (1980). The chapter begins with a short introduction, then lists primary and secondary sources in separate sections. Entries have brief annotations. In 1983, Horner published a second bibliography entitled "The Eighteenth Century" in her edited volume *The Present State of Scholarship in Historical and Contemporary Rhetoric*, which appeared in a revised edition in 1990 (coauthored with Kerri Morris Barton). This bibliographical essay begins with discussions of the major critical studies of the period, touches on eighteenth-century philosophy and aesthetics as they relate to the rhetoric, and then cites the research on rhetoricians and rhetorics in terms of neoclassical rhetorics, the old rhetoric, elocution, and belletristic rhetoric. A second good bibliographical source is James L. Golden and Edward P. J. Corbett's *The Rhetoric of Blair, Campbell, and Whately*, which in 1990 was reissued in a new edition with updated bibliographies. While not annotated, the "General Bibliography" is useful. One criticism is that it does not separate primary from secondary sources, which makes it cumbersome. The book also offers current bibliographies on Blair and Campbell, two of the most important theorists of the eighteenth century. The volume is also useful for its succinct, intelligent introductory essay on the rhetoric of the period and the essays introducing Blair and Campbell. Finally, Thomas P. Miller's extensive bibliography included in his "The Formation of College English: A Survey of the Archives of Eighteenth-Century Rhetorical Theory and Practice" (1990) collects much of the sociologically oriented background material on education in and the history and culture of Scotland, England, and America.

GENERAL STUDIES

Readers looking for overviews of the period will find several helpful sources. Douglas Ehninger's essay "Dominant Trends in English Rhetorical Thought, 1750–1800," offers a good place to start. He has identified four "movements" in the rhetoric of the last half of the eighteenth century: classicism, psychological-epistemological theories of discourse, elocutionism, and belletristic rhetoric. These categories are similar to those that Golden and Corbett have proposed in their introductory essay to *Blair, Campbell, and Whately*, although they have renamed Ehninger's second movement the "psychological-philosophical theories of public address" (9). A second overview is William Philips Sanford's 1929 dissertation (published in 1931) *English Theories of Public Address, 1530–1828*. As the dates in the title indicate, Sanford has discussed about 300 years of English rhetoric, a lot of territory to cover. His discussion of the eighteenth century appears in his third chapter. There he has evaluated the century's response to classical rhetoric, stylistic rhetorics, and the elocutionary movement. While now dated, the work remains useful for its summaries of obscure rhetorics. Several textbooks also provide good overviews of the period. Perhaps the best is Golden, Berquist, and Coleman's *The Rhetoric of Western Thought* (4th ed., 1989), in which Part Two is devoted largely to eighteenth-century theorists. Chapter 5 covers neoclassicism and Blair; 6, the epistemologists, including Locke and Hume, in addition to Continental thinkers; 7, Campbell and Whateley; and 8, the elocutionary movement. A second good textbook is Thomas M. Conley's *Rhetoric in the European Tradition* (1990), which, in Chapter 7, contains a discussion of European rhetoric of the century. Conley is particularly good at making connections between Continental and English rhetorical theory and practice. A third textbook is Corbett's *Classical Rhetoric for the Modern Student* (3d ed., 1990), which contains on pages 563–70 a good discussion of eighteenth-century rhetorical theory and practice. A fourth text is Patricia Bizzell and Bruce Herzberg's *The Rhetorical Tradition* (1990), a large anthology of readings in the history of rhetoric with ample introductions, overviews, and bibliographies. Part Four covers "Enlightenment Rhetoric," which includes selections from John Locke, Thomas Sheridan, George Campbell, and Hugh Blair. It also provides an essay that overviews the eighteenth century. A final textbook, Corbett, Golden, and Berquist's *Essays on the Rhetoric of the Western World* (1990), contains several essays on eighteenth-century rhetoricians.

The most important single study in the field remains Wilbur Samuel Howell's 1971 *Eighteenth-Century British Logic and Rhetoric*, which provides the most exhaustive treatment of English rhetoric and logic. The book has many strengths. It offers full discussions of all major and many minor figures, giving biographical as well as analytical treatments of each. Howell's readings of the rhetorics are almost always accurate and thorough; and although his prose is occasionally heavy, his observations are worth reading. The major weakness of the volume is its author's assumption that the best rhetorics of the period were those that incorporated the new psychology and philosophy. He therefore tends to read unsympathetically those theorists who retained strong classical elements. Howell has also published several important essays, including "John Locke and the New Rhetoric" (1967) and "Sources of the Elocutionary Movement in England" (1959).

No equivalent book-length study exists to date that examines rhetoric in America during the period. However, Warren Guthrie published in the 1940s and 1950s a series of essays on this subject, all titled "The Development of Rhetorical Theory in America," with various subtitles. In the first of these, subtitled "The Dominance of the Rhetoric of Style, 1635–1730" (1946), Guthrie has examined the influences of the rhetorics of Aristotle, Cicero, Ramus, Vossius, and others on American preparatory schools and colleges during the late seventeenth and early eighteenth centuries. In the second essay, subtitled "The Growth of the Classical Tradition, 1730–1785" (1947), the author has studied the influence of classical theorists, such as Aristotle and Cicero, and of classically influenced English and European rhetoricians, such as François Fénelon, John Lawson, and Joseph Priestley. In the third essay, subtitled "The Domination of English Rhetorics" (1948), Guthrie has discussed the influence in American education during the late eighteenth and early nineteenth centuries of the rhetorics of Blair, Campbell, Whately, and various minor works. In the fourth essay, subtitled "The Development of American Rhetorical Theory" (1949), the author has documented the rise of an indigenous American tradition that began with John Witherspoon, who lectured on the subject at Princeton between 1768 and 1794 (98). In the final essay, subtitled "The Elocution Movement—England" (1951), Witherspoon has discussed that movement's rise and development in England and its influence in America. Other theorists have also examined American rhetoric of the period. In "John Witherspoon, James Wilson, and the Influence of Scottish Rhetoric on America" (1991), David Daiches has traced the influences of Scottish rhetorical theory on the American Founding Fathers. Another good source on American theory and practice is Karl R. Wallace's edited volume, *History of Speech Education in America* (1954), which contains several essays on eighteenth-century rhetorical theory and practice, including Howell's "English Backgrounds of Rhetoric" and Frederick W. Haberman's "English Sources of American Elocution."

ELOCUTIONARY MOVEMENT

The elocutionary movement has received attention from other scholars. Charles A. Fritz examined the beginnings of the movement in "From Sheridan to Rush" (1930), Giles Wilkinson Gray has offered an overview of the movement in "What Was Elocution?" (1960), and G. P. Mohrmann has examined the movement's assumptions about language in "The Language of Nature and Elocutionary Theory" (1966). A book that contains an examination of American oratory of the period is Bernard K. Duffy and Halford R. Ryan's edited collection, *American Orators Before*

1900 (1987). Another book, Donald Weber's *Rhetoric and History in Revolutionary New England* (1988), contains an examination of Revolutionary pulpit oratory in the context of cultural and social upheaval.

INFLUENCE OF RHETORIC ON EDUCATION

Several recent studies have explored the influence of eighteenth-century rhetoric on British and American education. In *Our Colonial Curriculum* (1907), Colyer Meriwether has discussed in Chapter 8 the various forms that disputation took in eighteenth-century American and English colleges; in "The Colonial Period" (1943), George V. Bohman has discussed the intellectual background, training, and types of oratory conducted in American colleges at the time; and in "The Teaching of Rhetoric in the United States during the Classical Period of Education" (1943), Ota Thomas has examined speech education, in theory and practice, in eighteenth-century America. In "Where Did College English Studies Come From?" (1990), Thomas P. Miller has argued that instruction in English began, not in the elite English universities, but in the cultural provinces, such as America and Scotland, and in the Dissenting academies. "The Formation of College English" (1990) extends Miller's argument and cites research sources for those interested in pursing this issue. Horner's "The Roots of Writing Instruction" (1990) provides a good overview of English rhetorical instruction in schools at all levels, and in her 1993 *Nineteenth-Century Scottish Rhetoric* (which greatly extends James R. Irvine and G. Jack Gravlee's "Rhetorical Studies in Edinburgh" [1976] and Irvine's "Rhetoric and Moral Philosophy: A Selected Inventory of Lecture Notes and Dictates in Scottish Archives" [1978]), Horner has examined the influence of eighteenth-century Scottish rhetoric on nineteenth-century Scottish and American education. The book provides useful discussions of the Scottish university system during the eighteenth century, and provides annotated lists of many unpublished manuscripts of professors' lectures given during the late eighteenth century and throughout the nineteenth. The book ends with a chapter titled the "Scottish-American Connection," in which the author has discussed the influence of Scottish rhetoric on the development of writing instruction in the United States. Two other important books that explore this issue are James A. Berlin's *Writing Instruction in Nineteenth-Century American Colleges* (1984) and Nan Johnson's *Nineteenth-Century Rhetoric in North America* (1991). Berlin has argued that two eighteenth-century rhetoricians, Hugh Blair and George Campbell (along with Richard Whately), "dominated" American thinking about rhetoric during the following century (19). Johnson has argued that, while Blair and Campbell remained unchallenged during the first half of the nineteenth century, they continued to exert their influence through American rhetoricians who worked from the British rhetoricians' assumptions. Another useful influence study is Clarence W. Edney's essay, "English Sources of Rhetorical Theory in Nineteenth-Century America" (1954).

RHETORIC AND OTHER DISCIPLINES

The relationship between rhetoric and other disciplines—especially philosophy, aesthetics, literature, and linguistics—has received some attention. In "Philosophical Influences in the Development of English Rhetorical Theory, 1748 to 1783" (1968),

Vincent M. Bevilacqua has examined the influences of the new philosophies on the innovative rhetorics of the latter half of the century. In "The Mirror Image" (1962), Herman Cohen has discussed the influence of nominalism on the century's discussions of style. In his essay "Theories of Taste in the Eighteenth Century" (1938–1943), D. W. Jefferson has examined the idea of taste as various rhetoricians used the term, and Edward Niles Hooker has examined the topic more broadly in "The Discussion of Taste, from 1750 to 1770" (1934). Walter Jackson Bate offers a more general discussion of the concept in *From Classic to Romantic* (1946), in which he has discussed classical, neoclassical and romantic notions of taste used during the eighteenth century. In *Critical Responsiveness* (1949), Gordon McKenzie has analyzed the use of eighteenth-century philosophy in the literary criticism of Kames, Blair, and others. In a related book, *The Art of Poetry 1750–1820* (1967), P.W.K. Stone has argued that in the eighteenth century poetry was viewed as a rhetorical art; and the author has explored the relationships between the century's rhetoric theory and poetic practice in the first through the ninth chapters. Finally, in *Sensible Words* (1977), Murray Cohen has discussed eighteenth-century theories of linguistics, grammar, and stylistics, touching throughout on questions important to such rhetoricians as Hugh Blair and George Campbell.

SOCIAL CONTEXTS OF RHETORICAL THEORY

Work has begun that explores the social contexts of eighteenth-century rhetorics. Eric W. Skopec has applied systems theory to expressive theories of discourse of the period in his "Theory of Expression in Selected Eighteenth-Century Rhetorics" (1982). Stephen H. Browne in "The Gothic Voice in Eighteenth-Century Oratory" (1988) has argued that eighteenth-century oratory can be approached through its many "voices"; Browne has analyzed in detail the Gothic voice in Edmund Burke's oratory. Roy Porter in "The Language of Quackery in England, 1660–1800" (1987) has traced the rhetoric of the various medical quacks in the century. An especially important article is Paul G. Bator's "The Formation of the Regius Chair" (1989), in which the author has discussed the social and cultural influences on the establishment of this chair of rhetoric and belles lettres held originally by Hugh Blair at the University of Edinburgh. John W. Cairns in "Rhetoric, Language, and Roman Law" (1991) has discussed legal education in eighteenth-century Scotland. Finally, Robert T. Oliver in *The Influence of Rhetoric in the Shaping of Great Britain* (1986) has examined the various ways that rhetoric and rhetorical practice have helped shape English history.

One area that has received considerable cultural analysis is eighteenth-century Scotland, especially the Scottish Enlightenment, which included the development of the new rhetorics of Kames, Smith, Blair, Campbell, and others. I have already cited the work of Horner, Miller, Daiches, and Bator, much of which discusses the influence of Scottish rhetoric on England and America. A good short introduction to the period is George E. Davie's *The Scottish Enlightenment* (1981), which gives some attention to the philosophy of Smith, Hume, and others. Introductions to Scottish philosophy include James McCosh's *The Scottish Philosophy* (1875) and, more recently, S. A. Grave's *The Scottish Philosophy of Common Sense* (1960), which provides valuable philosophical background for the rhetoric. In *Church and University in the*

Scottish Enlightenment (1985), Richard B. Sher has discussed the nature of Scottish institutions and the status of its important men of letters. In *Henry Home, Lord Kames, and the Scottish Enlightenment* (1971), William C. Lehmann has discussed Kames's many contributions to Scottish intellectual life during the period. H. Lewis Ulman has edited *The Minutes of the Aberdeen Philosophical Society* (1990).

BIBLIOGRAPHY

Bate, Walter Jackson. *From Classic to Romantic: Premises of Taste in Eighteenth-Century England.* Cambridge, MA: Harvard University Press, 1946.

Bator, Paul G. "The Formation of the Regius Chair of Rhetoric and Belles Lettres at the University of Edinburgh." *Quarterly Journal of Speech* 75.1 (1989): 40–64.

Berlin, James A. *Writing Instruction in Nineteenth-Century American Colleges.* Carbondale: Southern Illinois University Press, 1984.

Bevilacqua, Vincent M. "Philosophical Influences in the Development of English Rhetorical Theory, 1748–1783." *Proceedings of the Leeds Philosophical and Literary Society, Literary and Historical Section* 12 (1968): 191–215.

———. "Two Newtonian Arguments Concerning 'Taste.' " *Philological Quarterly* 47.4 (1968): 585–90.

Bizzell, Patricia, and Bruce Herzberg, eds. *The Rhetorical Tradition: Readings from Classical Times to the Present.* Boston: Bedford, 1990.

Bohman, George V. "The Colonial Period." In *A History and Criticism of American Public Address.* 2 vols. I: 1–54. New York: McGraw-Hill, 1943.

Browne, Stephen H. "The Gothic Voice in Eighteenth-Century Oratory." *Communication Quarterly* 36.3 (1988): 227–36.

Cairns, John W. "Rhetoric, Language, and Roman Law: Legal Education and Improvement in Eighteenth-Century Scotland." *Law and History Review* 9.1 (1991): 31–58.

Cohen, Herman. "The Mirror Image: Eighteenth-Century Elocutio and the New Philosophy." *Western Speech* 26.1 (1962): 22–27.

Cohen, Murray. *Sensible Words: Linguistic Practice in England, 1640–1785.* Baltimore: Johns Hopkins University Press, 1977.

Conley, Thomas M. *Rhetoric in the European Tradition.* New York: Longman, 1990.

Corbett, Edward P. J. "English Rhetorics of the Eighteenth Century." In *Classical Rhetoric for the Modern Student.* 3d ed., 563–70. New York: Oxford University Press, 1990.

Corbett, Edward P. J., James L. Golden, and Goodwin F. Berquist, eds. *Essays on the Rhetoric of the Western World.* Dubuque, IA: Kendall/Hunt, 1990.

Daiches, David. "John Witherspoon, James Wilson, and the Influence of Scottish Rhetoric on America." *Eighteenth-Century Life* 15:1–2 (1991): 163–80.

Davie, George E. *The Scottish Enlightenment.* London: Historical Association, 1981.

Duffy, Bernard K., and Halford R. Ryan, eds. *American Orators Before 1900: Critical Studies and Sources.* Westport, CT: Greenwood, 1987.

Edney, Clarence W. "English Sources of Rhetorical Theory in Nineteenth-Century America." In *History of Speech Education in America*, edited by Karl R. Wallace. New York: Appleton-Century-Crofts, 1954.

Ehninger, Douglas. "Dominant Trends in English Rhetorical Thought, 1750–1800." *Southern Speech Journal* 18.1 (1952): 3–12.

Fritz, Charles A. "From Sheridan to Rush: The Beginnings of English Elocution." *Quarterly Journal of Speech* 16.1 (1930): 75–88.

Golden, James L., and Edward P. J. Corbett. *The Rhetoric of Blair, Campbell, and Whately: With Updated Bibliographies.* Carbondale: Southern Illinois University Press: 1990.

Golden, James L., Goodwin F. Berquist, and William E. Coleman. *The Rhetoric of Western Thought.* 4th ed. Dubuque, IA: Kendall/Hunt, 1989.

Grave, S. A. *The Scottish Philosophy of Common Sense.* Oxford: Clarendon Press, 1960.

Gray, Giles Wilkinson. "What Was Elocution?" *Quarterly Journal of Speech* 46 (1960): 1–7.

Guthrie, Warren. "The Development of Rhetorical Theory in America, 1635–1850: The Development of American Rhetorical Theory." *Speech Monographs* 16.1 (1949): 98–113.

———. "The Development of Rhetorical Theory in America, 1635–1850: Domination of the English Rhetorics." *Speech Monographs* 15.1 (1948): 61–71.

———. "The Development of Rhetorical Theory in America: The Dominance of the Rhetoric of Style, 1635–1730." *Speech Monographs* 13.1 (1946): 14–22.

———. "The Development of Rhetorical Theory in America, 1665–1850. 5: The Elocution Movement—England." *Speech Monographs* 18.1 (1951): 17–30.

———. "The Development of Rhetorical Theory in America, 1635–1850: The Growth of the Classical Tradition, 1730–1785." *Speech Monographs* 14.1 (1947): 38–54.

Haberman, Frederick W. "English Sources of American Elocution." In *History of Speech Education in America: Background Studies,* edited by Karl R. Wallace, 105–26. New York: Appleton-Century-Crofts, 1954.

Hooker, Edward Niles. "The Discussion of Taste, from 1750 to 1770." *Publications of the Modern Language Association* 49 (1934): 577–92.

Horner, Winifred Bryan. "American Rhetoric and Its Scottish Roots." In *The Carlyle Society Papers,* edited by Ian Campbell, 1–20. Edinburgh: Carlyle Society, 1992.

———. "The Eighteenth Century." In *Historical Rhetoric: An Annotated Bibliography of Selected Sources in English,* edited by Winifred Bryan Horner, 185–226. Boston: G. K. Hall, 1980.

———. "The Eighteenth Century." In *The Present State of Scholarship in Historical and Contemporary Rhetoric,* edited by Winifred Bryan Horner, 101–33. Columbia: Missouri University Press, 1983.

———. *Nineteenth-Century Scottish Rhetoric: The American Connection.* Carbondale: Southern Illinois University Press: 1993.

———. "The Roots of Writing Instruction: Eighteenth- and Nineteenth-Century Britain." *Rhetoric Review* 8.2 (1990): 322–45. Reprint. "Writing Instruction in Great Britain: Eighteenth and Nineteenth Centuries." In *A Short History of Writing Instruction from Ancient Greece to Twentieth-Century America,* edited by James J. Murphy, 121–49. Davis, CA: Hermagoras Press, 1990.

Horner, Winifred Bryan, and Kerri Morris Barton. "The Eighteenth Century." In *The Present State of Scholarship in Historical and Contemporary Rhetoric,* Rev. ed., edited by Winifred Bryan Horner, 114–50. Columbia: Missouri University Press, 1990.

Howell, Wilbur Samuel. *Eighteenth-Century British Logic and Rhetoric.* Princeton: Princeton University Press, 1971.

————. "English Backgrounds of Rhetoric." In *History of Speech Education in America: Background Studies*, edited by Karl R. Wallace, 1–47. New York: Appleton-Century-Crofts, 1954.

————. "John Locke and the New Rhetoric." *Quarterly Journal of Speech* 53 (1967): 319–33.

————. "Sources of the Elocutionary Movement in England, 1700–1748." *Quarterly Journal of Speech* 45 (1959): 1–18.

Irvine, James R. "Rhetoric and Moral Philosophy: A Selected Inventory of Lecture Notes and Dictates in Scottish Archives, 1700–1900." *Rhetoric Society Quarterly* 8.4 (1978): 159–64.

Irvine, James R., and G. Jack Gravlee. "Rhetorical Studies in Edinburgh: A Select Inventory of Manuscripts in Scottish Archives." *Communication Monographs* 43.4 (1976): 101–3.

Jefferson, D. W. "Theories of Taste in the Eighteenth Century." *Proceedings of the Leeds Philosophical and Literary Society, Literary and Historical Section* 5 (1938–1943): 1–9.

Johnson, Nan. *Nineteenth-Century Rhetoric in North America*. Carbondale: Southern Illinois University Press, 1991.

Lehmann, William C. *Henry Home, Lord Kames, and the Scottish Enlightenment: A Study in National Character and the History of Ideas*. The Hague: Martinus Nijhoff, 1971.

McCosh, James. *The Scottish Philosophy*. London, 1875.

McKenzie, Gordon. *Critical Responsiveness: A Study of the Psychological Current in Later Eighteenth-Century Criticism*. University of California Publications in English, 20 (1949).

Meriwether, Colyer. *Our Colonial Curriculum, 1607–1776*. Washington, DC: Capital Publishing, 1907.

Miller, Thomas P. "The Formation of College English: A Survey of the Archives of Eighteenth-Century Rhetorical Theory and Practice." *Rhetoric Society Quarterly* 20.3 (1990): 261–86.

————. "Where Did College English Studies Come From?" *Rhetoric Review* 9.1 (1990): 50–69.

Mohrmann, G. P. "The Language of Nature and Elocutionary Theory." *Quarterly Journal of Speech* 52 (1966): 116–24.

Oliver, Robert T. *The Influence of Rhetoric in the Shaping of Great Britain: From the Roman Invasion to the Early Nineteenth Century*. Newark: Delaware University Press, 1986.

Porter, Roy. "The Language of Quackery in England, 1660–1800." In *The Social History of Language*, edited by Peter Burke and Roy Porter, 73–103. Cambridge: Cambridge University Press, 1987.

Sanford, William P. *English Theories of Public Address, 1530–1828*. Columbus, OH: H. L. Hendrick, 1931.

Sher, Richard B. *Church and University in the Scottish Enlightenment: The Moderate Literati of Edinburgh*. Princeton: Princeton University Press, 1985.

Skopec, Eric W. "The Theory of Expression in Selected Eighteenth-Century Rhetorics." In *Explorations in Rhetoric: Studies in Honor of Douglas Ehninger*, edited by Ray E. McKerrow, 119–36. Glenview, IL: Scott, Foresman, 1982.

Stone, P.W.K. *The Art of Poetry 1750–1820: Theories of Poetic Composition and Style in the Late Neo-Classical and Early Romantic Periods.* New York: Barnes and Noble, 1967.

Thomas, Ota. "The Teaching of Rhetoric in the United States during the Classical Period of Education." In *A History and Criticism of American Public Address,* edited by William Norwood Brigance. 2 vols. 1:193–210. New York: Mc-Graw-Hill, 1943.

Ulman, H. Lewis, ed. *The Minutes of the Aberdeen Philosophical Society, 1758–1771.* Aberdeen: Aberdeen University Press, 1990.

Wallace, Karl R., ed. *History of Speech Education in America: Background Studies.* New York: Appleton-Century-Crofts, 1954.

Weber, Donald. *Rhetoric and History in Revolutionary New England.* New York: Oxford University Press, 1988.

INDEX

Page numbers in boldface indicate location of main entry.

ABOUT THE EDITOR AND CONTRIBUTORS

SHELLEY ALEY is assistant to Winifred Bryan Horner, the Lillian Redford Chair of Rhetoric and Composition at Texas Christian University. She is pursuing her Ph.D. at Texas Christian. She has done extensive archival research on Alexander Bain at the University of Aberdeen and is contributing a chapter on Bain to Horner's *Three Scottish Nineteenth-Century Rhetoricians: Jardine, Aytoun, and Bain* (in press). Her teaching and research interests include the history of Western rhetoric, rhetoric and science, environmental rhetoric, and eighteenth- and nineteenth-century British literature.

PAUL G. BATOR is Assistant Professor in the Department of English at Santa Clara University. He carried out his research under the support of grants from his university and the National Endowment for the Humanities. He has published articles on the history of rhetoric and on modern rhetorical theory in *College Composition and Communication, Philosophy and Rhetoric,* and *The Quarterly Journal of Speech.*

WILLIAM BENZIE is Professor of English at the University of Victoria, British Columbia. He has published two books, *The Dublin Orator* (1972) and *Dr. F. J. Furnivall: A Victorian Scholar Adventurer* (1983). His teaching and research interests include the history of rhetoric, nineteenth-century literary scholarship, and Edwardian fiction.

JO ALLEN BRADHAM is Professor of English at Kennesaw State College. Satire and drama are her special interests. Her articles appear in *Biography, Studies in Narrative Technique, Critique, University of Dayton Review, College Literature,* and the *CEA Critic,* among others.

BYRON K. BROWN is Associate Professor of English at Valdosta State College. His teaching and research interests include composition theory, late eighteenth-century and early nineteenth-century rhetoric, and British Romantic literature, especially William Wordsworth.

STEPHEN H. BROWNE is Associate Professor of Speech Communication at Pennsylvania State University. His teaching and research interests include rhetorical criticism, history of oratory and political argument, and rhetorical theory. He is the author of *Edmund Burke and the Discourse of Virtue* (in press).

BRENDA H. COX is Assistant Professor and Program Coordinator of English Education at the University of North Carolina, Greensboro. She is a former Assistant Director of the Freshman English Program at the University of Georgia and has recently completed a dissertation entitled "Woman and Composing in Academic Discourse," under the direction of Michael G. Moran. Her interests include writing theory and research, reader response, and teacher training.

CHRISTY DESMET, Associate Professor of English at the University of Georgia, is the author of *Reading Shakespeare's Characters: Rhetoric, Ethics, and Identity* (1992). Her teaching and research interests include Shakespeare and Renaissance literature, rhetorical theory, literary theory, and rhetoric and composition.

LARRY FERRARIO is Assistant Professor of Business Communication at the University of Southern California. He is interested in the history of rhetoric and has done research on eighteenth- and nineteenth-century British rhetoric, particularly focusing on the rhetorical views of Thomas De Quincey.

LINDA FERREIRA-BUCKLEY is Assistant Professor of English at the University of Texas at Austin, where she teaches graduate courses in eighteenth- and nineteenth-century rhetoric and the history of English Studies and undergraduate courses in writing, writing pedagogy, the history of language studies, and Victorian nonfiction prose. She is currently working on a book, *On the Origin of English Studies: The Influence of Belletristic Rhetoric on Victorian Education, Language Books, and Nonfiction Prose Writers.*

LYNÉE LEWIS GAILLET is Assistant Professor of English and Director of the Mentoring Program for Graduate Teaching Assistants at Georgia State University. Her teaching and research interests include the history of rhetoric, the connections between modern composition pedagogy and nineteenth-century writing instruction in Scotland, and the eighteenth-century

British novel. Currently, she is examining the work of George Jardine for inclusion in *Three Nineteenth-Century Rhetoricians: Jardine, Aytoun, and Bain*, edited by Winifred Bryan Horner (in press).

JOHN S. GENTILE is Associate Professor of Communication and Performance Studies at Kennesaw State College. He is the author of *Cast of One: One-Person Shows from the Chautauqua Platform of the Broadway Stage* (1989). His essays have appeared in *Text and Performance Quarterly, Literature in Performance,* and *Studies in Popular Culture.* His teaching and research interests include the history of performance, performance theory and pedagogy, and folklore and oral traditional literature, particularly heroic epics.

ROCHELLE S. GLENN teaches English at the University of Georgia. Her teaching and research interests include rhetorical theory and African-American literature.

RUSSELL GREER teaches English at the University of Georgia. His research and teaching interests include rhetoric, textual editing, and nineteenth- and twentieth-century British literature.

SUSAN GRIFFIN is a Lecturer in the UCLA Writing Programs, where she teaches both freshman composition/rhetoric courses and an introduction to legal writing for upper-division students. Her work on Shaftesbury's rhetorical theory appears in *Rhetoric Review* and the *Proceedings of the Second International Conference on Argumentation.* Her research interests include the history of rhetoric, particularly in the eighteenth century, and the problem of gender in legal discourse.

MAUREEN BYRNES HARDEGREE teaches English at the University of Georgia where she serves as the Assistant Director of Freshman English. Her research interests include the history of rhetoric and early twentieth-century American composition theory and pedagogy.

WINIFRED BRYAN HORNER is Professor of English and Lillian Radford Chair of Rhetoric and Composition at Texas Christian University. She has published extensively in the history of rhetoric. Her latest book is *Nineteenth-Century Scottish Rhetoric: The American Connection* (1993). Horner is past president of the Rhetoric Society of America and has served on the Council of the International Society for the History of Rhetoric. She has lectured nationally and internationally. Her international lectures have been presented in Scotland, England, France, Italy, and China.

KATHY M. HOUFF teaches English at the University of Georgia. Her teaching and research interests include composition and rhetoric, creative writing, American nineteenth- and twentieth-century writing, and feminist pedagogy.

SUSAN HUNTER is Associate Professor of English and Director of Writing Programs at Kennesaw State College. She has co-edited *Writing Ourselves into the Story: Unheard Voices from Composition Studies* (1993). She has published essays on gender and pedagogy and on professional issues in such journals as *Rhetoric Review* and *Journal of Advanced Composition*. She is a founding editor of *Dialogue: A Journal for Writing Specialists*.

MELISSA L. KING has taught English in various public schools in Georgia. She is currently doing graduate work at the University of Georgia in English literature and rhetorical theory.

ELIZABETH K. LARSEN is Professor of English and Director of Honors at West Chester University. A former director of Freshman Composition at WCU, she has published essays in composition studies and in historical rhetoric, particularly in the interrelationship of rhetoric, writing, and composition in the eighteenth and nineteenth centuries. Her work on Alexander Gerard was begun during a summer NEH seminar. She currently is working on a historical study of the composing process. Her teaching and research interests include managerial communication and women's autobiographical writing.

KATHLEEN MASSEY is Associate Professor of English at California State Polytechnic University, Pomona, where she coordinates the freshman composition program and teaches courses in rhetorical theory, history of rhetoric, and composition theory and pedagogy in the Composition and Rhetoric Master's degree program. Her research on Ward has been supported with funds granted by the NEH for a summer seminar conducted by Lloyd Bitzer at the British Library, and by an Affirmative Action grant from Cal Poly for work at the Huntington Library in San Marino, California.

YVONNE MERRILL teaches English at the University of Arizona. Her interests include the social construction of gender as reflected in historic women's discourse. She has published articles on teaching literature and composition and on writing across the curriculum.

MAE MILLER has taught English at Abraham Baldwin College and now teaches at the University of Georgia. Her interests include American literature, Southern literature, and eighteenth-century rhetoric.

THOMAS P. MILLER helped develop the Ph.D. program in Rhetoric, Composition, and the Teaching of English at the University of Arizona, and he also teaches and helps administer the undergraduate composition program there. His publications include *Selected Writings of John Witherspoon* (1990) and articles in *College English, Journal of Advanced Composition, Rhetoric Review, Rhetorica,* and *Rhetoric Society Quarterly.* His research on John Witherspoon and eighteenth-century rhetoric has been supported by the National Endowment for the Humanities. Miller is currently completing a book on eighteenth-century rhetoric and the formation of college English studies.

MARY HURLEY MORAN is Associate Professor in the English component of the Developmental Studies Division at the University of Georgia. She has published books and articles in the areas of modern British literature, technical writing, and composition.

MICHAEL G. MORAN is Associate Professor of English and Director of Freshman English at the University of Georgia. He has co-edited three books, *Research in Composition and Rhetoric* (1984), *Research in Technical Communication* (1985), and *Research in Basic Writing* (1990), all with Greenwood Press. His teaching and research interests include composition theory and pedagogy, the history of rhetoric, the history of technical communication, and eighteenth-century British literature, especially the novel.

DAVID PAYNE is Coordinator of the Writing Center at the University of Georgia. He has written on Herman Melville and Flannery O'Connor. His research interests include the appearance of language-origin theories in American literature and the use of computers in textual study.

ADAM POTKAY is Assistant Professor of English at the College of William and Mary, and an advisory editor of *Eighteenth-Century Life.* He has published a number of articles on eighteenth- and nineteenth-century literature, and has recently completed a book entitled *Of Eloquence: Literature and Politics in the Age of Hume.*

SUSAN SEYFARTH is Assistant Professor of English at Valdosta State College. She has published articles on pedagogy, popular culture, and eighteenth-century British literature. Her teaching and research interests include rhetoric and prose style, popular culture, and eighteenth-century British literature, especially Henry Fielding's rehearsal plays.

H. LEWIS ULMAN is Associate Professor of English at Ohio State University, where he teaches courses in composition, rhetorical and critical theory, and American literature. He has edited *The Minutes of the Aberdeen*

Philosophical Society, 1758–1773 (1990) and has published journal articles on eighteenth-century British philosophy and rhetoric and on the work of Henry James. His current research focuses on self-representation in American nature writing.

WILLIAM WALKER completed his Ph.D. in English at Johns Hopkins University in 1989, held a two-year postdoctoral fellowship at McGill University, and currently teaches part time at the University of Ottawa. He has published articles on Browning, Locke, Richardson, Nietzsche, and Milton and has written *Locke, Literary Criticism, and Philosophy* (in press).

PATRICIA B. WORRALL teaches English at the University of Georgia. Her teaching and research interests include the literature of the English Renaissance and using computers to teach literary analysis.